W9-BOO-601

Elementary Algebra
for TVI Math 100A

Alan S. Tussy

R. David Gustafson

Australia · Canada · Mexico · Singapore · Spain · United Kingdom · United States

THOMSON
™
BROOKS/COLE

Elementary Algebra
Tussy / Gustafson

Executive Editors:
Michele Baird, Maureen Staudt &
Michael Stranz

Project Development Manager:
Linda de Stefano

Marketing Coordinators:
Lindsay Annett and Sara Mercurio

Production/Manufacturing Supervisor:
Donna M. Brown

Pre-Media Services Supervisor:
Dan Plofchan

Kalina Hintz and Bahman Naraghi

Cover Image
Getty Images*

© 2006 Thomson Brooks/Cole, a part
of the Thomson Corporation. Thomson,
the Star logo, and Brooks/Cole are
trademarks used herein under license.

Printed in the
United States of America
2 3 4 5 6 7 8 08 07 06

For more information, please contact
Thomson Custom Solutions, 5191
Natorp Boulevard, Mason, OH 45040.
Or you can visit our Internet site at
www.thomsoncustom.com

Rights and Permissions Specialists:
ALL RIGHTS RESERVED. No part of
this work covered by the copyright
hereon may be reproduced or used in
any form or by any means — graphic,
electronic, or mechanical, including
photocopying, recording, taping, Web
distribution or information storage and
retrieval systems — without the written
permission of the publisher.

For permission to use material from this
text or product, contact
us by:
Tel (800) 730-2214
Fax (800) 730 2215
www.thomsonrights.com

The Adaptable Courseware Program
consists of products and additions to
existing Brooks/Cole products that are
produced from camera-ready copy.
Peer review, class testing, and
accuracy are primarily the responsibility
of the author(s).

Elementary Algebra / Tussy /
Gustafson
p. 336
ISBN 0-534-61702-6

International Divisions List

Asia (Including India):
Thomson Learning
(a division of Thomson Asia Pte Ltd)
5 Shenton Way #01-01
UIC Building
Singapore 068808
Tel: (65) 6410-1200
Fax: (65) 6410-1208

Australia/New Zealand:
Thomson Learning Australia
102 Dodds Street
Southbank, Victoria 3006
Australia

Latin America:
Thomson Learning
Seneca 53
Colonia Polano
11560 Mexico, D.F., Mexico
Tel (525) 281-2906
Fax (525) 281-2656

Canada:
Thomson Nelson
1120 Birchmount Road
Toronto, Ontario
Canada M1K 5G4
Tel (416) 752-9100
Fax (416) 752-8102

UK/Europe/Middle East/Africa:
Thomson Learning
High Holborn House
50-51 Bedford Row
London, WC1R 4L$
United Kingdom
Tel 44 (020) 7067-2500
Fax 44 (020) 7067-2600

Spain (Includes Portugal):
Thomson Paraninfo
Calle Magallanes 25
28015 Madrid
España
Tel 34 (0)91 446-3350
Fax 34 (0)91 445-6218

*Unless otherwise noted, all cover images used by Thomson Custom Solutions have been supplied courtesy of Getty Images with
the exception of the *Earthview* cover image, which has been supplied by the National Aeronautics and Space Administration (NASA).

Table of Contents

Preface

Algebra is a language in its own right. The purpose of this textbook is to teach students how to read, write, and think mathematically using the language of algebra. It is written for students studying algebra for the first time and for those who need a review of the basics. *Elementary Algebra,* Third Edition, employs a variety of instructional methods that reflect the recommendations of NCTM and AMATYC. You will find the vocabulary, practice, and well-defined pedagogy of a traditional approach. You will also find that we emphasize the reasoning, modeling, and communicating skills that are part of today's reform movement.

The third edition retains the basic philosophy of the second edition. However, we have made several improvements as a direct result of the comments and suggestions we received from instructors and students. Our goal has been to make the book more enjoyable to read, easier to understand, and more relevant.

■ NEW TO THIS EDITION

- Nine new chapter openers reference the *TLE* computer lessons that accompany each chapter.
- The new Language of Algebra features, along with Success Tips, Notation, Calculator Boxes, and Cautions, are presented in the margins to promote understanding and increased clarity.
- Many additional applications involving real-life data have been added.
- Answers to the popular *Self Check* feature have been relocated to the end of each section, right before the *Study Set.*
- Several high-level Challenge Problems have been added to each *Study Set.*
- The Accent on Teamwork feature has been redesigned to offer the instructor two or three collaborative activities per chapter that can be assigned as group work.
- More illustrations, diagrams, and color have been added for the visual learner.

■ REVISED TABLE OF CONTENTS

Chapter 1: *An Introduction to Algebra* Introductory concepts from Chapters 1 and 2 of the previous edition have been consolidated to create a less-repetitive, quicker-paced beginning for the course. More emphasis has been placed on simplifying and building fractions to ready students for Chapter 6, Rational Expressions and Equations. Addition, subtraction, multiplication, and division of signed numbers are now discussed in this chapter.

Chapter 2: *Equations, Inequalities, and Problem Solving* This chapter now contains two sections that are exclusively devoted to problem solving using the five-step problem-solving strategy. Circle graphs have been added to the study of percent.

Chapter 3: *Linear Equations and Inequalities in Two Variables* The nonlinear graphs previously in Section 3.2 were moved to Chapter 4. The slope section was rewritten so that slope of a line is introduced first, followed by a discussion of rates of change. Sections 3.5 and 3.6 have new titles: Slope–Intercept Form and Point–Slope Form. Graphing Linear Inequalities, previously a part of the Systems of Equations chapter, is now Section 3.7.

With its placement here, students graph inequalities at two well-separated times during the course: in Chapter 3 and Chapter 7. New graphs and linear models of real-world data have been added as examples and as exercises in the Study Sets.

Chapter 4: *Exponents and Polynomials* Section 4.4, Polynomials, now includes graphs of nonlinear equations, such as $y = x^2$ and $y = x^3$. A separate section has been devoted to special products. Sections 4.7 and 4.8 from the second edition were combined so that division of polynomials is now covered in one section.

Chapter 5: *Factoring and Quadratic Equations* Previously Chapter 6, this chapter has been extensively rewritten. Added attention has been given to the grouping method (key number method) for factoring trinomials.

Chapter 6: *Rational Expressions and Equations* Unit conversion is now introduced in Section 6.2. Addition and subtraction of rational expressions is now presented in two parts: In Section 6.3, the denominators are like, and in Section 6.4, the denominators are unlike. The concepts of unit price and best buy have been added to Section 6.8, Proportions and Similar Triangles.

Chapter 7: *Solving Systems of Equations and Inequalities* Previously Chapter 8, many new real-life applications have been added.

Chapter 8: *Radical Expressions and Equations* This chapter, which was previously Chapter 5, has been rewritten so that only square roots are discussed in the first six sections. Solving radical equations now follows the sections that discuss simplifying radical expressions. In Section 8.6, higher-order roots and rational exponents are introduced.

Chapter 9: *Solving Quadratic Equations; Functions* This chapter is the result of some reorganization of some topics previously in Chapter 3, Chapter 6, and Chapter 7. A section on Complex Numbers has been added. Section 9.5, Introduction to Functions, now introduces this important concept using a real-world example. Section 9.6, Variation, is a consolidation of material that had previously appeared in two different sections of two different chapters.

■ ACKNOWLEDGMENTS

We are grateful to the following people who reviewed the manuscript at various stages of its development. They all had valuable suggestions that have been incorporated into the text.

The first and second editions:

Julia Brown
Atlantic Community College

John Coburn
Saint Louis Community College–Florissant Valley

Sally Copeland
Johnson County Community College

Ben Cornelius
Oregon Institute of Technology

James Edmondson
Santa Barbara Community College

Judith Jones
Valencia Community College

Therese Jones
Amarillo College

Elizabeth Morrison
Valencia Community College

Angelo Segalla
Orange Coast College

June Strohm
Pennsylvania State Community College–DuBois

Rita Sturgeon
San Bernardino Valley College

Jo Anne Temple
Texas Technical University

Sharon Testone
Onondaga Community College

Marilyn Treder
Rochester Community College

The third edition:

Cynthia J. Broughton
Arizona Western College

Jamie McGill
East Tennessee State University

Don K. Brown
Macon State College

Margaret Michener
University of Nebraska, Kearney

Light Bryant
Arizona Western College

Bernard J. Pina
Dona Ana Branch Community College

John Scott Collins
Pima Community College

Carol Purcell
Century Community College

Lee Gibbs
Arizona Western College

Daniel Russow
Arizona Western College

Haile K. Haile
Minneapolis Community and Technical College

Donald W. Solomon
University of Wisconsin, Milwaukee

John Thoo
Yuba College

Suzanne Harris-Smith
Albuquerque Technical Vocational Institute

Susan M. Twigg
Wor-Wic Community College

Kamal Hennayake
Chesapeake College

Gizelle Worley
California State University, Stanislaus

Lynn Marecek
Santa Ana College

We want to express our gratitude to Karl Hunsicker, Cathy Gong, Dave Ryba, Terry Damron, Marion Hammond, Lin Humphrey, Doug Keebaugh, Robin Carter, Tanja Rinkel, Bob Billups, Liz Tussy, Alexander Lee, Steve Odrich, and the Citrus College Library staff (including Barbara Rugeley) for their help with some of the application problems in the textbook.

Without the talents and dedication of the editorial, marketing, and production staff of Brooks/Cole, this revision of *Elementary Algebra* could not have been so well accomplished. We express our sincere appreciation for the hard work of Bob Pirtle, Jennifer Huber, Helen Walden, Lori Heckleman, Vernon Boes, Kim Rokusek, Sarah Woicicki, Greta Kleinert, Jessica Bothwell, Bryan Vann, Kirsten Markson, Rebecca Subity, Hal Humphrey, Tammy Fisher-Vasta, Christine Davis, Ellen Brownstein, Diane Koenig, and Graphic World for their help in creating the book.

Alan S. Tussy
R. David Gustafson

For the Student

■ SUCCESS IN ALGEBRA

To be successful in mathematics, you need to know how to study it. The following check-list will help you develop your own personal strategy to study and learn the material. The suggestions below require some time and self-discipline on your part, but it will be worth the effort. This will help you get the most out of the course.

As you read each of the following statements, place a check mark in the box if you can truthfully answer Yes. If you can't answer Yes, think of what you might do to make the suggestion part of your personal study plan. You should go over this checklist several times during the semester to be sure you are following it.

Preparing for the Class
❏ I have made a commitment to myself to give this course my best effort.
❏ I have the proper materials: a pencil with an eraser, paper, a notebook, a ruler, a calculator, and a calendar or day planner.
❏ I am willing to spend a minimum of two hours doing homework for every hour of class.
❏ I will try to work on this subject every day.
❏ I have a copy of the class syllabus. I understand the requirements of the course and how I will be graded.
❏ I have scheduled a free hour after the class to give me time to review my notes and begin the homework assignment.

Class Participation
❏ I know my instructor's name.
❏ I will regularly attend the class sessions and be on time.
❏ When I am absent, I will find out what the class studied, get a copy of any notes or handouts, and make up the work that was assigned when I was gone.
❏ I will sit where I can hear the instructor and see the chalkboard.
❏ I will pay attention in class and take careful notes.
❏ I will ask the instructor questions when I don't understand the material.
❏ When tests, quizzes, or homework papers are passed back and discussed in class, I will write down the correct solutions for the problems I missed so that I can learn from my mistakes.

Study Sessions
❏ I will find a comfortable and quiet place to study.
❏ I realize that reading a math book is different from reading a newspaper or a novel. Quite often, it will take more than one reading to understand the material.
❏ After studying an example in the textbook, I will work the accompanying Self Check.
❏ I will begin the homework assignment only after reading the assigned section.
❏ I will try to use the mathematical vocabulary mentioned in the book and used by my instructor when I am writing or talking about the topics studied in this course.
❏ I will look for opportunities to explain the material to others.
❏ I will check all my answers to the problems with those provided in the back of the book (or with the *Student Solutions Manual*) and resolve any differences.
❏ My homework will be organized and neat. My solutions will show all the necessary steps.
❏ I will work some review problems every day.

❑ After completing the homework assignment, I will read the next section to prepare for the coming class session.

❑ I will keep a notebook containing my class notes, homework papers, quizzes, tests, and any handouts—all in order by date.

Special Help

❑ I know my instructor's office hours and am willing to go in to ask for help.

❑ I have formed a study group with classmates that meets regularly to discuss the material and work on problems.

❑ When I need additional explanation of a topic, I use the tutorial videos and the interactive CD, as well as the website.

❑ I make use of extra tutorial assistance that my school offers for mathematics courses.

❑ I have purchased the *Students Solutions Manual* that accompanies this text, and I use it.

To follow each of these suggestions will take time. It takes a lot of practice to learn mathematics, just as with any other skill.

No doubt, you will sometimes become frustrated along the way. This is natural. When it occurs, take a break and come back to the material after you have had time to clear your thoughts. Keep in mind that the skills and discipline you learn in this course will help make for a brighter future. Gook luck!

iLrn Tutorial Quick Start Guide

■ *iLrn* CAN HELP YOU SUCCEED IN MATH

iLrn is an online program that facilitates math learning by providing resources and practice to help you succeed in your math course. Your instructor chose to use *iLrn* because it provides online opportunities for learning (Explanations found by clicking **Read Book**), practice (Exercises), and evaluating (Quizzes). It also gives you a way to keep track of your own progress and manage your assignments.

The mathematical notation in *iLrn* is the same as that you see in your textbooks, in class, and when using other math tools like a graphing calculator. *iLrn* can also help you run calculations, plot graphs, enter expressions, and grasp difficult concepts. You will encounter various problem types as you work through *iLrn,* all of which are designed to strengthen your skills and engage you in learning in different ways.

■ LOGGING IN TO iLrn

Registering with the PIN Code on the iLrn Card   *Situation:* Your instructor has not given you a PIN code for an online course, but you have a textbook with a iLrn product PIN code.

Initial Log-in

1. Go to **http://iLrn.com.**
2. In the menu at the left, click on **Student Tutorial.**
3. Make sure that the name of your school appears in the "School" field. If your school name does not appear, follow steps a–d below. If your school is listed, go to step 4.
   a. Click on **Find Your School.**
   b. In the "State" field, select your state from the drop-down menu.

     c. In the "Name of school" field, type the first few letters of your school's name; then click on **Search.** The school list will appear at the right.

     d. Click on your school. The "First Time Users" screen will open.

4. In the "PIN Code" field, type the iLrn PIN code supplied on your iLrn card.

5. In the "ISBN" field, type the ISBN of your book (from the textbook's back cover), for example, 0-534-41914-3.

6. Click on **Register.**

7. Enter the appropriate information. Fields marked with a red asterisk must be filled in.

8. Click on **Register** and **Begin BCA/iLrn.**

You will be asked to select a user name and password. Save your user name and password in a safe place. You will need them to log in the next time you use iLrn. Only your user name and password will allow you to reenter iLrn.

Subsequent Log-in

1. Go to **http://iLrn.com.**

2. Click on **Login.**

3. Make sure the name of your school appears in the "School" field. If not, then follow steps 3a–d under "Initial Login" to identify your school.

4. Type your user name and password (see boxed information above); then click on **Login.** The "My Assignments" page will open.

■ NAVIGATING THROUGH iLrn

To navigate between chapters and sections, use the drop-down menu below the top navigation bar. This will give you access to the study activities available for each section.

    The view of a tutorial in iLrn looks like this.

Math Toolbar

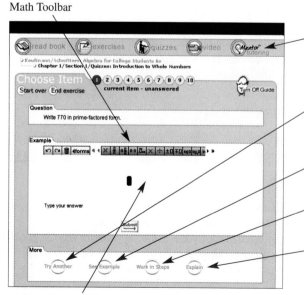

vMentor: Live online tutoring is only a click away. Tutors can take screen shots of your book and lead you through a problem with voice-over and visual aids.

Try Another: Click here to have iLrn create a new question or a new set of problems.

See Examples: Preworked examples provide you with additional help.

Work in Steps: iLrn can guide you through a problem step-by-step.

Explain: Additional explanation from your book can help you with a problem.

Type your answer here.

■ ONLINE TUTORING WITH *vMENTOR*

Access to iLrn also means access to online tutors and support through vMentor, which provides live homework help and tutorials. To access vMentor while you are working in the Exercises or "Tutorial" areas in iLrn, click on the **vMentor Tutoring** button at the top right of the navigation bar above the problem or exercise.

Next, click on the **vMentor** button; you will be taken to a Web page that lists the steps for entering a vMentor classroom. If you are a first-time user of vMentor, you might need to download Java software before entering the class for the first class. You can either take an Orientation Session or log in to a vClass from the links at the bottom of the opening screen.

All vMentor Tutoring is done through a vClass, an Internet-based virtual classroom that features two-way audio, a shared whiteboard, chat, messaging, and experienced tutors.

You can access vMentor Sunday through Thursday, as follows:

5 p.m. to 9 p.m. Pacific Time
6 p.m. to 10 p.m. Mountain Time
7 p.m. to 11 p.m. Central Time
8 p.m. to midnight Eastern Time

If you need additional help using vMentor, you can access the Participant Guide at this Website: **http://www.elluminate.com/support/guide/pdf.**

■ INTERACT WITH TLE ONLINE LABS

If your text came with TLE Online Labs, use the labs to explore and reinforce key concepts Introduced in this text. These electronic labs give you access to additional instruction and practice problems, so you can explore each concept interactively, at your own pace. Not only will you be better prepared, but you will perform better in the class overall.

To access TLE Online Labs:

1. Go to http://tle.brookscole.com.
2. In the "Pin Code" field, type the TLE PIN code supplied on your iLrn card.
3. Click on **Register.**
4. Enter the appropriate information. Fields marked with a red asterisk must be filled in.
5. Click on **Register** and **Begin TLE.**

> You will be asked to select a user name and password. Save your user name and password in a safe place. You will need them to login the next time you use TLE. Only your user name and password will allow you to reenter TLE.

Subsequent Log-in

1. Go to **http://tle.brookscole.com.**
2. Click on **Login.**
3. Make sure the name of your school appears in the "School" field. If not, then follow steps 3a–d under "Initial Login" to identify your school.
4. Type your user name and password (see boxed information above); then click on **Login.** The "My Assignments" page will open.

Applications Index

Examples that are applications are shown with boldface page numbers.
Exercises that are applications are shown with lightface page numbers.

1

An Introduction to Algebra

©Chuck Savage/CORBIS

Most banks are beehives of activity. Tellers and bank officials help customers make deposits and withdrawals, arrange loans, and set up credit card accounts. To describe these financial transactions, positive and negative numbers, fractions, and decimals are used. These numbers belong to a set that we call the *real numbers*.

To learn more about real numbers and how they are used in banking, visit *The Learning Equation* on the Internet at http://tle.brookscole.com. (The log-in instructions are in the Preface.) For Chapter 1, the online lessons are:

- *TLE* Lesson 1: The Real Numbers
- *TLE* Lesson 2: Order of Operations

Algebra is a mathematical language that can be used to solve many types of problems.

1.1   Introducing the Language of Algebra

- Tables and Graphs   • Vocabulary   • Notation
- Variables, Expressions, and Equations   • Constructing Tables

Algebra is the result of contributions from many cultures over thousands of years. The word *algebra* comes from the title of the book *Ihm Al-jabr wa'l muqābalah,* written by the Arabian mathematician al-Khwarizmi around A.D. 800. Using the vocabulary and notation of algebra, we can mathematically **model** many situations in the real world. In this section, we begin to explore the language of algebra by introducing some of its basic components.

■ TABLES AND GRAPHS

In algebra, we use tables to show relationships between quantities. For example, the following table lists the number of bicycle tires a production planner must order when a given number of bicycles are to be manufactured. For a production run of, say, 300 bikes, we locate 300 in the left-hand column and then scan across the table to see that the company must order 600 tires.

Bicycles to be manufactured	Tires to order
100	200
200	400
300	600
400	800

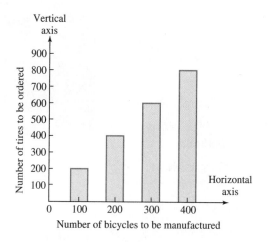

This information can also be presented using a graph. The **bar graph** (shown above) has a **horizontal axis** labeled "Number of bicycles to be manufactured." The labels are in units of 100 bicycles. The **vertical axis,** labeled "Number of tires to be ordered," is scaled in units of 100 tires. The height of a bar indicates the number of tires to order. For example, if 200 bikes are to be manufactured, we see that the bar extends to 400, meaning 400 tires are needed.

Another way to present this information is with a **line graph.** Instead of using a bar to denote the number of tires to order, we use a dot drawn at the correct height. After drawing the data points for 100, 200, 300, and 400 bicycles, we connect them with line segments to create the following graph, on the right.

The Language of Algebra

Horizontal is a form of the word *horizon.* Think of the sun setting over the *horizon.* *Vertical* means in an upright position, like *vertical* blinds in a window.

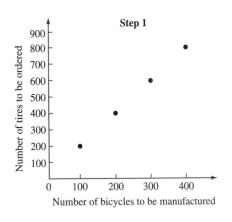

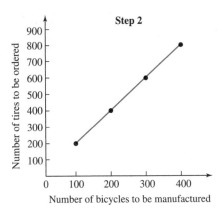

EXAMPLE 1

Use the following line graph to find the number of tires needed when 250 bicycles are to be manufactured.

Solution   We locate 250 between 200 and 300 on the horizontal axis and draw a dashed line upward to intersect the graph. From the point of intersection, we draw a dashed horizontal line to the left that intersects the vertical axis at 500. This means that 500 tires should be ordered if 250 bicycles are to be manufactured.

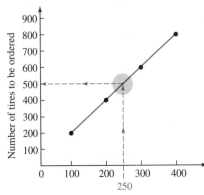

Success Tip

The video icons (see above) show which examples are taught on tutorial video tapes or disks.

Self Check 1   Use the graph to find the number of tires needed if 350 bicycles are to be manufactured.

■ VOCABULARY

From the table and graphs, it is clear that there is a relationship between the number of tires to order and the number of bicycles to be manufactured. Using words, we can express this relationship as a **verbal model:**

"The number of tires to order is two times the number of bicycles to be manufactured."

Since the word **product** indicates the result of a multiplication, we can write:

"The number of tires to order is the *product* of 2 and the number of bicycles to be manufactured."

To indicate other arithmetic operations, we will use the following words.

- A **sum** is the result of an addition: the sum of 5 and 6 is 11.
- A **difference** is the result of a subtraction: the difference of 3 and 2 is 1.
- A **quotient** is the result of a division: the quotient of 6 and 3 is 2.

■ NOTATION

Many symbols used in arithmetic are also used in algebra. For example, a + symbol is used to indicate addition, a − symbol is used to indicate subtraction, and an = symbol means *is equal to.*

Since the letter x is often used in algebra and could be confused with the multiplication symbol $\times$, we normally write multiplication in other ways.

Symbols for Multiplication	Symbol	Meaning	Example
	$\times$	Times sign	$6 \times 4 = 24$
	$\cdot$	Raised dot	$6 \cdot 4 = 24$
	$(\ )$	Parentheses	$(6)4 = 24$ or $6(4) = 24$ or $(6)(4) = 24$

In algebra, the symbol most often used to indicate division is the fraction bar.

Symbols for Division	Symbol	Meaning	Example
	$\div$	Division sign	$24 \div 4 = 6$
	$\overline{)}$	Long division	$\dfrac{6}{4\overline{)24}}$
	—	Fraction bar	$\dfrac{24}{4} = 6$

EXAMPLE 2

Express each statement in words, using one of the words *sum, product, difference,* or *quotient:*   **a.** $\frac{22}{11} = 2$ and   **b.** $22 + 11 = 33$.

Solution   **a.** We can represent the equal symbol = with the word *is.* Since the fraction bar indicates division, we have: the quotient of 22 and 11 is 2.

b. The + symbol indicates addition: the sum of 22 and 11 is 33.

Self Check 2   Express the following statement in words: $22 - 11 = 11$

■ VARIABLES, EXPRESSIONS, AND EQUATIONS

Another way to describe the tires–to–bicycles relationship uses *variables.* **Variables** are letters that stand for numbers. If we let the letter t stand for the number of tires to be ordered and b for the number of bicycles to be manufactured, we can translate the *verbal model* to mathematical symbols.

The Language of Algebra

The equal symbol = can be represented by words such as:

is   gives   yields   equals

The symbol ≠ is read as *"is not equal to."*

The number of tires to order	is	two	times	the number of bicycles to be manufactured.
t	$=$	2	$\cdot$	b

The statement $t = 2 \cdot b$ is called an *equation.* An **equation** is a mathematical sentence that contains an = symbol. Some examples are

$$3 + 5 = 8 \qquad x + 5 = 20 \qquad 17 - t = 14 - t \qquad p = 100 - d$$

When we multiply a variable by a number or multiply a variable by another variable, we can omit the symbol for multiplication.

$2b$ means $2 \cdot b$ xy means $x \cdot y$ abc means $a \cdot b \cdot c$

Using this form, we can write the equation $t = 2 \cdot b$ as $t = 2b$. The notation $2b$ on the right-hand side is called an **algebraic expression,** or more simply, an **expression.**

Algebraic Expressions	Variables and/or numbers can be combined with the operations of addition, subtraction, multiplication, and division to create **algebraic expressions.**

Here are some examples of algebraic expressions.

$4a + 7$ This expression is a combination of the numbers 4 and 7, the variable a, and the operations of multiplication and addition.

$\dfrac{10 - y}{3}$ This expression is a combination of the numbers 10 and 3, the variable y, and the operations of subtraction and division.

$15mn(2m)$ This expression is a combination of the numbers 15 and 2, the variables m and n, and the operation of multiplication.

In the bicycle manufacturing example, using the equation $t = 2b$ to describe the relationship has one major advantage over the other methods. It can be used to determine the number of tires needed for a production run of any size.

EXAMPLE 3   Use the equation $t = 2b$ to find the number of tires needed for a production run of 178 bicycles.

Solution $t = 2b$ This is the describing equation.

$t = 2(178)$ Replace b, which stands for the number of bicycles, with 178. Use parentheses to show the multiplication.

$t = 356$ Do the multiplication.

If 178 bicycles are manufactured, 356 tires will be needed.

Self Check 3   Use the equation $t = 2b$ to find the number of tires needed if 604 bicycles are to be manufactured.

■ **CONSTRUCTING TABLES**

Equations such as $t = 2b$, which express a relationship between two or more variables, are called **formulas.** Some applications require the repeated use of a formula.

EXAMPLE 4   Find the number of tires to order for production runs of 233 and 852 bicycles. Present the results in a table.

Solution   *Step 1:* We construct a two-column table. Since *b* represents the number of bicycles to be manufactured, we use it as the heading of the first column. Since *t* represents the number of tires needed, we use it as the heading of the second column. Then we enter the size of each production run in the first column, as shown.

Bicycles to be manufactured b	Tires needed t
233	466
852	1,704

Step 2: In $t = 2b$, we replace *b* with 233 and with 852 and find each corresponding value of *t*.

$$t = 2b$$
$$t = 2(233)$$
$$t = 466$$

$$t = 2b$$
$$t = 2(852)$$
$$t = 1,704$$

Step 3: These results are entered in the second column.

Self Check 4   Find the number of tires needed for production runs of 87 and 487 bicycles. Present the results in a table.

Answers to Self Checks   **1.** 700   **2.** The difference of 22 and 11 is 11.   **3.** 1,208   **4.**

b	t
87	174
487	974

1.1   STUDY SET

VOCABULARY   **Fill in the blanks.**

1. The answer to an addition problem is called the _____. The answer to a subtraction problem is called the _____.

2. The answer to a multiplication problem is called the _____. The answer to a division problem is called the _____.

3. _____ are letters that stand for numbers.

4. Variables and numbers can be combined with the operations of addition, subtraction, multiplication, and division to create algebraic _____.

5. An _____ is a mathematical sentence that contains an = symbol.

6. An equation such as $t = 2b$, which expresses a relationship between two or more variables, is called a _____.

7. The _____ axis of a graph extends left and right and the _____ axis extends up and down.

8. The word _____ comes from the title of a book written by an Arabian mathematician around A.D. 800.

CONCEPTS   **Classify each item as an algebraic expression or an equation.**

9. $18 + m = 23$

10. $18 + m$

11. $y - 1$

12. $y - 1 = 2$

13. $30x$

14. $t = 16b$

15. $r = \dfrac{2}{3}$

16. $\dfrac{c - 7}{5}$

17. a. What operations does the expression $5x - 16$ contain?

b. What variable does the expression contain?

18. a. What operations does the expression $\dfrac{12 + t}{25}$ contain?

   b. What variable does the expression contain?

19. a. What operations does the equation $4 + 1 = 20 - m$ contain?

   b. What variable does the equation contain?

20. a. What operations does the equation $y + 14 = 5(6)$ contain?

   b. What variable does the equation contain?

21. Construct a line graph using the data in the table.

Hours worked	Pay (dollars)
1	20
2	40
3	60
4	80
5	100

22. Use the data in the graph to complete the table.

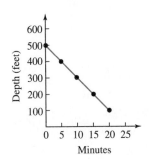

Minutes	Depth (feet)
0	
5	
10	
15	
20	

23. Explain what the dashed lines help us find in the graph.

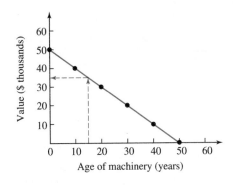

24. Use the line graph to find the income received from 30, 50, and 70 customers.

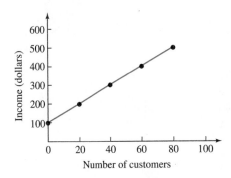

NOTATION   Write each multiplication using a raised dot and then parentheses.

25. 5×6 **26.** 4×7

27. 34×75 **28.** 90×12

Write each expression without using a multiplication symbol or parentheses.

29. $4 \cdot x$ **30.** $5 \cdot y$

31. $3 \cdot r \cdot t$ **32.** $22 \cdot q \cdot s$

33. $l \cdot w$ **34.** $b \cdot h$

35. $P \cdot r \cdot t$ **36.** $l \cdot w \cdot h$

37. $2(w)$ **38.** $2(l)$

39. $(x)(y)$ **40.** $(r)(t)$

Write each division using a fraction bar.

41. $32 \div x$ **42.** $y \div 15$

43. $30\overline{)90}$ **44.** $20\overline{)80}$

PRACTICE   Express each statement using one of the words *sum, difference, product,* or *quotient.*

45. $8(2) = 16$ **46.** $45 \cdot 12 = 540$

47. $11 - 9 = 2$ **48.** $65 + 89 = 154$

49. $2x = 10$ **50.** $16t = 4$

51. $\dfrac{66}{11} = 6$ **52.** $12 \div 3 = 4$

Translate each verbal model into an equation. (Answers may vary, depending on the variables chosen.)

53.

| The sale price | is | $100 | minus | the discount. |

54.

| The cost of dining out | equals | the cost of the meal | plus | $7 for parking. |

55.

| 7 | times | the age of a dog in years | gives | the dog's equivalent human age. |

56.

| The number of centuries | is | the number of years | divided by | 100. |

57. The amount of sand that should be used is the product of 3 and the amount of cement used.

58. The number of waiters needed is the quotient of the number of customers and 10.

59. The weight of the truck is the sum of the weight of the engine and 1,200.

60. The number of classes still open is the difference of 150 and the number of classes that are closed.

61. The profit is the difference of the revenue and 600.

62. The distance is the product of the rate and 3.

63. The quotient of the number of laps run and 4 is the number of miles run.

64. The sum of the tax and 35 is the total cost.

Use the formula to complete each table.

65. $d = 360 + L$

Lunch time (minutes) L	School day (minutes) d
30	
40	
45	

66. $b = 1,024k$

Kilobytes k	Bytes b
1	
5	
10	

67. $t = 1,500 - d$

Deductions d	Take-home pay t
200	
300	
400	

68. $w = \dfrac{s}{12}$

Inches of snow s	Inches of water w
12	
24	
72	

Use the data to find a formula that describes the relationship between the two quantities.

69.

Eggs e	Dozens d
24	2
36	3
48	4

70.

Couples c	Individuals I
20	40
100	200
200	400

APPLICATIONS

71. TRAFFIC SAFETY   As the railroad crossing guard drops, the measure of angle 1 ($\angle 1$) increases while the measure of $\angle 2$ decreases. At any instant the *sum* of the measures of the two angles is 90 degrees (denoted 90°). Complete the table. Then use the data to construct a line graph.

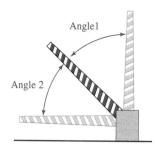

Angle 1 (degrees)	Angle 2 (degrees)
0	
30	
45	
60	
90	

72. U.S. CRIME STATISTICS   Property crimes include burglary, theft, and motor vehicle theft. Graph the following property crime rate data using a bar graph. Is an overall trend apparent?

Year	Crimes per 1,000 households
1991	354
1992	325
1993	319
1994	310
1995	291
1996	266

Year	Crimes per 1,000 households
1997	248
1998	217
1999	198
2000	178
2001	167

Source: Bureau of Justice Statistics

WRITING

73. Many people misuse the word *equation* when discussing mathematics. What is an equation? Give an example.

74. Explain the difference between an algebraic expression and an equation. Give an example of each.

75. In this section, four methods for describing numerical relationships were discussed: tables, words, graphs, and equations. Which method do you think is the most useful? Explain why.

76. In your own words, define *horizontal* and *vertical*.

CHALLENGE PROBLEMS

77. Complete the table and the formula.

s	t
10	
18	19
	34
47	48

$t = \rule{1cm}{0.4pt}$

78. Suppose $h = 4n$ and $n = 2g$. Complete the following formula: $h = \rule{0.5cm}{0.4pt}\, g$.

1.2	**Fractions**

- Factors and Prime Factorizations
- Multiplying and Dividing Fractions
- Simplifying Fractions
- Simplifying Answers
- The Meaning of Fractions
- Building Equivalent Fractions
- Adding and Subtracting Fractions
- Mixed Numbers

In arithmetic, you added, subtracted, multiplied, and divided **whole numbers:** 0, 1, 2, 3, 4, 5, and so on. Assuming that you have mastered those skills, we will now review the arithmetic of fractions.

■ FACTORS AND PRIME FACTORIZATIONS

The Language of Algebra

When we say "factor 8," we are using the word *factor* as a verb. When we say "2 is a *factor* of 8," we are using the word factor as a noun.

To compute with fractions, we need to know how to *factor* whole numbers. To **factor** a number means to express it as a product of two or more numbers. For example, some ways to factor 8 are

$$1 \cdot 8, \qquad 4 \cdot 2, \qquad \text{and} \qquad 2 \cdot 2 \cdot 2$$

The numbers 1, 2, 4, and 8 that were used to write the products are called **factors** of 8.

Sometimes a number has only two factors, itself and 1. We call these numbers *prime numbers.*

Prime Numbers and Composite Numbers	A **prime number** is a whole number greater than 1 that has only itself and 1 as factors. The first ten prime numbers are 2, 3, 5, 7, 11, 13, 17, 19, 23, and 29.
	A **composite number** is a whole number, greater than 1, that is not prime. The first ten composite numbers are 4, 6, 8, 9, 10, 12, 14, 15, 16, and 18.

Every composite number can be factored into the product of two or more prime numbers. This product of these prime numbers is called its **prime factorization.**

EXAMPLE 1

Find the prime factorization of 210.

Solution

First, write 210 as the product of two whole numbers other than 1.

The Language of Algebra

In Example 1, the prime factors are written in *ascending* order. To *ascend* means to move upward.

$$210 = 10 \cdot 21$$ The resulting prime factorization will be the same no matter which two factors of 210 you begin with.

Neither 10 nor 21 are prime numbers, so we factor each of them.

$$210 = 2 \cdot 5 \cdot 3 \cdot 7$$ Factor 10 as $2 \cdot 5$ and factor 21 as $3 \cdot 7$.

Writing the factors in ascending order, the **prime-factored form** of 210 is $2 \cdot 3 \cdot 5 \cdot 7$. Two other methods for prime factoring 210 are shown as follows.

Success Tip

When finding a prime factorization, remember that a whole number is divisible by

- 2 if it ends in 0, 2, 4, 6, or 8
- 3 if the sum of the digits is divisible by 3
- 5 if it ends in 0 or 5
- 10 if it ends in 0

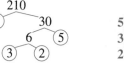

Factor tree

Work downward. Factor each number as a product of two numbers other than 1 and itself until all factors are prime.

Division ladder

$$\begin{array}{r} 7 \\ 5\overline{)35} \\ 3\overline{)105} \\ 2\overline{)210} \end{array}$$

Work upward. Perform repeated division by prime numbers until the final quotient is a prime number.

Either way, the factorization is $2 \cdot 3 \cdot 5 \cdot 7$.

Self Check 1

Find the prime factorization of 189.

■ THE MEANING OF FRACTIONS

In a fraction, the number above the **fraction bar** is called the **numerator,** and the number below is called the **denominator.**

fraction bar → $\dfrac{1}{2}$ ← numerator
← denominator

$\dfrac{5}{6}$

Fractions can describe the number of equal parts of a whole. To illustrate, we consider the circle with 5 of its 6 equal parts colored red. We say that $\frac{5}{6}$ (five-sixths) of the circle is shaded.

Fractions are also used to indicate division. For example, $\frac{8}{2}$ indicates that the numerator, 8, is to be divided by the denominator, 2:

$$\frac{8}{2} = 8 \div 2 = 4 \qquad \text{We know that } \tfrac{8}{2} = 4 \text{ because of its related multiplication}$$
$$\text{statement: } 4 \cdot 2 = 8.$$

A numerator can be any number, including 0. If it is 0 and the denominator is not, the fraction is equal to 0. For example, $\frac{0}{6} = 0$ because $0 \cdot 6 = 0$.

A denominator can be any number except 0. To see why, consider $\frac{6}{0}$. If there were an answer to the division, then $\frac{6}{0} = \text{answer}$. The related multiplication statement (answer $\cdot$ 0 = 6) is impossible because no number, when multiplied by 0, gives 6. Fractions such as $\frac{6}{0}$, that indicate division of a nonzero number by 0, are undefined.

If the numerator and denominator of a fraction are the same nonzero number, the fraction indicates division of a number by itself, and the result is 1. For example, $\frac{9}{9} = 1$.

If a denominator is 1, the fraction indicates division by 1, and the result is simply the numerator. For example, $\frac{5}{1} = 5$.

The facts about special fraction forms are summarized as follows.

The Language of Algebra

The word *undefined* is used in mathematics to describe an expression that has no meaning.

Special Fraction Forms   For any nonzero number a,

$$\frac{a}{a} = 1 \qquad \frac{a}{1} = a \qquad \frac{0}{a} = 0 \qquad \frac{a}{0} \text{ is undefined}$$

■ MULTIPLYING AND DIVIDING FRACTIONS

We now discuss how to add, subtract, multiply, and divide fractions. We begin with multiplication.

Multiplying Fractions   To multiply two fractions, multiply the numerators and multiply the denominators. Let a, b, c, and d represent numbers, where b and d are not 0,

$$\frac{a}{b} \cdot \frac{c}{d} = \frac{a \cdot c}{b \cdot d}$$

EXAMPLE 2

Multiply: $\dfrac{7}{8} \cdot \dfrac{3}{5}$.

Solution

$$\frac{7}{8} \cdot \frac{3}{5} = \frac{7 \cdot 3}{8 \cdot 5} \qquad \text{Multiply the numerators and multiply the denominators.}$$

$$= \frac{21}{40} \qquad \text{Do the multiplications.}$$

Self Check 2   Multiply: $\dfrac{5}{9} \cdot \dfrac{2}{3}$.

One number is called the **reciprocal** of another if their product is 1. To find the reciprocal of a fraction, we invert its numerator and denominator.

Success Tip

Every number, except 0, has a reciprocal. Zero has no reciprocal, because the product of 0 and a number cannot be 1.

$\frac{3}{4}$ is the reciprocal of $\frac{4}{3}$, because $\frac{3}{4} \cdot \frac{4}{3} = \frac{12}{12} = 1$.

$\frac{1}{10}$ is the reciprocal of 10, because $\frac{1}{10} \cdot 10 = \frac{10}{10} = 1$.

We use reciprocals to divide fractions.

Dividing Fractions   To divide fractions, multiply the first fraction by the reciprocal of the second. Let a, b, c, and d represent numbers, where b, c, and d are not 0,

$$\frac{a}{b} \div \frac{c}{d} = \frac{a}{b} \cdot \frac{d}{c}$$

EXAMPLE 3

Divide: $\frac{1}{3} \div \frac{4}{5}$.

Solution

$\frac{1}{3} \div \frac{4}{5} = \frac{1}{3} \cdot \frac{5}{4}$ Multiply the first fraction by the reciprocal of the second. The reciprocal of $\frac{4}{5}$ is $\frac{5}{4}$.

$= \frac{1 \cdot 5}{3 \cdot 4}$ Multiply the numerators and multiply the denominators.

$= \frac{5}{12}$ Do the multiplications.

Self Check 3   Divide: $\frac{6}{25} \div \frac{1}{2}$.

■ BUILDING EQUIVALENT FRACTIONS

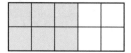

In the figure on the left, the rectangle is divided into 10 equal parts. Since 6 of those parts are red, $\frac{6}{10}$ of the figure is shaded.

Now consider the 5 equal parts of the rectangle created by the vertical lines. Since 3 of those parts are red, $\frac{3}{5}$ of the figure is shaded. We can conclude that $\frac{6}{10} = \frac{3}{5}$ because $\frac{6}{10}$ and $\frac{3}{5}$ represent the same shaded part of the rectangle. We say that $\frac{6}{10}$ and $\frac{3}{5}$ are *equivalent fractions*.

Equivalent Fractions   Two fractions are **equivalent** if they represent the same number.

Writing a fraction as an equivalent fraction with a larger denominator is called **building** the fraction. To build a fraction, we multiply it by a form of the number 1. Since any number multiplied by 1 remains the same (identical), 1 is called the **multiplicative identity.**

Multiplication Property of 1	The product of 1 and any number is that number.

For any number a,

$$1 \cdot a = a \qquad \text{and} \qquad a \cdot 1 = a$$

EXAMPLE 4   Write $\dfrac{3}{5}$ as an equivalent fraction with a denominator of 35.

Solution   We need to multiply the denominator of $\dfrac{3}{5}$ by 7 to obtain a denominator of 35. It follows that $\dfrac{7}{7}$ should be the form of 1 that is used to build $\dfrac{3}{5}$. Multiplying $\dfrac{3}{5}$ by $\dfrac{7}{7}$ does not change its value, because we are multiplying $\dfrac{3}{5}$ by 1.

$$\frac{3}{5} = \frac{3}{5} \cdot \frac{7}{7} \qquad \tfrac{7}{7} = 1$$

$$= \frac{3 \cdot 7}{5 \cdot 7} \qquad \text{Multiply the numerators and multiply the denominators.}$$

$$= \frac{21}{35}$$

Self Check 4   Write $\dfrac{5}{8}$ as an equivalent fraction with a denominator of 24.

■ SIMPLIFYING FRACTIONS

The Language of Algebra

The word *infinitely* is a form of the word *infinite*, which means endless.

Every fraction can be written in infinitely many equivalent forms. For example, some equivalent forms of $\dfrac{30}{36}$ are:

$$\frac{5}{6} = \frac{10}{12} = \frac{15}{18} = \frac{20}{24} = \frac{25}{30} = \frac{30}{36} = \frac{35}{42} = \frac{40}{48} = \frac{45}{54} = \frac{50}{60} = \cdots$$

Of all of the equivalent forms in which we can write a fraction, we often need to determine the one that is in *simplest form.*

Simplest Form of a Fraction	A fraction is in **simplest form,** or **lowest terms,** when the numerator and denominator have no common factors other than 1.

To **simplify a fraction,** we write it in simplest form by removing a factor equal to 1. For example, to simplify $\dfrac{30}{36}$, we note that the greatest factor common to the numerator and denominator is 6 and proceed as follows:

$$\frac{30}{36} = \frac{5 \cdot 6}{6 \cdot 6} \qquad \text{Factor 30 and 36, using their greatest common factor, 6.}$$

$$= \frac{5}{6} \cdot \frac{6}{6} \qquad \text{Use the rule for multiplying fractions in reverse: write } \tfrac{5 \cdot 6}{6 \cdot 6} \text{ as the product of two fractions, } \tfrac{5}{6} \text{ and } \tfrac{6}{6}.$$

$$= \frac{5}{6} \cdot 1 \qquad \text{A number divided by itself is equal to 1: } \tfrac{6}{6} = 1.$$

$$= \frac{5}{6} \qquad \text{Use the multiplication property of 1: any number multiplied by 1 remains the same.}$$

To simplify $\frac{30}{36}$, we removed a factor equal to 1 in the form of $\frac{6}{6}$. The result, $\frac{5}{6}$, is equivalent to $\frac{30}{36}$.

We can easily identify the greatest common factor of the numerator and the denominator of a fraction if we write them in prime-factored form.

EXAMPLE 5

Simplify each fraction, if possible: **a.** $\frac{63}{42}$ and   **b.** $\frac{33}{40}$.

Solution   **a.** After prime factoring 63 and 42, we see that the greatest common factor of the numerator and the denominator is $3 \cdot 7 = 21$.

Language of Algebra

What do Calvin Klein, Sheryl Swoopes, and Dustin Hoffman have in common? They all attended a community college. The word *common* means shared by two or more. In this section, we will work with *common* factors and *common* denominators.

$$\frac{63}{42} = \frac{3 \cdot 3 \cdot 7}{2 \cdot 3 \cdot 7} \qquad \text{Write 63 and 42 in prime-factored form.}$$

$$= \frac{3}{2} \cdot \frac{3 \cdot 7}{3 \cdot 7} \qquad \text{Write } \frac{3 \cdot 3 \cdot 7}{2 \cdot 3 \cdot 7} \text{ as the product of two fractions, } \frac{3}{2} \text{ and } \frac{3 \cdot 7}{3 \cdot 7}.$$

$$= \frac{3}{2} \cdot 1 \qquad \text{A nonzero number divided by itself is equal to 1: } \frac{3 \cdot 7}{3 \cdot 7} = 1.$$

$$= \frac{3}{2} \qquad \text{Any number multiplied by 1 remains the same.}$$

b. Prime factor 33 and 40.

$$\frac{33}{40} = \frac{3 \cdot 11}{2 \cdot 2 \cdot 2 \cdot 5}$$

Since the numerator and the denominator have no common factors other than 1, $\frac{33}{40}$ is in simplest form (lowest terms).

Self Check 5   Simplify each fraction, if possible: **a.** $\frac{24}{56}$ and   **b.** $\frac{16}{125}$.

To streamline the simplifying process, we can replace pairs of factors common to the numerator and denominator with the equivalent fraction $\frac{1}{1}$.

EXAMPLE 6

Simplify: $\frac{90}{105}$.

Solution $$\frac{90}{105} = \frac{2 \cdot 3 \cdot 3 \cdot 5}{3 \cdot 5 \cdot 7} \qquad \text{Write 90 and 105 in prime-factored form.}$$

$$= \frac{2 \cdot \overset{1}{\cancel{3}} \cdot 3 \cdot \overset{1}{\cancel{5}}}{\underset{1}{\cancel{3}} \cdot \underset{1}{\cancel{5}} \cdot 7} \qquad \text{Slashes and 1's are used to show that } \frac{3}{3} \text{ and } \frac{5}{5} \text{ are replaced by the equivalent fraction } \frac{1}{1}.$$

$$= \frac{6}{7}$$

Multiply to find the numerator: $2 \cdot 1 \cdot 3 \cdot 1 = 6$. Multiply to find the denominator: $1 \cdot 1 \cdot 7 = 7$.

Self Check 6   Simplify: $\dfrac{126}{70}$.

Simplifying a Fraction

1. Factor (or prime factor) the numerator and denominator to determine all the factors common to both.
2. Replace each pair of factors common to the numerator and denominator with the equivalent fraction $\frac{1}{1}$.
3. Multiply the remaining factors in the numerator and in the denominator.

Caution When all common factors of the numerator and the denominator of a fraction are removed, forgetting to write 1's above the slashes leads to a common mistake.

Correct

$$\frac{15}{45} = \frac{\overset{1}{\cancel{3}} \cdot \overset{1}{\cancel{5}}}{\underset{1}{\cancel{3}} \cdot 3 \cdot \underset{1}{\cancel{5}}} = \frac{1}{3}$$

Incorrect

$$\frac{15}{45} = \frac{\cancel{3} \cdot \cancel{5}}{\cancel{3} \cdot 3 \cdot \cancel{5}} = \frac{0}{3} = 0$$

ADDING AND SUBTRACTING FRACTIONS

To add or subtract fractions, they must have the same denominator.

Adding and Subtracting Fractions

To add (or subtract) two fractions with the same denominator, add (or subtract) their numerators and write the sum (or difference) over the common denominator.
Let a, b, and d represent numbers, where d is not 0,

$$\frac{a}{d} + \frac{b}{d} = \frac{a+b}{d} \qquad \frac{a}{d} - \frac{b}{d} = \frac{a-b}{d}$$

For example,

$$\frac{3}{7} + \frac{1}{7} = \frac{3+1}{7} = \frac{4}{7} \quad \text{and} \quad \frac{18}{25} - \frac{9}{25} = \frac{18-9}{25} = \frac{9}{25}$$

Caution Only factors common to the numerator and the denominator of a fraction can be removed. It is incorrect to remove the 5's in $\frac{5+8}{5}$, because 5 is not used as a factor in the expression $5 + 8$. This error leads to an incorrect answer of 9.

Correct

$$\frac{5+8}{5} = \frac{13}{5}$$

Incorrect

$$\frac{5+8}{5} = \frac{\overset{1}{\cancel{5}}+8}{\underset{1}{\cancel{5}}} = \frac{9}{1} = 9$$

To add (or subtract) fractions with different denominators, we express them as equivalent fractions that have a common denominator. The smallest common denominator, called the **least** or **lowest common denominator,** is usually the easiest common denominator to use.

Least Common Denominator (LCD)	The **least** or **lowest common denominator (LCD)** for a set of fractions is the smallest number each denominator will divide exactly (divide with no remainder).

Success Tip

To determine the LCD of two fractions, list the multiples of one of the denominators. The first number in the list that is exactly divisible by the other denominator is their LCD. For $\frac{2}{5}$ and $\frac{1}{3}$, the multiples of 5 are 5, 10, 15, 20, 25, ... Since 15 is the first number in the list that is exactly divisible by 3, the LCD is 15.

The denominators of $\frac{2}{5}$ and $\frac{1}{3}$ are 5 and 3. The numbers 5 and 3 divide many numbers exactly (30, 45, and 60, to name a few), but the smallest number that they divide exactly is 15. Thus, 15 is the LCD for $\frac{2}{5}$ and $\frac{1}{3}$.

To find $\frac{2}{5} + \frac{1}{3}$, we find equivalent fractions that have denominators of 15 and we use the rule for adding fractions.

$$\frac{2}{5} + \frac{1}{3} = \frac{2}{5} \cdot \frac{3}{3} + \frac{1}{3} \cdot \frac{5}{5}$$ Multiply $\frac{2}{5}$ by 1 in the form of $\frac{3}{3}$. Multiply $\frac{1}{3}$ by 1 in the form of $\frac{5}{5}$.

$$= \frac{6}{15} + \frac{5}{15}$$ Multiply the numerators and multiply the denominators. Note that the denominators are now the same.

$$= \frac{6 + 5}{15}$$ Add the numerators. Write the sum over the common denominator.

$$= \frac{11}{15}$$ Do the addition.

When adding (or subtracting) fractions with unlike denominators, the least common denominator is not always obvious. Prime factorization is helpful in determining the LCD.

EXAMPLE 7

Subtract: $\frac{3}{10} - \frac{5}{28}$.

Solution   To find the LCD, we find the prime factorization of both denominators and use each prime factor the *greatest* number of times it appears in any one factorization:

$$\left.\begin{array}{l} 10 = 2 \cdot 5 \\ 28 = 2 \cdot 2 \cdot 7 \end{array}\right\} \text{LCD} = 2 \cdot 2 \cdot 5 \cdot 7 = 140$$

2 appears twice in the factorization of 28.
5 appears once in the factorization of 10.
7 appears once in the factorization of 28.

Since 140 is the smallest number that 10 and 28 divide exactly, we write both fractions as fractions with the LCD of 140.

$$\frac{3}{10} - \frac{5}{28} = \frac{3}{10} \cdot \frac{14}{14} - \frac{5}{28} \cdot \frac{5}{5}$$ We must multiply 10 by 14 to obtain 140. We must multiply 28 by 5 to obtain 140.

$$= \frac{42}{140} - \frac{25}{140}$$ Do the multiplications.

$$= \frac{42 - 25}{140}$$ Subtract the numerators. Write the difference over the common denominator.

$$= \frac{17}{140}$$ Do the subtraction.

Self Check 7   Subtract: $\dfrac{11}{48} - \dfrac{7}{40}$.

■ SIMPLIFYING ANSWERS

When adding, subtracting, multiplying, or dividing fractions, remember to express the answer in simplest form.

EXAMPLE 8   Perform each operation: **a.** $45\left(\dfrac{4}{9}\right)$ and **b.** $\dfrac{5}{12} + \dfrac{3}{4}$.

Solution   **a.** $45\left(\dfrac{4}{9}\right) = \dfrac{45}{1}\left(\dfrac{4}{9}\right)$ Write 45 as a fraction: $45 = \dfrac{45}{1}$.

$= \dfrac{45 \cdot 4}{1 \cdot 9}$ Multiply the numerators. Multiply the denominators.

$= \dfrac{\overset{1}{\cancel{3}} \cdot \overset{1}{\cancel{3}} \cdot 5 \cdot 2 \cdot 2}{1 \cdot \underset{1}{\cancel{3}} \cdot \underset{1}{\cancel{3}}}$ To simplify the fraction, prime factor 45, 4, and 9. Then replace each $\frac{3}{3}$ with $\frac{1}{1}$.

$= 20$

b. Since the smallest number that 12 and 4 divide exactly is 12, the LCD is 12.

$\dfrac{5}{12} + \dfrac{3}{4} = \dfrac{5}{12} + \dfrac{3}{4} \cdot \dfrac{3}{3}$ $\frac{5}{12}$ already has a denominator of 12. Build $\frac{3}{4}$ so that its denominator is 12.

$= \dfrac{5}{12} + \dfrac{9}{12}$ Multiply the numerators and denominators in the second term. The denominators are now the same.

$= \dfrac{14}{12}$ Add the numerators, 5 and 9, to get 14. Write that sum over the common denominator.

$= \dfrac{\overset{1}{\cancel{2}} \cdot 7}{\underset{1}{\cancel{2}} \cdot 6}$ To simplify $\frac{14}{12}$, factor 14 and 12, using their greatest common factor, 2. Then remove $\frac{2}{2} = 1$.

$= \dfrac{7}{6}$

Self Check 8   Perform each operation: **a.** $24\left(\dfrac{8}{6}\right)$, **b.** $\dfrac{1}{15} + \dfrac{31}{30}$

■ MIXED NUMBERS

A **mixed number** represents the sum of a whole number and a fraction. For example, $5\frac{3}{4}$ means $5 + \frac{3}{4}$. To perform calculations involving mixed numbers, we often express them as improper fractions.

EXAMPLE 9

Divide: $5\frac{3}{4} \div 2$.

Solution

To write the mixed number $5\frac{3}{4}$ as a fraction, we use a two-step process.

The Language of Algebra

Fractions such as $\frac{23}{4}$, with a numerator greater than or equal to the denominator, are called **improper fractions.** This term is misleading. In algebra, such fractions are often preferable to their equivalent mixed number form.

$$5\frac{3}{4} = \frac{23}{4}$$

Step 1. Multiply the whole number by the denominator: $5 \cdot 4 = 20$. Then add that product to the numerator: $20 + 3 = 23$.
Step 2. Write the result from Step 1 over the denominator, 4.

Now we replace $5\frac{3}{4}$ with $\frac{23}{4}$ and divide.

$$5\frac{3}{4} \div 2 = \frac{23}{4} \div \frac{2}{1} \qquad \text{Write } 5\frac{3}{4} \text{ as } \frac{23}{4}. \text{ Write 2 as a fraction: } 2 = \frac{2}{1}.$$

$$= \frac{23}{4} \cdot \frac{1}{2} \qquad \text{Multiply by the reciprocal of } \frac{2}{1}, \text{ which is } \frac{1}{2}.$$

$$= \frac{23}{8} \qquad \text{Multiply the numerators. Multiply the denominators.}$$

To write the answer, $\frac{23}{8}$, as a mixed number, we use a two-step process.

$$\frac{23}{8} = 2\frac{7}{8}$$

Step 1. Divide the numerator, 23, by the denominator, 8.
Step 2. The quotient, 2, is the whole-number part of the mixed number. Its fractional part is the remainder, 7, over the original denominator, 8.

$$\begin{array}{r} 2 \\ 8\overline{)23} \\ \underline{16} \\ 7 \end{array}$$

Self Check 9

Multiply: $1\frac{1}{8} \cdot 9$.

Answers to Self Checks

1. $189 = 3 \cdot 3 \cdot 3 \cdot 7$ **2.** $\frac{10}{27}$ **3.** $\frac{12}{25}$ **4.** $\frac{15}{24}$ **5. a.** $\frac{3}{7}$,   **b.** in simplest form   **6.** $\frac{9}{5}$
7. $\frac{13}{240}$ **8. a.** 32,   **b.** $\frac{11}{10}$ **9.** $\frac{81}{8} = 10\frac{1}{8}$

1.2   STUDY SET

VOCABULARY   Fill in the blanks.

1. Numbers that have only 1 and themselves as factors, such as 23, 37, and 41, are called _____ numbers.

2. When we write 60 as $20 \cdot 3$, we say that we have _____ 60. When we write 60 as $5 \cdot 3 \cdot 2 \cdot 2$, we say that we have written 60 in _____ form.

3. The _____ of the fraction $\frac{3}{4}$ is 3, and the _____ is 4.

4. A fraction is in _____ form, or _____ terms, when the numerator and denominator have no common factors other than 1.

5. Two fractions that represent the same number, such as $\frac{1}{2}$ and $\frac{2}{4}$, are called _____ fractions.

6. The number $\frac{2}{3}$ is the _____ of the number $\frac{3}{2}$, because their product is 1.

7. The _____ common denominator for a set of fractions is the smallest number each denominator will divide exactly.

8. The _____ number $7\frac{1}{3}$ represents the sum of a whole number and a fraction: $7 + \frac{1}{3}$.

CONCEPTS

9. The prime factorization of a number is $2 \cdot 2 \cdot 3 \cdot 5$. What is the number?

10. Complete each fact about fractions. Assume $a \neq 0$.

$$\frac{a}{a} = \boxed{} \qquad \frac{a}{1} = \boxed{} \qquad \frac{0}{a} = \boxed{} \qquad \frac{a}{0} \text{ is } \boxed{}$$

11. What equivalent fractions are shown in the illustration?

12. Complete each rule.

a. $\dfrac{a}{b} \cdot \dfrac{c}{d} = \boxed{}$ **b.** $\dfrac{a}{b} \div \dfrac{c}{d} = \boxed{}$

c. $\dfrac{a}{d} + \dfrac{b}{d} = \boxed{}$ **d.** $\dfrac{a}{d} - \dfrac{b}{d} = \boxed{}$

13. Simplify $\dfrac{2 \cdot 2 \cdot 3}{2 \cdot 3 \cdot 5}$.

14. To express $\frac{3}{8}$ as an equivalent fraction with a denominator of 40, by what number must we multiply the numerator and the denominator?

15. Complete each statement.
   a. To build a fraction, we multiply it by ▪ in the form of $\frac{2}{2}$, $\frac{3}{3}$, or $\frac{4}{4}$, and so on.
   b. To simplify a fraction, we remove factors equal to ▪ in the form of $\frac{2}{2}$, $\frac{3}{3}$, or $\frac{4}{4}$, and so on.

16. a. Give three numbers that 4 and 6 divide exactly.

   b. What is the smallest number that 4 and 6 divide exactly?

17. The prime factorizations of 24 and 36 are

$$24 = 2 \cdot 2 \cdot 2 \cdot 3$$
$$36 = 2 \cdot 2 \cdot 3 \cdot 3$$

   a. What is the greatest number of times 2 appears in any one factorization?
   b. What is the greatest number of times 3 appears in any one factorization?

18. a. Write $2\dfrac{15}{16}$ as an improper fraction.

   b. Write $\dfrac{49}{12}$ as a mixed number.

NOTATION

19. Consider $\dfrac{5}{16} = \dfrac{5}{16} \cdot \dfrac{3}{3}$.

   a. What fraction is being built up?

   b. Fill in the blank: $\dfrac{3}{3} = \boxed{}$.

   c. What equivalent fraction is the result after building $\dfrac{5}{16}$?

20. Consider $\dfrac{70}{175} = \dfrac{\overset{1}{\cancel{7}} \cdot \overset{1}{\cancel{5}} \cdot 2}{\underset{1}{\cancel{7}} \cdot \underset{1}{\cancel{5}} \cdot 5}$.

   a. What fraction is being simplified?

   b. What are $\dfrac{7}{7}$ and $\dfrac{5}{5}$ replaced with?

   c. What equivalent fraction is the result after simplifying?

PRACTICE   List the factors of each number.

21. 20   **22.** 50
23. 28   **24.** 36

Give the prime factorization of each number.

25. 75   **26.** 20
27. 28   **28.** 54
29. 117   **30.** 147
31. 220   **32.** 270

Build each fraction or whole number to an equivalent fraction having the indicated denominator.

33. $\dfrac{1}{3}$, denominator 9   **34.** $\dfrac{3}{8}$, denominator 24

35. $\dfrac{4}{9}$, denominator 54   **36.** $\dfrac{9}{16}$, denominator 64

37. 7, denominator 5   **38.** 12, denominator 3

Write each fraction in lowest terms. If the fraction is in lowest terms, so indicate.

39. $\dfrac{6}{12}$ **40.** $\dfrac{3}{9}$

41. $\dfrac{24}{18}$ **42.** $\dfrac{35}{14}$

43. $\dfrac{15}{20}$ **44.** $\dfrac{22}{77}$

45. $\dfrac{72}{64}$ **46.** $\dfrac{26}{21}$

47. $\dfrac{33}{56}$ **48.** $\dfrac{26}{39}$

49. $\dfrac{36}{225}$ **50.** $\dfrac{175}{490}$

Perform each operation and simplify the result when possible.

51. $\dfrac{1}{2} \cdot \dfrac{3}{5}$ **52.** $\dfrac{3}{4} \cdot \dfrac{5}{7}$

53. $\dfrac{4}{3}\left(\dfrac{6}{5}\right)$ **54.** $\dfrac{7}{8}\left(\dfrac{6}{15}\right)$

55. $\dfrac{5}{12} \cdot \dfrac{18}{5}$ **56.** $\dfrac{5}{4} \cdot \dfrac{12}{10}$

57. $21\left(\dfrac{10}{3}\right)$ **58.** $28\left(\dfrac{4}{7}\right)$

59. $7\dfrac{1}{2} \cdot 1\dfrac{2}{5}$ **60.** $3\dfrac{1}{4}\left(1\dfrac{1}{5}\right)$

61. $6 \cdot 2\dfrac{7}{24}$ **62.** $7 \cdot 1\dfrac{3}{28}$

63. $\dfrac{3}{5} \div \dfrac{2}{3}$ **64.** $\dfrac{4}{5} \div \dfrac{3}{7}$

65. $\dfrac{3}{4} \div \dfrac{6}{5}$ **66.** $\dfrac{3}{8} \div \dfrac{15}{28}$

67. $\dfrac{21}{35} \div \dfrac{3}{14}$ **68.** $\dfrac{23}{25} \div \dfrac{46}{5}$

69. $6 \div \dfrac{3}{14}$ **70.** $23 \div \dfrac{46}{5}$

71. $3\dfrac{1}{3} \div 1\dfrac{5}{6}$ **72.** $2\dfrac{1}{2} \div 1\dfrac{5}{8}$

73. $8 \div 3\dfrac{1}{5}$ **74.** $15 \div 3\dfrac{1}{3}$

75. $\dfrac{3}{5} + \dfrac{3}{5}$ **76.** $\dfrac{4}{13} - \dfrac{3}{13}$

77. $\dfrac{1}{6} + \dfrac{1}{24}$ **78.** $\dfrac{17}{25} - \dfrac{2}{5}$

79. $\dfrac{3}{5} + \dfrac{2}{3}$ **80.** $\dfrac{4}{3} + \dfrac{7}{2}$

81. $\dfrac{5}{12} + \dfrac{1}{3}$ **82.** $\dfrac{7}{15} + \dfrac{1}{5}$

83. $\dfrac{9}{4} - \dfrac{5}{6}$ **84.** $\dfrac{2}{15} + \dfrac{7}{9}$

85. $\dfrac{7}{10} - \dfrac{1}{14}$ **86.** $\dfrac{7}{25} + \dfrac{3}{10}$

87. $\dfrac{5}{14} - \dfrac{4}{21}$ **88.** $\dfrac{2}{33} + \dfrac{3}{22}$

89. $3 - \dfrac{3}{4}$ **90.** $\dfrac{17}{3} + 4$

91. $3\dfrac{3}{4} - 2\dfrac{1}{2}$ **92.** $15\dfrac{5}{6} + 11\dfrac{5}{8}$

93. $8\dfrac{2}{9} - 7\dfrac{2}{3}$ **94.** $3\dfrac{4}{5} - 3\dfrac{1}{10}$

APPLICATIONS

95. BOTANY   To assess the effects of smog, botanists cut down a pine tree and measured the width of the growth rings for the last two years.
a. What was the growth over this two-year period?

b. What is the difference in the widths of the rings?

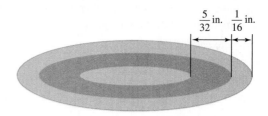

96. HARDWARE   To secure the bracket to the stock, a bolt and a nut are used. How long should the threaded part of the bolt be?

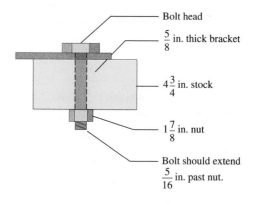

97. FRAMES How much molding is needed to produce the square picture frame shown?

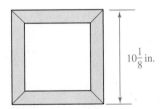

$10\frac{1}{8}$ in.

98. DECORATING The materials used to make a pillow are shown here. Examine the inventory list to decide how many pillows can be manufactured in one production run with the materials in stock.

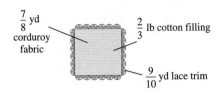

$\frac{7}{8}$ yd corduroy fabric

$\frac{2}{3}$ lb cotton filling

$\frac{9}{10}$ yd lace trim

Factory Inventory List

Materials	Amount in stock
Lace trim	135 yd
Corduroy fabric	154 yd
Cotton filling	98 lb

WRITING

99. Explain how to add two fractions having unlike denominators.

100. To multiply two fractions, must they have like denominators? Explain.

101. What are equivalent fractions?

102. Explain the error in the following work.

$$\text{Add: } \frac{4}{3} + \frac{3}{2} = \frac{4}{\cancel{3}} + \frac{\cancel{3}^{1}}{5}$$

$$= \frac{4}{1} + \frac{1}{5}$$

$$= 4 + \frac{1}{5}$$

$$= 4\frac{1}{5}$$

REVIEW **Express each statement using one of the words sum, difference, product, or quotient.**

103. $7 - 5 = 2$

104. $5(6) = 30$

105. $30 \div 15 = 2$

106. $12 + 12 = 24$

Use the formula to complete each table.

107. $T = 15g$

Number of gears g	Number of teeth T
10	
12	

108. $p = r - 200$

Revenue r	Profit p
1,000	
5,000	

CHALLENGE PROBLEMS

109. Which is larger: $\frac{11}{12}$ or $\frac{8}{9}$?

110. If the circle represents a whole, find the missing value.

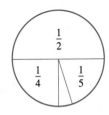

$\frac{1}{2}$

$\frac{1}{4}$

$\frac{1}{5}$

1.3   **The Real Numbers**

- The Integers   • Rational Numbers: Fractions and Mixed Numbers
- Rational Numbers: Decimals   • Irrational Numbers   • The Real Numbers
- Graphing on the Number Line   • Absolute Value

In this section, we will define many types of numbers. Then we will show that together they form a collection or **set** of numbers called the *real numbers*.

■ THE INTEGERS

Natural numbers are the numbers that we use for counting. To write this set, we list its **members** (or **elements**) within **braces** {   }.

Natural Numbers   The set of **natural numbers** is {1, 2, 3, 4, 5, . . .}.   Read as "the set containing one, two, three, four, five, and so on."

The three dots . . . in this definition mean that the list continues on forever. The natural numbers, together with 0, form the set of **whole numbers.**

Whole Numbers   The set of **whole numbers** is {0, 1, 2, 3, 4, 5, . . .}.

Although whole numbers are used in a wide variety of settings, they are not adequate for describing many real-life situations. For example, if you write a check for more than what's in your account, the account balance will be less than zero.

We can use the **number line** below to visualize numbers less than zero. A number line is straight and has uniform markings. The arrowheads indicate that it extends forever in both directions. For each natural number on the number line, there is a corresponding number, called its *opposite,* to the left of 0. In the illustration, we see that 3 and −3 (negative three) are opposites, as are −5 (negative five) and 5. Note that 0 is its own opposite.

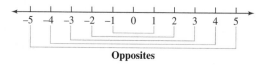

Opposites

Opposites   Two numbers that are the same distance from 0 on the number line, but on opposite sides of it, are called **opposites.**

The whole numbers, together with their opposites, form the set of **integers.**

Integers   The set of **integers** is {. . . , −4, −3, −2, −1, 0, 1, 2, 3, 4, . . .}.

The Language of Algebra

The *positive integers* are: 1, 2, 3, 4, 5, ...
The *negative integers* are: −1, −2, −3, −4, −5, ...

On the number line, numbers greater than 0 are to the right of 0. They are called **positive numbers.** Positive numbers can be written with or without a **positive sign** +. For example, 2 = +2 (positive two). They can be used to describe such quantities as an elevation above sea level (+3,000 ft) or a stock market gain (25 points).

Numbers less than 0 are to the left of 0 on the number line. They are called **negative numbers.** Negative numbers are always written with a **negative sign** −. They can be used to describe such quantities as an overdrawn checking account (−$75) or a below-zero temperature (−12°).

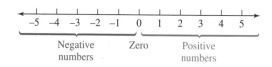

Negative numbers   Zero   Positive numbers

■ RATIONAL NUMBERS: FRACTIONS AND MIXED NUMBERS

Many situations cannot be described using integers. For example, a commute to work might take $\frac{1}{4}$ hour, or a hat might be size $7\frac{5}{8}$. To describe these situations, we need fractions, often called *rational numbers*.

| Rational Numbers | A **rational number** is any number that can be expressed as a fraction with an integer numerator and a nonzero integer denominator. |

Some examples of rational numbers are

$$\frac{1}{4}, \quad \frac{7}{8}, \quad \frac{25}{25}, \quad \text{and} \quad \frac{19}{12}$$

To show that negative fractions are rational numbers, we use the following fact.

| Negative Fractions | Let a and b represent numbers, where b is not 0. $$-\frac{a}{b} = \frac{-a}{b} = \frac{a}{-b}$$ |

To illustrate this rule, we consider $-\frac{11}{16}$. It is a rational number because it can be written as $\frac{-11}{16}$ or as $\frac{11}{-16}$.

Positive and negative mixed numbers are also rational numbers because they can be expressed as fractions. For example,

The Language of Algebra

Rational numbers are so named because they can be expressed as the ratio (quotient) of two integers.

$$7\frac{5}{8} = \frac{61}{8} \quad \text{and} \quad -6\frac{1}{2} = -\frac{13}{2} = \frac{-13}{2}$$

Any natural number, whole number, or integer can be expressed as a fraction with a denominator of 1. For example, $5 = \frac{5}{1}$, $0 = \frac{0}{1}$, and $-3 = \frac{-3}{1}$. Therefore, every natural number, whole number, and integer is also a rational number.

■ RATIONAL NUMBERS: DECIMALS

Many numerical quantities are written in decimal notation. For instance, a candy bar might cost $0.89, a dragster might travel at 203.156 mph, or a business loss might be −$4.7 million. These decimals are called **terminating decimals** because their representations terminate. As shown below, terminating decimals can be expressed as fractions. Therefore, terminating decimals are rational numbers.

The Language of Algebra

To *terminate* means to bring to an end. In the movie *The Terminator,* actor Arnold Schwarzenegger plays a heartless machine sent to Earth to bring an end to his enemies.

$$0.89 = \frac{89}{100} \qquad 203.156 = 203\frac{156}{1,000} = \frac{203,156}{1,000} \qquad -4.7 = -4\frac{7}{10} = \frac{-47}{10}$$

Decimals such as $0.3333\ldots$ and $2.8167167167\ldots$, which have a digit (or block of digits) that repeats, are called **repeating decimals**. Since any repeating decimal can be expressed as a fraction, repeating decimals are rational numbers.

The set of rational numbers cannot be listed as we listed other sets in this section. Instead, we use **set-builder** notation.

Rational Numbers

The set of rational numbers is

$$\left\{ \frac{a}{b} \,\middle|\, a \text{ and } b \text{ are integers, with } b \neq 0. \right\}$$

Read as "the set of all numbers of the form $\frac{a}{b}$, such that a and b are integers, with $b \neq 0$."

To find the decimal equivalent for a fraction, we divide its numerator by its denominator. For example, to write $\frac{1}{4}$ and $\frac{5}{22}$ as decimals, we proceed as follows:

The Language of Algebra

Since every natural number belongs to the set of whole numbers, we say the set of natural numbers is a *subset* of the set of whole numbers. Similarly, the set of whole numbers is a subset of the set of integers, and the set of integers is a subset of the set of rational numbers.

$$\begin{array}{r} 0.25 \\ 4\overline{)1.00} \\ \underline{8} \\ 20 \\ \underline{20} \\ 0 \end{array}$$

Write a decimal point and additional zeros to the right of 1.

The remainder is 0.

$$\begin{array}{r} 0.22727\ldots \\ 22\overline{)5.00000} \\ \underline{4\,4} \\ 60 \\ \underline{44} \\ 160 \\ \underline{154} \\ 60 \\ \underline{44} \\ 160 \end{array}$$

Write a decimal point and additional zeros to the right of 5.

60 and 160 continually appear as remainders. Therefore, 2 and 7 will continually appear in the quotient.

The decimal equivalent of $\frac{1}{4}$ is 0.25 and the decimal equivalent of $\frac{5}{22}$ is 0.2272727 . . . . We can use an **overbar** to write repeating decimals in more compact form: $0.2272727\ldots = 0.2\overline{27}$. Here are more fractions and their decimal equivalents.

Terminating decimals

$$\frac{1}{2} = 0.5$$

$$\frac{5}{8} = 0.625$$

$$\frac{3}{4} = 0.75$$

Repeating decimals

$$\frac{1}{6} = 0.16666\ldots \quad \text{or} \quad 0.1\overline{6}$$

$$\frac{1}{3} = 0.3333\ldots \quad \text{or} \quad 0.\overline{3}$$

$$\frac{5}{11} = 0.454545\ldots \quad \text{or} \quad 0.\overline{45}$$

■ IRRATIONAL NUMBERS

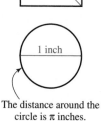

The distance around the circle is π inches.

Numbers that cannot be expressed as a fraction with an integer numerator and an integer denominator are called **irrational numbers.** One example is the square root of 2, denoted $\sqrt{2}$. It is the number that, when multiplied by itself, gives 2: $\sqrt{2} \cdot \sqrt{2} = 2$. It can be shown that a square with sides of length 1 inch has a diagonal that is $\sqrt{2}$ inches long.

The number represented by the Greek letter π (pi) is another example of an irrational number. A circle, with a 1-inch diameter, has a circumference of π inches.

Expressed in decimal form,

$$\sqrt{2} = 1.414213562\ldots \quad \text{and} \quad \pi = 3.141592654\ldots$$

These decimals neither terminate nor repeat.

Irrational Numbers

An **irrational number** is a nonterminating, nonrepeating decimal. An irrational number cannot be expressed as a fraction with an integer numerator and an integer denominator.

Other examples of irrational numbers are:

$$\sqrt{3} = 1.732050808 \ldots \qquad -\sqrt{5} = -2.236067977 \ldots$$
$$-\pi = -3.141592654 \ldots \qquad 3\pi = 9.424777961 \ldots \qquad \text{3}\pi \text{ means } 3 \cdot \pi.$$

We can use a calculator to approximate the decimal value of an irrational number. To approximate $\sqrt{2}$ using a scientific calculator, we use the square root key $\sqrt{}$. To approximate π, we use the *pi* key π.

$$\sqrt{2} \approx 1.414213562 \qquad \text{and} \qquad \pi \approx 3.141592654 \qquad \text{Read } \approx \text{ as "is approximately equal to."}$$

Rounded to the nearest thousandth, $\sqrt{2} \approx 1.414$ and $\pi \approx 3.142$.

■ THE REAL NUMBERS

The set of **real numbers** is formed by combining the set of rational numbers and the set of irrational numbers. Every real number has a decimal representation. If it is rational, its corresponding decimal terminates or repeats. If it is irrational, its decimal representation is nonterminating and nonrepeating.

The Real Numbers	A **real number** is any number that is a rational number or an irrational number.

The following diagram shows how various sets of numbers are related. Note that a number can belong to more than one set. For example, -6 is an integer, a rational number, and a real number.

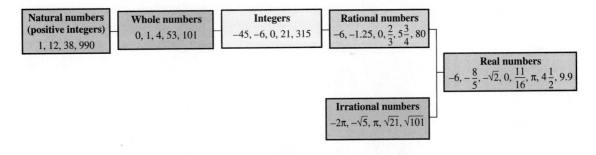

EXAMPLE 1

Which numbers in the following set are natural numbers, whole numbers, integers, rational numbers, irrational numbers, real numbers? $\left\{-3.4, \frac{2}{5}, 0, -6, 1\frac{3}{4}, \pi, 16\right\}$

Solution

Natural numbers: 16   16 is a member of $\{1, 2, 3, 4, 5, \ldots\}$.

Whole numbers: 0, 16   0 and 16 are members of $\{0, 1, 2, 3, 4, 5, \ldots\}$.

Integers: 0, -6, 16   0, -6, and 16 are members of $\{\ldots, -3, -2, -1, 0, 1, 2, 3, \ldots\}$.

Rational numbers:
$$-3.4, \frac{2}{5}, 0, -6, 1\frac{3}{4}, 16$$
A rational number can be expressed as a fraction: $-3.4 = \frac{-34}{10}, 0 = \frac{0}{1}, -6 = \frac{-6}{1}, 1\frac{3}{4} = \frac{7}{4}$, and $16 = \frac{16}{1}$.

Irrational numbers: π $\pi = 3.1415\ldots$ is a nonterminating, nonrepeating decimal.

Real numbers:
$$-3.4, \frac{2}{5}, 0, -6, 1\frac{3}{4}, \pi, 16$$
Every natural number, whole number, integer, rational number, and irrational number is a real number.

Self Check 1   Use the instructions for Example 1 with the set $\left\{0.1, \sqrt{2}, -\frac{2}{7}, 45, -2, \frac{13}{4}, -6\frac{7}{8}\right\}$.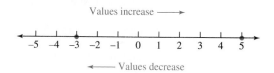

■ GRAPHING ON THE NUMBER LINE

Every real number corresponds to a point on the number line, and every point on the number line corresponds to exactly one real number. As we move right on the number line, the values of the numbers increase. As we move left, the values decrease. On the number line, we see that 5 is greater than -3, because 5 lies to the right of -3. Similarly, -3 is less than 5, because it lies to the left of 5.

Values increase ⟶

$$\xleftarrow{\quad} \;\; \underset{-5}{|} \;\; \underset{-4}{|} \;\; \underset{-3}{\bullet} \;\; \underset{-2}{|} \;\; \underset{-1}{|} \;\; \underset{0}{|} \;\; \underset{1}{|} \;\; \underset{2}{|} \;\; \underset{3}{|} \;\; \underset{4}{|} \;\; \underset{5}{\bullet} \;\; \xrightarrow{\quad}$$

⟵ Values decrease

The Language of Algebra

The prefix *in* means *not*. For example:

inaccurate ↔ not accurate
inexpensive ↔ not expensive
inequality ↔ not equal

The **inequality symbol** $>$ means "is greater than." It is used to show that one number is greater than another. The inequality symbol $<$ means "is less than." It is used to show that one number is less than another. For example,

$5 > -3$ Read as "5 is greater than -3."

$-3 < 5$ Read as "-3 is less than 5."

To distinguish between these inequality symbols, remember that each one points to the smaller of the two numbers involved.

$5 > -3$ $-3 < 5$

⎣———Points to the smaller number.———⎦

EXAMPLE 2

Use one of the symbols $>$ or $<$ to make each statement true: **a.** $-4 \;\; \square \;\; 4$,   **b.** $-2 \;\; \square \;\; -3$,   **c.** $4.47 \;\; \square \;\; 12.5$,   and   **d.** $\frac{3}{4} \;\; \square \;\; \frac{5}{8}$.

Solution   **a.** Since -4 is to the left of 4 on the number line, we have $-4 < 4$.

b. Since -2 is to the right of -3 on the number line, we have $-2 > -3$.

c. Since 4.47 is to the left of 12.5 on the number line, we have $4.47 < 12.5$.

The Language of Algebra

To state that a number x is positive, we can write $x > 0$. To state that a number x is negative, we can write $x < 0$.

d. To compare fractions, express them in terms of the same denominator, preferably the LCD. If we write $\frac{3}{4}$ as an equivalent fraction with denominator 8, we see that $\frac{3}{4} = \frac{3 \cdot 2}{4 \cdot 2} = \frac{6}{8}$. Therefore, $\frac{3}{4} > \frac{5}{8}$.

To compare the fractions, we could also convert each to its decimal equivalent. Since $\frac{3}{4} = 0.75$ and $\frac{5}{8} = 0.625$, we know that $\frac{3}{4} > \frac{5}{8}$.

Self Check 2   Use one of the symbols $>$ or $<$ to make each statement true: **a.** $1 \;\; \square \;\; -1$,   **b.** $-5 \;\; \square \;\; -4$,   **c.** $6.7 \;\; \square \;\; 4.999$,   **d.** $\frac{3}{5} \;\; \square \;\; \frac{2}{3}$.

To **graph a number** means to mark its position on the number line.

EXAMPLE 3   Graph each number in the following set: $\left\{-2.43, \sqrt{2}, 1, -0.\overline{3}, 2\frac{5}{6}, -\frac{3}{2}\right\}$.

Solution   We locate the position of each number on the number line, draw a bold dot, and label it. It is often helpful to approximate the value of a number or to write the number in an equivalent form to determine its location on the number line.

- To locate -2.43, we round it to the nearest tenth: $-2.43 \approx -2.4$.
- Use a calculator to find that $\sqrt{2} \approx 1.4$.
- Recall that $0.\overline{3} = 0.333 \ldots = \frac{1}{3}$. Therefore, $-0.\overline{3} = -\frac{1}{3}$.
- In mixed-number form, $-\frac{3}{2} = -1\frac{1}{2}$. This is midway between -1 and -2.

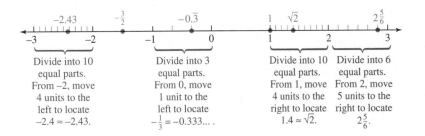

Self Check 3   Graph each number in the set: $\left\{1.7, \pi, -1\frac{3}{4}, 0.\overline{6}, \frac{5}{2}, -3\right\}$.

■ ABSOLUTE VALUE

A number line can be used to measure the distance from one number to another. For example, in the following figure we see that the distance from 0 to -4 is 4 units and the distance from 0 to 3 is 3 units.

To express the distance that a number is from 0 on a number line, we often use absolute values.

Absolute Value   The **absolute value** of a number is the distance from 0 to the number on the number line.

Success Tip

Since absolute value expresses distance, the absolute value of a number is always positive or zero.

To indicate the absolute value of a number, we write the number between two vertical bars. From the figure above, we see that $\left|-4\right| = 4$. This is read as "the absolute value of negative 4 is 4" and it tells us that the distance from 0 to -4 is 4 units. It also follows from the figure that $\left|3\right| = 3$.

EXAMPLE 4   Find each absolute value: **a.** $|18|$,   **b.** $\left|-\frac{7}{8}\right|$,   **c.** $|98.6|$,   and   **d.** $|0|$.

Solution   **a.** Since 18 is a distance of 18 from 0 on the number line, $|18| = 18$.
b. Since $-\frac{7}{8}$ is a distance of $\frac{7}{8}$ from 0 on the number line, $\left|-\frac{7}{8}\right| = \frac{7}{8}$.
c. Since 98.6 is a distance of 98.6 from 0 on the number line, $|98.6| = 98.6$.
d. Since 0 is a distance of 0 from 0 on the number line, $|0| = 0$.

Self Check 4   Find each absolute value: **a.** $|100|$,   **b.** $|-4.7|$,   **c.** $\left|-\sqrt{2}\right|$.

Answers to Self Checks   **1.** natural numbers: 45; whole numbers: 45; integers: 45, -2; rational numbers: 0.1, $-\frac{2}{7}$, 45, -2, $\frac{13}{4}$, $-6\frac{7}{8}$; irrational numbers: $\sqrt{2}$; real numbers: all   **2. a.** $>$,   **b.** $<$,   **c.** $>$,   **d.** $<$
3.

4. a. 100,   **b.** 4.7,   **c.** $\sqrt{2}$

1.3   STUDY SET

VOCABULARY   Fill in the blanks.

1. The set of _____ numbers is {0, 1, 2, 3, 4, 5, . . .}.
2. The set of _____ numbers is {1, 2, 3, 4, 5, . . .}.
3. The set of _____ is {. . . , -2, -1, 0, 1, 2, . . .}.
4. Two numbers represented by points on the number line that are the same distance away from 0, but on opposite sides of it, are called _____.
5. Numbers less than zero are _____, and numbers greater than zero are _____.
6. The symbols $<$ and $>$ are _____ symbols.
7. A _____ number is any number that can be expressed as a fraction with an integer numerator and a nonzero integer denominator.
8. A decimal such as 0.25 is called a _____ decimal, and 0.333. . . is called a _____ decimal.
9. An _____ number is a nonterminating, nonrepeating decimal.
10. An _____ number cannot be expressed as a fraction.
11. Every point on the number line corresponds to exactly one _____ number.
12. The _____ of a number is the distance on the number line between the number and 0.

CONCEPTS

13. What concept is illustrated here?

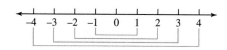

14. Fill in the blanks on the illustration.

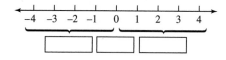

15. Show that each of the following numbers is a rational number by expressing it as a fraction with an integer numerator and a nonzero integer denominator: 6, -9, $-\frac{7}{8}$, $3\frac{1}{2}$, -0.3, 2.83.

16. Represent each situation using a signed number.
    a. A loss of \$15 million
    b. A rainfall total 0.75 inch below average
    c. A score $12\frac{1}{2}$ points under the standard
    d. A building foundation $\frac{5}{16}$ inch above grade

17. What numbers are a distance of 8 away from 5 on the number line?

18. Suppose *m* stands for a negative number. Use *m*, an inequality symbol, and 0 to express this fact.

19. Refer to the graph. Use an inequality symbol, < or >, to make each statement true.

 a. *a*   *b*
 b. *b*   *a*
 c. *b*   0 and *a*   0
 d. |*a*| |*b*|

20. What is the length of the diagonal of the square shown below?

21. What is the circumference of the circle?

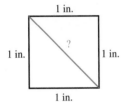

1 in.

1 in.   ?   1 in.

1 in.

1 inch

22. Place check marks in the table to show the set or sets to which each number belongs. For example, the checks show that $\sqrt{2}$ is an irrational and a real number.

	5	0	−3	$\frac{7}{8}$	0.17	$-9\frac{1}{4}$	$\sqrt{2}$	π
Real							✓	
Irrational							✓	
Rational								
Integer								
Whole								
Natural								

NOTATION   Fill in the blanks.

23. $\sqrt{2}$ is read "the _____ of 2."

24. |−15| is read "the _____ of −15."

25. The symbol ≠ means _____.

26. The symbols { }, called _____, are used when writing a set.

27. The symbol π is a letter from the _____ alphabet.

28. To find the decimal equivalent for the fraction $\frac{2}{3}$ we divide:

29. Write $-\frac{4}{5}$ in two other equivalent fractional forms.

30. Write each repeating decimal using an overbar.
 a. 0.666. . .
 b. 0.2444. . .
 c. 0.717171. . .
 d. 0.456456456. . .

PRACTICE   Write each fraction as a decimal. If the result is a repeating decimal, use an overbar.

31. $\frac{5}{8}$
32. $\frac{3}{32}$
33. $\frac{1}{30}$
34. $\frac{7}{9}$
35. $\frac{21}{50}$
36. $\frac{2}{125}$
37. $\frac{5}{11}$
38. $\frac{1}{60}$

Insert one of the symbols >, <, or = in the blank.

39. 5   4
40. −5   −4
41. −2   −3
42. 0   32
43. |3.4| $\sqrt{2}$
44. 0.08   0.079
45. |−1.1| 1.2
46. −5.5 $-5\frac{1}{2}$
47. $-\frac{5}{8}$ $-\frac{3}{8}$
48. $-19\frac{2}{3}$ $-19\frac{1}{3}$
49. $|-\frac{15}{2}|$ 7.5
50. $\sqrt{2}$ π
51. $\frac{99}{100}$ 0.99
52. |2| |−2|
53. 0.333. . .   0.3
54. $|-2\frac{2}{3}|$ $\frac{7}{3}$
55. 1 $|-\frac{15}{16}|$
56. −0.666. . .   0

Decide whether each statement is true or false.

57. a. Every whole number is an integer.
 b. Every integer is a natural number.
 c. Every integer is a whole number.
 d. Irrational numbers are nonterminating, nonrepeating decimals.

58. a. Irrational numbers are real numbers.
 b. Every whole number is a rational number.
 c. Every rational number can be written as a fraction.
 d. Every rational number is a whole number.

59. a. Write the statement $-6 < -5$ using an inequality symbol that points in the other direction.

b. Write the statement $16 > -25$ using an inequality symbol that points in the other direction.

60. If we begin with the number -4 and find its opposite, and then find the opposite of that result, what number do we obtain?

Graph each set of numbers on the number line.

61. $\left\{ -\pi, 4.25, -1\frac{1}{2}, -0.333 \ldots, \sqrt{2}, -\frac{35}{8}, 3 \right\}$

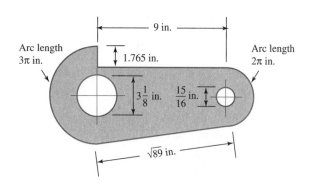

62. $\left\{ \pi, -2\frac{1}{8}, 2.75, -\sqrt{2}, \frac{17}{4}, 0.666 \ldots, -3 \right\}$

APPLICATIONS

63. DRAFTING The drawing shows the dimensions of an aluminum bracket. Which numbers shown are natural numbers, whole numbers, integers, rational numbers, irrational numbers, and real numbers?

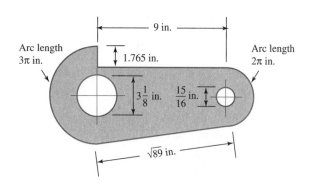

64. HISTORY Refer to the time line.
a. What basic unit was used to scale the time line?

b. On the time line, what symbolism is used to represent zero?

c. On the time line, which numbers could be thought of as positive and which as negative?

d. Express the dates for the Maya civilization using positive and negative numbers.

MAYA CIVILIZATION

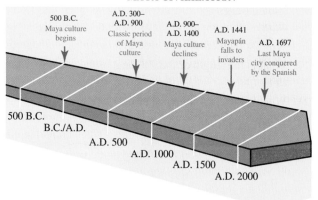

Based on data from *People in Time and Place, Western Hemisphere* (Silver Burdett & Ginn, 1991), p. 129

65. TARGET PRACTICE Which artillery shell landed farther from the target? How can the concept of absolute value be applied to answer this question?

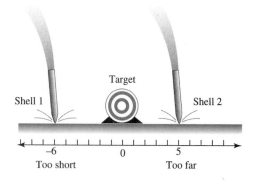

66. DRAFTING An architect's scale has several measuring edges. The edge marked 16 divides each inch into 16 equal parts. Find the decimal form for each fractional part of one inch that is highlighted on the scale.

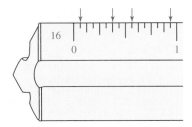

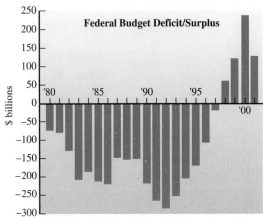

Source: U.S. Bureau of the Census

67. TRADE Each year from 1990 through 2002, the United States imported more goods and services from Japan than it exported to Japan. This caused trade deficits, which are represented by negative numbers on the graph.

a. In which three years was the deficit the worst? Estimate each of them.

b. In which year was the deficit the smallest? Estimate the deficit then.

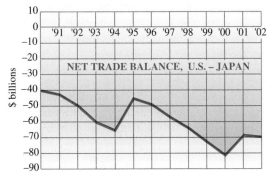

Source: U.S. Bureau of the Census

68. GOVERNMENT DEBT A budget deficit indicates that the government's expenditures were more than the revenue it took in that year. Deficits are represented by negative numbers on the graph.

a. For the years 1980–2001, when was the federal budget deficit the worst? Estimate the size of the deficit.

b. For the years 1980–2001, when did the first budget surplus occur? Estimate it. Explain what it means to have a budget surplus.

WRITING

69. Explain the difference between a rational and an irrational number.

70. Can two different numbers have the same absolute value? Explain.

71. Explain how to find the decimal equivalent of a fraction.

72. What is a real number?

REVIEW

73. Simplify: $\dfrac{24}{54}$.

74. Prime factor 60.

75. Find: $\dfrac{3}{4}\left(\dfrac{8}{5}\right)$.

76. Find: $5\dfrac{2}{3} \div 2\dfrac{5}{9}$.

77. Find: $\dfrac{3}{10} + \dfrac{2}{15}$.

78. Classify each of the following as an *expression* or an *equation*.

a. $2x$

b. $x = 2$

CHALLENGE PROBLEMS

79. Find the set of nonnegative integers.

80. Is $0.10100100010000\ldots$ a repeating decimal? Explain.

1.4   Adding Real Numbers

- Adding Two Numbers with the Same Sign
- Adding Two Numbers with Different Signs   • Properties of Addition
- Opposites or Additive Inverses

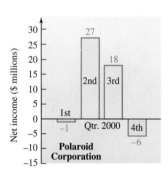

Source: Hoover's Online

Positive and negative numbers are called **signed numbers.** In the graph on the left, signed numbers are used to denote the financial performance of the Polaroid Corporation for the year 2000. The positive numbers indicate *profits* and the negative numbers indicate *losses*. To find Polaroid's net earnings (in millions of dollars), we need to calculate the following sum:

$$\text{Net earnings} = -1 + 27 + 18 + (-6)$$

In this section, we discuss how to perform this addition and others involving signed numbers.

ADDING TWO NUMBERS WITH THE SAME SIGN

A number line can be used to explain the addition of signed numbers. For example, to compute $5 + 2$, we begin at 0 and draw an arrow five units long that points right. It represents 5. From the tip of that arrow, we draw a second arrow two units long that points right. It represents 2. Since we end up at 7, it follows that $5 + 2 = 7$.

The Language of Algebra

The names of the parts of an addition fact are:

Addend   Addend   Sum
$$5 + 2 = 7$$

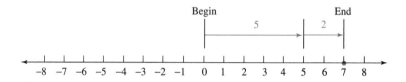

Notation

To avoid confusion, we write negative numbers within parentheses to separate the negative sign $-$ from the addition symbol $+$.

$$-5 + (-2)$$

To compute $-5 + (-2)$, we begin at 0 and draw an arrow five units long that points left. It represents -5. From the tip of that arrow, we draw a second arrow two units long that points left. It represents -2. Since we end up at -7, it follows that $-5 + (-2) = -7$.

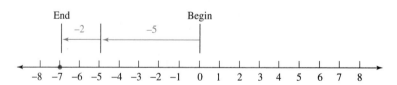

To check this result, think of the problem in terms of money. If you lost \$5 (-5) and then lost another \$2 (-2), you would have lost a total of \$7 (-7).

When we use a number line to add numbers with the same sign, the arrows point in the same direction and they build upon each other. Furthermore, the answer has the same sign as the numbers that we added. We can conclude that *the sum of two positive numbers is positive* and *the sum of two negative numbers is negative.*

Adding Two Numbers with the Same Sign

1. To add two positive numbers, add them. The answer is positive.

2. To add two negative numbers, add their absolute values and make the answer negative.

EXAMPLE 1   Find each sum: **a.** $-20 + (-15)$,   **b.** $-7.89 + (-0.6)$,   and   **c.** $-\dfrac{1}{3} + \left(-\dfrac{1}{2}\right)$.

Solution   **a.** $-20 + (-15) = -35$ Add their absolute values, 20 and 15, to get 35.
Make the answer negative.

b. Add their absolute values and make the answer negative: $-7.89 + (-0.6) = -8.49$.

c. Add their absolute values

$$\frac{1}{3} + \frac{1}{2} = \frac{2}{6} + \frac{3}{6}$$ The LCD is 6. Build each fraction: $\dfrac{1}{3} \cdot \dfrac{2}{2} = \dfrac{2}{6}$ and $\dfrac{1}{2} \cdot \dfrac{3}{3} = \dfrac{3}{6}$.

$$= \frac{5}{6}$$ Add the numerators and write the sum over the LCD.

and make the answer negative: $-\dfrac{1}{3} + \left(-\dfrac{1}{2}\right) = -\dfrac{5}{6}$.

Self Check 1   Find the sum: **a.** $-51 + (-9)$,   **b.** $-12.3 + (-0.88)$,   **c.** $-\dfrac{1}{4} + \left(-\dfrac{2}{3}\right)$.

■ ADDING TWO NUMBERS WITH DIFFERENT SIGNS

To compute $5 + (-2)$, we begin at 0 and draw an arrow five units long that points right. From the tip of that arrow, we draw a second arrow two units long that points left. Since we end up at 3, it follows that $5 + (-2) = 3$. In terms of money, if you won $5 and then lost $2, you would have $3 left.

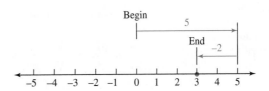

To compute $-5 + 2$, we begin at 0 and draw an arrow five units long that points left. From the tip of that arrow, we draw a second arrow two units long that points right. Since we end up at -3, it follows that $-5 + 2 = -3$. In terms of money, if you lost $5 and then won $2, you have lost $3.

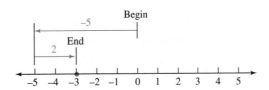

When we use a number line to add numbers with different signs, the arrows point in opposite directions and the longer arrow determines the sign of the answer. If the longer arrow represents a positive number, the sum is positive. If it represents a negative number, the sum is negative.

Adding Two Numbers with Different Signs	To add a positive number and a negative number, subtract the smaller absolute value from the larger.

1. If the positive number has the larger absolute value, the answer is positive.

2. If the negative number has the larger absolute value, make the answer negative.

EXAMPLE 2

Find each sum: **a.** $-20 + 32$,   **b.** $5.7 + (-7.4)$,   and   **c.** $-\dfrac{19}{25} + \dfrac{2}{5}$.

Solution   **a.** $-20 + 32 = 12$ Subtract the smaller absolute value from the larger: $32 - 20 = 12$. The positive number, 32, has the larger absolute value, so the answer is positive.

b. Subtract the smaller absolute value, 5.7, from the larger, 7.4, and determine the sign of the answer.

$$5.7 + (-7.4) = -1.7$$ The negative number, -7.4, has the larger absolute value, so we make the answer negative.

Calculators
Entering negative numbers

When using a calculator to add positive and negative numbers, we don't do anything special to enter positive numbers. To enter a negative number, say -1, on a scientific calculator, we press the *sign change* key $+/-$ after entering 1. If we use a graphing calculator, we press the *negation* key $(-)$ and then enter 1.

c. Since $\dfrac{2}{5} = \dfrac{10}{25}$, $-\dfrac{19}{25}$ has the larger absolute value. We subtract the smaller absolute value from the larger:

$$\frac{19}{25} - \frac{2}{5} = \frac{19}{25} - \frac{10}{25}$$ Replace $\dfrac{2}{5}$ with the equivalent fraction $\dfrac{10}{25}$.

$$= \frac{9}{25}$$ Subtract the numerators and write the difference over the LCD.

and determine the sign of the answer.

$$-\frac{19}{25} + \frac{10}{25} = -\frac{9}{25}$$ Since $-\dfrac{19}{25}$ has the larger absolute value, make the answer negative.

Self Check 2   Find each sum: **a.** $63 + (-87)$,   **b.** $-6.27 + 8$,   **c.** $-\dfrac{1}{10} + \dfrac{1}{2}$

EXAMPLE 3

Corporate earnings.   Find the net earnings of Polaroid Corporation for the year 2000 using the data in the graph on page 32.

Solution   To find the net earnings, we add the quarterly profits and losses (in millions of dollars), performing the additions as they occur from left to right.

$$-1 + 27 + 18 + (-6) = 26 + 18 + (-6)$$ Add: $-1 + 27 = 26$.
$$= 44 + (-6)$$ Add: $26 + 18 = 44$.
$$= 38$$

In 2000, Polaroid's net earnings were $38 million.

Self Check 3   Add: $7 + (-13) + 8 + (-10)$.

■ PROPERTIES OF ADDITION

The addition of two numbers can be done in any order and the result is the same. For example, $8 + (-1) = 7$ and $-1 + 8 = 7$. This example illustrates that addition is **commutative.**

The Commutative Property of Addition	Changing the order when adding does not affect the answer. Let a and b represent real numbers, $a + b = b + a$

The Language of Algebra

Commutative is a form of the word *commute,* meaning to go back and forth.

In the following example, we add $-3 + 7 + 5$ in two ways. We will use grouping symbols ( ), called **parentheses,** to show this. Standard practice requires that the operation within the parentheses be performed first.

Method 1: Group −3 and 7

$(-3 + 7) + 5 = 4 + 5$
$= 9$

Method 2: Group 7 and 5

$-3 + (7 + 5) = -3 + 12$
$= 9$

It doesn't matter how we group the numbers in this addition; the result is 9. This example illustrates that addition is **associative.**

The Associative Property of Addition	Changing the grouping when adding does not affect the answer. Let a, b, and c represent real numbers, $(a + b) + c = a + (b + c)$

Sometimes, an application of the associative property can simplify a computation.

EXAMPLE 4

Find the sum: $98 + (2 + 17)$.

Solution

If we use the associative property of addition to regroup, we have a convenient pair of numbers to add: $98 + 2 = 100$.

$$98 + (2 + 17) = (98 + 2) + 17$$
$$= 100 + 17$$
$$= 117$$

The Language of Algebra

Associative is a form of the word *associate,* meaning to join a group.

Self Check 4   Find the sum: $(39 + 25) + 75$.

EXAMPLE 5

Game shows.   A contestant on *Jeopardy!* correctly answered the first question to win $100, missed the second to lose $200, correctly answered the third to win $300, and missed the fourth to lose $400. What is her score after answering four questions?

Solution

WHO'S WHO	WHODUNIT	WHO'S ON FIRST	HOUDINI	HOOVER	HOULIGANS
100	100	100	100	100	100
200	200	200	200	200	200
300	300	300	300	300	300
400	400	400	400	400	400
500	500	500	500	500	500

We can represent money won by a positive number and money lost by a negative number. Her score is the sum of 100, -200, 300, and -400. Instead of doing the additions from left to right, we will use another approach. Applying the commutative and associative properties, we add the positives, add the negatives, and then add those results.

$$100 + (-200) + 300 + (-400)$$
$$= (100 + 300) + [(-200) + (-400)]$$ Reorder the numbers. Group the positives together. Group the negatives together using brackets [ ].
$$= 400 + (-600)$$ Add the positives. Add the negatives.
$$= -200$$ Add the results.

After four questions, her score was $-\$200$, a loss of $200.

Self Check 5   Find $-6 + 1 + (-4) + (-5) + 9$.

The Language of Algebra

Identity is a form of the word *identical,* meaning the same. You have probably seen *identical* twins.

Whenever we add 0 to a number, the number remains the same:

$$8 + 0 = 8, \qquad 2.3 + 0 = 2.3, \qquad \text{and} \qquad 0 + (-16) = -16$$

These examples illustrate the **addition property of 0.** Since any number added to 0 remains the same, 0 is called the **identity element** for addition.

Addition Property of 0

When 0 is added to any real number, the result is the same real number.
For any real number a,

$$a + 0 = a \qquad \text{and} \qquad 0 + a = a$$

■ OPPOSITES OR ADDITIVE INVERSES

The Language of Algebra

Don't confuse the words *opposite* and *reciprocal.* The opposite of 4 is -4. The reciprocal of 4 is $\frac{1}{4}$.

Recall that two numbers that are the same distance from 0 on a number line, but on opposite sides of it, are called **opposites.** To develop a property of opposites, we will find $-4 + 4$ using a number line. We begin at 0 and draw an arrow four units long that points left, to represent -4. From the tip of that arrow, we draw a second arrow, four units long that points right, to represent 4. We end up at 0; therefore, $-4 + 4 = 0$.

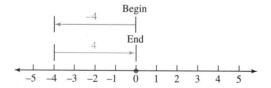

This example illustrates that when we add opposites, the result is 0. It also follows that whenever the sum of two numbers is 0, those numbers are opposites. For these reasons, opposites are also called **additive inverses.**

Addition Property of Opposites (Inverse Property of Addition)

The sum of a number and its opposite (additive inverse) is 0.
For any real number a and its opposite or additive inverse $-a$,

$$a + (-a) = 0 \qquad \text{Read } -a \text{ as "the opposite of } a\text{."}$$

EXAMPLE 6   Find the sum: $12 + (-5) + 6 + 5 + (-12)$.

Solution   The commutative and associative properties of addition enable us to add pairs of opposites: $12 + (-12) = 0$ and $-5 + 5 = 0$.

opposites

$$12 + (-5) + 6 + 5 + (-12) = 0 + 0 + 6$$
$$= 6$$

opposites

Self Check 6   Find the sum: $8 + (-1) + 6 + 5 + (-8) + 1$.

Answers to Self Checks   **1. a.** -60,   **b.** -13.18,   **c.** $-\frac{11}{12}$ **2. a.** -24,   **b.** 1.73,   **c.** $\frac{2}{5}$ **3.** -8 **4.** 139
5. -5 **6.** 11

1.4   STUDY SET

VOCABULARY   Fill in the blanks.

1. Positive and negative numbers are called _____ numbers.

2. In the addition statement $-2 + 5 = 3$, the result, 3, is called the _____.

3. Two numbers that are the same distance from 0 on a number line, but on opposite sides of it, are called _____.

4. The _____ property of addition states that changing the order when adding does not affect the answer. The _____ property of addition states that changing the grouping when adding does not affect the answer.

5. Since any number added to 0 remains the same (is identical), the number 0 is called the _____ element for addition.

6. The sum of a number and its opposite or additive _____ is 0.

CONCEPTS   What addition fact is represented by each illustration?

7.

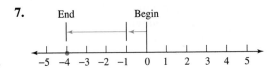

8.

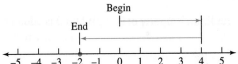

Add using a number line.

9. $-3 + (-2)$ **10.** $4 + (-6)$

11. $1 + (-4)$ **12.** $-3 + (-1)$

13. Complete each property of addition.
   a. $a + (-a) =$ **b.** $a + 0 =$
   c. $a + b = b +$
   d. $(a + b) + c = a +$

For each addition, determine the sign of the answer.

14. $59 + (-64)$

15. $-87 + 98$

16. Circle any opposites in the following expression.

$$12 + (-3) + (-6) + 3 + 1$$

17. Use the commutative property of addition to complete each statement.

   a. $-5 + 1 = $ _____

   b. $15 + (-80.5) = $ _____

   c. $-20 + (4 + 20) = -20 + $ _____

18. Use the associative property of addition to complete each statement.

   a. $(-6 + 2) + 8 = $ _____

   b. $-7 + (7 + 3) = $ _____

19. Find each sum.

   a. $5 + (-5)$ **b.** $-2.2 + 2.2$

   c. $0 + (-6)$ **d.** $-\dfrac{15}{16} + 0$

   e. $-\dfrac{3}{4} + \dfrac{3}{4}$ **f.** $19 + (-19)$

20. Consider $-3 + 6 + (-9) + 8 + (-4)$.

   a. Add all the positives in the expression.

   b. Add all of the negatives.

   c. Add the results from parts **a** and **b**.

NOTATION

21. Express the commutative property of addition using the variables x and y.

22. Express the associative property of addition using the variables x, y, and z.

23. In $7 + (8 + 9)$, which addition should be done first?

24. Insert parentheses where they are needed.

$$6 + -8 + -10$$

PRACTICE   Add.

25. $6 + (-8)$ **26.** $4 + (-3)$

27. $-6 + 8$ **28.** $-21 + (-12)$

29. $-4 + (-4)$ **30.** $-5 + (-5)$

31. $9 + (-1)$ **32.** $11 + (-2)$

33. $-16 + 16$ **34.** $-25 + 25$

35. $-65 + (-12)$ **36.** $75 + (-13)$

37. $15 + (-11)$ **38.** $27 + (-30)$

39. $300 + (-335)$ **40.** $240 + (-340)$

41. $-10.5 + 2.3$ **42.** $-2.1 + 0.4$

43. $-9.1 + (-11)$ **44.** $-6.7 + (-7.1)$

45. $0.7 + (-0.5)$ **46.** $0.9 + (-0.2)$

47. $-\dfrac{9}{16} + \dfrac{7}{16}$ **48.** $-\dfrac{3}{4} + \dfrac{1}{4}$

49. $-\dfrac{1}{4} + \dfrac{2}{3}$ **50.** $\dfrac{3}{16} + \left(-\dfrac{1}{2}\right)$

51. $-\dfrac{4}{5} + \left(-\dfrac{1}{10}\right)$ **52.** $-\dfrac{3}{8} + \left(-\dfrac{1}{3}\right)$

53. $8 + (-5) + 13$ **54.** $17 + (-12) + (-23)$

55. $21 + (-27) + (-9)$ **56.** $-32 + 12 + 17$

57. $-27 + (-3) + (-13) + 22$

58. $53 + (-27) + (-32) + (-7)$

59. $-20 + (-16 + 10)$

60. $-13 + (-16 + 4)$

61. $19 + (-20 + 1)$

62. $33 + (-35 + 2)$

63. $(-7 + 8) + 2 + (-12 + 13)$

64. $(-9 + 5) + 10 + (-8 + 1)$

65. $-7 + 5 + (-10) + 7$

66. $-3 + 6 + (-9) + (-6)$

67. $-8 + 11 + (-11) + 8 + 1$

68. $2 + 15 + (-15) + 8 + (-2)$

69. $-2.1 + 6.5 + (-8.2) + 0.6$

70. $0.9 + 0.5 + (-0.2) + (-0.9)$

71. $-60 + 70 + (-10) + (-10) + 20$

72. $-100 + 200 + (-300) + (-100) + 200$

Apply the associative property of addition, and find the sum.

73. $-99 + (99 + 215)$

74. $67 + (-67 + 127)$

75. $(-112 + 56) + (-56)$

76. $(-67 + 5) + (-5)$

APPLICATIONS

77. MILITARY SCIENCE   During a battle, an army retreated 1,500 meters, regrouped, and advanced 2,400 meters. The next day, it advanced another 1,250 meters. Find the army's net gain.

78. HEALTH   Find the point total for the six risk factors (in blue) on the medical questionnaire. Then use the table to determine the patient's risk of contracting heart disease in the next 10 years.

Age		Total Cholesterol	
Age	Points	Reading	Points
34	−1	150	−3

Cholesterol		Blood Pressure	
HDL	Points	Systolic/Diastolic	Points
62	−2	124/100	3

Diabetic		Smoker	
	Points		Points
Yes	2	Yes	2

10-Year Heart Disease Risk			
Total Points	Risk	Total Points	Risk
−2 or less	1%	5	4%
−1 to 1	2%	6	6%
2 to 3	3%	7	6%
4	4%	8	7%

79. GOLF The leaderboard shows the top finishers from the 1997 Masters Golf Tournament. Scores for each round are compared to *par*, the standard number of strokes necessary to complete the course. A score of −2, for example, indicates that the golfer used two strokes less than par to complete the course. A score of +5 indicates five strokes more than par. Determine the tournament total for each golfer.

Leaderboard

	Round				
	1	2	3	4	Total
Tiger Woods	−2	−6	−7	−3	
Tom Kite	+5	−3	−6	−2	
Tommy Tolles	0	0	0	−5	
Tom Watson	+3	−4	−3	0	

80. SUBMARINES A submarine was cruising at a depth of 1,250 feet. The captain gave the order to climb 550 feet. Relative to sea level, find the new depth of the sub.

81. CREDIT CARDS
  a. What amounts in the monthly credit card statement could be represented by negative numbers?
  b. Express the new balance as a negative number.

Previous Balance	New Purchases, Fees, Advances & Debts	Payments & Credits	New Balance
3,660.66	1,408.78	3,826.58	

04/21/03 Billing Date	05/16/03 Date Payment Due	9,100 Credit Line

Periodic rates may vary.
See reverse for explanation and important information.
Please allow sufficient time for mail to reach us.

82. POLITICS The following proposal to limit campaign contributions was on the ballot in a state election, and it passed. What will be the net fiscal impact on the state government?

212 Campaign Spending Limits	YES ☐ NO ☐

Limits contributions to $200 in state campaigns. Fiscal impact: Costs of $4.5 million for implementation and enforcement. Increases state revenue by $6.7 million by eliminating tax deductions for lobbying.

83. MOVIE LOSSES According to the *Guinness Book of World Records 2000,* MGM's *Cutthroat Island* (1995), starring Geena Davis, cost about $100 million to produce, promote, and distribute. It has reportedly earned back just $11 million since being released. What dollar loss did the studio suffer on this film?

84. STOCK EXCHANGE Many newspapers publish daily summaries of the stock market's activity. The last entry on the line for June 12 indicates that one share of Walt Disney Co. stock lost $0.81 in value that day. How much did the value of a share of Disney stock rise or fall over the five-day period shown?

June 12	43.88	23.38	Disney	.21	0.5	87	−43	40.75	−.81
June 13	43.88	23.38	Disney	.21	0.5	86	−15	40.19	−.56
June 14	43.88	23.38	Disney	.21	0.5	87	−50	41.00	+.81
June 15	43.88	23.38	Disney	.21	0.5	89	−28	41.81	+.81
June 16	43.88	23.38	Disney				−15	41.19	−.63

Based on data from the *Los Angeles Times*

85. SAHARA DESERT   From 1980 to 1990, a satellite was used to trace the expansion and contraction of the southern boundary of the Sahara Desert in Africa. If movement southward is represented with a negative number and movement northward with a positive number, use the data in the table to determine the net movement of the Sahara Desert boundary over the 10-year period.

Years	Distance/Direction
1980–1984	240 km/South
1984–1985	110 km/North
1985–1986	30 km/North
1986–1987	55 km/South
1987–1988	100 km/North
1988–1990	77 km/South

Sahara Desert

Based on data from A. Dolgoff, *Physical Geology* (D.C. Heath, 1996), p. 496

86. ELECTRONICS   A closed circuit contains two batteries and three resistors. The sum of the voltages in the loop must be 0. Is it?

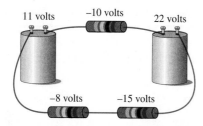

11 volts   −10 volts   22 volts

−8 volts   −15 volts

87. PROFITS AND LOSSES   The 2001 quarterly profits and losses of Greyhound Bus Lines are shown in the table. Losses are denoted using parentheses. Use the data to construct a line graph. Then calculate the company's total net income for 2001.

Quarter	Net income ($ million)
1st	(10.7)
2nd	4.0
3rd	12.2
4th	(3.4)

Source: Edgar Online

88. POLITICS   Six months before an election, the incumbent trailed the challenger by 18 points. To overtake her opponent, the campaign staff decided to use a four-part strategy. Each part of this plan is shown, with the anticipated point gain. With these gains, will the incumbent overtake the challenger on election day?

1. Intense TV ad blitz   +10
2. Ask for union endorsement   +2
3. Voter mailing   +3
4. Get-out-the-vote campaign   +1

REVIEW

89. True or false: Every real number can be expressed as a decimal.

90. Multiply: $\dfrac{1}{3} \cdot \dfrac{1}{3}$.

91. What two numbers are a distance of 6 away from -3 on the number line?

92. Graph $\left\{ -2.5, \sqrt{2}, \dfrac{11}{3}, -0.333\ldots, 0.75 \right\}$.

WRITING

93. Explain why the sum of two positive numbers is always positive and the sum of two negative numbers is always negative.

94. Explain why the sum of a negative number and a positive number is sometimes positive, sometimes negative, and sometimes zero.

CHALLENGE PROBLEMS

95. A set is said to be *closed under addition* if the sum of any two of its members is also a member of the set. Is the set $\{-1, 0, 1\}$ a closed set under addition? Explain.

96. Think of two numbers. First, add the absolute value of the two numbers, and write your answer. Second, add the two numbers, take the absolute value of that sum, and write that answer. Do the two answers agree? Can you find two numbers that produce different answers? When do you get answers that agree, and when don't you?

1.5   Subtracting Real Numbers

• Subtraction   • Applications Involving Subtraction

In this section, we discuss a rule to use when subtracting signed numbers.

■ SUBTRACTION

A minus symbol $-$ is used to indicate subtraction. However, this symbol is also used in two other ways, depending on where it appears in an expression.

$5 - 18$ This is read as "five minus eighteen."

-5 This is usually read as "negative five." It could also be read as "the additive inverse of five" or "the opposite of five."

$-(-5)$ This is usually read as "the opposite of negative five." It could also be read as "the additive inverse of negative five."

In $-(-5)$, parentheses are used to write the opposite of a negative number. When such expressions are encountered in computations, we simplify them by finding the opposite of the number within the parentheses.

$-(-5) = 5$ The opposite of negative five is five.

This observation illustrates the following rule.

Opposite of an Opposite	The opposite of the opposite of a number is that number. For any real number a, $\qquad -(-a) = a$ Read as "the opposite of the opposite of a is a."

EXAMPLE 1

Simplify each expression: **a.** $-(-45)$,   **b.** $-(-h)$,   and   **c.** $-|-10|$.

Solution   **a.** The number within the parentheses is -45. Its opposite is 45. Therefore, $-(-45) = 45$.

b. The opposite of the opposite of h is h. Therefore, $-(-h) = h$.

c. The notation $-|-10|$ means "the opposite of the absolute value of negative ten." Since $|-10| = 10$, we have:

$$-|-10| = -10$$

Self Check 1   Simplify each expression: **a.** $-(-1)$,   **b.** $-(-y)$,   and   **c.** $-|-500|$.

The subtraction $5 - 2$ can be thought of as taking away 2 from 5. To use a number line to illustrate this, we begin at 0 and draw an arrow 5 units long that points to the right. From the tip of that arrow, we move back two units to the left. Since we end up at 3, it follows that $5 - 2 = 3$.

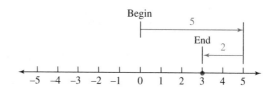

The Language of Algebra

The names of the parts of a subtraction fact are:

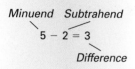

The previous illustration could also serve as a representation of the addition problem $5 + (-2)$. In the problem $5 - 2$, we subtracted 2 from 5. In the problem $5 + (-2)$, we added -2 to 5. In each case, the result is 3.

Subtracting 2.

Adding the opposite of 2.

$$5 - 2 = 3 \qquad\qquad 5 + (-2) = 3$$

The results are the same.

These observations suggest the following definition.

Subtraction of Real Numbers   To subtract two real numbers, add the first number to the opposite (additive inverse) of the number to be subtracted.

Let a and b represent real numbers,

$$a - b = a + (-b)$$

EXAMPLE 2   Subtract: **a.** $-13 - 8$,   **b.** $-7 - (-45)$,   and   **c.** $\dfrac{1}{4} - \left(-\dfrac{1}{8}\right)$.

Solution   **a.** We read $-13 - 8$ as "negative thirteen *minus* eight."

Change the subtraction to addition.

$$-13 - 8 \quad = \quad -13 + (-8) \quad = \quad -21 \qquad \text{To subtract, add the opposite.}$$

Change the number being subtracted to its opposite.

To check, we add the difference, -21, and the subtrahend, 8, to obtain the minuend, -13.

The Language of Algebra

The rule for subtracting real numbers is often summarized as: *Subtraction is the same as adding the opposite.*

$$-21 + 8 = -13$$

b. We read $-7 - (-45)$ as "negative seven *minus* negative forty-five."

Add

$$-7 - (-45) \quad = \quad -7 + 45 \quad = \quad 38 \qquad \text{To subtract, add the opposite.}$$

the opposite.

Check the result: $38 + (-45) = -7$.

Calculators
The subtraction key

When using a calculator to subtract signed numbers, be careful to distinguish between the *subtraction* key $-$ and the keys that are used to enter negative values: $+/-$ on a scientific calculator and $(-)$ on a graphing calculator.

c.
$$\frac{1}{4} - \left(-\frac{1}{8}\right) = \frac{2}{8} - \left(-\frac{1}{8}\right) \qquad \text{Build } \frac{1}{4}\text{: } \frac{1}{4} \cdot \frac{2}{2} = \frac{2}{8}.$$
$$= \frac{2}{8} + \frac{1}{8} \qquad \text{To subtract, add the opposite.}$$
$$= \frac{3}{8}$$

Check the result: $\dfrac{3}{8} + \left(-\dfrac{1}{8}\right) = \dfrac{2}{8} = \dfrac{1}{4}.$

Self Check 2   Subtract: **a.** $-32 - 25$, **b.** $17 - (-12)$, and **c.** $-\dfrac{1}{3} - \left(-\dfrac{3}{4}\right)$.

EXAMPLE 3

Translate from words to symbols: **a.** Subtract 0.5 from 4.6, and **b.** subtract 4.6 from 0.5.

Solution   **a.** The number to be subtracted is 0.5. When we translate to mathematical symbols, we must reverse the order in which 0.5 and 4.6 appear in the sentence.

Caution

When subtracting two numbers, it is important that we write them in the correct order, because, in general, $a - b \neq b - a.$

Subtract 0.5 from 4.6.

$$4.6 - 0.5 = 4.1$$

b. The number to be subtracted is 4.6. When we translate to mathematical symbols, we must reverse the order in which 4.6 and 0.5 appear in the sentence.

Subtract 4.6 from 0.5.

$$0.5 - 4.6 = 0.5 + (-4.6) \qquad \text{Add the opposite of 4.6.}$$
$$= -4.1$$

Self Check 3   **a.** Subtract 2.2 from 4.9, and **b.** subtract 4.9 from 2.2.

EXAMPLE 4

Find: $-9 - 15 + 20 - (-6).$

Solution   We write each subtraction as addition of the opposite and add.

$$-9 - 15 + 20 - (-6) = -9 + (-15) + 20 + 6$$
$$= -24 + 26$$
$$= 2$$

Self Check 4   Find: $-40 - (-10) + 7 - (-15).$

■ APPLICATIONS INVOLVING SUBTRACTION

Subtraction finds the difference between two numbers. When we find the difference between the maximum value and the minimum value of a collection of measurements, we are finding the **range** of the values.

EXAMPLE 5

U.S. temperatures.   The record high temperature in the United States was 134°F in Death Valley, California, on July 10, 1913. The record low was −80°F at Prospeck Creek, Alaska, on January 23, 1971. Find the temperature range for these extremes.

Solution   To find the temperature range, we subtract the lowest temperature from the highest temperature.

$$134 - (-80) = 134 + 80$$
$$= 214$$

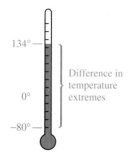

The temperature range for these extremes is 214°F.

Many things change in our lives. The price of a gallon of gasoline, the amount of money we have in the bank, and our ages are just a few examples. In general, to find the change in a quantity, we subtract the earlier value from the later value.

EXAMPLE 6

Water levels.   In one week, the water level in a storage tank went from 16 feet above normal to 14 feet below normal. Find the change in the water level.

Solution   We can represent a water level above normal using a positive number and a water level below normal using a negative number. To find the change in the water level, we subtract the previous measurement, 16, from the most recent measurement, −14.

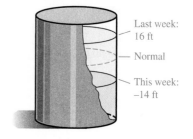

$$-14 - 16 = -14 + (-16)$$
$$= -30$$

The negative result indicates that the water level fell 30 feet that week.

Answers to Self Checks   **1. a.** 1,   **b.** *y*,   **c.** −500   **2. a.** −57,   **b.** 29,   **c.** $\frac{5}{12}$ **3. a.** 2.7,   **b.** −2.7
4. −8

1.5   STUDY SET

VOCABULARY   **Fill in the blanks.**

1. Two numbers that are the same distance from 0 on a number line, but on opposite sides of it, are called _____, or additive _____.

2. In the subtraction −2 − 5 = −7, the result of −7 is called the _____.

3. The difference between the maximum and the minimum value of a collection of measurements is called the _____ of the values.

4. To find the _____ in a quantity, subtract the earlier value from the later value.

CONCEPTS

5. Find the opposite, or additive inverse, of each number.

   a. 12   **b.** $-\frac{1}{5}$

   c. 2.71   **d.** 0

6. Complete each statement.
  a. $a - b = a + $ ____   **b.** $-(-a) = $ ____
  c. In general, $a - b$ ___ $b - a$.

7. Fill in the blanks.
  a. The opposite of the opposite of a number is that
  _____.

  b. To subtract two numbers, add the first number to
  the _____ of the number to be subtracted.

8. In each case, determine what number is being
  subtracted.
  a. $5 - 8$ **b.** $5 - (-8)$
  c. $-5 - 8$ **d.** $-5 - (-8)$

Apply the rule for subtraction and fill in the blanks.

9. $-1 - 9 = -1$

10. $1 - (-9) = 1$

11. Use addition to check this subtraction:
  $15 - (-8) = 7$. Is the result correct?

12. Which expression below represents the phrase
  subtract 6 from 2?

$$2 - 6 \quad \text{or} \quad 6 - 2$$

13. Write each subtraction in the following expression as
  addition of the opposite.

$$-10 - 8 + (-23) + 5 - (-34)$$

14. Simplify each expression.
  a. $-(-1)$ **b.** $-(-0.5)$

15. Simplify each expression.
  a. $-|-500|$ **b.** $-(-y)$

NOTATION

16. Write each phrase using symbols.
  a. Negative four
  b. One minus negative seven
  c. The opposite of negative two
  d. The opposite of the absolute value of negative
  three
  e. The opposite of the opposite of m

PRACTICE   Subtract.

17. $4 - 7$ **18.** $1 - 6$
19. $2 - 15$ **20.** $3 - 14$
21. $8 - (-3)$ **22.** $17 - (-21)$
23. $-12 - 9$ **24.** $-25 - 17$
25. $0 - 6$ **26.** $0 - 9$
27. $0 - (-1)$ **28.** $0 - (-8)$
29. $10 - (-2)$ **30.** $11 - (-3)$
31. $-1 - (-3)$ **32.** $-1 - (-7)$
33. $20 - (-20)$ **34.** $30 - (-30)$
35. $-3 - (-3)$ **36.** $-6 - (-6)$
37. $-2 - (-7)$ **38.** $-9 - (-1)$
39. $-4 - 5$ **40.** $-3 - 4$
41. $-44 - 44$ **42.** $-33 - 33$
43. $0 - (-12)$ **44.** $0 - 12$
45. $-25 - (-25)$ **46.** $13 - (-13)$
47. $0 - 4$ **48.** $0 - (-3)$
49. $-19 - (-17)$ **50.** $-30 - (-11)$
51. $-\dfrac{1}{8} - \dfrac{3}{8}$ **52.** $-\dfrac{3}{4} - \dfrac{1}{4}$
53. $-\dfrac{9}{16} - \left(-\dfrac{1}{4}\right)$ **54.** $-\dfrac{1}{2} - \left(-\dfrac{1}{4}\right)$
55. $\dfrac{1}{3} - \dfrac{3}{4}$ **56.** $\dfrac{1}{6} - \dfrac{5}{8}$
57. $-0.9 - 0.2$ **58.** $-0.3 - 0.2$
59. $6.3 - 9.8$ **60.** $2.1 - 9.4$
61. $-1.5 - 0.8$ **62.** $-1.5 - (-0.8)$
63. $2.8 - (-1.8)$ **64.** $4.7 - (-1.9)$

65. Subtract -5 from 17.
66. Subtract 45 from -50.
67. Subtract 12 from -13.
68. Subtract -11 from -20.

Perform the operations.

69. $8 - 9 - 10$
70. $1 - 2 - 3$
71. $-25 - (-50) - 75$
72. $-33 - (-22) - 44$
73. $-6 + 8 - (-1) - 10$
74. $-4 + 5 - (-3) - 13$
75. $61 - (-62) + (-64) - 60$

76. $93 - (-92) + (-94) - 95$

77. $-6 - 7 - (-3) + 9$

78. $-1 - 3 - (-8) + 5$

79. $-20 - (-30) - 50 + 40$

80. $-24 - (-28) - 48 + 44$

APPLICATIONS

81. TEMPERATURE RECORDS   Find the difference between the record high temperature of 108°F set in 1926 and the record low of -52°F set in 1979 for New York State.

82. LIE DETECTOR TESTS   A burglar scored -18 on a lie detector test, a score that indicates deception. However, on a second test, he scored $+3$, a score that is inconclusive. Find the change in the scores.

83. LAND ELEVATIONS   The elevation of Death Valley, California, is 282 feet below sea level. The elevation of the Dead Sea in Israel is 1,312 feet below sea level. Find the change in their elevations.

84. CARD GAMES   Gonzalo won the second round of a card game and earned 50 points. Matt and Hydecki had to deduct the value of each of the cards left in their hands from their score on the first round. Use this information to update the score sheet. (Face cards are counted as 10 points and aces as 1 point.)

Matt   Hydecki

Running point total	Round 1	Round 2
Matt	+50	
Gonzalo	−15	
Hydecki	−2	

85. RACING   To improve handling, drivers often adjust the angle of the wheels of their car. When the wheel leans out, the degree measure is considered positive. When the wheel leans in, the degree measure is considered negative. Find the change in the position of the wheel shown.

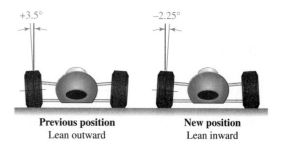

Previous position
Lean outward

New position
Lean inward

86. EYESIGHT   Nearsightedness, the condition where near objects are clear and far objects are blurry, is measured using negative numbers. Farsightedness, the condition where far objects are clear and near objects are blurry, is measured using positive numbers. Find the range in the measurements shown.

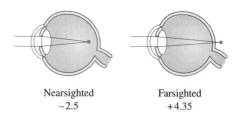

Nearsighted
−2.5

Farsighted
+4.35

87. HISTORY   Plato, a famous Greek philosopher, died in 347 B.C. (-347) at the age of 81. When was he born?

88. HISTORY   Julius Caesar, a famous Roman leader, died in 44 B.C. (-44) at the age of 56. When was he born?

89. GAUGES   Many automobiles have an ammeter like that shown. If the headlights, which draw a current of 7 amps, and the radio, which draws a current of 6 amps, are both turned on, which way will the arrow move? What will be the new reading?

90. U.S. JOBS   The graph shows the number of jobs gained or lost each month during the year 2002.
   a. In what month were the most jobs gained? Estimate the number.

b. In what month were the most jobs lost? Estimate the number.

c. Find the range for these two extremes.

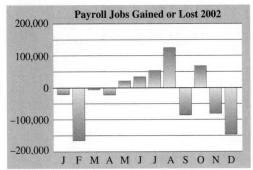

Source: Bureau of Labor Statistics

WRITING

91. Is subtracting 2 from 10 the same as subtracting 10 from 2? Explain.

92. How is $-1 - (-8)$ read?

93. Why is addition of signed numbers taught before subtraction of signed numbers?

94. Explain why we know that the answer to $4 - 10$ is negative without having to do any computation.

REVIEW

95. Find the prime factorization of 30.

96. What factor do the numerator and denominator of the fraction $\frac{15}{18}$ have in common? Simplify the fraction.

97. Build the fraction $\frac{3}{8}$ to an equivalent fraction with a denominator of 56.

98. Write the set of integers.

99. True or false: $-4 > -5$?

100. Use the associative property of addition to simplify the calculation: $-18 + (18 + 89)$.

CHALLENGE PROBLEMS

101. Suppose x is positive and y is negative. Determine whether each statement is true or false.
   a. $x - y > 0$ **b.** $y - x < 0$
   c. $-x < 0$ **d.** $-y < 0$

102. Find:

$$1 - 2 + 3 - 4 + 5 - 6 + \cdots + 99 - 100.$$

1.6 Multiplying and Dividing Real Numbers

- Multiplying Signed Numbers
- Properties of Multiplication
- Dividing Signed Numbers
- Properties of Division

In this section, we will develop rules for multiplying and dividing positive and negative numbers.

■ MULTIPLYING SIGNED NUMBERS

The Language of Algebra

The names of the parts of a multiplication fact are:

Factor   Factor   Product
$$4(3) = 12$$

Multiplication represents repeated addition. For example, $4(3)$ equals the sum of four 3's.

$$4(3) = 3 + 3 + 3 + 3$$
$$= 12$$

This example illustrates that *the product of two positive numbers is positive.*

To develop a rule for multiplying a positive number and a negative number, we will find $4(-3)$, which equals the sum of four -3's.

$$4(-3) = -3 + (-3) + (-3) + (-3)$$
$$= -12$$

We see that the result is negative. As a check, think of the problem in terms of money. If you lose $3 four times, you have lost a total of $12, which is denoted −$12. This example illustrates that *the product of a positive number and a negative number is negative.*

Multiplying Two Numbers with Unlike Signs	To multiply a positive number and a negative number, multiply their absolute values. Then make the product negative.

EXAMPLE 1

Multiply: **a.** $8(-12)$,   **b.** $-15 \cdot 5$,   and   **c.** $\dfrac{3}{4}\left(-\dfrac{4}{15}\right)$.

Solution   **a.** $8(-12) = -96$ Multiply the absolute values, 8 and 12, to get 96. The signs are unlike. Make the product negative.

The Language of Algebra

A positive number and a negative number are said to have *unlike* signs.

b. $-15 \cdot 5 = -75$ Multiply the absolute values, 15 and 5, to get 75. The signs are unlike. Make the product negative.

c. $\dfrac{3}{4}\left(-\dfrac{4}{15}\right) = -\dfrac{3 \cdot 4}{4 \cdot 15}$ Multiply the absolute values $\frac{3}{4}$ and $\frac{4}{15}$. The signs are unlike. Make the product negative.

$$= -\dfrac{\overset{1}{\cancel{3}} \cdot \overset{1}{\cancel{4}}}{\underset{1}{\cancel{4}} \cdot \underset{1}{\cancel{3}} \cdot 5}$$ To simplify the fraction, factor 15 as 3 · 5. Remove the common factors 3 and 4 in the numerator and denominator.

$$= -\dfrac{1}{5}$$

Self Check 1   Multiply: **a.** $20(-3)$,   **b.** $-3 \cdot 5$,   **c.** $-\dfrac{5}{8} \cdot \dfrac{16}{25}$

EXAMPLE 2

Medicine.   A doctor changes the setting on a heart monitor so that the screen display is magnified by a factor of 1.5. If the current low reading is −14, what will it be after the setting is changed?

Solution   To *magnify by a factor of 1.5* means to multiply by 1.5. Therefore, the new low will be $1.5(-14)$. To find this product, we multiply the absolute values, 1.5 and 14 and make the product negative.

$1.5(-14) = -21$ Multiply absolute values, 1.5 and 14, to get 21. Since 1.5 and −14 have unlike signs, the product is negative.

When the setting is changed, the low reading will be −21.

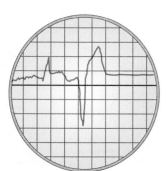

To develop a rule for multiplying negative numbers, we will find $-4(-1)$, $-4(-2)$, and $-4(-3)$. In the following list, we multiply −4 and a series of factors that decrease by 1. We know how to find the first four products. Graphing those results on a number line is helpful in determining the last three products.

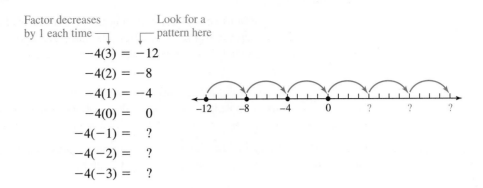

From the pattern, we see that the product increases by 4 each time. Thus,

$$-4(-1) = 4, \qquad -4(-2) = 8, \qquad \text{and} \qquad -4(-3) = 12$$

The Language of Algebra

Two negative numbers, as well as two positive numbers, are said to have *like* signs.

These results illustrate that *the product of two negative numbers is positive.* As a check, think of $-4(-3)$ as losing four debts of \$3. This is equivalent to gaining \$12. Therefore, $-4(-\$3) = \$12$.

Since the product of two positive numbers is positive, and the product of two negative numbers is also positive, we can summarize the multiplication rule as follows.

Multiplying Two Numbers with Like Signs	To multiply two real numbers with the same sign, multiply their absolute values. The product is positive.

EXAMPLE 3   Multiply: **a.** $-5(-6)$ and **b.** $\left(-\dfrac{1}{2}\right)\left(-\dfrac{5}{8}\right)$.

Solution   **a.** $-5(-6) = 30$ Multiply the absolute values, 5 and 6, to get 30. Since both factors are negative, the product is positive.

b. $\left(-\dfrac{1}{2}\right)\left(-\dfrac{5}{8}\right) = \dfrac{5}{16}$ Multiply the absolute values, $\frac{1}{2}$ and $\frac{5}{8}$, to get $\frac{5}{16}$. Since the factors have like signs, the product is positive.

Self Check 3   Multiply: **a.** $-15(-8)$, **b.** $-\dfrac{1}{4}\left(-\dfrac{1}{3}\right)$.

■ PROPERTIES OF MULTIPLICATION

The multiplication of two numbers can be done in any order; the result is the same. For example, $-6(5) = -30$ and $5(-6) = -30$. This shows that multiplication is **commutative.**

The Commutative Property of Multiplication	Changing the order when multiplying does not affect the answer. Let a and b represent real numbers, $ab = ba$

In the following example, we multiply $-3 \cdot 7 \cdot 5$ in two ways. Recall that the operation within the parentheses should be performed first.

Method 1: Group -3 and 7	**Method 2: Group 7 and 5**
$(-3 \cdot 7)5 = (-21)5$	$-3(7 \cdot 5) = -3(35)$
$\qquad\qquad\quad = -105$	$\qquad\qquad\quad = -105$

It doesn't matter how we group the numbers in this multiplication; the result is -105. This example illustrates that multiplication is **associative.**

The Associative Property of Multiplication	Changing the grouping when multiplying does not affect the answer. Let a, b, and c represent real numbers, $$(ab)c = a(bc)$$

EXAMPLE 4

Multiply: **a.** $-5(-37)(-2)$ and   **b.** $-4(-3)(-2)(-1)$.

Solution   Using the commutative and associative properties of multiplication, we can reorder and regroup the factors to simplify computations.

a. Since it is easy to multiply by 10, we will find $-5(-2)$ first.

$$-5(-37)(-2) = 10(-37)$$
$$\qquad\qquad\quad = -370$$

b. $-4(-3)(-2)(-1) = 12(2)$ Multiply the first two factors and multiply the last two factors.
$$\qquad\qquad\qquad\quad = 24$$

Self Check 4   Multiply: **a.** $-25(-3)(-4)$,   **b.** $-1(-2)(-3)(-3)$.

In Example 4a, we multiplied three negative numbers. In Example 4b, we multiplied four negative numbers. The results illustrate the following fact.

Multiplying Negative Numbers	The product of an even number of negative numbers is positive. The product of an odd number of negative numbers is negative.

Success Tip

If 0 is a factor in a multiplication, the product is 0. For example,

$$25(-6)(0)(-17) = 0$$

Whenever we multiply 0 and a number, the product is 0:

$$0 \cdot 8 = 0, \qquad 6.5(0) = 0, \qquad \text{and} \qquad 0(-12) = 0$$

These examples illustrate the **multiplication property of 0.**

Multiplication Property of 0	The product of 0 and any real number is 0. For any real number a, $$0 \cdot a = 0 \qquad \text{and} \qquad a \cdot 0 = 0$$

Whenever we multiply a number by 1, the number remains the same:

$$1 \cdot 6 = 6, \qquad 4.57 \cdot 1 = 4.57, \qquad \text{and} \qquad 1(-9) = -9$$

These examples illustrate the **multiplication property of 1.** Since any number multiplied by 1 remains the same (is identical), the number 1 is called the **identity element** for multiplication.

Multiplication Property of 1 (Identity Property of Multiplication)	The product of 1 and any number is that number. For any real number a, $$1 \cdot a = a \quad \text{and} \quad a \cdot 1 = a$$

Two numbers whose product is 1 are **reciprocals** or **multiplicative inverses** of each other. For example, 8 is the multiplicative inverse of $\frac{1}{8}$, and $\frac{1}{8}$ is the multiplicative inverse of 8, because $8 \cdot \frac{1}{8} = 1$. Likewise, $-\frac{3}{4}$ and $-\frac{4}{3}$ are multiplicative inverses because $-\frac{3}{4}\left(-\frac{4}{3}\right) = 1$. All real numbers, except 0, have a multiplicative inverse.

Multiplicative Inverses (Inverse Property of Multiplication)	The product of any number and its multiplicative inverse (reciprocal) is 1. For any nonzero real number a, $$a\left(\frac{1}{a}\right) = 1$$

EXAMPLE 5

Find the reciprocal of each number.   **a.** $\frac{2}{3}$,   **b.** $-\frac{2}{3}$,   and   **c.** -11.

Solution   **a.** The reciprocal of $\frac{2}{3}$ is $\frac{3}{2}$ because $\frac{2}{3}\left(\frac{3}{2}\right) = 1$.

b. The reciprocal of $-\frac{2}{3}$ is $-\frac{3}{2}$ because $-\frac{2}{3}\left(-\frac{3}{2}\right) = 1$.

c. The reciprocal of -11 is $-\frac{1}{11}$ because $-11\left(-\frac{1}{11}\right) = 1$.

Self Check 5   Find the reciprocal of each number: **a.** $-\frac{15}{16}$,   **b.** $\frac{15}{16}$,   **c.** -27.

■ DIVIDING SIGNED NUMBERS

Every division fact can be written as an equivalent multiplication fact.

Division	Let a, b, and c represent real numbers, where $b \neq 0$, $$\frac{a}{b} = c \qquad \text{provided that} \qquad c \cdot b = a$$

We can use this relationship between multiplication and division to develop rules for dividing signed numbers. For example,

$$\frac{15}{5} = 3 \qquad \text{because} \qquad 3(5) = 15$$

From this example, we see that *the quotient of two positive numbers is positive.*

To determine the quotient of two negative numbers, we consider $\frac{-15}{-5}$.

The Language of Algebra

The names of the parts of a division fact are:

Dividend   Quotient

$$\frac{15}{5} = 3$$

Divisor

$$\frac{-15}{-5} = 3 \qquad \text{because} \qquad 3(-5) = -15$$

From this example, we see that the *quotient of two negative numbers is positive.*

To determine the quotient of a positive number and a negative number, we consider $\frac{15}{-5}$.

$$\frac{15}{-5} = -3 \qquad \text{because} \qquad -3(-5) = 15$$

From this example, we see that *the quotient of a positive number and a negative number is negative.*

To determine the quotient of a negative number and a positive number, we consider $\frac{-15}{5}$.

$$\frac{-15}{5} = -3 \qquad \text{because} \qquad -3(5) = -15$$

From this example, we see that *the quotient of a negative number and a positive number is negative.*

We summarize the rules from the previous examples and note that they are similar to the rules for multiplication.

Dividing Two Real Numbers

To divide two real numbers, divide their absolute values.

1. The quotient of two numbers with *like* signs is positive.

2. The quotient of two numbers with *unlike* signs is negative.

EXAMPLE 6   Find each quotient: **a.** $\dfrac{-81}{-9}$,   **b.** $\dfrac{45}{-9}$,   and   **c.** $-2.87 \div 0.7$.

Solution   **a.** $\dfrac{-81}{-9} = 9$ Divide the absolute values, 81 by 9, to get 9. Since the signs are like, the quotient is positive.

Multiply to check the result: $9(-9) = -81$.

b. $\dfrac{45}{-9} = -5$ Divide the absolute values, 45 by 9, to get 5. Since the signs are unlike, make the quotient negative.

Multiply to check the result: $-5(-9) = 45$.

c. $-2.87 \div 0.7 = -4.1$ Since the signs are unlike, make the quotient negative.

Multiply to check the result: $-4.1(0.7) = -2.87$.

Self Check 6   Find each quotient: **a.** $\dfrac{-28}{-4}$,   **b.** $\dfrac{75}{-25}$,   **c.** $0.32 \div (-1.6)$.

EXAMPLE 7   Divide: $-\dfrac{5}{16} \div \left(-\dfrac{1}{2}\right)$.

Solution

$$-\frac{5}{16} \div \left(-\frac{1}{2}\right) = -\frac{5}{16}\left(-\frac{2}{1}\right)$$

Multiply the first fraction by the reciprocal of the second fraction. The reciprocal of $-\frac{1}{2}$ is $-\frac{2}{1}$.

$$= \frac{5 \cdot 2}{16 \cdot 1}$$

Multiply the absolute values $\frac{5}{16}$ and $\frac{2}{1}$. Since the signs are like, the product is positive.

$$= \frac{5 \cdot \overset{1}{\cancel{2}}}{\cancel{2} \cdot 8 \cdot 1}$$

To simplify the fraction, factor 16 as $2 \cdot 8$. Replace $\frac{2}{2}$ with $\frac{1}{1}$.

$$= \frac{5}{8}$$

Self Check 7   Divide: $\dfrac{3}{4} \div \left(-\dfrac{5}{8}\right)$.

EXAMPLE 8

Depreciation.   Over an 8-year period, the value of a \$150,000 house fell at a uniform rate to \$110,000. Find the amount of depreciation per year.

Solution   First, we find the change in the value of the house.

$$110,000 - 150,000 = -40,000$$ Subtract the previous value from the current value.

The result represents a drop in value of \$40,000. Since the depreciation occurred over 8 years, we divide $-40,000$ by 8.

$$\frac{-40,000}{8} = -5,000$$ Divide the absolute values, 40,000 by 8, to get 5,000, and make the quotient negative.

The house depreciated \$5,000 per year.

The Language of Algebra

Depreciation is a form of the word *depreciate,* meaning to lose value. You've probably heard that the minute you drive a new car off the lot, it has depreciated.

■ PROPERTIES OF DIVISION

Whenever we divide a number by 1, the quotient is that number:

$$\frac{12}{1} = 12, \qquad \frac{-80}{1} = -80, \qquad \text{and} \qquad 7.75 \div 1 = 7.75$$

Furthermore, whenever we divide a nonzero number by itself, the quotient is 1:

$$\frac{35}{35} = 1, \qquad \frac{-4}{-4} = 1, \qquad \text{and} \qquad 0.9 \div 0.9 = 1$$

These observations suggest the following properties of division.

Division Properties   Any number divided by 1 is the number itself. Any number (except 0) divided by itself is 1.

For any real number a,

$$\frac{a}{1} = a \qquad \text{and} \qquad \frac{a}{a} = 1 \qquad \text{(where } a \neq 0)$$

We will now consider division that involves zero. First, we examine division of zero. As an example, let's consider $\frac{0}{2}$. We know that

$$\frac{0}{2} = 0 \qquad \text{because} \qquad 0(2) = 0$$

The Language of Algebra

When we say a division by 0, such as $\frac{2}{0}$, is *undefined*, we mean that $\frac{2}{0}$ does not represent a real number.

From this example, we see that *0 divided by a nonzero number is 0.*

Next, we consider division by zero by considering $\frac{2}{0}$. We know that $\frac{2}{0}$ has no answer because there is no number we can multiply 0 by to get 2. We say that such a division is **undefined.**

These results suggest the following division facts.

Division Involving 0   For any nonzero real number a,

$$\frac{0}{a} = 0 \qquad \text{and} \qquad \frac{a}{0} \text{ is undefined.}$$

EXAMPLE 9   Find each quotient, if possible: **a.** $\dfrac{0}{13}$ and **b.** $\dfrac{-13}{0}$.

Solution   **a.** $\dfrac{0}{13} = 0$ because $0(13) = 0$.

b. Since $\dfrac{-13}{0}$ involves division by zero, the division is undefined.

Self Check 9   Find each quotient, if possible: **a.** $\dfrac{4}{0}$, **b.** $\dfrac{0}{17}$.

Answers to Self Checks   **1. a.** -60,   **b.** -15,   **c.** $-\frac{2}{5}$ **3. a.** 120,   **b.** $\frac{1}{12}$ **4. a.** -300,   **b.** 18
5. a. $-\frac{16}{15}$,   **b.** $\frac{16}{15}$,   **c.** $-\frac{1}{27}$ **6. a.** 7,   **b.** -3,   **c.** -0.2 **7.** $-\frac{6}{5}$
9. a. undefined,   **b.** 0

1.6   STUDY SET

VOCABULARY   Fill in the blanks.

1. The answer to a multiplication problem is called a _____. The answer to a division problem is called a _____.

2. The numbers -4 and -6 are said to have _____ signs. The numbers -10 and 12 are said to have _____ signs.

3. The _____ property of multiplication states that changing the order when multiplying does not affect the answer.

4. The _____ property of multiplication states that changing the grouping when multiplying does not affect the answer.

5. Division of a nonzero number by zero is _____.

6. If the product of two numbers is 1, the numbers are called _____ or _____ inverses.

CONCEPTS   Fill in the blanks.

7. The expression $-5 + (-5) + (-5) + (-5)$ can be represented by the multiplication $4(\quad)$.

8. The quotient of two numbers with _____ signs is negative.

9. The product of two negative numbers is _____.

10. The product of zero and any number is ___.

11. The product of ___ and any number is that number.

12. We know that $\frac{20}{-2} = -10$ because $-10(\quad) = 20$.

13. a. If we multiply two different numbers and the answer is 0, what must be true about one of the numbers?

   b. If we multiply two different numbers and the answer is 1, what must be true about the numbers?

14. a. If we divide two numbers and the answer is 1, what must be true about the numbers?

   b. If we divide two numbers and the answer is 0, what must be true about the numbers?

Let POS stand for a positive number and NEG stand for a negative number. Determine the sign of each result, if possible.

15. a. POS $\cdot$ NEG   **b.** POS + NEG

   c. POS $-$ NEG   **d.** $\dfrac{\text{POS}}{\text{NEG}}$

16. a. NEG $\cdot$ NEG   **b.** NEG + NEG

   c. NEG $-$ NEG   **d.** $\dfrac{\text{NEG}}{\text{NEG}}$

17. Complete each property of multiplication.
   a. $a \cdot b = b \cdot$ ___   **b.** $(ab)c = $ ___
   c. $0 \cdot a = $ ___   **d.** $1 \cdot a = $ ___
   e. $a\left(\dfrac{1}{a}\right) = $ ___ $(a \neq 0)$

18. Complete each property of division.
   a. $\dfrac{a}{1} = $ ___   **b.** $\dfrac{a}{a} = $ ___ $(a \neq 0)$
   c. $\dfrac{0}{a} = $ ___ $(a \neq 0)$ **d.** $\dfrac{a}{0}$ is ___

19. Which property justifies each statement?
   a. $-5(2 \cdot 17) = (-5 \cdot 2)17$

   b. $-5\left(-\dfrac{1}{5}\right) = 1$

   c. $-5 \cdot 2 = 2(-5)$

   d. $-5(1) = -5$

20. Complete the table.

Number	Opposite (additive inverse)	Reciprocal (multiplicative inverse)
2		
$-\dfrac{4}{5}$		
-55		
1.75		

NOTATION

21. Write each sentence using symbols.
   a. The product of negative four and negative five is twenty.
   b. The quotient of sixteen and negative eight is negative two.

22. Write each expression without $-$ signs.
   a. $\dfrac{-1}{-2}$ **b.** $\dfrac{-7}{-8}$

PRACTICE   Perform each operation.

23. $-2 \cdot 8$ **24.** $-3 \cdot 4$

25. $(-6)(-9)$ **26.** $(-8)(-7)$

27. $12(-5)$ **28.** $(-9)(11)$

29. $-6 \cdot 4$ **30.** $-8 \cdot 9$

31. $-20(40)$ **32.** $-10(10)$

33. $(-6)(-6)$ **34.** $(-1)(-1)$

35. $-0.6(-4)$ **36.** $-0.7(-8)$

37. $1.2(-0.4)$ **38.** $0(-0.2)$

39. $-1.1(-0.9)$ **40.** $-2.3(-3.1)$

41. $7.2(-2.1)$ **42.** $4.6(-5.4)$

43. $\dfrac{1}{2}\left(-\dfrac{3}{4}\right)$ **44.** $\dfrac{1}{3}\left(-\dfrac{5}{16}\right)$

45. $\left(-\dfrac{7}{8}\right)\left(-\dfrac{2}{21}\right)$ **46.** $\left(-\dfrac{5}{6}\right)\left(-\dfrac{2}{15}\right)$

47. $-\dfrac{16}{25} \cdot \dfrac{15}{64}$ **48.** $-\dfrac{15}{16} \cdot \dfrac{8}{25}$

49. $-1\dfrac{1}{4}\left(-\dfrac{3}{4}\right)$ **50.** $-1\dfrac{1}{8}\left(-\dfrac{3}{8}\right)$

51. $-5.2 \cdot 100$ **52.** $-1.17 \cdot 1,000$

53. $0(-22)$

54. $-8 \cdot 0$

55. $-3(-4)(0)$

56. $15(0)(-22)$

57. $3(-4)(-5)$

58. $(-2)(-4)(-5)$

59. $(-4)3(-7)$

60. $5(-3)(-4)$

61. $(-2)(-3)(-4)(-5)$

62. $(-3)(-4)(5)(-6)$

63. $\dfrac{1}{2}\left(-\dfrac{1}{3}\right)\left(-\dfrac{1}{4}\right)$

64. $\dfrac{1}{3}\left(-\dfrac{1}{5}\right)\left(-\dfrac{1}{7}\right)$

65. $-2(-3)(-4)(-5)(-6)$

66. $-9(-7)(-5)(-3)(-1)$

67. $-30 \div (-3)$

68. $-12 \div (-2)$

69. $\dfrac{-6}{-2}$

70. $\dfrac{-36}{9}$

71. $\dfrac{4}{-2}$

72. $\dfrac{-9}{3}$

73. $\dfrac{80}{-20}$

74. $\dfrac{-66}{33}$

75. $\dfrac{17}{-17}$

76. $\dfrac{-24}{24}$

77. $\dfrac{-110}{-110}$

78. $\dfrac{-200}{-200}$

79. $\dfrac{-160}{40}$

80. $\dfrac{-250}{-50}$

81. $\dfrac{320}{-16}$

82. $\dfrac{-180}{36}$

83. $\dfrac{0.5}{-100}$

84. $\dfrac{-1.7}{10}$

85. $\dfrac{0}{150}$

86. $\dfrac{225}{0}$

87. $\dfrac{-17}{0}$

88. $\dfrac{0}{-12}$

89. $-\dfrac{1}{3} \div \dfrac{4}{5}$

90. $-\dfrac{2}{3} \div \dfrac{7}{8}$

91. $-\dfrac{9}{16} \div \left(-\dfrac{3}{20}\right)$

92. $-\dfrac{4}{5} \div \left(-\dfrac{8}{25}\right)$

93. $-3\dfrac{3}{8} \div \left(-2\dfrac{1}{4}\right)$

94. $-3\dfrac{4}{15} \div \left(-2\dfrac{1}{10}\right)$

95. $\dfrac{-23.5}{5}$

96. $\dfrac{-337.8}{6}$

97. $\dfrac{-24.24}{-0.8}$

98. $\dfrac{-55.02}{-0.7}$

Use the associative property of multiplication to find each product.

99. $-\dfrac{1}{2}(2 \cdot 67)$

100. $\left(-\dfrac{5}{16} \cdot \dfrac{1}{7}\right)7$

101. $-0.2(10 \cdot 3)$

102. $-1.5(100 \cdot 4)$

APPLICATIONS

103. TEMPERATURE CHANGE   In a lab, the temperature of a fluid was decreased 6° per hour for 12 hours. What signed number indicates the change in temperature?

104. BACTERIAL GROWTH   To slowly warm a bacterial culture, biologists programmed a heating pad under the culture to increase the temperature 4° every hour for 6 hours. What signed number indicates the change in the temperature of the pad?

105. GAMBLING   A gambler places a $40 bet and loses. He then decides to go "double or nothing" and loses again. Feeling that his luck has to change, he goes "double or nothing" once more and, for the third time, loses. What signed number indicates his gambling losses?

106. REAL ESTATE   A house has depreciated $1,250 each year for 8 years. What signed number indicates its change in value over that time period?

107. PLANETS   The temperature on Pluto gets as low as −386° F. This is twice as low as the lowest temperature reached on Jupiter. What is the lowest temperature on Jupiter?

108. CAR RADIATORS   The instructions on the back of a container of antifreeze state, "A 50/50 mixture of antifreeze and water protects against freeze-ups down to −34° F, while a 60/40 mix protects against freeze-ups down to one and one-half times that temperature." To what temperature does the 60/40 mixture protect?

109. ACCOUNTING   For 1999, the total net income for Converse, the sports shoe company, was about −$22.8 million. The company's losses for 2000 were even worse, by a factor of about 1.9. What signed number indicates the company's total net income that year?

110. AIRLINES In the income statement for Trans World Airlines, numbers within parentheses represent a loss. Complete the statement given these facts. The second and fourth quarter losses were approximately the same and totaled −$1,000 million. The third quarter loss was about $\frac{3}{5}$ of the first quarter loss.

TWA INCOME STATEMENT				2002
All amounts in millions of US dollars	1st Qtr (1,550)	2nd Qtr (?)	3rd Qtr (?)	4th Qtr (?)

111. THE QUEEN MARY The ocean liner Queen Mary was commissioned in 1936 and cost $22,500,000 to build. In 1967, the ship was purchased by the city of Long Beach, California for $3,450,000 and now serves as a hotel and convention center. What signed number indicates the annual average depreciation of the Queen Mary over the 31-year period from 1936 to 1967? Round to the nearest dollar.

112. COMPUTERS The formula = A1*B1*C1 in cell D1 of the following spreadsheet instructs the computer to multiply the values in cells A1, B1, and C1 and to print the result *in place of the formula* in cell D1. (The symbol * represents multiplication.) What value will the computer print in the cell D1? What values will be printed in cells D2 and D3?

	A	B	C	D
1	4	−5	−17	= A1*B1*C1
2	22	−30	14	= A2*B2*C2
3	−60	−20	−34	= A3*B3*C3
4				

Microsoft Excel-Book 1 — File Edit View Insert Format Tools — Sheet 1 / Sheet 2 / Sheet 3 / Sheet 4 / Sheet 5

113. PHYSICS An oscilloscope displays electrical signals which appear as wavy lines on a screen. By switching the magnification setting to × 2, for example, the height of the "peak" and the depth of the "valley" of a graph will be doubled. Use signed numbers to indicate the height and depth of the display for each setting of the magnification dial.
a. normal
b. × 0.5
c. × 1.5
d. × 2

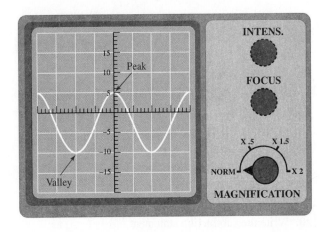

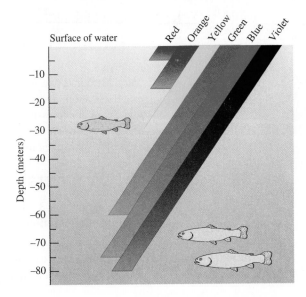

114. LIGHT Water acts as a selective filter of light. In the illustration, we see that red light waves penetrate water only to a depth of about 5 meters. How many times deeper does
a. yellow light penetrate than red light?
b. green light penetrate than orange light?
c. blue light penetrate than yellow light?

WRITING

115. When a calculator was used to compute 16 ÷ 0, the message shown appeared on the display screen. Explain what the message means.

116. a. Find $-1(8)$. In general, what is the result when a number is multiplied by -1?

   b. Find $\frac{8}{-1}$. In general, what is the result when a number is divided by -1?

117. What is wrong with the following statement?

   A negative and a positive is a negative.

118. Is 80 divided by -5 the same as -5 divided by 80? Explain.

REVIEW

119. Add: $-3 + (-4) + (-5) + 4 + 3$.

120. Write the subtraction statement $-3 - (-5)$ as addition of the opposite.

121. Find $\frac{1}{2} + \frac{1}{4} + \frac{1}{3}$ and express the result as a decimal.

122. Describe the balance in a checking account that is overdrawn $65 using a signed number.

123. Remove the common factors of the numerator and denominator to simplify the fraction: $\frac{2 \cdot 3 \cdot 5 \cdot 5}{2 \cdot 5 \cdot 5 \cdot 7}$.

124. Find $|-2{,}345|$.

CHALLENGE PROBLEMS

125. If the product of five numbers is negative, how many of them could be negative? Explain.

126. Suppose a is a positive number and b is a negative number. Determine whether the given expression is positive or negative.

   a. $-a(-b)$ **b.** $\dfrac{-a}{b}$

   c. $\dfrac{-a}{a}$ **d.** $\dfrac{1}{b}$

1.7 Exponents and Order of Operations

- Exponents   • Order of Operations   • Grouping Symbols   • The Mean (Average)

In this course, we will perform six operations with real numbers: addition, subtraction, multiplication, division, raising to a power, and finding a root. Often, we will have to find the value of expressions that involve more than one operation. In this section, we introduce an order-of-operations rule to follow in such cases. But first, we discuss a way to write repeated multiplication using *exponents*.

■ EXPONENTS

In the expression $3 \cdot 3 \cdot 3 \cdot 3 \cdot 3$, the number 3 repeats as a factor five times. We can use **exponential notation** to write this product more concisely.

Exponent and Base	An **exponent** is used to indicate repeated multiplication. It tells how many times the **base** is used as a factor.

The Language of Algebra

5^2 represents the area of a square with sides 5 units long. 4^3 represents the volume of a cube with sides 4 units long.

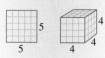

$$\underbrace{3 \cdot 3 \cdot 3 \cdot 3 \cdot 3}_{\text{Five repeated factors of 3.}} = 3^5$$

The exponent is 5.

The base is 3.

In the **exponential expression** 3^5, 3 is the base, and 5 is the exponent. The expression 3^5 is called a power of 3. Some other examples of exponential expressions are:

5^2 Read as "5 to the second power" or "5 squared."

4^3 Read as "4 to the third power" or "4 cubed."

$(-2)^5$ Read as "-2 to the fifth power."

EXAMPLE 1   Write each expression using exponents: **a.** $7 \cdot 7 \cdot 7$, **b.** $(-5)(-5)(-5)(-5)(-5)$, **c.** sixteen cubed, and **d.** $8 \cdot 8 \cdot 15 \cdot 15 \cdot 15 \cdot 15$.

Solution   **a.** We can represent this repeated multiplication with an exponential expression having a base of 7 and an exponent of 3: $7 \cdot 7 \cdot 7 = 7^3$.

b. The factor -5 is repeated five times: $(-5)(-5)(-5)(-5)(-5) = (-5)^5$.

c. Sixteen cubed can be written as 16^3.

d. $8 \cdot 8 \cdot 15 \cdot 15 \cdot 15 \cdot 15 = 8^2 \cdot 15^4$

Self Check 1   Write each expression using exponents: **a.** $(12)(12)(12)(12)(12)(12)$, **b.** $2 \cdot 9 \cdot 9 \cdot 9$, **c.** fifty squared, **d.** $(-30)(-30)(-30)$.

EXAMPLE 2   Write each product using exponents: **a.** $a \cdot a \cdot a \cdot a \cdot a \cdot a$ and **b.** $4 \cdot \pi \cdot r \cdot r$.

Solution   **a.** $a \cdot a \cdot a \cdot a \cdot a \cdot a = a^6$ a is repeated as a factor 6 times.

b. $4 \cdot \pi \cdot r \cdot r = 4\pi r^2$ r is repeated as a factor 2 times.

Self Check 2   Write each product using exponents: **a.** $y \cdot y \cdot y \cdot y$, **b.** $12 \cdot b \cdot b \cdot b \cdot c$.

EXAMPLE 3   Find the value of each expression: **a.** 5^3, **b.** 10^1, **c.** $(-3)^4$, and **d.** $(-3)^5$.

Solution   **a.** $5^3 = 5 \cdot 5 \cdot 5 = 125$ The base is 5, the exponent is 3.

b. $10^1 = 10$ The base is 10. Since the exponent is 1, we write the base once.

Notation

If a number or a variable is written without an exponent, we assume the number or variable has an understood exponent of 1. For example,

$x = x^1$ and $8 = 8^1$

c. $(-3)^4 = (-3)(-3)(-3)(-3)$ Write -3 as a factor four times.
$= 9(-3)(-3)$ Work from left to right.
$= -27(-3)$
$= 81$

d. $(-3)^5 = (-3)(-3)(-3)(-3)(-3)$ Write -3 as a factor five times.
$= 9(-3)(-3)(-3)$ Work from left to right.
$= -27(-3)(-3)$
$= 81(-3)$
$= -243$

Self Check 3   Evaluate: **a.** 2^5, **b.** 9^1, **c.** $(-6)^2$, **d.** $(-5)^3$.

Caution   A common mistake when evaluating an exponential expression is to multiply the base and the exponent. For example, $5^3 \neq 15$. As we saw in Example 3a, $5^3 = 5 \cdot 5 \cdot 5 = 125$.

In part c of Example 3, we raised -3 to an even power, and the result was positive. In part d, we raised -3 to an odd power, and the result was negative. These results illustrate the following rule.

Even and Odd Powers of a Negative Number	When a negative number is raised to an even power, the result is positive.
	When a negative number is raised to an odd power, the result is negative.

Calculators
Finding a power

The squaring key x^2 can be used to find the square of a number. To raise a number to a power, we use the y^x key on a scientific calculator and the $\wedge$ key on a graphing calculator.

Although the expressions $(-4)^2$ and -4^2 look alike, they are not. When we find the value of each expression, it becomes clear that they are not equivalent.

$(-4)^2 = (-4)(-4)$ The base is -4, the exponent is 2.

$= 16$

$-4^2 = -(4 \cdot 4)$ The base is 4, the exponent is 2.

$= -16$

Different results

EXAMPLE 4

Evaluate: -2^4.

Solution

$-2^4 = -(2 \cdot 2 \cdot 2 \cdot 2)$ Since the base is 2, and the exponent is 4, write 2 as a factor four times within parentheses.

$= -16$ Do the multiplication within the parentheses.

Self Check 4   Evaluate: -5^4.

EXAMPLE 5

Evaluate: **a.** $\left(-\dfrac{2}{3}\right)^3$ and **b.** $(0.6)^2$.

Solution **a.** $\left(-\dfrac{2}{3}\right)^3 = \left(-\dfrac{2}{3}\right)\left(-\dfrac{2}{3}\right)\left(-\dfrac{2}{3}\right)$ Since $-\dfrac{2}{3}$ is the base and 3 is the exponent, we write $-\dfrac{2}{3}$ as a factor three times.

$= \dfrac{4}{9}\left(-\dfrac{2}{3}\right)$ Work from left to right. $\left(-\dfrac{2}{3}\right)\left(-\dfrac{2}{3}\right) = \dfrac{4}{9}$

$= -\dfrac{8}{27}$ We say $-\dfrac{8}{27}$ is the *cube* of $-\dfrac{2}{3}$.

b. $(0.6)^2 = (0.6)(0.6)$ Since 0.6 is the base and 2 is the exponent, we write 0.6 as a factor two times.

$= 0.36$ We say 0.36 is the *square* of 0.6.

Self Check 5   Evaluate: **a.** $\left(-\dfrac{3}{4}\right)^3$, **b.** $(-0.3)^2$.

■ ORDER OF OPERATIONS

Suppose you have been asked to contact a friend if you see a Rolex watch for sale when you are traveling in Europe. While in Switzerland, you find the watch and send the e-mail message shown on the left. The next day, you get the response shown on the right.

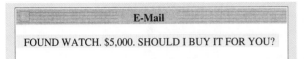

E-Mail
FOUND WATCH. $5,000. SHOULD I BUY IT FOR YOU?

E-Mail
NO PRICE TOO HIGH! REPEAT...NO! PRICE TOO HIGH.

Something is wrong. The first part of the response (No price too high!) says to buy the watch at any price. The second part (No! Price too high.) says not to buy it, because it's too expensive. The placement of the exclamation point makes us read the two parts of the response differently, resulting in different meanings. When reading a mathematical statement, the same kind of confusion is possible. For example, consider the expression

$$2 + 3 \cdot 6$$

We can evaluate this expression in two ways. We can add first, and then multiply. Or we can multiply first, and then add. However, the results are different.

$$2 + 3 \cdot 6 = 5 \cdot 6 \quad \text{Add 2 and 3 first.} \qquad 2 + 3 \cdot 6 = 2 + 18 \quad \text{Multiply 3 and 6 first.}$$
$$= 30 \quad \text{Multiply 5 and 6.} \qquad\qquad\qquad = 20 \quad \text{Add 2 and 18.}$$

Different results

If we don't establish a uniform order of operations, the expression has two different values. To avoid this possibility, we will always use the following set of priority rules.

Order of Operations

1. Perform all calculations within parentheses and other grouping symbols following the order listed in Steps 2–4 below, working from the innermost pair of grouping symbols to the outermost pair.
2. Evaluate all exponential expressions.
3. Perform all multiplications and divisions as they occur from left to right.
4. Perform all additions and subtractions as they occur from left to right.

When grouping symbols have been removed, repeat Steps 2–4 to complete the calculation.

    If a fraction is present, evaluate the expression above and the expression below the bar separately. Then do the division indicated by the fraction bar, if possible.

It isn't necessary to apply all of these steps in every problem. For example, the expression $2 + 3 \cdot 6$ does not contain any parentheses, and there are no exponential expressions. So we look for multiplications and divisions to perform and proceed as follows:

$$2 + 3 \cdot 6 = 2 + 18 \quad \text{Do the multiplication first: } 3 \cdot 6 = 18.$$
$$= 20 \quad \text{Do the addition.}$$

EXAMPLE 6

Evaluate: $3 \cdot 2^3 - 4$.

Solution   Three operations need to be performed to find the value of this expression. By the rules for the order of operations, we evaluate 2^3 first.

$$3 \cdot 2^3 - 4 = 3 \cdot 8 - 4 \qquad \text{Evaluate the exponential expression: } 2^3 = 8.$$
$$= 24 - 4 \qquad \text{Do the multiplication: } 3 \cdot 8 = 24.$$
$$= 20 \qquad \text{Do the subtraction.}$$

Self Check 6   Evaluate: $2 \cdot 3^2 + 17$.

EXAMPLE 7

Evaluate: $-30 - 4 \cdot 5 + 9$.

Solution   This expression involves subtraction, multiplication, and addition. The rules for the order of operations tell us to multiply first.

The Language of Algebra

Sometimes, the word *simplify* is used in place of the word *evaluate.*

$$-30 - 4 \cdot 5 + 9 = -30 - 20 + 9 \qquad \text{Do the multiplication: } 4 \cdot 5 = 20.$$
$$= -50 + 9 \qquad \text{Working from left to right, do the subtraction:}$$
$$-30 - 20 = -30 + (-20) = -50.$$
$$= -41 \qquad \text{Do the addition.}$$

Self Check 7   Evaluate: $-40 - 9 \cdot 4 + 10$.

EXAMPLE 8

Evaluate: $160 \div (-4) - 6(-2)3$.

Solution   Although this expression contains parentheses, there are no operations to perform within them. Since there are no exponents, we do multiplications and divisions as they are encountered from left to right.

$$160 \div (-4) - 6(-2)3 = -40 - 6(-2)3 \qquad \text{Do the division: } 160 \div (-4) = -40.$$
$$= -40 - (-12)3 \qquad \text{Do the multiplication: } 6(-2) = -12.$$
$$= -40 - (-36) \qquad \text{Do the multiplication: } (-12)3 = -36.$$
$$= -40 + 36 \qquad \text{Write the subtraction as addition of the opposite.}$$
$$= -4 \qquad \text{Do the addition.}$$

Self Check 8   Evaluate: $240 \div (-8) - 3(-2)4$.

■ GROUPING SYMBOLS

Grouping symbols serve as mathematical punctuation marks. They help determine the order in which an expression is to be evaluated. Examples of grouping symbols are parentheses ( ), brackets [ ], absolute value symbols | |, and the fraction bar —.

EXAMPLE 9

Evaluate: $(6 - 3)^2$.

Solution   This expression contains parentheses. By the rules for the order of operations, we must perform the operation within the parentheses first.

$$(6 - 3)^2 = 3^2 \quad \text{Do the subtraction: } 6 - 3 = 3.$$
$$= 9 \quad \text{Evaluate the exponential expression.}$$

Self Check 9   Evaluate: $(12 - 6)^3$.

EXAMPLE 10   Evaluate: $5^3 + 2(-8 - 3 \cdot 2)$.

Solution   We begin by performing the operations within the parentheses in the proper order: multiplication first, and then subtraction.

Notation

Multiplication is indicated when a number is next to a grouping symbol.

$$\downarrow$$
$$5^3 + 2(-8 - 3 \cdot 2)$$

$$5^3 + 2(-8 - 3 \cdot 2) = 5^3 + 2(-8 - 6) \quad \text{Do the multiplication: } 3 \cdot 2 = 6.$$
$$= 5^3 + 2(-14) \quad \text{Do the subtraction: } -8 - 6 = -14.$$
$$= 125 + 2(-14) \quad \text{Evaluate } 5^3.$$
$$= 125 + (-28) \quad \text{Do the multiplication.}$$
$$= 97 \quad \text{Do the addition.}$$

Self Check 10   Evaluate: $1^3 + 6(-6 - 3 \cdot 0)$.

Expressions can contain two or more pairs of grouping symbols. To evaluate the following expression, we begin by working within the innermost pair of grouping symbols. Then we work within the outermost pair.

Innermost pair
$$\downarrow \quad \downarrow$$
$$-4[-2 - 3(4 - 8^2)] - 2$$
$$\uparrow \qquad \uparrow$$
Outermost pair

EXAMPLE 11   Evaluate: $-4[-2 - 3(4 - 8^2)] - 2$.

Solution   We do the work within the innermost grouping symbols (the parentheses) first.

$$-4[-2 - 3(4 - 8^2)] - 2$$
$$= -4[-2 - 3(4 - 64)] - 2 \quad \text{Evaluate the exponential expression within the parentheses: } 8^2 = 64.$$
$$= -4[-2 - 3(-60)] - 2 \quad \text{Do the subtraction within the parentheses: } 4 - 64 = 4 + (-64) = -60.$$
$$= -4[-2 - (-180)] - 2 \quad \text{Do the multiplication within the brackets: } 3(-60) = -180.$$
$$= -4[178] - 2 \quad \text{Do the subtraction within the brackets: } -2 - (-180) = -2 + 180 = 178.$$
$$= -712 - 2 \quad \text{Do the multiplication: } -4[178] = -712.$$
$$= -714 \quad \text{Do the subtraction.}$$

Self Check 11   Evaluate: $-5[2(5^2 - 15) + 4] - 10$

EXAMPLE 12

Evaluate: $\dfrac{-3(3 + 2) + 5}{17 - 3(-4)}$.

Solution   We simplify the numerator and the denominator separately.

Calculators
Order of operations

Calculators have the order of operations built in. A left parenthesis key (and a right parenthesis key) should be used when grouping symbols, including a fraction bar, are needed.

$$\dfrac{-3(3 + 2) + 5}{17 - 3(-4)} = \dfrac{-3(5) + 5}{17 - (-12)}$$ In the numerator, do the addition within the parentheses. In the denominator, do the multiplication.

$$= \dfrac{-15 + 5}{17 + 12}$$ In the numerator, do the multiplication. In the denominator, write the subtraction as addition of the opposite of -12, which is 12.

$$= \dfrac{-10}{29}$$ Do the additions.

$$= -\dfrac{10}{29}$$ Write the $-$ sign in front of the fraction: $\dfrac{-10}{29} = -\dfrac{10}{29}$.

Self Check 12   Evaluate: $\dfrac{-4(-2 + 8) + 6}{8 - 5(-2)}$.

EXAMPLE 13

Evaluate: $10|9 - 15| - 2^5$.

Solution   The absolute value bars are grouping symbols. We do the calculation within them first.

$$10|9 - 15| - 2^5 = 10|-6| - 2^5$$ Subtract: $9 - 15 = 9 + (-15) = -6$.

$$= 10(6) - 2^5$$ Find the absolute value: $|-6| = 6$.

$$= 10(6) - 32$$ Evaluate the exponential expression: $2^5 = 32$.

$$= 60 - 32$$ Do the multiplication: $10(6) = 60$.

$$= 28$$ Do the subtraction.

Self Check 13   Evaluate: $10^3 + 3|24 - 25|$.

■ THE MEAN (AVERAGE)

The **arithmetic mean** (or **average**) of a set of numbers is a value around which the values of the numbers are grouped.

Finding an Arithmetic Mean   To find the **mean** of a set of values, divide the sum of the values by the number of values.

EXAMPLE 14

Customer service.   To measure its effectiveness in serving customers, a store had the telephone company electronically record the number of times the telephone rang before an employee answered it. The results of the week-long survey are shown in the table. We see that for 11 calls, the phone was answered after it rang 1 time. For 46 calls, the phone was answered after it rang 2 times, and so on. Find the *average* number of times the phone rang before an employee answered it that week.

Number of rings	Number of calls
1	11
2	46
3	45
4	28
5	20

Solution   To find the total number of rings, we multiply each *number of rings* (1, 2, 3, 4, and 5 rings) by the respective number of occurrences and add those subtotals.

$$\text{Total number of rings} = 11(1) + 46(2) + 45(3) + 28(4) + 20(5)$$

The total number of calls received was $11 + 46 + 45 + 28 + 20$. To find the average, we divide the total number of rings by the total number of calls.

$$\text{Average} = \frac{11(1) + 46(2) + 45(3) + 28(4) + 20(5)}{11 + 46 + 45 + 28 + 20}$$

In the numerator, do the multiplications. In the denominator, do the additions.

$$= \frac{11 + 92 + 135 + 112 + 100}{150}$$

$$= \frac{450}{150}$$

Do the addition.

$$= 3$$

The average number of times the phone rang before it was answered was 3.

Answers to Self Checks **1. a.** 12^6, **b.** $2 \cdot 9^3$, **c.** 50^2, **d.** $(-30)^3$ **2. a.** y^4, **b.** $12b^3c$ **3. a.** 32, **b.** 9, **c.** 36, **d.** -125 **4.** -625 **5. a.** $-\frac{27}{64}$, **b.** 0.09 **6.** 35 **7.** -66 **8.** -6 **9.** 216 **10.** -35 **11.** -130 **12.** -1 **13.** 1,003

1.7   STUDY SET

VOCABULARY   **Fill in the blanks.**

1. In the exponential expression 3^2, 3 is the _____, and 2 is the _____.
2. 10^2 can be read as ten _____, and 10^3 can be read as ten _____.
3. 7^5 is the fifth _____ of seven.
4. An _____ is used to represent repeated multiplication.
5. The rules for the _____ of operations guarantee that an evaluation of a numerical expression will result in a single answer.
6. The arithmetic _____ or _____ of a set of numbers is a value around which the values of the numbers are grouped.

CONCEPTS

7. Given: $4 + 5 \cdot 6$.
   a. Evaluate the expression in two different ways and state the two possible results.
   b. Which result from part a is correct, and why?
8. **a.** What repeated multiplication does 5^3 represent?
   b. Write a multiplication statement in which the factor x is repeated 4 times. Then write the expression in simpler form using an exponent.
9. In the expression $-8 + 2[15 - (-6 + 1)]$, which grouping symbols are innermost, and which are outermost?
10. **a.** What operations does the expression $12 + 5^2(-3)$ contain?
    b. In what order should they be performed?
11. **a.** What operations does the expression $20 - (-2)^2 + 3(-1)$ contain?
    b. In what order should they be performed?

12. Consider the expression $\frac{36 - 4(7)}{2(10 - 8)}$. In the numerator, what operation should be done first? In the denominator, what operation should be done first?

13. To evaluate each expression, what operation should be done first?
  a. $24 - 4 + 2$ **b.** $24 \div 4 \cdot 2$

14. To evaluate each expression, what operation should be done first?
  a. $-80 - 3 + 5 - 2^2$
  b. $-80 - (3 + 5) - 2^2$
  c. $-80 - 3 + (5 - 2)^2$

15. To evaluate each expression, what operation should be done first?
  a. $(65 - 3)^3$
  b. $65 - 3^3$
  c. $6(5) - (3)^3$ **d.** $65 \cdot 3^3$

16. a. How is the mean (or average) of a set of scores found?

  b. Find the average of 75, 81, 47, and 53.

NOTATION

17. Fill in the blanks.
  a. $3^1 =$ **b.** $x^1 =$
  c. $9 = 9$ **d.** $y = y$

18. Tell the name of each grouping symbol: ( ), [ ], | |, and —.

19. a. In the expression $(-5)^2$, what is the base?
  b. In the expression -5^2, what is the base?

20. Write each expression using symbols.
  a. Negative two squared.
  b. The opposite of two squared.

Complete the evaluation of each expression.

21. $-19 - 2[(1 + 2) \cdot 3] = -19 - 2[\cdot 3]$
$$= -19 - 2[]$$
$$= -19 - $$
$$= -37$$

22. $\dfrac{46 - 2^3}{-3(5) - 4} = \dfrac{46 - }{ - 4}$

$$= \dfrac{}{}$$

$$= -2$$

PRACTICE   Write each product using exponents.

23. $3 \cdot 3 \cdot 3 \cdot 3$ **24.** $m \cdot m \cdot m \cdot m \cdot m$
25. $10 \cdot 10 \cdot k \cdot k \cdot k$ **26.** $5(5)(5)(i)(i)$

27. $8 \cdot \pi \cdot r \cdot r \cdot r$ **28.** $4 \cdot \pi \cdot r \cdot r$
29. $6(x)(x)(y)(y)(y)$ **30.** $76 \cdot s \cdot s \cdot s \cdot s \cdot t$

Evaluate each expression.

31. $(-6)^2$ **32.** -6^2
33. -4^4 **34.** $(-4)^4$
35. $(-5)^3$ **36.** -5^3
37. $-(-6)^4$ **38.** $-(-7)^2$
39. $(-0.4)^2$ **40.** $(-0.5)^2$
41. $\left(-\dfrac{2}{5}\right)^3$ **42.** $\left(-\dfrac{1}{4}\right)^3$
43. $3 - 5 \cdot 4$ **44.** $-4 \cdot 6 + 5$
45. $3 \cdot 8^2$ **46.** $(3 \cdot 4)^2$
47. $8 \cdot 5^1 - 4 \div 2$ **48.** $9 \cdot 5^1 - 6 \div 3$
49. $100 - 8(10) + 60$ **50.** $50 - 2(5) - 7$
51. $-22 - (15 - 3)$ **52.** $-(33 - 8) - 10$
53. $-2(9) - 2(5)$ **54.** $-75 - 7^2$
55. $5^2 + 13^2$ **56.** $3^3 - 2^3$
57. $-4(6 + 5)$ **58.** $-3(5 - 4)$
59. $(9 - 3)(9 - 9)$ **60.** $-(-8 - 6)(6 - 6)$
61. $(-1 - 18)2$ **62.** $-5(128 - 5^3)^2$
63. $-2(-1)^2 + 3(-1) - 3$ **64.** $-4(-3)^2 + 3(-3) - 1$
65. $4^2 - (-2)^2$ **66.** $(-5 - 2)^2$
67. $12 + 2\left(-\dfrac{9}{3}\right) - (-2)$ **68.** $2 + 3\left(-\dfrac{25}{5}\right) - (-4)$

69. $\dfrac{-2 - 5}{-7 - (-7)}$ **70.** $\dfrac{-3 - (-1)}{-2 - (-2)}$

71. $200 - (-6 + 5)^3$

72. $19 - (-45 + 41)^3$

73. $|5 \cdot 2^2 \cdot 4| - 30$

74. $2 + |3 \cdot 2^2 \cdot 4|$

75. $[6(5) - 5(5)]4$

76. $175 - 2 \cdot 3^4$

77. $-6(130 - 4^3)$

78. $-5(150 - 3^3)$

79. $(17 - 5 \cdot 2)^3$

80. $(4 + 2 \cdot 3)^4$

81. $-5(-2)^3(3)^2$

82. $-3(-2)^5(2)^2$

83. $-2\left(\dfrac{15}{-5}\right) - \dfrac{6}{2} + 9$

84. $-6\left(\dfrac{25}{-5}\right) - \dfrac{36}{9} + 1$

85. $\dfrac{5 \cdot 50 - 160}{-9}$

86. $\dfrac{5(68 - 32)}{-9}$

87. $\dfrac{2(6 - 1)}{16 - (-4)^2}$

88. $\dfrac{6 - (-1)}{4 - 2^2}$

89. $5(10 + 2) - 1$

90. $14 + 3(7 - 5)$

91. $64 - 6[15 + (-3)3]$

92. $4 + 2[26 + 5(-3)]$

93. $(12 - 2)^3$

94. $(-2)^3\left(\dfrac{-6}{2}\right)(-1)$

95. $(-3)^3\left(\dfrac{-4}{2}\right)(-1)$

96. $\dfrac{-5 - 3^3}{2^3}$

97. $\dfrac{1}{2}\left(\dfrac{1}{8}\right) + \left(-\dfrac{1}{4}\right)^2$

98. $-\dfrac{1}{9}\left(\dfrac{1}{4}\right) + \left(-\dfrac{1}{6}\right)^2$

99. $-2|4 - 8|$

100. $-5|1 - 8|$

101. $|7 - 8(4 - 7)|$

102. $|9 - 5(1 - 8)|$

103. $3 + 2[-1 - 4(5)]$

104. $4 + 2[-7 - 3(9)]$

105. $-3[5^2 - (7 - 3)^2]$

106. $3 - [3^3 + (3 - 1)^3]$

107. $-(2 \cdot 3 - 4)^3$

108. $-(3 \cdot 5 - 2 \cdot 6)^2$

109. $\dfrac{(3 + 5)^2 + |-2|}{-2(5 - 8)}$

110. $\dfrac{|-25| - 8(-5)}{2^4 - 29}$

111. $\dfrac{2[-4 - 2(3 - 1)]}{3(-3)(-2)}$

112. $\dfrac{3[-9 + 2(7 - 3)]}{(5 - 8)(7 - 9)}$

113. $\dfrac{|6 - 4| + 2|-4|}{26 - 2^4}$

114. $\dfrac{4|9 - 7| + |-7|}{3^2 - 2^2}$

115. $\dfrac{(4^3 - 10) + (-4)}{5^2 - (-4)(-5)}$

116. $\dfrac{(6 - 5)^4 - (-21)}{(-9)(-3) - 4^2}$

117. $\dfrac{72 - (2 - 2 \cdot 1)}{10^2 - (90 + 2^2)}$

118. $\dfrac{13^2 - 5^2}{-3(5 - 9)}$

119. $-\left(\dfrac{40 - 1^3 - 2^4}{3(2 + 5) + 2}\right)$

120. $-\left(\dfrac{8^2 - 10}{2(3)(4) - 5(3)}\right)$

APPLICATIONS

121. LIGHT The illustration shows that the light energy that passes through the first unit of area, 1 yard away from the bulb, spreads out as it travels away from the source. How much area does that light energy cover 2 yards, 3 yards, and 4 yards from the bulb? Express each answer using exponents.

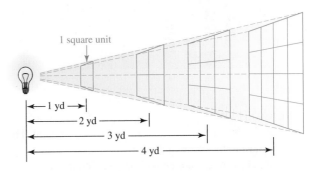

1 square unit

1 yd

2 yd

3 yd

4 yd

122. CHAIN LETTERS A store owner sent two friends a letter advertising her store's low prices. The ad closed with the following request: "Please send a copy of this letter to two of your friends."

a. Assume that all those receiving letters respond and that everyone in the chain receives just one letter. Complete the table.

b. How many letters will be circulated in the 10th level of the mailing?

Level	Numbers of letters circulated
1st	$2 = 2^1$
2nd	$ = 2^{}$
3rd	$ = 2^{}$
4th	$ = 2^{}$

123. AUTO INSURANCE See the following premium comparison. What is the average six-month insurance premium?

Allstate	$2,672	Mercury	$1,370
Auto Club	$1,680	State Farm	$2,737
Farmers	$2,485	20th Century	$1,692

Criteria: Six-month premium. Husband, 45, drives a 1995 Explorer, 12,000 annual miles. Wife, 43, drives a 1996 Dodge Caravan, 12,000 annual miles. Son, 17, is an occasional operator. All have clean driving records.

124. ENERGY USAGE   Find the average number of therms of natural gas used per month.

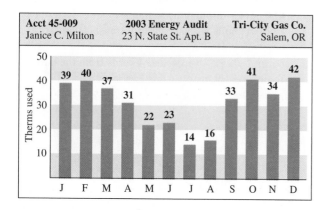

Acct 45-009   2003 Energy Audit   Tri-City Gas Co.
Janice C. Milton   23 N. State St. Apt. B   Salem, OR

125. CASH AWARDS   A contest is to be part of a promotional kickoff for a new children's cereal. The prizes to be awarded are shown.
  a. How much money will be awarded in the promotion?
  b. What is the average cash prize?

> ### Coloring Contest
> **Grand prize: Disney World vacation plus $2,500**
> Four 1st place prizes of $500
> Thirty-five 2nd place prizes of $150
> Eighty-five 3rd place prizes of $25

126. SURVEYS   Some students were asked to rate the food at their college cafeteria on a scale from 1 to 5. The responses are shown on the tally sheet. Find the average rating.

Poor		Fair		Excellent
1	2	3	4	5
	|||	|||	₸₸₸	₸₸₸ ||||

127. WRAPPING GIFTS
How much ribbon is needed to wrap the package if 15 inches of ribbon are needed to make the bow?

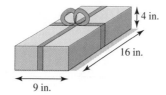

4 in.
16 in.
9 in.

128. SCRABBLE   Illustration (a) shows a portion of the game board before and Illustration (b) shows it after the word *QUARTZY* is played. Determine the score. (The number on each tile gives the point value of the letter.)

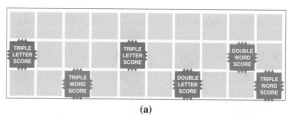

(a)

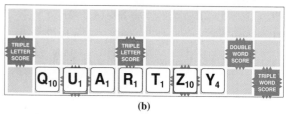

(b)

WRITING

129. Explain the difference between 2^3 and 3^2.

130. Explain why rules for the order of operations are necessary.

131. What does it mean when we say, do all additions and subtractions as they occur from left to right?

132. In what settings do you encounter or use the concept of arithmetic mean (average) in your everyday life?

REVIEW

133. Match each term with the proper operation.
  a. sum   **i.** division
  b. difference   **ii.** addition
  c. product   **iii.** subtraction
  d. quotient   **iv.** multiplication

134. a. What is the opposite of -8?
  b. What is the reciprocal of -8?

CHALLENGE PROBLEMS

135. Using each of the numbers 2, 3, and 4 only once, what is the greatest value that the following expression can have?

$$\left(\square^{\square}\right)^{\square}$$

136. Insert a pair of parentheses into the expression so that it has a value of 40.

$$4 \cdot 3^2 - 4 \cdot 2$$

1.8 Algebraic Expressions

- Algebraic Expressions
- Writing Algebraic Expressions
- Number and Value Problems
- Translating from Words to Symbols
- Analyzing Problems
- Evaluating Algebraic Expressions

Since problems in algebra are often presented in words, the ability to interpret what you read is important. In this section, we will introduce several strategies that will help you translate words into algebraic expressions.

◼ ALGEBRAIC EXPRESSIONS

Recall that variables and/or numbers can be combined with the operations of arithmetic to create **algebraic expressions.** Addition symbols separate these expressions into parts called *terms*. For example, the expression $x + 8$ has two terms.

$$\underset{\text{First term}}{x} \quad + \quad \underset{\text{Second term}}{8}$$

The Language of Algebra

Note the difference between *terms* and *factors*. In the expression $x + 8$, x and 8 are *terms*. In the expression $8x$, x and 8 are *factors*.

Since subtraction can be written as addition of the opposite, the expression $a^2 - 3a - 9$ has three terms.

$$a^2 - 3a - 9 = \underset{\text{First term}}{a^2} \quad + \quad \underset{\text{Second term}}{(-3a)} \quad + \quad \underset{\text{Third term}}{(-9)}$$

In general, a **term** is a product or quotient of numbers and/or variables. A single number or variable is also a term. Examples of terms include:

$$8, \quad y, \quad 6r, \quad -w^3, \quad 3.7x^5, \quad \frac{3}{n}, \quad -15ab^2$$

Notation

By the commutative property of multiplication, $r6 = 6r$ and $-15b^2a = -15ab^2$. However, we usually write the numerical factor first and the variable factors in alphabetical order.

The numerical factor of a term is called the **coefficient** of the term. For example, the term $6r$ has a coefficient of 6 because $6r = 6 \cdot r$. The coefficient of $-15ab^2$ is -15 because $-15ab^2 = -15 \cdot ab^2$. More examples are shown in the following table.

Term	Coefficient	
$8y^2$	8	
$-0.9pq$	-0.9	
$\frac{3}{4}b$	$\frac{3}{4}$	This term could be written $\frac{3b}{4}$.
$-\frac{x}{6}$	$-\frac{1}{6}$	This term could be written $-\frac{1}{6}x$.
x	1	$x = 1x$.
$-t$	-1	$-t = -1t$.
15	15	

The Language of Algebra

Terms such as x and yz^3 have *implied* coefficients of 1. *Implied* means suggested without being precisely expressed.

A term, such as 15, that consists of a single number is called a **constant term.**

EXAMPLE 1

Identify the coefficient of each term in the expression $7x^2 - x + 6$.

Solution   If we write $7x^2 - x + 6$ as $7x^2 + (-x) + 6$, we see that it has three terms: $7x^2$, $-x$, and 6.

The coefficient of $7x^2$ is 7.
The coefficient of $-x$ is -1.
The coefficient of 6 is 6.

Self Check 1   Identify the coefficient of each term in the expression $p^3 - 12p^2 + 3p - 4$.

■ TRANSLATING FROM WORDS TO SYMBOLS

In the following tables, we list words and phrases and show how they can be translated into algebraic expressions.

Addition	
the sum of a and 8	$a + 8$
4 plus c	$4 + c$
16 added to m	$m + 16$
4 more than t	$t + 4$
20 greater than F	$F + 20$
T increased by r	$T + r$
exceeds y by 35	$y + 35$

Subtraction	
the difference of 23 and P	$23 - P$
550 minus h	$550 - h$
18 less than w	$w - 18$
7 decreased by j	$7 - j$
M reduced by x	$M - x$
12 subtracted from L	$L - 12$
5 less f	$5 - f$

The Language of Algebra

When a translation involves the phrase *less than,* note how the terms are reversed.

18 less than w

$w - 18$

Multiplication	
the product of 4 and x	$4x$
20 times B	$20B$
twice r	$2r$
triple the profit P	$3P$
$\frac{3}{4}$ of m	$\frac{3}{4}m$

Division	
the quotient of R and 19	$\frac{R}{19}$
s divided by d	$\frac{s}{d}$
the ratio of c to d	$\frac{c}{d}$
k split into 4 equal parts	$\frac{k}{4}$

EXAMPLE 2

Write each phrase as an algebraic expression: **a.** one-half of the profit P,   **b.** 5 less than the capacity c,   and   **c.** the product of the weight w and 2,000, increased by 300.

Solution   **a. Key phrase:** *One-half of*   **Translation:** multiply by $\frac{1}{2}$

The translation is: $\frac{1}{2}P$.

b. Key phrase: *less than*   **Translation:** subtract

Sometimes, thinking in terms of specific numbers makes translating easier. Suppose the capacity was 100. Then 5 *less than* 100 would be $100 - 5$. If the capacity is c, then we need to make it 5 less. The translation is: $c - 5$.

c. We are given: The product of the weight w and 2,000, increased by 300.

> **Key word:** *product*   **Translation:** multiply
>
> **Key phrase:** *increased by*   **Translation:** add

The comma after 2,000 means w is first multiplied by 2,000 and then 300 is added to that product. The translation is: $2{,}000w + 300$.

Self Check 2   Write each phrase as an algebraic expression: **a.** 80 less than the total t,   **b.** $\frac{2}{3}$ of the time T,   **c.** the difference of twice a and 15.

■ WRITING ALGEBRAIC EXPRESSIONS

When solving problems, we usually begin by letting a variable stand for an unknown quantity.

EXAMPLE 3

Swimming. The pool shown is x feet wide. If it is to be sectioned into 8 equally wide swimming lanes, write an algebraic expression that represents the width of each lane.

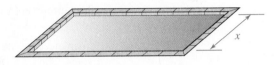

Solution   We let $x =$ the width of the swimming pool (in feet).

> **Key phrase:** *sectioned into 8 equally wide lanes*   **Translation:** divide

The width of each lane is $\dfrac{x}{8}$ feet.

Self Check 3   When a secretary rides the bus to work, it takes her m minutes. If she drives her own car, her travel time exceeds this by 15 minutes. How long does it take her to get to work by car?

EXAMPLE 4

Painting. A 10-inch-long paintbrush has two parts: a handle and bristles. Choose a variable to represent the length of one of the parts. Then write an expression to represent the length of the other part.

Solution   There are two approaches. First, refer to the following drawing on the left. If we let $h =$ the length of the handle (in inches), the length of the bristles is $10 - h$.

Now refer to the drawing on the right. If we let $b =$ the length of the bristles (in inches), the length of the handle is $10 - b$.

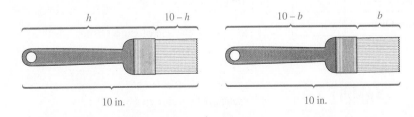

Self Check 4   Part of a $900 donation to a preschool was designated to go to the scholarship fund, the remainder to the building fund. Choose a variable to represent the amount donated to one of the funds. Write an expression for the amount donated to the other fund.

EXAMPLE 5

College enrollments.   In the second semester, enrollment in a retraining program at a college was 32 more than twice that of the first semester. Choose a variable to represent the enrollment in one of the semesters. Then write an expression for the enrollment in the other semester.

Solution   Since the second-semester enrollment is expressed in terms of the first-semester enrollment, we let x = the enrollment in the first semester.

Key phrase: *more than*   **Translation:** add
Key word: *twice*   **Translation:** multiply by 2

The enrollment for the second semester is $2x + 32$.

Self Check 5   In an election, the incumbent received 55 fewer votes than three times the challenger's votes. Choose a variable to represent the number of votes received by one candidate. Write an expression for the number of votes received by the other.

■ ANALYZING PROBLEMS

When solving problems, we aren't always given key words or key phrases to help establish what mathematical operation to use. Sometimes a careful reading of the problem is needed to determine any hidden operations.

EXAMPLE 6

Vacationing.   Disneyland, in California, was in operation 16 years before the opening of Disney World in Florida. Euro Disney, in France, was constructed 21 years after Disney World. Write an algebraic expression to represent the age (in years) of each Disney attraction.

Solution   The ages of Disneyland and Euro Disney are both related to the age of Disney World. Therefore, we will let x = the age of Disney World.

In carefully reading the problem, we see that Disneyland was built 16 years *before* Disney World. That makes its age 16 years more than that of Disney World.

Attraction	Age
Disneyland	$x + 16$
Disney World	x
Euro Disney	$x - 21$

$x + 16$ = the age of Disneyland

Euro Disney was built 21 years *after* Disney World. That makes its age 21 years less than that of Disney World.

$x - 21$ = the age of Euro Disney

EXAMPLE 7

How many months are in x years?

Solution   Since there are no key words, we must carefully analyze the problem. It is often helpful to
consider some specific cases. For example,
let's calculate the number of months in 1 year,
2 years, and 3 years. When we write the results
in a table, a pattern is apparent.

Number of years	Number of months
1	12
2	24
3	36
x	$12x$

We multiply the number of years
by 12 to find the number of months.

The number of months in x years is $12 \cdot x$ or $12x$.

Self Check 7   How many days is h hours?

■ **NUMBER AND VALUE PROBLEMS**

In some problems, we must distinguish between *the number of* and *the value of* the
unknown quantity. For example, to find the value of 3 quarters, we multiply the number of
quarters by the value (in cents) of one quarter. Therefore, the value of 3 quarters is
$3 \cdot 25$ cents $= 75$ cents.

   The same distinction must be made if the number is unknown. For example, the value
of n nickels is not n cents. The value of n nickels is $n \cdot 5$ cents $= 5n$ cents. For problems of
this type, we will use the relationship

   Number · value = total value

EXAMPLE 8   Find the total value of   **a.** five dimes,   **b.** q quarters,   and   **c.** $x + 1$ half-dollars.

Solution   To find the total value (in cents) of each collection of coins, we multiply the number of
coins by the value (in cents) of one coin, as shown in the table.

Type of coin	Number	· Value	= Total value
Dime	5	10	50
Quarter	q	25	$25q$
Half-dollar	$x + 1$	50	$50(x + 1)$

←— $q \cdot 25$ is written $25q$.

Self Check 8   Find the value of   **a.** six fifty-dollar savings bonds,   **b.** t one-hundred-dollar savings
bonds,   **c.** $x - 4$ one-thousand-dollar savings bonds.

■ **EVALUATING ALGEBRAIC EXPRESSIONS**

To evaluate an algebraic expression, we substitute given numbers for each variable and do
the necessary calculations.

EXAMPLE 9   Evaluate each expression if $x = 3$ and $y = -4$:   **a.** $y^3 + y^2$,   **b.** $-y - x$,   **c.** $|5xy - 7|$,
and   **d.** $\dfrac{y - 0}{x - (-1)}$.

Solution   **a.** $y^3 + y^2 = (-4)^3 + (-4)^2$ Substitute -4 for each y. We must write -4 within parentheses so that it is the base of each exponential expression.

$= -64 + 16$ Evaluate each exponential expression.

$= -48$

Caution

When replacing a variable with its numerical value, we must often write the replacement number within parentheses to convey the proper meaning.

b. $-y - x = -(-4) - 3$ Substitute 3 for x and -4 for y.

$= 4 - 3$ Simplify: $-(-4) = 4$.

$= 1$

c. $|5xy - 7| = |5(3)(-4) - 7|$ Substitute 3 for x and -4 for y.

$= |-60 - 7|$ Do the multiplication within the absolute value symbols, working left to right: $5(3)(-4) = 15(-4) = -60$.

$= |-67|$ Do the subtraction: $-60 - 7 = -60 + (-7) = -67$.

$= 67$ Find the absolute value of -67.

d. $\dfrac{y - 0}{x - (-1)} = \dfrac{-4 - 0}{3 - (-1)}$ Substitute 3 for x and -4 for y.

$= \dfrac{-4}{4}$ In the denominator, do the subtraction: $3 - (-1) = 3 + 1 = 4$.

$= -1$

Self Check 9   Evaluate each expression if $a = -2$ and $b = 5$:   **a.** $|a^3 + b^2|$,   **b.** $-a + 2ab$,   and   **c.** $\dfrac{a + 2}{b - 3}$.

EXAMPLE 10

Diving.   Fins are used by divers to provide a larger area to push against the water. The fin shown on the right is in the shape of a trapezoid. The expression $\frac{1}{2}h(b + d)$ gives the area of a trapezoid, where h is the height and b and d are the lengths of the lower and upper bases, respectively. Find the area of the fin.

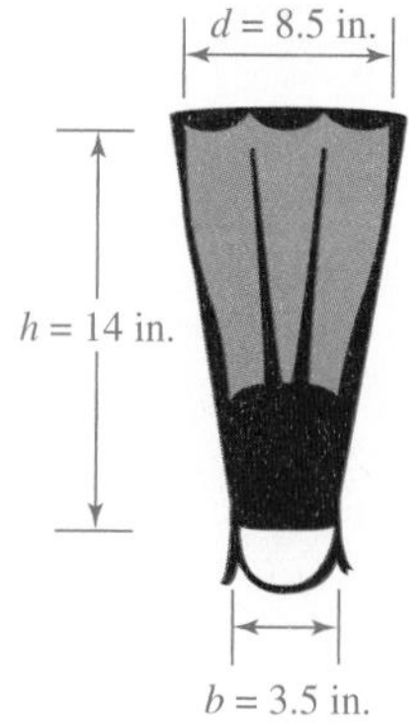

Solution $\dfrac{1}{2}h(b + d) = \dfrac{1}{2}(14)(3.5 + 8.5)$ Substitute 14 for h, 3.5 for b, and 8.5 for d.

$= \dfrac{1}{2}(14)(12)$ Do the addition within the parentheses.

$= 84$ $\frac{1}{2}(14) = 7$ and $7(12) = 84$.

$d = 8.5$ in.

$h = 14$ in.

$b = 3.5$ in.

The area of the fin is 84 square inches.

EXAMPLE 11

Rocketry.   If a toy rocket is shot into the air with an initial velocity of 80 feet per second, its height (in feet) after t seconds in flight is given by

$80t - 16t^2$

How many seconds after the launch will it hit the ground?

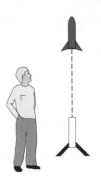

Solution   We can substitute positive values for t, the time in flight, until we find the one that gives a height of 0. At that time, the rocket will be on the ground. We begin by finding the height after the rocket has been in flight for 1 second ($t = 1$).

$$80t - 16t^2 = 80(1) - 16(1)^2 \quad \text{Substitute 1 for } t.$$
$$= 64$$

As we evaluate $80t - 16t^2$ for several more values of t, we record each result in a table.

t	$80t - 16t^2$
1	64
2	96
3	96
4	64
5	0

Evaluate for $t = 2$: $80t - 16t^2 = 80(2) - 16(2)^2 = 96$

Evaluate for $t = 3$: $80t - 16t^2 = 80(3) - 16(3)^2 = 96$

Evaluate for $t = 4$: $80t - 16t^2 = 80(4) - 16(4)^2 = 64$

Evaluate for $t = 5$: $80t - 16t^2 = 80(5) - 16(5)^2 = 0$

The height of the rocket is 0 when $t = 5$. The rocket will hit the ground 5 seconds after being launched.

Self Check 11   In Example 11, suppose the height of the rocket is given by $112t - 16t^2$. In how many seconds after launch would the rocket hit the ground?

The two columns of the table in Example 11 can be headed with the terms **input** and **output**. The values of t are the inputs into the expression $80t - 16t^2$, and the resulting values are the outputs.

Input	Output
1	64
2	96
3	96
4	64
5	0

Answers to Self Checks   **1.** $1, -12, 3, -4$ **2. a.** $t - 80$,   **b.** $\frac{2}{3}T$,   **c.** $2a - 15$ **3.** $(m + 15)$ minutes
4. $s =$ amount donated to scholarship fund in dollars; $900 - s =$ amount donated to building fund
5. $x =$ the number of votes received by the challenger; $3x - 55 =$ the number of votes received
by the incumbent   **7.** $\frac{h}{24}$ **8. a.** \$300,   **b.** \$100t,   **c.** \$1,000(x - 4)
9. a. 17,   **b.** -18,   **c.** 0   **11.** 7 sec

1.8   STUDY SET

VOCABULARY   Fill in the blanks.

1. Variables and/or numbers can be combined with the operations of arithmetic to create algebraic _____.

2. Addition symbols separate algebraic expressions into parts called _____.

3. A term, such as 27, that consists of a single number is called a _____ term.

4. The _____ of $10x$ is 10.

5. To _____ an algebraic expression, we substitute the values for the variables and simplify.

6. Consider the expression $2a + 8$. When we replace a with 4, we say we are _____ a value for the variable.

7. $2x + 5$ is an example of an algebraic _____, whereas $2x + 5 = 7$ is an example of an _____.

8. When we evaluate an expression for several values of x, we can keep track of the results in an input/output _____.

CONCEPTS

9. Consider the expression $11x^2 - 6x - 9$.
  a. How many terms does this expression have?
  b. What is the coefficient of the first term?
  c. What is the coefficient of the second term?
  d. What is the constant term?

10. Complete the table.

Term	Coefficient
$6m$	
$-75t$	
w	
$\frac{1}{2}bh$	
$\frac{x}{5}$	

11. In each expression, tell whether c is used as a *factor* or as a *term*.
  a. $c + 32$ **b.** $5c$
  c. $-18bc$ **d.** $a + b + c$
  e. $24c + 6$ **f.** $c - 9$

12. a. Write a term that has an implied coefficient of 1.

  b. Write a term that has an implied coefficient of -1.

13. a. Complete the table on the left to determine how many days are in w weeks.
  b. Complete the table on the right.

Number of weeks	Number of days		Number of seconds	Number of minutes
1			60	
2			120	
3			180	
w			s	

14. a. If the knife is 12 inches long, how long is the blade?

  b. A student inherited \$5,000 and deposits x dollars in American Savings. Write an expression to show how much she has left to deposit in a City Mutual account.

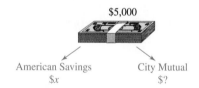

  c. Suppose solution 1 is poured into solution 2. Write an expression to show how many ounces of the mixture there will be.

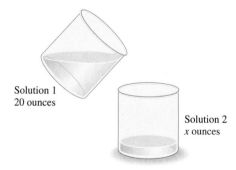

15. a. The weight of the van in the illustration is 500 pounds less than twice the weight of the car. Express the weight of the van and the car using the variable x.

b. If the actual weight of the car is 2,000 pounds, what is the weight of the van?

16. a. If we let b represent the length of the beam, write an algebraic expression for the length of the pipe.

b. If we let p represent the length of the pipe, write an algebraic expression for the length of the beam.

15 ft

17. Complete the table.

Type of coin	Number ·	Value (in cents) =	Total value (in cents)
Nickel	6		
Dime	d		
Half-dollar	$x + 5$		

18. If $x = -9$, find the value of $-x$.

NOTATION   Complete each solution.

19. Evaluate the expression $9a - a^2$ for $a = 5$.

$$9a - a^2 = 9(\quad) - (5)^2$$
$$= 9(5) - \quad$$
$$= \quad - 25$$
$$= 20$$

20. Evaluate $-x + 6y$ for $x = -2$ and $y = 4$.

$$-x + 6y = -(\quad) + 6(\quad)$$
$$= \quad + 24$$
$$= 26$$

21. Write each term in standard form.
  a. $y8$ **b.** $c2d$
  c. $15xs$ **d.** $b^2(-9)a^3$

Fill in the blanks.

22. a. $\dfrac{2}{3}m = \dfrac{\quad}{3}$ **b.** $\dfrac{t}{3} = \quad t$

  c. $-\dfrac{w}{2} = \quad w$ **d.** $-\dfrac{5}{3}s = -\dfrac{\quad}{3}$

  e. $d = \quad d$ **f.** $-h = \quad h$

PRACTICE   Translate each phrase to an algebraic expression. If no variable is given, use x as the variable.

23. The sum of the length l and 15

24. The difference of a number and 10

25. The product of a number and 50

26. Three-fourths of the population p

27. The ratio of the amount won w and lost l

28. The tax t added to c

29. P increased by p

30. 21 less than the total height h

31. The square of k minus 2,005

32. s subtracted from S

33. J reduced by 500

34. Twice the attendance a

35. 1,000 split n equal ways

36. Exceeds the cost c by 25,000

37. 90 more than the current price p

38. 64 divided by the cube of y

39. The total of 35, h, and 300

40. x decreased by 17

41. 680 fewer than the entire population p

42. Triple the number of expected participants

43. The product of d and 4, decreased by 15

44. Forty-five more than the quotient of y and 6

45. Twice the sum of 200 and t

46. The square of the quantity 14 less than x

47. The absolute value of the difference of a and 2

48. The absolute value of a, decreased by 2

49. How many minutes are there in   **a.** 5 hours   and **b.** h hours?

50. A woman watches television x hours a day. Express the number of hours she watches TV   **a.** in a week and   **b.** in a year.

51. a. How many feet are in y yards?

  b. How many yards are in f feet?

52. A sales clerk earns $\$x$ an hour. How much does he earn in   **a.** an 8-hour day   and   **b.** a 40-hour week?

53. If a car rental agency charges 29¢ a mile, express the rental fee if a car is driven x miles.

54. A model's skirt is x inches long. The designer then lets the hem down 2 inches. How can we express the length (in inches) of the altered skirt?

55. A soft drink manufacturer produced c cans of cola during the morning shift. Write an expression for how many six-packs of cola can be assembled from the morning shift's production.

56. The tag on a new pair of 36-inch-long jeans warns that after washing, they will shrink x inches in length. Express the length (in inches) of the jeans after they are washed.

57. A caravan of b cars, each carrying 5 people, traveled to the state capital for a political rally. Express how many people were in the caravan.

58. A caterer always prepares food for 10 more people than the order specifies. If p people are to attend a reception, write an expression for the number of people she should prepare for.

59. Tickets to a circus cost $\$5$ each. Express how much tickets will cost for a family of x people if they also pay for two of their neighbors.

60. If each egg is worth e¢, express the value (in cents) of a dozen eggs.

Complete each table.

61.

x	$x^3 - 1$
0	
-1	
-3	

62.

g	$g^2 - 7g + 1$
0	
7	
-10	

63.

s	$\dfrac{5s + 36}{s}$
1	
6	
-12	

64.

a	$2{,}500a + a^3$
2	
4	
-5	

65.

Input x	Output $2x - \dfrac{x}{2}$
100	
-300	

66.

Input x	Output $\dfrac{x}{3} + \dfrac{x}{4}$
12	
-36	

67.

x	$(x + 1)(x + 5)$
-1	
-5	
-6	

68.

x	$\dfrac{1}{x + 8}$
-7	
-9	
-8	

Evaluate each expression, given that $x = 3$, $y = -2$, and $z = -4$.

69. $3y^2 - 6y - 4$

70. $-z^2 - z - 12$

71. $(3 + x)y$

72. $(4 + z)y$

73. $(x + y)^2 - |z + y|$

74. $[(z - 1)(z + 1)]^2$

75. $(4x)^2 + 3y^2$

76. $4x^2 + (3y)^2$

77. $-\dfrac{2x + y^3}{y + 2z}$

78. $-\dfrac{2z^2 - y}{2x - y^2}$

Evaluate each expression for the given values of the variables.

79. $b^2 - 4ac$ for $a = -1$, $b = 5$, and $c = -2$

80. $(x - a)^2 + (y - b)^2$ for $x = -2$, $y = 1$, $a = 5$, and $b = -3$

81. $a^2 + 2ab + b^2$ for $a = -5$ and $b = -1$

82. $\dfrac{x - a}{y - b}$ for $x = -2$, $y = 1$, $a = 5$, and $b = 2$

83. $\dfrac{n}{2}[2a + (n - 1)d]$ for $n = 10$, $a = -4$, and $d = 6$

84. $\dfrac{a(1 - r^n)}{1 - r}$ for $a = -5$, $r = 2$, and $n = 3$

85. $\dfrac{a^2 + b^2}{2}$ for $a = 0$ and $b = -10$

86. $(y^3 - 52y^2)^2$ for $y = 0$

APPLICATIONS

87. ROCKETRY   The expression $64t - 16t^2$ gives the height of a toy rocket (in feet) t seconds after being launched. Find the height of the rocket for each of the times shown.

t	h
1	
2	
3	
4	

88. AMUSEMENT PARK RIDES The distance in feet that an object will fall in t seconds is given by the expression $16t^2$. Find the distance that riders on "Drop Zone" will fall during the times listed in the table.

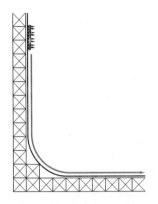

Time (seconds)	Distance (feet)
1	
2	
3	
4	

89. ANTIFREEZE The expression $\frac{5(F - 32)}{9}$ converts a temperature in degrees Fahrenheit (given as F) to degrees Celsius. Convert the temperatures listed on the container of antifreeze shown to degrees Celsius. Round to the nearest degree.

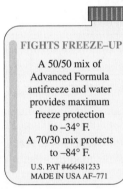

FIGHTS FREEZE–UP

A 50/50 mix of Advanced Formula antifreeze and water provides maximum freeze protection to –34° F.
A 70/30 mix protects to –84° F.

U.S. PAT #466481233
MADE IN USA AF–771

90. MARS The expression $\frac{9C + 160}{5}$ converts a temperature in degrees Celsius (represented by C) to a temperature in degrees Fahrenheit. On Mars, daily temperatures average $-33°$ C. Convert this to degrees Fahrenheit. Round to the nearest degree.

91. TOOLS The utility knife blade shown is in the shape of a trapezoid. Find the area of the front face of the blade.

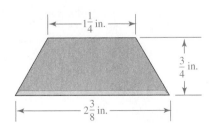

92. GROWING SOD To determine the number of square feet of sod remaining in a field after filling an order, the manager of a sod farm uses the expression $20{,}000 - 3s$ (where s is the number of strips the customer has ordered). To sod a soccer field, a city orders 7,000 strips of sod. Evaluate the expression for this value of s and explain the result.

Strips of sod, cut and ready to be loaded on a truck for delivery

WRITING

93. What is an algebraic expression? Give some examples.

94. What is a variable? How are variables used in this section?

95. In this section, we substituted a number for a variable. List some other uses of the word *substitute* that you encounter in everyday life.

96. Explain why d dimes are not worth $d¢$.

REVIEW

97. Find the LCD for $\frac{5}{12}$ and $\frac{1}{15}$.

98. Remove the common factors of the numerator and denominator to simplify: $\frac{3 \cdot 5 \cdot 5}{3 \cdot 5 \cdot 5 \cdot 11}$.

99. Evaluate: $(-2 \cdot 3)^3 - 10 + 1$.

100. Find the result when $\frac{7}{8}$ is multiplied by its reciprocal.

CHALLENGE PROBLEMS

101. Evaluate:
$(8 - 1)(8 - 2)(8 - 3) \cdot \cdot \cdot \cdot \cdot (8 - 49)(8 - 50)$

102. If the values of x and y were doubled, what would happen to the value of $17xy$?

ACCENT ON TEAMWORK

WRITING FRACTIONS AS DECIMALS

Overview: This is a good activity to try at the beginning of the course. You can become acquainted with other students in your class while you review the process for finding decimal equivalents of fractions.

Instructions: Form groups of 6 students. Select one person from your group to record the group's responses on the questionnaire. Express the results in fraction form and in decimal form.

What fraction (decimal) of the students in your group . . .	Fraction	Decimal
have the letter *a* in their first names?		
have a birthday in January or February?		
work full-time or part-time?		
have ever been on television?		
live more than 10 miles from the campus?		
say that summer is their favorite season of the year?		

WRITING MATHEMATICAL SOLUTIONS

Overview: A major objective of this course is to learn how to put your thinking on paper in a form that can be read and understood by others. This activity will help you develop that ability.

Instructions: Form groups of 2 or 3 students. Have someone read the following problem out loud. Discuss it in your group. Then work together to present a written solution. Exchange your solution with another group and see whether you understand their explanation.

When three professors attending a convention in Las Vegas registered at the hotel, they were told that the room rate was $120. Each professor paid his $40 share. Later the desk clerk realized that the cost of the room should have been $115. To fix the mistake, she sent a bellhop to the room to refund the $5 overcharge. Realizing that $5 could not be evenly divided among the three professors and not wanting to start a quarrel, the bellhop refunded only $3 and kept the other $2. Since each professor received a $1 refund, each paid $39 for the room, and the bellhop kept $2. This gives $39 + $39 + $39 + $2, or $119. What happened to the other $1?

KEY CONCEPT: VARIABLES

One of the major objectives of this course is for you to become comfortable working with **variables.** In Chapter 1, we have used the concept of variables in several ways.

STATING MATHEMATICAL PROPERTIES

Variables have been used to state properties of mathematics. Match each statement in words with its proper description expressed with a variable (or variables). Assume that a, b, and c are real numbers and that there are no divisions by zero.

1. A nonzero number divided by itself is 1.

2. When we add opposites, the result is 0.

3. Two numbers can be multiplied in either order to get the same result.

4. It doesn't matter how we group numbers in multiplication.

5. When we multiply a number and its reciprocal, the result is 1.

6. When we multiply a number and 0, the result is 0.

7. It doesn't matter how we group numbers in addition.

8. Any number divided by 1 is the number itself.

9. Two numbers can be added in either order to get the same result.

10. When we add a number and 0, the number remains the same.

a. $(ab)c = a(bc)$

b. $a\left(\dfrac{1}{a}\right) = 1$

c. $(a + b) + c = a + (b + c)$

d. $a + b = b + a$

e. $a \cdot 0 = 0$

f. $\dfrac{a}{a} = 1$

g. $a + 0 = a$

h. $ab = ba$

i. $\dfrac{a}{1} = a$

j. $a + (-a) = 0$

STATING RELATIONSHIPS BETWEEN QUANTITIES

Variables are letters that stand for numbers. We have used **formulas** to express known relationships between two or more variables.

11. Translate the word model to an equation (formula) that mathematically describes the situation: The total cost is the sum of the purchase price of the item and the sales tax.

12. Use the data in the table to state the relationship between the quantities using a formula.

Picnic tables	Benches needed
2	4
3	6
4	8

WRITING ALGEBRAIC EXPRESSIONS

We have combined variables and numbers with the operations of arithmetic to create **algebraic expressions.**

13. One year, a cruise company did x million dollars' worth of business. After a celebrity was signed as a spokeswoman for the company, its business increased by \$4 million the next year. Write an expression that represents the amount of business the cruise company had in the year the celebrity was the spokeswoman.

14. Evaluate the expression for the given values of the variable, and enter the results in the table.

x	$3x^2 - 2x + 1$
0	
4	
6	

CHAPTER REVIEW

SECTION 1.1	Introducing the Language of Algebra

CONCEPTS

Tables, bar graphs, and *line graphs* are used to describe numerical relationships.

REVIEW EXERCISES

The line graph shows the number of cars parked in a parking structure from 6 P.M. to 12 midnight on a Saturday.

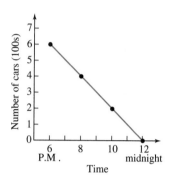

1. What units are used to scale the horizontal and vertical axes?

2. How many cars were in the parking structure at 11 P.M.?

3. At what time did the parking structure have 500 cars in it?

The result of an addition is called the *sum;* of a subtraction, the *difference;* of a multiplication, the *product;* and of a division, the *quotient.*

Express each statement in words.

4. $15 - 3 = 12$

5. $15 + 3 = 18$

6. $15 \div 3 = 5$

7. $15 \cdot 3 = 45$

8. Write the multiplication 4×9 with a raised dot and then with parentheses.

9. Write the division $9 \div 3$ using a fraction bar.

Variables are letters used to stand for numbers.

An *equation* is a mathematical sentence that contains an = symbol. Variables and/or numbers can be combined with the operations of arithmetic to create *algebraic expressions.*

Equations that express a known relationship between two or more variables are called *formulas.*

Write each multiplication without a multiplication symbol.

10. $8 \cdot b$

11. $P \cdot r \cdot t$

Classify each item as either an expression or an equation.

12. $5 = 2x + 3$

13. $2x + 3$

14. Use the formula $n = b + 5$ to complete the table.

Number of brackets (b)	Number of nails (n)
5	
10	
20	

| SECTION 1.2 | **Fractions** |

Whole numbers can be written as the product of two or more whole-number *factors*.

A *prime number* is a whole number greater than 1 that has only 1 and itself as factors.

Division by 0 is *undefined*.

15. a. Write 24 as the product of two factors.
   b. Write 24 as the product of three factors.
   c. List the factors of 24.

Give the prime factorization of each number, if possible.

16. 54   **17.** 147   **18.** 385   **19.** 41

Perform each division, if possible.

20. $\dfrac{12}{12}$ **21.** $\dfrac{0}{10}$

Simplify each fraction.

22. $\dfrac{20}{35}$ **23.** $\dfrac{24}{18}$

Build each number to an equivalent fraction with the indicated denominator.

24. $\dfrac{5}{8}$, denominator 64   **25.** 12, denominator 3

To multiply two fractions, multiply their numerators and multiply their denominators.

To divide two fractions, multiply the first fraction by the reciprocal of the second fraction.

To add (or subtract) fractions with the same denominator, add (or subtract) the numerators and keep the common denominator.

The *least common denominator (LCD)* for a set of fractions is the smallest number each denominator will divide exactly.

Perform each operation.

26. $\dfrac{1}{8} \cdot \dfrac{7}{8}$ **27.** $\dfrac{16}{35} \cdot \dfrac{25}{48}$ **28.** $\dfrac{1}{3} \div \dfrac{15}{16}$ **29.** $16\dfrac{1}{4} \div 5$

30. $\dfrac{17}{25} - \dfrac{7}{25}$ **31.** $\dfrac{8}{11} - \dfrac{1}{2}$ **32.** $\dfrac{1}{4} + \dfrac{2}{3}$ **33.** $4\dfrac{1}{9} - 3\dfrac{5}{6}$

34. MACHINE SHOPS   How much must be milled off the $\frac{17}{24}$-inch-thick steel rod so that the collar will slip over it?

Steel rod

SECTION 1.3   The Real Numbers

The *natural numbers:*
$\{1, 2, 3, 4, 5, 6, \ldots\}$
The *whole numbers:*
$\{0, 1, 2, 3, 4, 5, 6, \ldots\}$
The *integers:*
$\{\ldots, -2, -1, 0, 1, 2, \ldots\}$

Two *inequality symbols* are
$>$ "is greater than"
$<$ "is less than"

A *rational number* is any number that can be expressed as a fraction with an integer numerator and a nonzero integer denominator.

To write a fraction as a decimal, divide the numerator by the denominator.

An *irrational number* is a nonterminating, nonrepeating decimal. Irrational numbers cannot be written as the ratio of two integers.

A *real number* is any number that is either a rational or an irrational number.

The natural numbers are a *subset* of the whole numbers. The whole numbers are a subset of the integers. The integers are a subset of the rational numbers. The rational numbers are a subset of the real numbers.

35. Which number is a whole number but not a natural number?

Represent each of these situations with a signed number.

36. A budget deficit of $65 billion

37. 206 feet below sea level

Use one of the symbols $>$ or $<$ to make each statement true.

38. 0   5

39. -12 -13

Show that each of the following numbers is a rational number by expressing it as a fraction.

40. 0.7

41. $4\dfrac{2}{3}$

Write each fraction as a decimal. Use an overbar if the result is a repeating decimal.

42. $\dfrac{1}{250}$

43. $\dfrac{17}{22}$

44. Graph each number on a number line: $\left\{\pi, 0.333\ldots, 3.75, \sqrt{2}, -\dfrac{17}{4}, \dfrac{7}{8}, -2\right\}$.

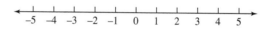

Decide whether each statement is true or false.

45. All integers are whole numbers.

46. π is a rational number.

47. The set of real numbers corresponds to all points on the number line.

48. A real number is either rational or irrational.

49. Tell which numbers in the given set are natural numbers, whole numbers, integers, rational numbers, irrational numbers, and real numbers.

$$\left\{-\tfrac{4}{5}, 99.99, 0, \sqrt{2}, -12, 4\tfrac{1}{2}, 0.666\ldots, 8\right\}$$

The *absolute value* of a number is the distance on the number line between the number and 0.

Insert one of the symbols $>$, $<$, or $=$ in the blank to make each statement true.

50. $|-6|$ ___ $|5|$

51. -9 ___ $|-10|$

| SECTION 1.4 | **Adding Real Numbers** |

To add two real numbers with *like signs*, add their absolute values and attach their common sign to the sum.

To add two real numbers with *unlike signs*, subtract their absolute values, the smaller from the larger. To that result, attach the sign of the number with the larger absolute value.

The *commutative* and *associative* properties of addition:

$$a + b = b + a$$

$$(a + b) + c$$
$$= a + (b + c)$$

Add the numbers.

52. $-45 + (-37)$

53. $25 + (-13)$

54. $0 + (-7)$

55. $-7 + 7$

56. $12 + (-8) + (-15)$

57. $-9.9 + (-2.4)$

58. $\dfrac{5}{16} + \left(-\dfrac{1}{2}\right)$

59. $35 + (-13) + (-17) + 6$

Tell what property of addition guarantees that the quantities are equal.

60. $-2 + 5 = 5 + (-2)$

61. $(-2 + 5) + 1 = -2 + (5 + 1)$

62. $80 + (-80) = 0$

63. $-5.75 + 0 = -5.75$

64. ATOMS   An atom is composed of protons, neutrons, and electrons. A proton has a positive charge (represented by $+1$), a neutron has no charge, and an electron has a negative charge (-1). A simple model of an atom is shown here. What is its net charge?

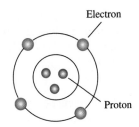

Electron

Proton

| **SECTION 1.5** | **Subtracting Real Numbers** |

Two numbers represented by points on a number line that are the same distance away from 0, but on opposite sides of it, are called *opposites*.

To *subtract* real numbers, add the opposite:

$$a - b = a + (-b)$$

Write the expression in simpler form.

65. The opposite of 10

66. The opposite of -3

67. $-\left(-\dfrac{9}{16}\right)$

68. $-|-4|$

Perform the operations.

69. $45 - 64$

70. $-17 - 32$

71. $-27 - (-12)$

72. $3.6 - (-2.1)$

73. $0 - 10$

74. $-33 + 7 - 5 - (-2)$

75. GEOGRAPHY   The tallest peak on Earth is Mount Everest, at 29,028 feet, and the greatest ocean depth is the Mariana Trench, at $-36,205$ feet. Find the difference in the two elevations.

| **SECTION 1.6** | **Multiplying and Dividing Real Numbers** |

To multiply two real numbers, multiply their absolute values.

1. The product of two real numbers with *like signs* is positive.

2. The product of two real numbers with *unlike signs* is negative.

The *commutative* and *associative* properties of multiplication:

$$ab = ba$$

$$(ab)c = a(bc)$$

Multiply.

76. $-8 \cdot 7$

77. $(-9)(-6)$

78. $2(-3)(-2)$

79. $(-4)(-1)(-3)(-3)$

80. $-1.2(-5.3)$

81. $0.002(-1,000)$

82. $-\dfrac{2}{3}\left(\dfrac{1}{5}\right)$

83. $-6(-3)(0)(-1)$

Tell what property of multiplication guarantees that the quantities are equal.

84. $(2 \cdot 3)5 = 2(3 \cdot 5)$

85. $(-5)(-6) = (-6)(-5)$

86. $-6 \cdot 1 = -6$

87. $\dfrac{1}{2}(2) = 1$

88. What is the additive inverse (opposite) of -3?

89. What is the multiplicative inverse (reciprocal) of -3?

To divide two real numbers, divide their absolute values.

1. The quotient of two real numbers with *like signs* is positive.
2. The quotient of two real numbers with *unlike signs* is negative.

Division *of zero* by a nonzero number is 0. Division *by zero* is undefined.

Perform each division.

90. $\dfrac{44}{-44}$

91. $\dfrac{-100}{25}$

92. $\dfrac{-81}{-27}$

93. $-\dfrac{3}{5} \div \dfrac{1}{2}$

94. $\dfrac{-60}{0}$

95. $\dfrac{-4.5}{1}$

96. Find the high and low reading that is displayed on the screen of the emissions-testing device.

97. The picture on the screen can be magnified by switching a setting on the monitor. What would be the new high and low if every value were to be doubled?

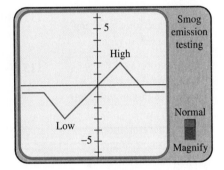

| SECTION 1.7 | **Exponents and Order of Operations** |

An *exponent* is used to represent repeated multiplication. In the *exponential expression* a^n, a is the *base,* and n is the *exponent.*

Write each expression using exponents.

98. $8 \cdot 8 \cdot 8 \cdot 8 \cdot 8$

99. $a(a)(a)(a)$

100. $9 \cdot \pi \cdot r \cdot r$

101. $x \cdot x \cdot x \cdot y \cdot y \cdot y \cdot y$

Order of operations:

1. Do all calculations within grouping symbols, working from the innermost pair to the outermost pair, in the following order:

2. Evaluate all exponential expressions.

3. Do all multiplications and divisions, working from left to right.

4. Do all additions and subtractions, working from left to right.

If the expression does not contain grouping symbols, begin with Step 2. In a fraction, simplify the numerator and denominator separately. Then simplify the fraction, if possible.

The *arithmetic mean* (or *average*) is a value around which number values are grouped.

$$\text{Mean} = \frac{\text{sum of values}}{\text{number of values}}$$

Evaluate each expression.

102. 9^2

103. $\left(-\dfrac{2}{3}\right)^3$

104. 2^5

105. 50^1

106. How many operations does the expression $5 \cdot 4 - 3^2 + 1$ contain, and in what order should they be performed?

Evaluate each expression.

107. $2 + 5 \cdot 3$

108. $24 - 3(6)(4)$

109. $-(6 - 3)^2$

110. $4^3 + 2(-6 - 2 \cdot 2)$

111. $10 - 5[-3 - 2(5 - 7^2)] - 5$

112. $\dfrac{-4(4 + 2) - 4}{|-18 - 4(5)|}$

113. $(-3)^3\left(\dfrac{-8}{2}\right) + 5$

114. $-9^2 + (-9)^2$

115. WALK-A-THONS   Use the data in the table to find the average (mean) donation to a charity walk-a-thon.

Donation	Number received
$5	20
$10	65
$20	25
$50	5
$100	10

SECTION 1.8   **Algebraic Expressions**

Addition signs separate algebraic expressions into terms.

How many terms are in each expression?

116. $3x^2 + 2x - 5$

117. $-12xyz$

In a term, the numerical factor is called the *coefficient.*

Identify the coefficient of each term.

118. $2x - 5$

119. $16x^2 - 5x + 25$

120. $\dfrac{x}{2} + y$

121. $9.6t^2 - t$

In order to describe numerical relationships, we need to translate the words of a problem into mathematical symbols.

Write each phrase as an algebraic expression.

122. 25 more than the height h

123. 15 less than the cutoff score s

124. $\frac{1}{2}$ of the time t

125. If we let n represent the length of the nail, write an algebraic expression for the length of the bolt (in inches).

126. If we let b represent the length of the bolt, write an algebraic expression for the length of the nail (in inches).

4 in.

Sometimes we must rely on common sense and insight to find *hidden operations.*

127. How many years are in d decades?

128. Five years after a house was constructed, a patio was added. How old, in years, is the patio if the house is x years old?

Number · value
    = total value

129. Complete the table.

Type of coin	Number	Value (¢)	Total value (¢)
Nickel	6	5	
Dime	d	10	

When we replace the variable, or variables, in an algebraic expression with specific numbers and then apply the rules for the order of operations, we are *evaluating* the algebraic expression.

130. Complete the table.

x	$20x - x^3$
0	
1	
-4	

Evaluate each algebraic expression for the given value(s) of the variable(s).

131. $b^2 - 4ac$ for $b = -10$, $a = 3$, and $c = 5$

132. $\dfrac{x + y}{-x - z}$ for $x = 19$, $y = 17$, and $z = -18$

CHAPTER 1 TEST

The line graph shows the cost to hire a security guard. Use the graph to answer Problems 1 and 2.

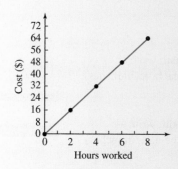

1. What will it cost to hire a security guard for 3 hours?

2. If a school was billed $40 for hiring a security guard for a dance, for how long did the guard work?

3. Use the formula $f = \dfrac{a}{5}$ to complete the table.

Area in square miles (a)	Number of fire stations (f)
15	
100	
350	

4. Give the prime factorization of 180.

5. Simplify: $\dfrac{42}{105}$.

6. Divide: $\dfrac{15}{16} \div \dfrac{5}{8}$.

7. Subtract: $\dfrac{11}{12} - \dfrac{2}{9}$.

8. Add: $1\dfrac{2}{3} + 8\dfrac{2}{5}$.

9. SHOPPING   Find the cost of the fruit on the scale.

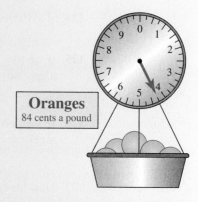

Oranges
84 cents a pound

10. Write $\dfrac{5}{6}$ as a decimal.

11. Graph each member of the set on the number line.
$$\left\{-1\tfrac{1}{4},\ \sqrt{2},\ -3.75,\ \tfrac{7}{2},\ 0.5,\ -3\right\}$$

12. Decide whether each statement is true or false.

a. Every integer is a rational number.
b. Every rational number is an integer.
c. π is an irrational number.
d. 0 is a whole number.

13. Describe the set of real numbers.

14. Insert the proper symbol, $>$ or $<$, in the blank to make each statement true.

a. -2 ___ -3 **b.** $-|-7|$ ___ 8
c. $|-4|$ ___ $-(-5)$ **d.** $\left|-\dfrac{7}{8}\right|$ ___ 0.5

15. SWEEPS WEEK   During "sweeps week," television networks make a special effort to gain viewers by showing unusually flashy programming. Use the information in the graph to determine the average daily gain (or loss) of ratings points by a network for the 7-day "sweeps period."

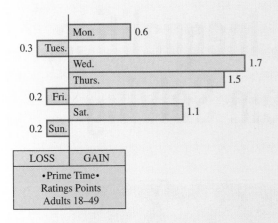

Perform the operations.

16. $(-6) + 8 + (-4)$

17. $-\dfrac{1}{2} + \dfrac{7}{8}$

18. $-10 - (-4)$

19. $(-2)(-3)(-5)$

20. $\dfrac{-22}{-11}$

21. $-6.1(0.4)$

22. $\dfrac{0}{-3}$

23. $0 - 3$

24. $3 + (-3)$

25. $-30 + 50 - 10 - (-40)$

26. $\left(-\dfrac{3}{5}\right)^3$

27. ASTRONOMY *Magnitude* is a term used in astronomy to designate the brightness of celestial objects as viewed from Earth. Smaller magnitudes are associated with brighter objects, and larger magnitudes refer to fainter objects. By how many magnitudes do a full moon and the sun differ?

Object	Magnitude
Sun	-26.5
Full moon	-12.5

28. What property of real numbers is illustrated below? $(-12 + 97) + 3 = -12 + (97 + 3)$.

29. Write each product using exponents:
   a. $9(9)(9)(9)(9)$ **b.** $3 \cdot x \cdot x \cdot z \cdot z \cdot z$.

30. Evaluate: $8 + 2 \cdot 3^4$.

31. Evaluate: $9^2 - 3[45 - 3(6 + 4)]$.

32. Evaluate: $\dfrac{3(40 - 2^3)}{-2(6 - 4)^2}$.

33. Evaluate: -10^2.

34. Evaluate $3(x - y) - 5(x + y)$ for $x = 2$ and $y = -5$.

35. Complete the table.

x	$2x - \dfrac{30}{x}$
5	
10	
-30	

36. Translate to an algebraic expression: seven more than twice the width w.

37. A rock band recorded x songs for a CD. Technicians had to delete two songs from the album because of poor sound quality. Express the number of songs on the CD using an algebraic expression.

38. Find the value of q quarters in cents.

39. Explain the difference between an expression and an equation.

40. How many terms are in the expression $4x^2 + 5x - 7$? What is the coefficient of the second term?

2 Equations, Inequalities, and Problem Solving

Comstock/Getty Images

When shopping for big-ticket items such as appliances, automobiles, or home furnishings, we often have to stay within a budget. Besides price, the quality and dependability of an item must also be considered. The problem-solving skills that we will discuss can help you make wise decisions when making large purchases such as these.

To learn more about the use of algebra in the marketplace, visit *The Learning Equation* on the Internet at http://tle.brookscole.com. (Log-in instructions are in the Preface.) For Chapter 2, the online lessons are:

- *TLE* Lesson 3: Translating Written Phrases
- *TLE* Lesson 4: Solving Equations Part 1
- *TLE* Lesson 5: Solving Equations Part 2

One of the most useful concepts in algebra is the equation. Writing and then solving an equation is a powerful problem-solving strategy.

2.1 Solving Equations

- Equations and Solutions   • The Addition Property of Equality
- The Subtraction Property of Equality   • The Multiplication Property of Equality
- The Division Property of Equality   • Geometry

In this section, we introduce basic types of equations and discuss four fundamental properties that are used to solve them.

■ EQUATIONS AND SOLUTIONS

An **equation** is a statement indicating that two expressions are equal. An example is $x + 5 = 15$. The equal symbol separates the equation into two parts: The expression $x + 5$ is the **left-hand side** and 15 is the **right-hand side.** The letter x is the **variable** (or the **unknown**). The sides of an equation can be reversed, so we can write $x + 5 = 15$ or $15 = x + 5$.

- An equation can be true: $6 + 3 = 9$.
- An equation can be false: $2 + 4 = 7$.
- An equation can be neither true nor false. For example, $x + 5 = 15$ is neither true nor false because we don't know what number x represents.

An equation that contains a variable is made true or false by substituting a number for the variable. If we substitute 10 for x in $x + 5 = 15$, the resulting equation is true: $10 + 5 = 15$. If we substitute 1 for x, the resulting equation is false: $1 + 5 = 15$. A number that makes an equation true is called a **solution** and it is said to *satisfy* the equation. Therefore, 10 is a solution of $x + 5 = 15$, and 1 is not.

EXAMPLE 1

Is 9 a solution of $3y - 1 = 2y + 7$?

Solution   We begin by substituting 9 for each y in the equation. Then we evaluate each side separately. If 9 is a solution, we will obtain a true statement.

The Language of Algebra

Read $\stackrel{?}{=}$ as "is possibly equal to."

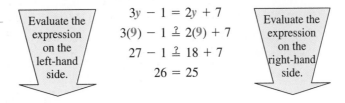

$$3y - 1 = 2y + 7$$
$$3(9) - 1 \stackrel{?}{=} 2(9) + 7$$
$$27 - 1 \stackrel{?}{=} 18 + 7$$
$$26 = 25$$

Evaluate the expression on the left-hand side.

Evaluate the expression on the right-hand side.

Since $26 = 25$ is false, 9 is not a solution.

Self Check 1   Is 25 a solution of $10 - x = 35 - 2x$?

■ THE ADDITION PROPERTY OF EQUALITY

To **solve an equation** means to find all values of the variable that make the equation true. We can develop an understanding of how to solve equations by referring to the scales shown on the right.

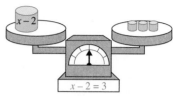

The first scale represents the equation $x - 2 = 3$. The scale is in balance because the weight on the left-hand side, $(x - 2)$ grams, and the weight on the right-hand side, 3 grams, are equal. To find x, we must add 2 grams to the left-hand side. To keep the scale in balance, we must also add 2 grams to the right-hand side. After doing this, we see in the second illustration that x grams is balanced by 5 grams. Therefore, x must be 5. We say that we have solved the equation $x - 2 = 3$ and that the solution is 5.

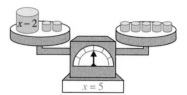

In this example, we solved $x - 2 = 3$ by transforming it to a simpler *equivalent equation*, $x = 5$.

Equivalent Equations	Equations with the same solutions are called **equivalent equations.**

The procedure that we used suggests the following property of equality.

Addition Property of Equality	Adding the same number to both sides of an equation does not change its solution. For any real numbers a, b, and c, if $a = b$, then $a + c = b + c$

When we use this property, the resulting equation is equivalent to the original one. We will now show how it is used to solve $x - 2 = 3$ algebraically.

EXAMPLE 2

Solve: $x - 2 = 3$.

Solution   To isolate x on the left-hand side of the equation, we use the addition property of equality. We can undo the subtraction of 2 by adding 2 to both sides.

The Language of Algebra

When solving an equation, we want to *isolate* the variable on one side of the equation. The word *isolate* means to be alone or by itself.

$$x - 2 = 3$$
$$x - 2 + 2 = 3 + 2 \quad \text{Add 2 to both sides.}$$
$$x + 0 = 5 \quad \text{Do the addition: } -2 + 2 = 0.$$
$$x = 5 \quad \text{When 0 is added to a number, the result is the same number.}$$

To check, we substitute 5 for x in the original equation and simplify. If 5 is a solution, we will obtain a true statement.

$$x - 2 = 3 \quad \text{This is the original equation.}$$
$$5 - 2 \stackrel{?}{=} 3 \quad \text{Substitute 5 for } x.$$
$$3 = 3 \quad \text{True.}$$

Since the statement is true, 5 is the solution.

Self Check 2   Solve: $n - 16 = 33$.

EXAMPLE 3

Solve: $-19 = y - 7$.

Solution   To isolate y on the right-hand side, we use the addition property of equality. We can undo the subtraction of 7 by adding 7 to both sides.

Notation

We may solve an equation so that the variable is isolated on either side of the equation. In Example 3, note that $-12 = y$ is equivalent to $y = -12$.

$$-19 = y - 7$$
$$-19 + 7 = y - 7 + 7 \quad \text{Add 7 to both sides.}$$
$$-12 = y \quad \text{Do the addition: } -7 + 7 = 0.$$

To check, we substitute -12 for y in the original equation and simplify.

$$-19 = y - 7 \qquad \text{This is the original equation.}$$
$$-19 \stackrel{?}{=} -12 - 7 \quad \text{Substitute } -12 \text{ for } y.$$
$$-19 = -19 \qquad \text{True.}$$

Since the statement is true, the solution is -12.

Self Check 3   Solve: $-5 = b - 38$.

EXAMPLE 4

Solve: $-27 + g = -3$.

Solution   To isolate g, we use the addition property of equality. We can eliminate -27 on the left-hand side by adding its opposite (additive inverse) to both sides.

Caution

After checking a result, be careful when stating your conclusion. For Example 4, it would be incorrect to say:

The solution is -3.

The number we were checking was 24, not -3.

$$-27 + g = -3$$
$$-27 + g + 27 = -3 + 27 \quad \text{Add 27 to both sides.}$$
$$g = 24 \quad \text{Do the addition: } -27 + 27 = 0.$$

Check: $-27 + g = -3$ This is the original equation.
$$-27 + 24 \stackrel{?}{=} -3 \quad \text{Substitute 24 for } g.$$
$$-3 = -3 \quad \text{True.}$$

The solution is 24.

Self Check 4   Solve: $-20 + n = 29$.

■ THE SUBTRACTION PROPERTY OF EQUALITY

The first scale shown on the next page represents the equation $x + 2 = 5$. The scale is in balance because the weight on the left-hand side, $(x + 2)$ grams, and the weight on the right-hand side, 5 grams, are equal. To find x, we isolate it by subtracting 2 grams from the left-hand side. To keep the scale in balance, we must also subtract 2 grams from the right-hand side. After doing this, we see in the second illustration that x grams is balanced by 3 grams. Therefore, x must be 3. We say that we have solved the equation $x + 2 = 5$ and that the solution is 3.

In this example, we solved $x + 2 = 5$ by transforming it to a simpler equivalent equation, $x = 3$. The process that we used to isolate x on the left-hand side of the scale suggests the following property of equality.

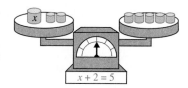

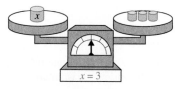

Subtraction Property of Equality	Subtracting the same number from both sides of an equation does not change its solution. For any real numbers a, b, and c,
	$$\text{if } a = b, \text{ then } a - c = b - c$$

When we use this property, the resulting equation is equivalent to the original one. We will now show how it is used to solve $x + 2 = 5$ algebraically.

EXAMPLE 5

Solve: $x + 2 = 5$.

Solution   To isolate x on the left-hand side, we use the subtraction property of equality. We can undo the addition of 2 by subtracting 2 from both sides.

$$x + 2 = 5$$
$$x + 2 - 2 = 5 - 2 \qquad \text{Subtract 2 from both sides.}$$
$$x + 0 = 3$$
$$x = 3$$

Check: $x + 2 = 5$ This is the original equation.
$3 + 2 \stackrel{?}{=} 5$ Substitute 3 for x.
$5 = 5$ True.

The solution is 3.

Self Check 5   Solve: $x + 24 = 50$.

EXAMPLE 6

Solve: $54.9 + m = 45.2$.

Solution   To isolate m, we can undo the addition of 54.9 by subtracting 54.9 from both sides.

$$54.9 + m = 45.2$$
$$54.9 + m - 54.9 = 45.2 - 54.9 \qquad \text{Subtract 54.9 from both sides.}$$
$$m = -9.7$$

Check: $54.9 + m = 45.2$ This is the original equation.

$54.9 + (-9.7) \stackrel{?}{=} 45.2$ Substitute -9.7 for m.

$45.2 = 45.2$ True.

The solution is -9.7.

Self Check 6   Solve: $0.7 + a = 0.2$

■ THE MULTIPLICATION PROPERTY OF EQUALITY

We can think of the first scale shown below as representing the equation $\frac{x}{3} = 25$. The weight on the left-hand side is $\frac{x}{3}$ grams, and the weight on the right-hand side is 25 grams. Because the weights are equal, the scale is in balance. To find x, we can triple (multiply by 3) the weight on each side. When we do this, the scale will remain in balance. We see that x grams will be balanced by 75 grams. Therefore, x is 75.

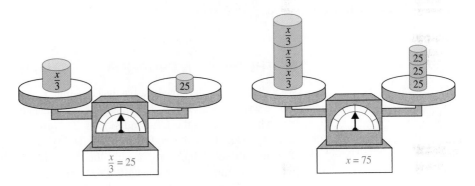

The process used to isolate x on the left-hand side of the scale suggests the following property of equality.

Multiplication Property of Equality	Multiplying both sides of an equation by the same nonzero number does not change its solution.
	For any real numbers a, b, and c, where c is not 0,
	if $a = b$, then $ca = cb$

When we use this property, the resulting equation is equivalent to the original one. We will now show how it is used to solve $\frac{x}{3} = 25$ algebraically.

EXAMPLE 7   Solve: $\dfrac{x}{3} = 25$.

Solution   To isolate x on the left-hand side, we use the multiplication property of equality. We can undo the division by 3 by multiplying both sides by 3.

$$\frac{x}{3} = 25$$

$$3 \cdot \frac{x}{3} = 3 \cdot 25 \qquad \text{Multiply both sides by 3.}$$

$$\frac{3x}{3} = 75 \qquad \text{Do the multiplications.}$$

$$1x = 75 \qquad \text{Simplify the fraction by removing the common factor of 3 in the}$$
$$\text{numerator and denominator: } \tfrac{3}{3} = 1.$$

$$x = 75 \qquad \text{The product of 1 and any number is that number.}$$

Check: $\dfrac{x}{3} = 25$ This is the original equation.

$$\frac{75}{3} \overset{?}{=} 25 \qquad \text{Substitute 75 for } x.$$

$$25 = 25 \qquad \text{True.}$$

The solution is 75.

Self Check 7   Solve: $\dfrac{b}{24} = 3$.

■ THE DIVISION PROPERTY OF EQUALITY

We will now consider how to solve the equation $2x = 8$. Since $2x$ means $2 \cdot x$, the equation can be written as $2 \cdot x = 8$. The first scale represents this equation.

The weight on the left-hand side is $2 \cdot x$ grams and the weight on the right-hand side is 8 grams. Because these weights are equal, the scale is in balance. To find x, we remove half of the weight from each side. This is equivalent to dividing the weight on both sides by 2. When we do this, the scale remains in balance. We see that x grams is balanced by 4 grams. Therefore, x is 4. We say that we have solved the equation $2x = 8$ and that the solution is 4.

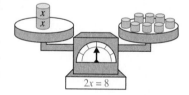

In this example, we solved $2x = 8$ by transforming it to a simpler equivalent equation, $x = 4$. The procedure that we used suggests the following property of equality.

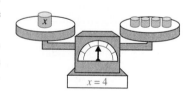

Division Property of Equality	Dividing both sides of an equation by the same nonzero number does not change its solution.

For any real numbers a, b, and c, where c is not 0,

$$\text{if } a = b, \text{ then } \frac{a}{c} = \frac{b}{c}$$

When we use this property, the resulting equation is equivalent to the original one. We will now show how it is used to solve $2x = 8$ algebraically.

EXAMPLE 8   Solve: $2x = 8$.

Solution   To isolate x on the left-hand side, we use the division property of equality to undo the multiplication by 2 by dividing both sides of the equation by 2.

$$2x = 8$$

$$\frac{2x}{2} = \frac{8}{2} \quad \text{Divide both sides by 2.}$$

$$1x = 4 \quad \text{Simplify the fraction by removing the common factor of 2 in the}$$
$$\text{numerator and denominator: } \frac{2}{2} = 1.$$

$$x = 4 \quad \text{The product of 1 and any number is that number: } 1x = x.$$

Check: $2x = 8$ This is the original equation.

$$2(4) \overset{?}{=} 8 \quad \text{Substitute 4 for } x.$$

$$8 = 8 \quad \text{True.}$$

The solution is 4.

Self Check 8   Solve: $16x = 176$.

EXAMPLE 9

Solve: $-6.02 = -8.6t$.

Solution   To isolate t on the right-hand side, we can undo the multiplication by -8.6 by dividing both sides by -8.6.

$$-6.02 = -8.6t$$

$$\frac{-6.02}{-8.6} = \frac{-8.6t}{-8.6} \quad \text{Divide both sides by } -8.6.$$

$$0.7 = t \quad \text{Do the divisions.}$$

The check is left to the student. The solution is 0.7.

Notation

In Example 9, if you prefer to isolate the variable on the left-hand side, you can solve $-6.02 = -8.6t$ by reversing both sides and solving $-8.6t = -6.02$.

Self Check 9   Solve: $10.04 = -0.4r$.

■ GEOMETRY

The following three figures are called **angles.** Angles are measured in **degrees,** denoted by the symbol °. If an angle measures 90° (ninety degrees), it is called a **right angle.** If an angle measures 180°, it is called a **straight angle.**

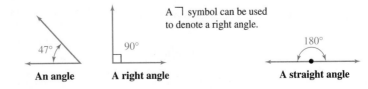

A ⌐ symbol can be used to denote a right angle.

47°   90°   180°

An angle   **A right angle**   **A straight angle**

EXAMPLE 10

Lawn mowers. Find x, the angle that the mower's handle makes with the ground.

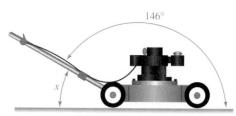

Solution We can use algebra to find the unknown angle labeled x. Since the sum of the measures of the angles is 180°, we have

$$x + 146 = 180$$
$$x + 146 - 146 = 180 - 146 \qquad \text{Subtract 146 from both sides.}$$
$$x = 34$$

The angle that the handle makes with the ground is 34°.

Answers to Self Checks **1.** yes **2.** 49 **3.** 33 **4.** 49 **5.** 26 **6.** −0.5 **7.** 72 **8.** 11 **9.** −25.1

2.1 STUDY SET

VOCABULARY Fill in the blanks.

1. An _____ is a statement indicating that two expressions are equal.

2. Any number that makes an equation true when substituted for its variable is said to _____ the equation. Such numbers are called _____.

3. To _____ the solution of an equation, we substitute the value for the variable in the original equation and see whether the result is a true statement.

4. In $30 = t - 12$, the _____ side of the equation is $t - 12$.

5. Equations with the same solutions are called _____ equations.

6. To _____ an equation means to find all values of the variable that make the equation true.

7. To solve an equation, we _____ the variable on one side of the equal symbol.

8. When solving an equation, the objective is to find all values of the _____ that will make the equation true.

CONCEPTS

9. **a.** What equation does the balanced scale represent?

   b. What must be done to isolate x on the left-hand side?

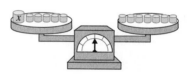

10. **a.** What equation does the balanced scale represent?

    b. What must be done to isolate x on the left-hand side?

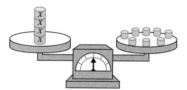

11. Given $x + 6 = 12$,
    a. What forms the left-hand side of the equation?

    b. Is this equation true or false?

    c. Is 5 a solution?

    d. Does 6 satisfy the equation?

12. For each equation, tell what operation is performed on the variable. Then tell how to undo that operation to isolate the variable.
    a. $x - 8 = 24$
    b. $x + 8 = 24$

c. $\dfrac{x}{8} = 24$

d. $8x = 24$

Complete each flow chart.

13.
| Begin with the number 24. |
↓
| Add 6. |
↓
| Subtract 6. |
↓
The result is ▢ .

14.
| Begin with a number x. |
↓
| Multiply by 10. |
↓
| Divide by 10. |
↓
The result is ▢ .

15.
| Begin with a number n. |
↓
| Divide by 5. |
↓
| Multiply by 5. |
↓
The result is ▢ .

16.
| Begin with the number 45. |
↓
| Subtract 9. |
↓
| Add 9. |
↓
The result is ▢ .

17. Complete the following properties of equality.
   a. If $x = y$, then $x + c = y +$ ▢ and $x - c = y -$ ▢ .

   b. If $x = y$, then $cx =$ ▢ y and $\dfrac{x}{c} = \dfrac{y}{▢}$ $(c \neq 0)$.

18. a. When solving $\dfrac{h}{10} = 20$, do we multiply both sides of the equation by 10 or 20?

   b. When solving $4k = 16$, do we subtract 4 from both sides of the equation or divide both sides by 4?

19. Simplify each expression.
   a. $x + 7 - 7$ **b.** $y - 2 + 2$

   c. $\dfrac{5t}{5}$ **d.** $6 \cdot \dfrac{h}{6}$

20. Complete each equation.
   a. $x + 20 =$ ▢   **b.** $x + 20 =$ ▢

   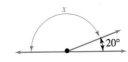

NOTATION   **Complete each solution.**

21. Solve: $x + 15 = 45$
$$x + 15 - ▢ = 45 - ▢$$
$$x = 30$$

   Check: $x + 15 = 45$
$$▢ + 15 \overset{?}{=} 45$$
$$45 = 45$$
   ▢ is a solution.

22. Solve: $8x = 40$
$$\dfrac{8x}{▢} = \dfrac{40}{▢}$$
$$x = 5$$

   Check: $8x = 40$
$$8(\;) \overset{?}{=} 40$$
$$40 = 40$$
   ▢ is a solution.

23. a. What does the symbol $\overset{?}{=}$ mean?

   b. Write twenty-seven degrees using symbols.

24. If you solve an equation and obtain $50 = x$, can you write $x = 50$?

PRACTICE   **Check to see whether the given number is a solution of the equation.**

25. $6, x + 12 = 18$

26. $110, x - 50 = 60$

27. $-8, 2b + 3 = -15$

28. $-2, 5t - 4 = -16$

29. $5, 0.5x = 2.9$

30. $3.5, 1.2 + x = 4.7$

31. $-6, 33 - \dfrac{x}{2} = 30$

32. $-8, \dfrac{x}{4} + 98 = 100$

33. $20, |c - 8| = 10$

34. $20, |30 - r| = 15$

35. $12, 3x - 2 = 4x - 5$

36. $5, 5y + 8 = 3y - 2$

37. $-3, x^2 - x - 6 = 0$

38. $-2, y^2 + 5y - 3 = 0$

39. $1, \dfrac{2}{a+1} + 5 = \dfrac{12}{a+1}$

40. $4, \dfrac{2t}{t-2} - \dfrac{4}{t-2} = 1$

41. $-3, (x-4)(x+3) = 0$

42. $5, (2x+1)(x-5) = 0$

Use a property of equality to solve each equation. Then check the result.

43. $x + 7 = 10$ **44.** $y + 15 = 24$

45. $a - 5 = 66$ **46.** $x - 34 = 19$

47. $0 = n - 9$ **48.** $3 = m - 20$

49. $9 + p = 9$ **50.** $88 + j = 88$

51. $x - 16 = -25$ **52.** $y - 12 = -13$

53. $a + 3 = 0$ **54.** $m + 1 = 0$

55. $f + 3.5 = 1.2$ **56.** $h + 9.4 = 8.1$

57. $-8 + p = -44$ **58.** $-2 + k = -41$

59. $8.9 = -4.1 + t$ **60.** $7.7 = -3.2 + s$

61. $d - \dfrac{1}{9} = \dfrac{7}{9}$ **62.** $\dfrac{7}{15} = b - \dfrac{1}{15}$

63. $s + \dfrac{4}{25} = \dfrac{11}{25}$ **64.** $\dfrac{8}{3} = h + \dfrac{1}{3}$

65. $4x = 16$ **66.** $5y = 45$

67. $369 = 9c$ **68.** $840 = 105t$

69. $4f = 0$ **70.** $0 = 60k$

71. $23b = 23$ **72.** $16 = 16h$

73. $-8h = 48$ **74.** $-9a = 72$

75. $-100 = -5g$ **76.** $-80 = -5w$

77. $-3.4y = -1.7$ **78.** $-2.1x = -1.26$

79. $\dfrac{x}{15} = 3$ **80.** $\dfrac{y}{7} = 12$

81. $0 = \dfrac{v}{11}$ **82.** $\dfrac{d}{49} = 0$

83. $\dfrac{w}{-7} = 15$ **84.** $\dfrac{h}{-2} = 3$

85. $\dfrac{d}{-7} = -3$ **86.** $\dfrac{c}{-2} = -11$

87. $\dfrac{y}{0.6} = -4.4$ **88.** $\dfrac{y}{0.8} = -2.9$

89. $a + 456,932 = 1,708,921$

90. $229,989 = x - 84,863$

91. $-1,563x = 43,764$

92. $999 = \dfrac{y}{-5,565}$

APPLICATIONS

93. SYNTHESIZERS Find the unknown angle measure.

94. PHYSICS   A 15-pound block is suspended with two ropes, one of which is horizontal. Find the unknown angle measure.

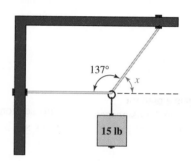

95. AVIATION   How many degrees from the horizontal position are the wings of the airplane?

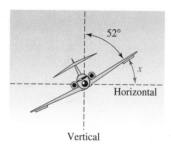

96. PLAYING A FLUTE   How many degrees from the horizontal is the position of the flute?

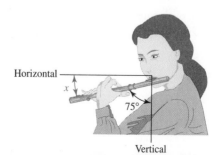

WRITING

97. What does it mean to solve an equation?

98. When solving an equation, we *isolate* the variable on one side of the equation. Write a sentence in which the word *isolate* is used in a different context.

99. Explain the error in the following work.

$$\text{Solve:} \quad x + 2 = 40$$
$$x + 2 - 2 = 40$$
$$x = 40$$

100. After solving an equation, how do we check the result?

REVIEW

101. Evaluate $-9 - 3x$ for $x = -3$.

102. Write a formula that would give the number of eggs in d dozen.

103. Translate to symbols: Subtract x from 45.

104. Evaluate: $\dfrac{2^3 + 3(5 - 3)}{15 - 4 \cdot 2}$.

CHALLENGE PROBLEMS

105. If $a + 80 = 50$, what is $a - 80$?

106. Find two solutions of $|x + 1| = 100$.

2.2 Problem Solving

- A Problem-Solving Strategy
- Drawing Diagrams
- Constructing Tables
- Solving Percent Problems

The Language of Algebra

A *strategy* is a plan for achieving a goal. Businesses often hire firms to develop an advertising *strategy* that will increase the sales of their products.

In this section, we combine the translating skills discussed in Chapter 1 and the equation-solving skills discussed in Section 2.1 to solve many applied problems.

■ A PROBLEM-SOLVING STRATEGY

To become a good problem solver, you need a plan to follow, such as the following five-step strategy.

Strategy for Problem Solving

1. **Analyze the problem** by reading it carefully to understand the given facts. What information is given? What are you asked to find? What vocabulary is given? Often, a diagram or table will help you visualize the facts of the problem.
2. **Form an equation** by picking a variable to represent the numerical value to be found. Then express all other unknown quantities as expressions involving that variable. Key words or phrases can be helpful. Finally, translate the words of the problem into an equation.
3. **Solve the equation.**
4. **State the conclusion.**
5. **Check the result** in the words of the problem.

EXAMPLE 1

Systems analysis. A company's telephone use would have to increase by 350 calls per hour before the system would reach the maximum capacity of 1,500 calls per hour. Currently, how many calls are being made each hour on the system?

Analyze the Problem

- The maximum capacity of the system is 1,500 calls per hour.
- If the number of calls increases by 350, the system will reach capacity.
- We are to find the number of calls currently being made each hour.

Form an Equation   Let n = the number of calls currently being made each hour. To form an equation, we look for a key word or phrase in the problem.

Key phrase: *increase by 350*   **Translation:** addition

The key phrase tells us to add 350 to the current number of calls to obtain an expression for the maximum capacity of the system. Now we translate the words of the problem into an equation.

The current number of calls per hour	increased by	350	equals	the maximum capacity of the system.
n	+	350	=	1,500

Solve the Equation

$$n + 350 = 1,500$$
$$n + 350 - 350 = 1,500 - 350 \quad \text{To undo the addition of 350, subtract 350 from both sides.}$$
$$n = 1,150 \quad \text{Do the subtractions.}$$

State the Conclusion   Currently, 1,150 calls are being made per hour.

Check the Result   If 1,150 calls are currently being made each hour and an increase of 350 calls per hour occurs, then $1,150 + 350 = 1,500$ calls will be made each hour. This is the capacity of the system. The answer, 1,150, checks.

■ DRAWING DIAGRAMS

Diagrams are often helpful because they enable us to visualize the given facts of a problem.

EXAMPLE 2

Airline travel.   On a book tour that took her from New York City to Chicago to Los Angeles and back to New York City, an author flew a total of 4,910 miles. The flight from New York to Chicago was 714 miles, and the flight from Chicago to L.A. was 1,745 miles. How long was the direct flight back to New York City?

Analyze the Problem
- The total miles flown on the tour was 4,910.
- The flight from New York to Chicago was 714 miles.
- The flight from Chicago to L.A. was 1,745 miles.
- We are to find the length of the flight from L.A. to New York City.

In the diagram, we see that the three parts of the tour form a triangle. We know the lengths of two of the sides of the triangle, 714 and 1,745, and the perimeter of the triangle, 4,910.

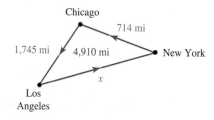

Form an Equation   We will let x = the length (in miles) of the flight from L.A. to New York and label the appropriate side of the triangle in the diagram. We then have:

The miles from New York to Chicago	plus	the miles from Chicago to L.A.	plus	the miles from L.A. to New York	is	4,910.
714	+	1,745	+	x	=	4,910

Notation

When forming an equation, we usually don't include the units.

714 ~~mi~~ + 1,745 ~~mi~~ + x ~~mi~~
= 4,910 ~~mi~~

Solve the Equation

$714 + 1,745 + x = 4,910$

$2,459 + x = 4,910$ Simplify the left-hand side of the equation: $714 + 1,745 = 2,459$.

$2,459 + x - 2,459 = 4,910 - 2,459$ Subtract 2,459 from both sides to isolate x.

$x = 2,451$ Do the subtractions.

State the Conclusion   The flight from L.A. to New York was 2,451 miles.

Check the Result   If we add the three flight lengths, we get $714 + 1,745 + 2,451 = 4,910$. This was the total number of miles flown on the book tour. The answer, 2,451, checks.

EXAMPLE 3

Eye surgery.   A technique called **radial keratotomy** is sometimes used to correct nearsightedness. This procedure involves equally spaced incisions in the cornea, as shown in the figure. Find the angle between each incision. (Round to the nearest tenth of a degree.)

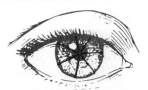

Analyze the Problem   A diagram labeled with the known and unknown information is shown.

- There are 7 angles of equal measure.
- One complete revolution is 360°.
- Find the measure of one angle.

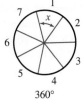

Form an Equation   We will let x = the measure of one of the angles. We then have:

7	times	the measure of one of the angles	is	360°
7	·	x	=	360

Solve the Equation

$7x = 360$

$\dfrac{7x}{7} = \dfrac{360}{7}$ Divide both sides by 7.

$x = 51.42\ldots$ Do the division.

$x \approx 51.4$ Round to the nearest tenth of a degree.

State the Conclusion   The incisions are approximately 51.4° apart.

Check the Result   The angle measure is approximately 51°. Since 51 · 7 = 357, and this is close to 360, the result of 51.4° seems reasonable.

■ CONSTRUCTING TABLES

Sometimes it is helpful to organize the given facts of the problem in a table.

EXAMPLE 4

Labor statistics.   The number of women (16 years or older) in the U.S. labor force has grown steadily over the past 40 years. From 1960 to 1970, the number grew by 8 million. By 1980, it had increased an additional 12 million. By 2000, the number rose another 21 million; by the end of that year, 63 million women were in the labor force. How many women were in the labor force in 1960?

Analyze the Problem
- The number grew by 8 million, increased by 12 million, and rose 21 million.
- The number of women in the labor force in 2000 was 63 million.
- We are to find the number of women in the U.S. labor force in 1960.

Form an Equation   We will let x = the number of women (in millions) in the labor force in 1960. We can write algebraic expressions to represent the number of women in the work force in 1970, 1980, and 2000 by translating key words.

The Language of Algebra

The word *cumulative* means to increase by successive additions. You've probably heard of a *cumulative* final exam—one that covers all of the material that was studied in the course.

Year	Women in the labor force (millions)
1960	x
1970	$x + 8$
1980	$x + 8 + 12$
2000	$x + 8 + 12 + 21$

This table helps us keep track of the cumulative total as the number of women in the work force increased over the years.

Key word: *grew*   **Translation:** addition

Key word: *increased*   **Translation:** addition

Key word: *rose*   **Translation:** addition

There are two ways to represent the number of women (in millions) in the 2000 labor force: $x + 8 + 12 + 21$ and 63. Therefore,

$$x + 8 + 12 + 21 = 63$$

Solve the Equation

$$x + 8 + 12 + 21 = 63$$
$$x + 41 = 63 \qquad \text{Simplify: } 8 + 12 + 21 = 41.$$
$$x + 41 - 41 = 63 - 41 \qquad \text{To undo the addition of 41, subtract 41 from both sides.}$$
$$x = 22 \qquad \text{Do the subtractions.}$$

State the Conclusion   There were 22 million women in the U.S. labor force in 1960.

Check the Result   Adding the number of women (in millions) in the labor force in 1960 and the increases, we get $22 + 8 + 12 + 21 = 63$. In 2000 there were 63 million, so the answer, 22, checks.

■ SOLVING PERCENT PROBLEMS

Percents are often used to present numeric information. Stores use them to advertise discounts, manufacturers use them to describe the contents of their products, and banks use them to list interest rates for loans and savings accounts.

Percent means parts per one hundred. For example, 93% means 93 out of 100 or $\frac{93}{100}$. There are three types of percent problems. Examples of these are as follows:

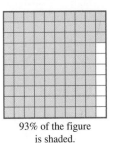

93% of the figure
is shaded.

- What number is 8% of 215?
- 14 is what percent of 52?
- 82 is 20.3% of what number?

EXAMPLE 5

What number is 8% of 215?

Solution First, we translate the words into an equation. Here the word *of* indicates multiplication, and the word *is* means equals.

What number	is	8%	of	215?
↓	↓	↓	↓	↓
x	=	8%	·	215

Translate to mathematical symbols.

To do the multiplication on the right-hand side of the equation, we must change the percent to a decimal (or a fraction). To change 8% to a decimal, we proceed as follows.

$8\% = 8.0\%$ The number 8 has an understood decimal point to the right of the 8.

$= .08\,0$ Drop the % symbol and divide 8.0 by 100 by moving the decimal point 2 places to the left.

The Language of Algebra

The names of the parts of a percent sentence are:

17.2	is	8%	of	215.
amount		percent		base

They are related by the formula:

Amount = percent · base

To complete the solution, we replace 8% with its decimal equivalent, 0.08, and do the multiplication.

$x = 8\% \cdot 215$ This is the original equation.

$x = 0.08 \cdot 215$ $8\% = 0.08$

$x = 17.2$ Do the multiplication.

We have found that 17.2 is 8% of 215.

Self Check 5 What number is 5.6% of 40?

One method for solving applied percent problems is to read the problem carefully, and use the given facts to write a **percent sentence** of the form:

is   %   of   ?

We enter the appropriate numbers in the first two blanks, and the word "what" in the remaining blank. Then we translate the sentence to mathematical symbols and solve the resulting equation.

EXAMPLE 6

Best-selling songs.   In 1993, Whitney Houston's "I Will Always Love You" led the *Billboard*'s music charts for 14 weeks. What percent of the year did she have the #1 song? (Round to the nearest one percent.)

Analyze the Problem
- For 14 out of 52 weeks in a year, she had the #1 song.
- We are to find what percent of the year she had the #1 song.

Form an Equation   Let x = the unknown percent and translate the words of the problem into an equation.

14	is	what percent	of	52?

$$14 \quad = \quad x \quad \cdot \quad 52$$

14 is the amount, x is the percent, and 52 is the base.

Solve the Equation

$$14 = x \cdot 52$$
$$14 = 52x \qquad \text{Write } x \cdot 52 \text{ as } 52x.$$
$$\frac{14}{52} = \frac{52x}{52} \qquad \text{To isolate } x, \text{ undo the multiplication by 52 by dividing both sides by 52.}$$
$$0.2692308 \approx x \qquad \text{Use a calculator to do the division.}$$

We were asked to find what *percent* of the year she had the #1 song. To change the decimal 0.2692307 to a percent, we proceed as follows.

$$0\,26.92308\% \approx x \qquad \text{Multiply 0.2692308 by 100 by moving the decimal point 2 places to the right, and then insert a \% symbol.}$$

$$26.92308\% \approx x$$

$$27\% \approx x \qquad \text{Round 26.92308\% to the nearest one percent.}$$

State the Conclusion   To the nearest one percent, Whitney Houston had the #1 song for 27% of the year.

Check the Result   We can check this result using estimation. Fourteen out of 52 weeks is approximately $\frac{14}{50}$ or $\frac{28}{100}$, which is 28%. The answer, 27%, seems reasonable.

EXAMPLE 7

Aging population.   By the year 2050, the U.S. Bureau of the Census predicts that about 82 million residents will be 65 years of age or older. The **circle graph** (or **pie chart**) indicates that age group will make up 20.3% of the population. If the prediction is correct, what will the population of the United States be in 2050? (Round to the nearest million.)

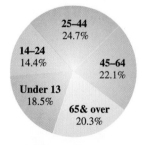

Projection of the 2050 U.S. Population by Age

25–44
24.7%

14–24
14.4%

45–64
22.1%

Under 13
18.5%

65& over
20.3%

Source: U.S. Bureau of the Census (2002).

Analyze the Problem
- 82 million people will be 65 years of age or older in 2050.
- 20.3% of the population will be 65 years of age or older in 2050.
- We are to find the predicted U.S. population for the year 2050.

Form an Equation   Let x = the predicted population in 2050. Translate to form an equation.

82	is	20.3%	of	what number?

$$82 = 20.3\% \cdot x$$

82 is the amount, 20.3% is the percent, and x is the base.

Solve the Equation

$$82 = 20.3\% \cdot x$$
$$82 = 0.203 \cdot x \quad \text{Change 20.3\% to a decimal: } 20.3\% = 0.203.$$
$$82 = 0.203x \quad \text{Write } 0.203 \cdot x \text{ as } 0.203x.$$
$$\frac{82}{0.203} = \frac{0.203x}{0.203} \quad \text{To undo the multiplication by 0.203, divide both sides by 0.203.}$$
$$403.94 \approx x \quad \text{Use a calculator to do the division.}$$
$$404 \approx x \quad \text{Round to the nearest one million.}$$

State the Conclusion   The census bureau is predicting a population of about 404 million in the year 2050.

Check the Result   82 million out of a population of 404 million is about $\frac{80}{400} = \frac{40}{200} = \frac{20}{100}$, or 20%. The answer of 404 million seems reasonable.

Percents are often used to describe how a quantity has changed. For example, a health care provider might increase the cost of medical insurance by 3%, or a police department might decrease the number of officers assigned to street patrols by 10%. To describe such changes, we use **percent of increase** or **percent of decrease.**

EXAMPLE 8

Identity theft.   The Federal Trade Commission receives complaints involving the theft of someone's identity information, such as a credit card/Social Security number or cell phone account. Refer to the data in the table. What was the percent of increase in the number of complaints from 2001 to 2002? (Round to the nearest percent.)

Number of Complaints

Year	2001	2002
	86,000	162,000

Analyze the Problem   To find the *amount of increase,* we subtract the number of complaints in 2001 from the number of complaints in 2002.

$$162,000 - 86,000 = 76,000 \quad \text{Subtract the earlier number from the later number.}$$

- The number of complaints increased by 76,000.
- Find what percent of the previous number of complaints a 76,000 increase is.

Caution

Always find the percent of increase (or decrease) with respect to the *original* amount.

Form an Equation   Let x = the unknown percent and translate the words to an equation.

76,000	is	what percent	of	86,000?

$$76,000 = x \cdot 86,000$$

76,000 is the amount, x is the percent, and 86,000 is the base.

Solve the Equation

$$76,000 = x \cdot 86,000$$

$$76,000 = 86,000x \qquad \text{Write } x \cdot 86,000 \text{ as } 86,000x.$$

$$\frac{76,000}{86,000} = \frac{86,000x}{86,000} \qquad \begin{array}{l}\text{To undo the multiplication by 86,000, divide both}\\ \text{sides by 86,000.}\end{array}$$

$$0.88372093 \approx x \qquad \text{Use a calculator to do the division.}$$

$$0\,88.372093\% \approx x \qquad \begin{array}{l}\text{To write the decimal as a percent, multiply by 100 by}\\ \text{moving the decimal point two places to the right and}\\ \text{insert a \% symbol.}\end{array}$$

$$88\% \approx x \qquad \text{Round to the nearest percent.}$$

State the Conclusion   In 2002, the number of complaints increased by about 88%.

Check the Result   A 100% increase in complaints would be 86,000 more complaints. Therefore, it seems reasonable that 76,000 complaints is an 88% increase.

Answer to Self Check   **5.** 2.24

2.2   STUDY SET

VOCABULARY   **Fill in the blanks.**

1. A letter that is used to represent a number is called a
_____.

2. An _____ is a mathematical statement that two quantities are equal. To _____ an equation means to find all the values of the variable that make the equation true.

3. To solve an applied problem, we let a _____ represent the unknown quantity. Then we write an _____ that models the situation. Finally, we _____ the equation for the variable to find the unknown.

4. _____ means parts per one hundred.

5. In the statement "10 is 50% of 20," 10 is called the _____, 50% is the _____, and 20 is the _____.

6. In mathematics, the word *of* often indicates _____, and ____ means equals.

Write an equation to describe each situation.

7. A college choir's tour of three cities covers 1,240 miles.

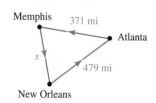

Memphis   371 mi   Atlanta
x   479 mi
New Orleans

8. A woman participated in a triathlon.

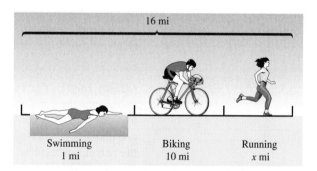

16 mi

Swimming   Biking   Running
1 mi   10 mi   x mi

9. An airliner changed its altitude to avoid storm clouds.

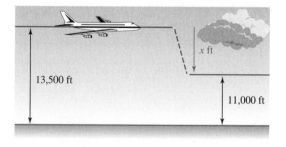

13,500 ft   x ft   11,000 ft

10. The sections of a 430-page book were assembled.

Section	Number of pages
Table of Contents	4
Preface	x
Text	400
Index	12

11. A hamburger chain sold a total of 31 million hamburgers in its first 4 years of business.

Year in business	Running total of hamburgers sold (millions)
1	x
2	$x + 5$
3	$x + 5 + 8$
4	$x + 5 + 8 + 16$

12. A pie was cut into equal-sized slices.

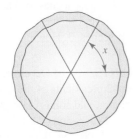

13. One method for solving percent problems is to read the problem carefully and use the given facts to write a percent sentence. What is the basic form of a percent sentence? ▭ ▭ ▭

14.

High School Sports Programs Girl's Water Polo—Number of Participants	
1981	**2001**
282	14,792

Source: National Federation of State High School Associations

a. Find the *amount* of increase in participation.

b. Fill in blanks to find the percent of increase in participation: ▭ is ▭ % of ▭

NOTATION **Translate each sentence into an equation.**

15. 12 is 40% of what number?

16. 99 is what percent of 200?

17. When computing with percents, the percent must be changed to a decimal or a fraction. Change each percent to a decimal.
   a. 35%   **b.** 3.5%
   c. 350%   **d.** $\frac{1}{2}\%$

18. Change each decimal to a percent.
   a. 0.9   **b.** 0.09
   c. 9   **d.** 0.999

PRACTICE **Translate each sentence into an equation, and then solve it.**

19. What number is 48% of 650?

20. What number is 60% of 200?

21. What percent of 300 is 78?

22. What percent of 325 is 143?

23. 75 is 25% of what number?

24. 78 is 6% of what number?

25. What number is 92.4% of 50?

26. What number is 2.8% of 220?

27. What percent of 16.8 is 0.42?

28. What percent of 2,352 is 199.92?

29. 128.1 is 8.75% of what number?

30. 1.12 is 140% of what number?

APPLICATIONS

31. GRAVITY   Suppose an astronaut, in full gear, was weighed on Earth. (See the illustration.) The weight of an object on Earth is 6 times greater than what it is on the moon. If we let $x =$ the weight the scale would read on the moon, which equation is true?

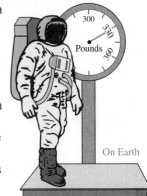

$$330x = 6 \qquad x + 6 = 330 \qquad \frac{x}{6} = 330 \qquad 6x = 330$$

32. POWER OUTAGE The electrical system in a building automatically shuts down when the meter shown reads 85. Suppose we let x = the amount the reading must increase to cause the system to shut down. Which equation is true?

$$85 + x = 60 \quad 60 + x = 85 \quad 60x = 85 \quad 60 - 85 = x$$

You can probably solve Problems 33–38 without algebra. Nevertheless, use the methods discussed in this section so that you can gain experience with writing and then solving an equation to find the unknown.

33. MONARCHY George III reigned as king of Great Britain for 59 years. This is 4 years less than the longest-reigning British monarch, Queen Victoria. For how many years did Queen Victoria rule?

34. TENNIS Billie Jean King won 40 Grand Slam tennis titles in her career. This is 14 less than the all-time leader, Martina Navratilova. How many Grand Slam titles did Navratilova win?

35. ATM RECEIPT Use the information on the automatic-teller receipt to find the balance in the account before the withdrawal.

HOME SAVINGS OF AMERICA			
TRAN.	DAT	TIM	T RM
0286.	1/16/03	11:46 AM	HSOA822
CARD NO.			61258
WITHDRAWAL OF			$35.00
FROM CHECKING ACCT.			3325256-612
CHECKING BAL.			$287.00

36. ENTERTAINMENT According to *Forbes* magazine, Oprah Winfrey made an estimated $150 million in 2002. This was $92 million more than Mariah Carey's estimated earnings for that year. How much did Mariah Carey make in 2002?

37. TV NEWS An interview with a world leader was edited into equally long segments and broadcast in parts over a 3-day period on a TV news program. If each daily segment of the interview lasted 9 minutes, how long was the original interview?

38. FLOODING Torrential rains caused the width of a river to swell to 84 feet. If this was twice its normal size, how wide was the river before the flooding?

Use a table to help organize the facts of the problem, then find the solution.

39. STATEHOOD From 1800 to 1850, 15 states joined the Union. From 1851 to 1900, an additional 14 states entered. Three states joined from 1901 to 1950. Since then, Alaska and Hawaii are the only others to enter the Union. How many states were part of the Union prior to 1800?

40. STUDIO TOUR Over a 4-year span, improvements in a Hollywood movie studio tour caused it to take longer. The first year, 10 minutes were added to the tour length. In the second, third, and fourth years, 5 minutes were added each year. If the tour now lasts 135 minutes, how long was it originally?

41. THEATER The play *Romeo and Juliet*, by William Shakespeare, has 5 acts and a total of 24 scenes. The second act has the most scenes, 6. The third and fourth acts each have 5 scenes. The last act has the least number of scenes, 3. How many scenes are in the first act?

42. U.S. PRESIDENTS As of December 31, 1999, there had been 42 presidents of the United States. George Washington and John Adams were the only presidents in the 18th century (1700–1799). During the 19th century (1800–1899), there were 23 presidents. How many presidents were there during the 20th century (1900–1999)?

43. ORCHESTRAS A 98-member orchestra is made up of a woodwind section with 19 musicians, a brass section with 23 players, a two-person percussion section, and a large string section. How many musicians make up the string section of the orchestra?

44. ANATOMY A premed student has to know the names of all 206 bones that make up the human skeleton. So far, she has memorized the names of the 60 bones in the feet and legs, the 31 bones in the torso, and the 55 bones in the neck and head. How many more names does she have to memorize?

Draw a diagram to help organize the facts of the problem, and then find the solution.

45. BERMUDA TRIANGLE   The Bermuda Triangle is a triangular region in the Atlantic Ocean where many ships and airplanes have disappeared. The perimeter of the triangle is about 3,075 miles. It is formed by three imaginary lines. The first, 1,100 miles long, is from Melbourne, Florida, to Puerto Rico. The second, 1,000 miles long, stretches from Puerto Rico to Bermuda. The third extends from Bermuda back to Florida. Find its length.

46. FENCING   To cut down on vandalism, a lot on which a house was to be constructed was completely fenced. The north side of the lot was 205 feet in length. The west and east sides were 275 and 210 feet long, respectively. If 945 feet of fencing was used, how long is the south side of the lot?

47. SPACE TRAVEL   The 364-foot-tall *Saturn V* rocket carried the first astronauts to the moon. Its first, second, and third stages were 138, 98, and 46 feet tall, respectively. Atop the third stage was the lunar module, and from it extended a 28-foot escape tower. How tall was the lunar module?

48. PLANETS   Mercury, Venus, and Earth have approximately circular orbits around the sun. Earth is the farthest from the sun, at 93 million miles, and Mercury is the closest, at 36 million miles. The orbit of Venus is about 31 million miles from that of Mercury. How far is Earth's orbit from that of Venus?

49. STOP SIGNS   Find the measure of one angle of the octagonal stop sign. (*Hint:* The sum of the measures of the angles of an octagon is 1,080°.)

50. FERRIS WHEELS   What is the measure of the angle between each of the "spokes" of the Ferris wheel?

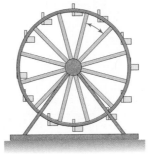

PERCENT PROBLEMS

51. ANTISEPTICS   Use the facts on the label to determine the amount of pure hydrogen peroxide in the bottle.

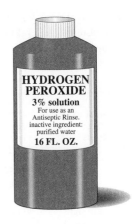

52. TIPPING   When paying with a Visa card, the user must fill in the amount of the gratuity (tip) and then compute the total. Complete the sales receipt if a 15% tip, rounded up to the nearest dollar, is to be left for the waiter.

STEAK STAMPEDE
Bloomington, MN
Server #12\ AT

VISA	67463777288
NAME	DALTON/ LIZ
AMOUNT	$75.18
GRATUITY $	_____
TOTAL $	_____

53. FEDERAL OUTLAYS   The **circle graph** shows the breakdown of the U.S. federal budget for fiscal year 2001. If total spending was approximately $1,900 billion, how much was paid for Social Security, Medicare, and other retirement programs?

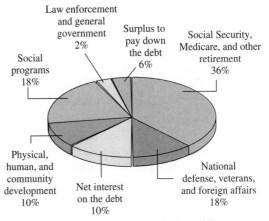

Based on 2002 Federal Income Tax Form 1040

54. INCOME TAX   Use the tax table to compute the amount of federal income tax if the amount of taxable income entered on Form 1040, line 40, is $39,909.

If the amount on Form 1040, line 40, is: Over—	But not over—	Enter on Form 1040, line 41	of the amount over—
$0	$7,000	.... 10%	$0
7,000	28,400	$700.00 + 15%	7,000
28,400	68,800	3,910.00 + 25%	28,400
68,800	143,500	14,010.00 + 28%	68,800
143,500	311,950	34,926.00 + 33%	143,500
311,950	....	90,514.50 + 35%	311,950

55. COLLEGE ENTRANCE EXAMS   On the Scholastic Aptitude Test, or SAT, a high school senior scored 550 on the mathematics portion and 700 on the verbal portion. What percent of the maximum 1,600 points did this student receive?

56. GENEALOGY   Through an extensive computer search, a genealogist determined that worldwide, 180 out of every 10 million people had his last name. What percent is this?

57. DENTAL RECORDS   On the dental chart for an adult patient, the dentist marks each tooth that has had a filling. To the nearest percent, what percent of this patient's teeth have fillings?

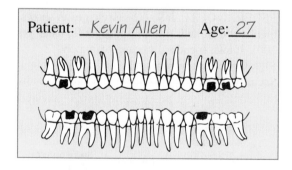

Patient: _Kevin Allen_   Age: _27_

58. AREAS   The total area of the 50 states and the District of Columbia is 3,618,770 square miles. If Alaska covers 591,004 square miles, what percent is this of the U.S. total (to the nearest percent)?

59. CHILD CARE   After the first day of registration, 84 children had been enrolled in a new day care center. That represented 70% of the available slots. What was the maximum number of children the center could enroll?

60. RACING PROGRAMS   One month before a stock car race, the sale of ads for the official race program was slow. Only 12 pages, or just 60% of the available pages, had been sold. What was the total number of pages devoted to advertising in the program?

61. NUTRITION   The Nutrition Facts label from a can of clam chowder is shown.
   a. Find the number of grams of saturated fat in one serving. What percent of a person's recommended daily intake is this?

Nutrition Facts
Serving Size 1 cup (240mL)
Servings Per Container about 2

Amount per serving	
Calories 240 Calories from Fat 140	

	% Daily Value*
Total Fat 15 g	**23%**
Saturated Fat 5 g	**25%**
Cholesterol 10 mg	**3%**
Sodium 980 mg	**41%**
Total Carbohydrate 21 g	**7%**
Dietary Fiber 2 g	**8%**
Sugars 1 g	
Protein 7 g	

   b. Determine the recommended number of grams of saturated fat that a person should consume daily.

62. CUSTOMER GUARANTEES   To assure its customers of low prices, the Home Club offers a "10% Plus" guarantee. If the customer finds the same item selling for less somewhere else, he or she receives the difference in price plus 10% of the difference. A woman bought miniblinds at the Home Club for $120 but later saw the same blinds on sale for $98 at another store. How much can she expect to be reimbursed?

63. EXPORTS   The bar graph shows United States exports to Mexico for the years 1992 through 2001. Between what two years was there the greatest percent of decrease in exports?

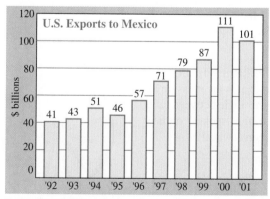

Based on data from www.census.gov/foreign-trade

64. AUCTIONS A pearl necklace of former First Lady Jacqueline Kennedy Onassis, originally valued at $700, was sold at auction in 1996 for $211,500. What was the percent of increase in the value of the necklace? (Round to the nearest percent.)

65. INSURANCE COSTS A college student's good grades earned her a student discount on her car insurance premium. What was the percent of decrease, to the nearest percent, if her annual premium was lowered from $1,050 to $925?

66. U.S. LIFE EXPECTANCY Use the following life expectancy data for 1900 and 2000 to determine the percent of increase for males and for females. Round to the nearest percent.

Years of life expected at birth		
	Male	Female
1900	46.3 yr	48.3 yr
2000	74.1 yr	79.5 yr

WRITING

67. Explain the relationship in a percent problem between the amount, the percent, and the base.

68. Write a real-life situation that could be described by "9 is what percent of 20?"

69. Explain why 150% of a number is more than the number.

70. Explain why "Find 9% of 100" is an easy problem to solve.

REVIEW

71. Divide: $-\dfrac{16}{25} \div \left(-\dfrac{4}{15}\right)$.

72. What two numbers are a distance of 8 away from 4 on the number line?

73. Is -34 a solution of $x + 15 = -49$?

74. Evaluate: $2 + 3[24 - 2(2 - 5)]$.

CHALLENGE PROBLEMS

75. SOAP A soap advertises itself as $99\frac{44}{100}\%$ pure. First, tell what percent of the soap is impurities. Then express your answer as a decimal.

76. Express $\frac{1}{20}$ of 1% as a percent using decimal notation.

2.3 Simplifying Algebraic Expressions

• Simplifying Products   • The Distributive Property   • Like Terms
• Combining Like Terms

In algebra, we frequently replace one algebraic expression with another that is equivalent and simpler in form. That process, called *simplifying an algebraic expression,* often involves the use of one or more properties of real numbers.

■ SIMPLIFYING PRODUCTS

Recall that the associative property of multiplication enables us to change the grouping of factors involved in a multiplication. The commutative property of multiplication enables us to change the order of the factors. These properties can be used to simplify certain products. For example, let's simplify $8(4x)$.

$$8(4x) = 8 \cdot (4 \cdot x) \quad \text{\small 4x = 4 · x.}$$
$$= (8 \cdot 4) \cdot x \quad \text{\small Use the associative property of multiplication to group 4 with 8.}$$
$$= 32x \quad \text{\small Do the multiplication within the parentheses.}$$

We have found that $8(4x) = 32x$. We say that $8(4x)$ and $32x$ are **equivalent expressions** because for each value of x, they represent the same number.

If x = 10	*If x = −3*
$8(4x) = 8[4(10)]$ $32x = 32(10)$	$8(4x) = 8[4(−3)]$ $32x = 32(−3)$
$= 8(40)$ $= 320$	$= 8(−12)$ $= −96$
$= 320$	$= −96$

EXAMPLE 1

Simplify each expression: **a.** $−9(3b)$, **b.** $15a(6)$, **c.** $35\left(\dfrac{4}{5}x\right)$, **d.** $\dfrac{8}{3}\cdot\dfrac{3}{8}r$, and **e.** $3(7p)(−5)$.

Solution

a. $−9(3b) = −27b$

b. $15a(6) = 90a$ Use the commutative property of multiplication to reorder the factors.

The Language of Algebra

Two of the most often encountered instructions in algebra are *simplify* and *solve*. Remember that we *simplify* expressions and we *solve* equations.

---

c. $35\left(\dfrac{4}{5}x\right) = \left(35\cdot\dfrac{4}{5}\right)x$ Use the associative property of multiplication to regroup the factors.

$\phantom{35\left(\dfrac{4}{5}x\right)} = 28x$ Factor 35 as $5 \cdot 7$ to do the multiplication.

d. $\dfrac{8}{3}\cdot\dfrac{3}{8}r = \left(\dfrac{8}{3}\cdot\dfrac{3}{8}\right)r$ Use the associative property of multiplication to regroup the factors.

$\phantom{\dfrac{8}{3}\cdot\dfrac{3}{8}r} = 1r$ Multiply.

$\phantom{\dfrac{8}{3}\cdot\dfrac{3}{8}r} = r$ Simplify.

e. $3(7p)(−5) = −105p$ Use the commutative property of multiplication to reorder the factors.

Self Check 1   Multiply: **a.** $9 \cdot 6s$, **b.** $36\left(\dfrac{2}{9}y\right)$, **c.** $\dfrac{2}{3}\cdot\dfrac{3}{2}m$, and **d.** $−4(6u)(−2)$.

■ THE DISTRIBUTIVE PROPERTY

Another property that is used to simplify algebraic expressions is the **distributive property**. To introduce it, we will evaluate $4(5 + 3)$ in two ways.

Method 1   *Order of operations:*   Compute the sum within the parentheses first.

$4(5 + 3) = 4(8)$

$ = 32$ Do the multiplication.

Method 2   *The distributive property:*   Multiply 5 and 3 by 4 and then add the results.

$4(5 + 3) = 4(5) + 4(3)$ Distribute the multiplication by 4.

$ = 20 + 12$ Do the multiplications.

$ = 32$

Each method gives a result of 32. This observation suggests the following property.

The Distributive Property   For any real numbers a, b, and c,

$$a(b + c) = ab + ac$$

The Language of Algebra

Formally, it is called the distributive property of multiplication over addition. When we use it to write a product, such as $5(x + 2)$ as a sum, $5x + 10$, we say that we have *removed* or *cleared* the parentheses.

To illustrate one use of the distributive property, let's consider the expression $5(x + 2)$. Since we are not given the value of x, we cannot add x and 2 within the parentheses. However, we can distribute the multiplication by the factor of 5 that is outside the parentheses to x and to 2 and add those products.

$$5(x + 2) = 5(x) + 5(2) \quad \text{Distribute the multiplication by 5.}$$
$$= 5x + 10$$

Since subtraction is the same as adding the opposite, the distributive property also holds for subtraction.

$$a(b - c) = ab - ac$$

EXAMPLE 2   Use the distributive property to remove parentheses: **a.** $6(a + 9)$,   **b.** $3(3b - 8)$,   **c.** $-12(a + 1)$,   **d.** $-6(-3y - 8)$,   and   **e.** $15\left(\frac{x}{3} + \frac{2}{5}\right)$.

Solution   **a.** $6(a + 9) = 6 \cdot a + 6 \cdot 9 \quad \text{Distribute the multiplication by 6.}$
$$= 6a + 54$$

The Language of Algebra

We read $6(a + 9)$ as "six times the *quantity* of a plus nine." The word *quantity* alerts us to the grouping symbols in the expression.

b. $3(3b - 8) = 3(3b) - 3(8) \quad \text{Distribute the multiplication by 3.}$
$$= 9b - 24 \quad \text{Do the multiplications.}$$

c. $-12(a + 1) = -12(a) + (-12)(1) \quad \text{Distribute the multiplication by } -12.$
$$= -12a - 12$$

d. $-6(-3y - 8) = -6(-3y) - (-6)(8) \quad \text{Distribute the multiplication by } -6.$
$$= 18y + 48$$

e. $15\left(\frac{x}{3} + \frac{2}{5}\right) = 15 \cdot \frac{x}{3} + 15 \cdot \frac{2}{5} \quad \text{Distribute the multiplication by 15.}$
$$= 5x + 6$$

Self Check 2   Use the distributive property to remove parentheses: **a.** $5(p + 2)$,   **b.** $4(2x - 1)$,   **c.** $-8(2x - 4)$,   and   **d.** $24\left(\frac{y}{6} + \frac{3}{8}\right)$.

Caution   The distributive property does not apply to every expression that contains parentheses—only those where multiplication is distributed over addition (or subtraction). For example, to simplify $6(5x)$, we do not use the distributive property.

Correct	*Incorrect*
$6(5x) = (6 \cdot 5)x = 30x$	$6(5x) = 30 \cdot 6x = 180x$

The distributive property can be extended to several other useful forms. Since multiplication is commutative:

$$(b + c)a = ba + ca \qquad\qquad (b - c)a = ba - ca$$

For situations in which there are more than two terms within parentheses:

$$a(b + c + d) = ab + ac + ad \qquad a(b - c - d) = ab - ac - ad$$

EXAMPLE 3

Multiply: **a.** $(6x + 4y)\dfrac{1}{2}$,   **b.** $2(a - 3b)8$,   and   **c.** $-0.3(3a - 4b + 7)$.

Solution   **a.** $(6x + 4y)\dfrac{1}{2} = (6x)\dfrac{1}{2} + (4y)\dfrac{1}{2}$ Distribute the multiplication by $\dfrac{1}{2}$.

$$= 3x + 2y \qquad\qquad\text{Do the multiplications.}$$

b. $2(a - 3b)8 = 2 \cdot 8(a - 3b)$ Use the commutative property of multiplication to reorder the factors.

$$= 16(a - 3b) \qquad\text{Do the multiplication.}$$

$$= 16a - 48b \qquad\text{Distribute the multiplication by 16.}$$

c. $-0.3(3a - 4b + 7) = -0.3(3a) - (-0.3)(4b) + (-0.3)(7)$ Distribute the multiplication by -0.3.

$$= -0.9a + 1.2b - 2.1 \qquad\text{Do the three multiplications.}$$

Self Check 3   Multiply: **a.** $(-6x - 24y)\dfrac{1}{3}$,   **b.** $6(c - 2d)9$,   **c.** $-0.7(2r + 5s - 8)$

Success Tip

Note that distributing the multiplication by -1 changes the sign of each term within the parentheses.

We can use the distributive property to find the opposite of a sum. For example, to find $-(x + 10)$, we interpret the $-$ symbol as a factor of -1, and proceed as follows:

$$-(x + 10) = -1(x + 10) \qquad\text{Replace the } - \text{ symbol with } -1.$$

$$= -1(x) + (-1)(10) \qquad\text{Distribute the multiplication by } -1.$$

$$= -x - 10 \qquad\qquad\text{Multiply.}$$

In general, we have the following property of real numbers.

The Opposite of a Sum   The opposite of a sum is the sum of the opposites. For any real numbers a and b,

$$-(a + b) = -a + (-b)$$

EXAMPLE 4

Simplify: $-(-9s - 3)$.

Solution $-(-9s - 3) = -1(-9s - 3)$ Replace the $-$ symbol in front of the parentheses with -1.

$$= -1(-9s) - (-1)(3) \qquad\text{Distribute the multiplication by } -1.$$

$$= 9s + 3$$

Self Check 4   Simplify: $-(-5x + 18)$.

■ LIKE TERMS

The distributive property can be used to simplify certain sums and differences. But before we can discuss this, we need to introduce some new vocabulary.

Like Terms	**Like terms** are terms with exactly the same variables raised to exactly the same powers. Any constant terms in an expression are considered to be like terms. Terms that are not like terms are called **unlike terms.**

Here are several examples.

Like terms	*Unlike terms*	
$4x$ and $7x$	$4x$ and $7y$	Different variables
$-10p^2$ and $25p^2$	$-10p$ and $25p^2$	Same variable, different powers
$\frac{1}{3}c^3d$ and c^3d	$\frac{1}{3}c^3d$ and c^3	Different variables

EXAMPLE 5

List the like terms in each expression: **a.** $7r + 5 + 3r$,   **b.** $6x^4 - 6x^2 - 6x$,   and   **c.** $-17m^3 + 3 - 2 + m^3$.

Solution   **a.** $7r + 5 + 3r$ contains the like terms $7r$ and $3r$.

b. $6x^4 - 6x^2 - 6x$ contains no like terms.

c. $-17m^3 + 3 - 2 + m^3$ contains two pairs of like terms: $-17m^3$ and m^3 are like terms, and the constant terms, 3 and -2, are like terms.

Self Check 5   List the like terms: **a.** $5x - 2y + 7y$ and   **b.** $-5p^2 - 12 + 17p^2 + 2$.

■ COMBINING LIKE TERMS

To add or subtract objects, they must have the same units. For example, we can add dollars to dollars and inches to inches, but we cannot add dollars to inches. When simplifying algebraic expressions, we can only add or subtract like terms.

Success Tip

When looking for like terms, don't look at the coefficients of the terms. Consider only the variable factors of each term.

This expression can be simplified, because it contains like terms.
$$3x + 4x$$

This expression cannot be simplified, because its terms are not like terms.
$$3x + 4y$$

Recall that the distributive property can be written in the following forms:

$$(b + c)a = ba + ca \qquad (b - c)a = ba - ca$$

We can use these forms of the distributive property in reverse to simplify a sum or difference of like terms. For example, we can simplify $3x + 4x$ as follows:

$$3x + 4x = (3 + 4)x$$
$$= 7x$$

We can simplify $15m^2 - 9m^2$ in a similar way:

$$15m^2 - 9m^2 = (15 - 9)m^2$$
$$= 6m^2$$

In each case, we say that we *combined like terms*. These examples suggest the following general rule.

Combining Like Terms   To add or subtract like terms, combine their coefficients and keep the same variables with the same exponents.

EXAMPLE 6   Simplify each expression, if possible: **a.** $-2x + 11x$,   **b.** $-8p + (-2p) + 4p$,   **c.** $0.5s^2 - 0.3s^2$,   and   **d.** $4w + 6$.

Solution   **a.** $-2x + 11x = 9x$ Think: $(-2 + 11)x = 9x$.
b. $-8p + (-2p) + 4p = -6p$ Think: $[-8 + (-2) + 4]p = -6p$.
c. $0.5s^2 - 0.3s^2 = 0.2s^2$ Think: $(0.5 - 0.3)s^2 = 0.2s^2$.
d. Since $4w$ and 6 are not like terms, they cannot be combined.

Self Check 6   Simplify, if possible: **a.** $-3x + 5x$,   **b.** $-6y + (-6y) + 9y$,   **c.** $4.4s^4 - 3.9s^4$,   and   **d.** $4a - 2$.

EXAMPLE 7   Simplify by combining like terms: **a.** $16t - 15t$,   **b.** $16t - t$,   **c.** $15t - 16t$,   and   **d.** $16t + t$.

Solution   **a.** $16t - 15t = t$ Think: $(16 - 15)t = 1t = t$.
b. $16t - t = 15t$ Think: $16t - 1t = (16 - 1)t = 15t$.
c. $15t - 16t = -t$ Think: $(15 - 16)t = -1t = -t$.
d. $16t + t = 17t$ Think: $16t + 1t = (16 + 1)t = 17t$.

Self Check 7   Simplify: **a.** $9h - h$,   **b.** $9h + h$,   **c.** $9h - 8h$,   and   **d.** $8h - 9h$.

EXAMPLE 8   Simplify: $6t - 8 - 4t + 1$.

Solution   We combine the like terms that involve the variable t and we combine the constant terms.

Think: $(6 - 4)t = 2t$

$$6t - 8 - 4t + 1 = 2t - 7$$

Think: $-8 + 1 = -7$

Self Check 8   Simplify: $50 + 70a - 60 - 10a$.

EXAMPLE 9   Simplify: $4(x + 5) - 5 - (2x - 4)$.

Solution   To simplify, we use the distributive property and combine like terms.

$$4(x + 5) - 5 - (2x - 4) = 4(x + 5) - 5 - 1(2x - 4)$$
$$= 4x + 20 - 5 - 2x + 4 \qquad \text{Distribute the multiplication}$$
$$\text{by 4 and } -1.$$
$$= 2x + 19 \qquad \text{Simplify.}$$

Self Check 9   Simplify: $6(3y - 1) + 2 - (-3y + 4)$.

Answers to Self Checks   **1. a.** $54s$,   **b.** $8y$,   **c.** m,   **d.** $48u$ **2. a.** $5p + 10$,   **b.** $8x + 4$,   **c.** $-16x + 32$,
d. $4y + 9$ **3. a.** $-2x - 8y$,   **b.** $54c - 108d$,   **c.** $-1.4r - 3.5s + 5.6$ **4.** $5x - 18$
5. a. $-2y$ and $7y$ **b.** $-5p^2$ and $17p^2$; -12 and 2 **6. a.** $2x$,   **b.** $-3y$,   **c.** $0.5s^4$,
d. $4a - 2$ **7. a.** $8h$,   **b.** $10h$,   **c.** h,   **d.** $-h$ **8.** $60a - 10$ **9.** $21y - 8$

2.3   STUDY SET

VOCABULARY   Fill in the blanks.

1. We can use the associative property of multiplication to _____ the expression $5(6x)$.

2. The _____ property of multiplication allows us to reorder factors. The _____ property of multiplication allows us to regroup factors.

3. We simplify _____ and we solve _____.

4. We can use the _____ property to remove or clear parentheses in the expression $2(x + 8)$.

5. We call $-(c + 9)$ the _____ of a sum.

6. Terms such as $7x^2$ and $5x^2$, which have the same variables raised to exactly the same exponents, are called _____ terms.

7. The _____ of the term $-23y$ is -23.

8. When we write $9x + x$ as $10x$, we say we have _____ like terms.

CONCEPTS

9. Fill in the blanks to simplify each product.
a. $5 \cdot 6t = (\quad \cdot \quad)t = \quad t$
b. $-8(2x)(4) = (\quad \cdot \quad \cdot \quad)x = \quad x$

10. Fill in the blanks.
a. $a(b + c) = ab +$ ____   **b.** $a(b - c) =$ ____ $- ac$
c. $(b + c)a = ba +$ ____   **d.** $(b - c)a =$ ____ $- ca$
e. $a(b + c + d) =$ ____ $+ ac +$ ____
f. $-(a + b) = -a +$ ____

11. Consider $3(x + 6)$. Why can't we add x and 6 within the parentheses?

12. Fill in the blanks.
a. $2(x + 4) = 2x \quad 8$
b. $2(x - 4) = 2x \quad 8$
c. $-2(x + 4) = -2x \quad 8$
d. $-2(-x - 4) = 2x \quad 8$

13. Fill in the blanks.

$$-(x + 10) = \quad (x + 10)$$

Distributing the multiplication by -1 changes the _____ of each term within the parentheses.

14. Consider $33x - 8x^2 - 21x + 6$. Identify the terms of the expression and the coefficient of each term.

15. For each expression, identify any like terms.
a. $3a + 8 + 2a$ **b.** $10 - 13h + 12$
c. $3x^2 + 3x + 3$ **d.** $9y^2 - 9m - 8y^2$

16. Complete this statement: To add like terms, add their _____ and keep the same _____ and exponents.

17. Fill in the blanks to combine like terms.
a. $4m + 6m = (\quad)m = \quad m$
b. $30n - 50n = (\quad)n = \quad n$
c. $12 - 32d + 15 = -32d +$ ____

18. Simplify each expression, if possible.

   a. $5(2x)$ and $5 + 2x$

   b. $6(-7x)$ and $6 - 7x$

   c. $2(3x)(3)$ and $2 + 3x + 3$

NOTATION   Complete each solution.

19. Translate to symbols.

   a. Six times the quantity of h minus four.

   b. The opposite of the sum of z and sixteen.

20. Write an equivalent expression for the given expression using fewer symbols.

   a. $1x$ **b.** $-1d$ **c.** $0m$

   d. $5x - (-1)$ **e.** $16t + (-6)$

21. A student compared her answers to six homework problems to the answers in the back of the book. Are her answers equivalent? Write *yes* or *no*.

Student's answer	Book's answer	Equivalent?
$10x$	$10 + x$	
$3 + y$	$y + 3$	
$5 - 8a$	$8a - 5$	
$3x + 4$	$3(x + 4)$	
$3 - 2x$	$-2x + 3$	
$h^2 + (-16)$	$h^2 - 16$	

22. Draw arrows to illustrate how we distribute the factor outside the parentheses over the terms within the parentheses.

   a. $8(6g + 7)$ **b.** $(4x^2 - x + 6)2$

PRACTICE   Simplify each expression.

23. $9(7m)$ **24.** $12n(8)$

25. $5(-7q)$ **26.** $-7(5t)$

27. $5t \cdot 60$ **28.** $70a \cdot 10$

29. $(-5.6x)(-2)$ **30.** $(-4.4x)(-3)$

31. $\dfrac{5}{3} \cdot \dfrac{3}{5}g$ **32.** $\dfrac{9}{7} \cdot \dfrac{7}{9}k$

33. $12\left(\dfrac{5}{12}x\right)$ **34.** $15\left(\dfrac{4}{15}w\right)$

35. $8\left(\dfrac{3}{4}y\right)$ **36.** $27\left(\dfrac{2}{3}x\right)$

37. $-\dfrac{15}{4}\left(-\dfrac{4s}{15}\right)$ **38.** $-\dfrac{50}{3}\left(-\dfrac{3h}{50}\right)$

39. $24\left(-\dfrac{5}{6}r\right)$ **40.** $\dfrac{3}{4} \cdot \dfrac{1}{2}g$

41. $5(4c)(3)$ **42.** $9(2h)(2)$

43. $-4(-6)(-4m)$ **44.** $-5(-9)(-4n)$

Remove parentheses, and simplify.

45. $5(x + 3)$ **46.** $4(x + 2)$

47. $6(6c - 7)$ **48.** $9(9d - 3)$

49. $(3t + 2)8$ **50.** $(2q + 1)9$

51. $0.4(x - 4)$ **52.** $-2.2(2q + 1)$

53. $-5(-t - 1)$ **54.** $-8(-r - 1)$

55. $-4(3x + 5)$ **56.** $-4(6r + 4)$

57. $(13c - 3)(-6)$ **58.** $(10s - 11)(-2)$

59. $-\dfrac{2}{3}(3w - 6)$ **60.** $\dfrac{1}{2}(2y - 8)$

61. $45\left(\dfrac{x}{5} + \dfrac{2}{9}\right)$ **62.** $35\left(\dfrac{y}{5} + \dfrac{8}{7}\right)$

63. $60\left(\dfrac{3}{20}r - \dfrac{4}{15}\right)$ **64.** $72\left(\dfrac{7}{8}f - \dfrac{8}{9}\right)$

65. $-(x - 7)$ **66.** $-(y + 1)$

67. $-(-5.6y + 7)$ **68.** $-(-4.8a - 3)$

69. $2(4d + 5)5$ **70.** $4(2w + 3)5$

71. $-6(r + 5)2$ **72.** $-7(b + 3)3$

73. $-(-x - y + 5)$ **74.** $-(-14 + 3p - t)$

75. $5(1.2x - 4.2y - 3.2z)$

76. $5(2.4a + 5.4b - 6.4c)$

Simplify each expression.

77. $3x + 17x$ **78.** $12y - 15y$

79. $-4x + 4x$ **80.** $-16y + 16y$

81. $-7b^2 + 7b^2$ **82.** $-2c^3 + 2c^3$

83. $13r - 12r$ **84.** $25s + s$

85. $36y + y$

86. $32a - a$

87. $43s^3 - 44s^3$

88. $8j^3 - 9j^3$

89. $23w + 5 - 23w$

90. $19x + 3 - 19x$

91. $-4r - 7r + 2r - r$

92. $-v - 3v + 6v + 2v$

93. $a + a + a$

94. $t - t - t - t$

95. $0 - 3x$

96. $0 - 4a$

97. $3x + 5x - 7x$

98. $-5.7m + 4.3m$

99. $\dfrac{3}{5}t + \dfrac{1}{5}t$

100. $\dfrac{3}{16}x - \dfrac{5}{16}x$

101. $-0.2r - (-0.6r)$

102. $-1.1m - (-2.4m)$

103. $2z + 5(z - 3)$

104. $12(m + 11) - 11$

105. $3x + 4 - 5x + 1$

106. $4b + 9 - 9b + 9$

107. $10(2d - 7) + 4$

108. $5(3x - 2) + 5$

109. $-(c + 7) - 2(c - 3)$

110. $-(z + 2) + 5(3 - z)$

111. $2(s - 7) - (s - 2)$

112. $4(d - 3) - (d - 1)$

113. $6 - 4(-3c - 7)$

114. $10 - 5(-5g - 1)$

115. $36\left(\dfrac{2}{9}x - \dfrac{3}{4}\right) + 36\left(\dfrac{1}{2}\right)$

116. $40\left(\dfrac{3}{8}y - \dfrac{1}{4}\right) + 40\left(\dfrac{4}{5}\right)$

APPLICATIONS

117. THE AMERICAN RED CROSS
In 1891, Clara Barton founded the
Red Cross. Its symbol is a white
flag bearing a red cross. If each
side of the cross has length x, write
an algebraic expression for the
perimeter of the cross.

118. BILLIARDS   Billiard tables vary in size, but all
tables are twice as long as they are wide.
a. If the billiard table is x feet wide, write an
expression involving x that represents its length.

b. Write an expression for the perimeter of the
table.

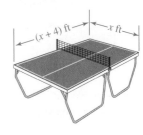

119. PING-PONG   Write an
expression for the
perimeter of the Ping-
Pong table.

120. SEWING   Write an expression for the length of the
yellow trim needed to outline a pennant with the
given side lengths.

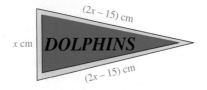

WRITING

121. Explain why the distributive property applies to
$2(3 + x)$ but not to $2(3x)$.

122. Tell how to combine like terms.

REVIEW   **Evaluate each expression for $x = -3$,
$y = -5$, and $z = 0$.**

123. $x^2z(y^3 - z)$

124. $\left| y^3 - z \right|$

125. $\dfrac{x - y^2}{2y - 1 + x}$

126. $\dfrac{2y + 1}{x} - x$

CHALLENGE PROBLEMS

127. The quantities below do not have the same units and
cannot be added as shown. Is there a way to find the
sum? If so, what is it?

$$2 \text{ inches} + 2 \text{ feet} + 2 \text{ yards}$$

128. Fill in the blanks: $\boxed{}\left(\boxed{} - \boxed{}\right) = -75x + 40.$

Simplify.

129. $-2[x + 4(2x + 1)]$

130. $-5[y + 2(3y + 4)]$

2.4   More about Solving Equations

- Using More Than One Property of Equality
- Simplifying Expressions to Solve Equations   • Identities and Contradictions

We have solved simple equations by using properties of equality. We will now expand our equation-solving skills by considering more complicated equations. The objective is to develop a general strategy that we can use to solve any kind of *linear equation in one variable*.

Linear Equation in One Variable	A **linear equation in one variable** can be written in the form $$ax + b = c$$ where a, b, and c are real numbers and $a \neq 0$.

■ USING MORE THAN ONE PROPERTY OF EQUALITY

Sometimes we must use several properties of equality to solve an equation. For example, on the left-hand side of $2x + 6 = 10$, the variable is multiplied by 2, and then 6 is added to that product. To isolate x, we use the order of operations rules in reverse. First, we undo the addition of 6, and then we undo the multiplication by 2.

$$2x + 6 = 10$$
$$2x + 6 - 6 = 10 - 6 \qquad \text{To undo the addition of 6, subtract 6 from both sides.}$$
$$2x = 4 \qquad \text{Do the subtractions.}$$
$$\frac{2x}{2} = \frac{4}{2} \qquad \text{To undo the multiplication by 2, divide both sides by 2.}$$
$$x = 2$$

The solution is 2.

EXAMPLE 1

Solve: $-12x + 5 = 17$.

Solution   On the left-hand side of the equation, x is multiplied by -12, and then 5 is added to that product. To isolate x, we undo the operations in the opposite order.

- To undo the addition of 5, we subtract 5 from both sides.
- To undo the multiplication by -12, we divide both sides by -12.

$$-12x + 5 = 17$$
$$-12x + 5 - 5 = 17 - 5 \qquad \text{Subtract 5 from both sides.}$$
$$-12x = 12 \qquad \text{Do the subtractions: } 5 - 5 = 0 \text{ and } 17 - 5 = 12.$$
$$\frac{-12x}{-12} = \frac{12}{-12} \qquad \text{Divide both sides by } -12.$$
$$x = -1 \qquad \text{Do the divisions.}$$

Caution
When checking solutions, always use the original equation.

Check:

$$-12x + 5 = 17$$

$$-12(-1) + 5 \stackrel{?}{=} 17 \quad \text{Substitute } -1 \text{ for } x.$$

$$12 + 5 \stackrel{?}{=} 17 \quad \text{Do the multiplication.}$$

$$17 = 17 \quad \text{True.}$$

The solution is -1.

Self Check 1   Solve: $8x - 13 = 43$.

EXAMPLE 2

Solve: $\dfrac{2x}{3} = -6$.

Solution   On the left-hand side, x is multiplied by 2, and then that product is divided by 3. To solve this equation, we must undo these operations in the opposite order.

- To undo the division of 3, we multiply both sides by 3.
- To undo the multiplication by 2, we divide both sides by 2.

$$\frac{2x}{3} = -6$$

$$3\left(\frac{2x}{3}\right) = 3(-6) \quad \text{Multiply both sides by 3.}$$

$$2x = -18 \quad \text{On the left-hand side: } 3\left(\frac{2x}{3}\right) = \frac{\cancel{3} \cdot 2 \cdot x}{\cancel{3}} = 2x.$$

$$\frac{2x}{2} = \frac{-18}{2} \quad \text{Divide both sides by 2.}$$

$$x = -9 \quad \text{Do the divisions.}$$

Check:

$$\frac{2x}{3} = -6$$

$$\frac{2(-9)}{3} \stackrel{?}{=} -6 \quad \text{Substitute } -9 \text{ for } x.$$

$$\frac{-18}{3} \stackrel{?}{=} -6 \quad \text{Do the multiplication.}$$

$$-6 = -6 \quad \text{True.}$$

The solution is -9.

Self Check 2   Solve: $\dfrac{7h}{16} = -14$.

Recall that the product of a number and its **reciprocal,** or **multiplicative inverse,** is 1. We can use this fact to solve the equation from Example 2 in a different way. Since $\frac{2x}{3}$ is the same as $\frac{2}{3}x$, the equation can be written

$$\frac{2}{3}x = -6 \quad \text{Note that the coefficient of } x \text{ is } \frac{2}{3}.$$

When the coefficient of the variable is a fraction, we can isolate the variable by multiplying both sides by the reciprocal.

$$\frac{3}{2}\left(\frac{2}{3}x\right) = \frac{3}{2}(-6)$$ Multiply both sides by the reciprocal of $\frac{2}{3}$, which is $\frac{3}{2}$.

$$\left(\frac{3}{2} \cdot \frac{2}{3}\right)x = \frac{3}{2}(-6)$$ On the left-hand side, regroup the factors.

$$1x = -9$$ Do the multiplications: $\frac{3}{2} \cdot \frac{2}{3} = 1$ and $\frac{3}{2}(-6) = -9$.

$$x = -9$$ Simplify.

EXAMPLE 3   Solve: $-\dfrac{5}{8}m - 2 = -12$.

Solution   The coefficient of m is the fraction $-\dfrac{5}{8}$. We proceed as follows.

- To undo the subtraction of 2, we add 2 to both sides.
- To undo the multiplication by $-\frac{5}{8}$, we multiply both sides by its reciprocal, $-\frac{8}{5}$.

$$-\frac{5}{8}m - 2 = -12$$

$$-\frac{5}{8}m - 2 + 2 = -12 + 2$$ Add 2 to both sides.

$$-\frac{5}{8}m = -10$$ Do the additions: $-2 + 2 = 0$ and $-12 + 2 = -10$.

$$-\frac{8}{5}\left(-\frac{5}{8}m\right) = -\frac{8}{5}(-10)$$ Multiply both sides by $-\frac{8}{5}$.

$$m = 16$$ On the left-hand side: $-\frac{8}{5}(-\frac{5}{8})m = 1m = m$.

On the right-hand side: $-\frac{8}{5}(-10) = \frac{8 \cdot 2 \cdot \overset{1}{\cancel{5}}}{\underset{1}{\cancel{5}}} = 16$.

Check that 16 is the solution.

Self Check 3   Solve: $\dfrac{7}{12}a - 6 = -27$.

EXAMPLE 4   Solve: $-0.2 = -0.8 - y$.

Solution   We begin by eliminating -0.8 from the right-hand side. We can do this by adding 0.8 to both sides.

$$-0.2 = -0.8 - y$$

$$-0.2 + \mathbf{0.8} = -0.8 - y + \mathbf{0.8}$$ Add 0.8 to both sides.

$$0.6 = -y$$ Do the additions.

Since the term $-y$ has an understood coefficient of -1, the equation can be rewritten as $0.6 = -1y$. To isolate y, either multiply both sides or divide both sides by -1.

Method 1

$$0.6 = -1y$$

$$-1(0.6) = -1(-1y) \quad \text{Multiply both sides by } -1.$$

$$-0.6 = y$$

Method 2

$$0.6 = -1y$$

$$\frac{0.6}{-1} = \frac{-1y}{-1} \quad \text{To undo the multiplication by } -1, \text{ divide both sides by } -1.$$

$$-0.6 = y$$

Check that -0.6 is the solution.

Self Check 4   Solve: $-6.6 - m = -2.7$.

■ SIMPLIFYING EXPRESSIONS TO SOLVE EQUATIONS

When solving equations, we should simplify the expressions that make up the left- and right-hand sides before applying any properties of equality. Often, that involves removing parentheses and/or combining like terms.

EXAMPLE 5

Solve: $3(k + 1) - 5k = 0$.

Solution

$$3(k + 1) - 5k = 0$$

$$3k + 3 - 5k = 0 \qquad \text{Distribute the multiplication by 3.}$$

$$-2k + 3 = 0 \qquad \text{Combine like terms: } 3k - 5k = -2k.$$

$$-2k + 3 - 3 = 0 - 3 \qquad \text{To undo the addition of 3, subtract 3 from both sides.}$$

$$-2k = -3 \qquad \text{Do the subtractions: } 3 - 3 = 0 \text{ and } 0 - 3 = -3.$$

$$\frac{-2k}{-2} = \frac{-3}{-2} \qquad \text{To undo the multiplication by } -2, \text{ divide both sides by } -2.$$

$$k = \frac{3}{2} \qquad \text{Simplify: } \frac{-3}{-2} = \frac{3}{2}.$$

Check:

$$3(k + 1) - 5k = 0$$

$$3\left(\frac{3}{2} + 1\right) - 5\left(\frac{3}{2}\right) \stackrel{?}{=} 0 \qquad \text{Substitute } \frac{3}{2} \text{ for } k.$$

$$3\left(\frac{5}{2}\right) - 5\left(\frac{3}{2}\right) \stackrel{?}{=} 0 \qquad \begin{array}{l}\text{Do the addition within the parentheses.} \\ \text{Think of 1 as } \frac{2}{2} \text{ and then add: } \frac{3}{2} + \frac{2}{2} = \frac{5}{2}.\end{array}$$

$$\frac{15}{2} - \frac{15}{2} \stackrel{?}{=} 0 \qquad \text{Do the multiplications.}$$

$$0 = 0 \qquad \text{True.}$$

The solution is $\frac{3}{2}$.

Self Check 5   Solve: $-5(x - 3) + 3x = 11$.

EXAMPLE 6

Solve: $3x - 15 = 4x + 36$.

Solution

To solve for x, all the terms containing x must be on the same side of the equation. We can eliminate $3x$ from the left-hand side by subtracting $3x$ from both sides.

Success Tip

We could have eliminated $4x$ from the right-hand side by subtracting $4x$ from both sides:

$3x - 15 - 4x = 4x + 36 - 4x$
$\quad -x - 15 = 36$

However, it is usually easier to isolate the variable term on the side that will result in a *positive* coefficient.

$$3x - 15 = 4x + 36$$
$$3x - 15 - 3x = 4x + 36 - 3x \qquad \text{Subtract } 3x \text{ from both sides.}$$
$$-15 = x + 36 \qquad \text{Combine like terms: } 3x - 3x = 0 \text{ and } 4x - 3x = x.$$
$$-15 - 36 = x + 36 - 36 \qquad \text{To undo the addition of 36, subtract 36 from both sides.}$$
$$-51 = x \qquad \text{Do the subtractions.}$$

Check:
$$3x - 15 = 4x + 36$$
$$3(-51) - 15 \stackrel{?}{=} 4(-51) + 36 \qquad \text{Substitute } -51 \text{ for } x.$$
$$-153 - 15 \stackrel{?}{=} -204 + 36 \qquad \text{Do the multiplications.}$$
$$-168 = -168 \qquad \text{True.}$$

The solution is -51.

Self Check 6

Solve: $30 + 6n = 4n - 2$.

Equations are usually easier to solve if they don't involve fractions. We can use the multiplication property of equality to *clear* an equation of fractions by multiplying both sides of the equation by the least common denominator.

EXAMPLE 7

Solve: $\dfrac{x}{6} + \dfrac{5}{2} = \dfrac{1}{3}$.

Solution

To clear the equation of fractions, we multiply both sides by the LCD, 6.

Success Tip

Before multiplying both sides of an equation by the LCD, enclose the left-hand side and enclose the right-hand side with parentheses:

$$\left(\frac{x}{6} + \frac{5}{2}\right) = \left(\frac{1}{3}\right)$$

$$\frac{x}{6} + \frac{5}{2} = \frac{1}{3}$$

$$6\left(\frac{x}{6} + \frac{5}{2}\right) = 6\left(\frac{1}{3}\right) \qquad \text{Multiply both sides by the LCD of } \frac{x}{6}, \frac{5}{2}, \text{ and } \frac{1}{3}, \text{ which is 6. The parentheses are used to show that both } \frac{x}{6} \text{ and } \frac{5}{2} \text{ must be multiplied by 6.}$$

$$6\left(\frac{x}{6}\right) + 6\left(\frac{5}{2}\right) = 6\left(\frac{1}{3}\right) \qquad \text{On the left-hand side, distribute the multiplication by 6.}$$

$$x + 15 = 2 \qquad \text{Simplify.}$$

$$x + 15 - 15 = 2 - 15 \qquad \text{To undo the addition of 15, subtract 15 from both sides.}$$

$$x = -13$$

Check that -13 is the solution.

Self Check 7

Solve: $\dfrac{x}{4} + \dfrac{1}{2} = -\dfrac{1}{8}$.

The preceding examples suggest the following strategy for solving equations.

Strategy for Solving Equations	1. Clear the equation of fractions.
	2. Use the distributive property to remove parentheses, if necessary.
	3. Combine like terms, if necessary.
	4. Undo the operations of addition and subtraction to get the variables on one side and the constant terms on the other.
	5. Undo the operations of multiplication and division to isolate the variable.
	6. Check the result.

The next example illustrates an important point: not all of these steps are necessary to solve every equation.

EXAMPLE 8

Solve: $\dfrac{7m + 5}{5} = -4m + 1$.

Solution

$$\frac{7m + 5}{5} = -4m + 1$$

$$5\left(\frac{7m + 5}{5}\right) = 5(-4m + 1)$$ Clear the equation of the fraction by multiplying both sides by 5.

$$7m + 5 = -20m + 5$$ On the left-hand side, divide out the common factor of 5 in the numerator and denominator. On the right-hand side, distribute the multiplication by 5.

$$7m + 5 + 20m = -20m + 5 + 20m$$ To eliminate the term $-20m$ on the right-hand side, add $20m$ to both sides.

$$27m + 5 = 5$$ Combine like terms: $7m + 20m = 27m$ and $-20m + 20m = 0$.

$$27m + 5 - 5 = 5 - 5$$ To undo the addition of 5 on the left-hand side, subtract 5 from both sides.

$$27m = 0$$ Do the subtractions.

$$\frac{27m}{27} = \frac{0}{27}$$ To undo the multiplication by 27, divide both sides by 27.

$$m = 0$$ 0 divided by any nonzero number is 0.

Substitute 0 for m in $\dfrac{7m + 5}{5} = -4m + 1$ to check that the solution is 0.

Caution

Remember that when you multiply one side of an equation by a nonzero number, you must multiply the other side of the equation by the same number.

Self Check 8   Solve: $6c + 2 = \dfrac{-c + 18}{9}$.

■ IDENTITIES AND CONTRADICTIONS

Each of the equations in Examples 1 through 8 had exactly one solution. However, some equations have no solutions while others have infinitely many solutions.

An equation that is true for all values of its variable is called an **identity**. An example is

$$x + x = 2x$$ If we substitute -10 for x, we get the true statement $-20 = -20$. If we substitute 0 for x, we get $0 = 0$. If we substitute 7 for x, we get $14 = 14$, and so on.

It is apparent that in an identity, we can replace x with any number and the equation will be true. We say that $x + x = 2x$ has infinitely many solutions.

An equation that is not true for any values of its variable is called a **contradiction.** An example is

$$x = x + 1 \quad \text{No number is 1 greater than itself.}$$

We say that $x = x + 1$ has no solutions.

EXAMPLE 9   Solve: $3(x + 8) + 5x = 2(12 + 4x)$.

Solution

$3(x + 8) + 5x = 2(12 + 4x)$	
$3x + 24 + 5x = 24 + 8x$	Distribute the multiplication by 3 and by 2.
$8x + 24 = 24 + 8x$	Combine like terms: $3x + 5x = 8x$. Note that the sides of the equation are identical.
$8x + 24 - 8x = 24 + 8x - 8x$	To eliminate the term $8x$ on the right-hand side, subtract $8x$ from both sides.
$24 = 24$	Combine like terms: $8x - 8x = 0$.

The terms involving x drop out and the result, $24 = 24$, is true. This means that any number substituted for x in the original equation will yield a true statement. Therefore, every real number is a solution and this equation is an identity.

Self Check 9   Solve: $3(x + 5) - 4(x + 4) = -x - 1$.

EXAMPLE 10   Solve: $3(d + 7) - d = 2(d + 10)$.

Solution

$3(d + 7) - d = 2(d + 10)$	
$3d + 21 - d = 2d + 20$	Distribute the multiplication by 3 and by 2.
$2d + 21 = 2d + 20$	Combine like terms: $3d - d = 2d$.
$2d + 21 - 2d = 2d + 20 - 2d$	To eliminate the term $2d$ on the right-hand side, subtract $2d$ from both sides.
$21 = 20$	Combine like terms: $2d - 2d = 0$.

The Language of Algebra

Contradiction is a form of the word *contradict,* meaning conflicting ideas. During a trial, evidence might be introduced that *contradicts* the testimony of a witness.

The terms involving d drop out and the result, $21 = 20$, is false. This means that any number that is substituted for x in the original equation will yield a false statement. This equation has no solution and it is a contradiction.

Self Check 10   Solve: $-4(c - 3) + 2c = 2(10 - c)$.

Answers to Self Checks   **1.** 7   **2.** -32 **3.** -36 **4.** -3.9 **5.** 2   **6.** -16 **7.** $-\frac{5}{2}$ **8.** 0   **9.** all real numbers; this equation is an identity   **10.** no solution; this equation is a contradiction

2.4   STUDY SET

VOCABULARY   Fill in the blanks.

1. An equation is a statement indicating that two expressions are _____.

2. To _____ an equation means to find all of the values of the variable that make the equation a true statement.

3. After solving an equation, we can check our result by substituting that value for the variable in the _____ equation.

4. The product of a number and its _____ is 1.

5. An equation that is true for all values of its variable is called an _____.

6. An equation that is not true for any values of its variable is called a _____.

CONCEPTS   Fill in the blanks.

7. To solve the equation $2x - 7 = 21$, we first undo the _____ of 7 by adding 7 to both sides. Then we undo the _____ by 2 by dividing both sides by 2.

8. To solve the equation $\frac{x}{2} + 3 = 5$, we first undo the _____ of 3 by subtracting 3 from both sides. Then we undo the _____ by 2 by multiplying both sides by 2.

9. To solve $\frac{s}{3} + \frac{1}{4} = -\frac{1}{2}$, we can clear the equation of the fractions by _____ both sides by 12.

10. To solve $15d = -2(3d + 7) + 2$, we begin by using the _____ property to remove parentheses.

11. One method of solving $-\frac{4}{5}x = 8$ is to multiply both sides of the equation by the reciprocal of $-\frac{4}{5}$. What is the reciprocal of $-\frac{4}{5}$?

12. **a.** Combine like terms on the left-hand side of $6x - 8 - 8x = -24$.
    b. Combine like terms on the right-hand side of $5a + 1 = 9a + 16 + a$.
    c. Combine like terms on both sides of $12 - 3r + 5r = -8 - r - 2$.

13. Find the LCD of the fractions in the equation $\frac{x}{3} - \frac{4}{5} = \frac{1}{2}$.

14. Simplify: $20\left(\frac{3}{5}x\right)$.

15. What must you multiply both sides of $\frac{2}{3} - \frac{b}{2} = -\frac{4}{3}$ by to clear the equation of fractions?

16. **a.** Simplify: $3x + 5 - x$.
    b. Solve: $3x + 5 - x = 9$.
    c. Evaluate $3x + 5 - x$ for $x = 9$.
    d. Check: Is -1 a solution of $3x + 5 - x = 9$?

NOTATION   Complete the solution.

17.
$$2x - 7 = 21$$
$$2x - 7 + \boxed{} = 21 + \boxed{}$$
$$2x = \boxed{}$$
$$\frac{2x}{\boxed{}} = \frac{28}{\boxed{}}$$
$$x = 14$$

18. Identify the like terms on the right-hand side of $5(9a + 1) = a + 6 - 7a$.

19. Fill in the blanks.
    a. $-x = \boxed{} x$.   **b.** $\frac{3x}{5} = \boxed{} x$.

20. What does the symbol $\stackrel{?}{=}$ mean?

PRACTICE   Solve each equation and check all solutions.

21. $2x + 5 = 17$

22. $3x - 5 = 13$

23. $5q - 2 = 23$

24. $4p + 3 = 43$

25. $-33 = 5t + 2$

26. $-55 = 3w + 5$

27. $20 = -x$

28. $10 = -a$

29. $-g = -4$

30. $-u = -20$

31. $1.2 - x = -1.7$

31. $0.6 = 4.1 - x$

33. $-3p + 7 = -3$

34. $-2r + 8 = -1$

35. $0 - 2y = 8$

36. $0 - 7x = -21$

37. $-8 - 3c = 0$

38. $-5 - 2d = 0$

39. $\frac{5}{6}k = 10$

40. $\frac{2c}{5} = 2$

41. $-\frac{7}{16}h = 21$

42. $-\frac{5}{8}h = 15$

43. $-\frac{t}{3} + 2 = 6$

44. $\frac{x}{5} - 5 = -12$

45. $2(-3) + 4y = 14$

46. $4(-1) + 3y = 8$

47. $7(0) - 4y = 17$

48. $3x - 4(0) = 2$

49. $10.08 = 4(0.5x + 2.5)$

50. $-3.28 = 8(1.5y - 0.5)$

51. $-(4 - m) = -10$

52. $-(6 - t) = -12$

53. $15s + 8 - s = 7 + 1$

54. $-7t - 9 + t = -10 + 1$

55. $-3(2y - 2) - y = 5$

56. $-(3a + 1) + a = 2$

57. $3x - 8 - 4x - 7x = -2 - 8$

58. $-6t - 7t - 5t - 1 = 12 - 3$

59. $4(5b) + 2(6b - 1) = -34$

60. $2(3x) + 5(3x - 1) = 58$

61. $9(x + 11) + 5(13 - x) = 0$

62. $-(19 - 3s) - (8s + 1) = 35$

63. $60r - 50 = 15r - 5$

64. $100f - 75 = 50f + 75$

65. $8y - 3 = 4y + 15$

66. $7 + 3w = 4 + 9w$

67. $5x + 7.2 = 4x$

68. $3x + 2.5 = 2x$

69. $8y + 328 = 4y$

70. $9y + 369 = 6y$

71. $15x = x$

72. $7y = 8y$

73. $3(a + 2) = 2(a - 7)$

74. $9(t - 1) = 6(t + 2) - t$

75. $2 - 3(x - 5) = 4(x - 1)$

76. $2 - (4x + 7) = 3 + 2(x + 2)$

77. $\dfrac{x + 5}{3} = 11$

78. $\dfrac{x + 2}{13} = 3$

79. $\dfrac{y}{6} + \dfrac{y}{4} = -1$

80. $\dfrac{x}{3} + \dfrac{x}{4} = -2$

81. $-\dfrac{2}{9} = \dfrac{5x}{6} - \dfrac{1}{3}$

82. $\dfrac{2}{3} = -\dfrac{2x}{3} + \dfrac{3}{4}$

83. $\dfrac{2}{3}y + 2 = \dfrac{1}{5} + y$

84. $\dfrac{2}{5}x + 1 = \dfrac{1}{3} + x$

85. $-\dfrac{3}{4}n + 2n = \dfrac{1}{2}n + \dfrac{13}{3}$

86. $-\dfrac{5}{6}n - 3n = \dfrac{1}{3}n + \dfrac{11}{9}$

87. $\dfrac{10 - 5s}{3} = s$

88. $\dfrac{40 - 8s}{5} = -2s$

89. $\dfrac{5(1 - x)}{6} = -x$

90. $\dfrac{3(14 - u)}{8} = -3u$

91. $\dfrac{3(d - 8)}{4} = \dfrac{2(d + 1)}{3}$

92. $\dfrac{3(c - 2)}{2} = \dfrac{2(2c + 3)}{5}$

93. $\dfrac{1}{2}(x + 3) + \dfrac{3}{4}(x - 2) = x + 1$

94. $\dfrac{3}{2}(t + 2) + \dfrac{1}{6}(t + 2) = 2 + t$

95. $8x + 3(2 - x) = 5(x + 2) - 4$

96. $5(x + 2) = 5x - 2$

97. $-3(s + 2) = -2(s + 4) - s$

98. $21(b - 1) + 3 = 3(7b - 6)$

99. $2(3z + 4) = 2(3z - 2) + 13$

100. $x + 7 = \dfrac{2x + 6}{2} + 4$

101. $4(y - 3) - y = 3(y - 4)$

102. $5(x + 3) - 3x = 2(x + 8)$

Solve each equation.

103. $\dfrac{h}{709} - 23{,}898 = -19{,}678$

104. $9.35 - 1.4y = 7.32 + 1.5y$

WRITING

105. To solve $3x - 4 = 5x + 1$, one student began by subtracting $3x$ from both sides. Another student solved the same equation by first subtracting $5x$ from both sides. Will the students get the same solution? Explain why or why not.

106. What does it mean to clear an equation such as $\frac{1}{4} + \frac{x}{2} = \frac{3}{8}$ of the fractions?

107. Explain the error in the following solution.

Solve: $2x + 4 = 30$.

$$2x + 4 = 30$$
$$\dfrac{2x}{2} + 4 = \dfrac{30}{2}$$
$$x + 4 = 15$$
$$x + 4 - 4 = 15 - 4$$
$$x = 11$$

108. Write an equation that is an identity. Explain why every number is a solution.

REVIEW

109. Subtract: $-8 - (-8)$.

110. Add: $\dfrac{1}{8} + \dfrac{1}{8}$.

111. Multiply: $\dfrac{1}{8} \cdot \dfrac{1}{8}$.

112. Divide: $\dfrac{0.8}{8}$.

113. Simplify: $8x + 8 + 8x - 8$.

114. Evaluate: -1^8.

CHALLENGE PROBLEMS

115. In this section, we discussed equations that have no solution, one solution, and an infinite number of solutions. Do you think an equation could have exactly two solutions? If so, give an example.

116. The equation $4x - 3y = 5$ contains two different variables. Solve the equation by determining a value of x and a value for y that make the equation true.

2.5 Formulas

- Formulas from Business
- Formulas from Science
- Formulas from Geometry
- Solving for a Specified Variable

A **formula** is an equation that states a known relationship between two or more variables. Formulas are used in fields such as economics, physical education, biology, automotive repair, and nursing. In this section, we will consider formulas from business, science, and geometry.

■ FORMULAS FROM BUSINESS

A formula for retail price: To make a profit, a merchant must sell an item for more than he or she paid for it. The price at which the merchant sells the product, called the **retail price,** is the sum of what the item cost the merchant plus the **markup.**

   Retail price = cost + markup

Using r to represent the retail price, c the cost, and m the markup, we can write this formula as

$$r = c + m$$

A formula for profit: The **profit** a business makes is the difference between the **revenue** (the money it takes in) and the costs.

   Profit = revenue − costs

Using p to represent the profit, r the revenue, and c the costs, we can write this formula as

$$p = r - c$$

EXAMPLE 1

Charitable giving.   In 2001, the Salvation Army received $2.31 billion in revenue. Of that amount, $1.92 billion went directly toward program services. Find the 2001 administrative costs of the organization.

Solution   The charity collected $2.31 billion. We can think of the $1.92 billion that was spent on programs as profit. We need to find the administrative costs, c.

$$p = r - c$$ This is the formula for profit.

$$1.92 = 2.31 - c$$ Substitute 1.92 for p and 2.31 for r.

$$1.92 - 2.31 = 2.31 - c - 2.31$$ To eliminate 2.31, subtract 2.31 from both sides.

$$-0.39 = -c$$ Do the subtractions.

$$\frac{-0.39}{-1} = \frac{-c}{-1}$$ Since $-c = -1c$, divide (or multiply) both sides by -1.

$$0.39 = c$$

In 2001, the Salvation Army had administrative costs of $0.39 billion.

Self Check 1   A PTA spaghetti dinner made a profit of $275.50. If the cost to host the dinner was $1,235, how much revenue did it generate?

The Language of Algebra

The word *annual* means occurring once a year. An *annual* interest rate is the interest rate paid per year.

A formula for simple interest: When money is borrowed, the lender expects to be paid back the amount of the loan plus an additional charge for the use of the money. The additional charge is called **interest.** When money is deposited in a bank, the depositor is paid for the use of the money. The money the deposit earns is also called interest.

Interest is computed in two ways: either as **simple interest** or as **compound interest.** Simple interest is the product of the principal (the amount of money that is invested, deposited, or borrowed), the annual interest rate, and the length of time in years.

Interest = principal · rate · time

Using I to represent the simple interest, P the principal, r the annual interest rate, and t the time in years, we can write this formula as

$$I = Prt$$

EXAMPLE 2

Retirement income.   One year after investing $15,000, a retired couple received a check for $1,125 in interest. Find the interest rate their money earned that year.

Solution   The couple invested $15,000 (the principal) for 1 year (the time) and made $1,125 (the interest). We need to find the annual interest rate, r.

$$I = Prt$$ This is the formula for simple interest.

$$1,125 = 15,000r(1)$$ Substitute 1,125 for I, 15,000 for P, and 1 for t.

$$1,125 = 15,000r$$ Simplify.

$$\frac{1,125}{15,000} = \frac{15,000r}{15,000}$$ To solve for r, undo the multiplication by 15,000 by dividing both sides by 15,000.

$$0.075 = r$$ Do the divisions.

$$7.5\% = r$$ To write 0.075 as a percent, multiply 0.075 by 100 by moving the decimal point two places to the right and inserting a % symbol.

Caution

When using the formula $I = Prt$, always write the interest rate r (which is given as a percent) as a decimal or fraction before performing any calculations.

The couple received an annual rate of 7.5% that year on their investment.

	P	·	r	·	$t =$	I
Investment	15,000		0.075		1	1,125

Self Check 2   A father loaned his daughter $12,200 at a 2% annual simple interest rate for a down payment on a house. If the interest on the loan amounted to $610, for how long was the loan?

■ **FORMULAS FROM SCIENCE**

A formula for distance traveled: If we know the average rate (of speed) at which we will be traveling and the time we will be traveling at that rate, we can find the distance traveled.

Distance = rate · time

Using d to represent the distance, r the average rate, and t the time, we can write this formula as

$d = rt$

EXAMPLE 3

Finding the rate.   As they migrate from the Bering Sea to Baja California, gray whales swim for about 20 hours each day, covering a distance of approximately 70 miles. Estimate their average swimming rate in miles per hour (mph).

Solution   Since the distance d is 70 miles and the time t is 20 hours, we substitute 70 for d and 20 for t in the formula $d = rt$ and solve for r.

Caution

When using the formula $d = rt$, make sure the units are consistent. For example, if the rate is given in miles per hour, the time must be expressed in hours.

$d = rt$

$70 = r(20)$ Substitute 70 for d and 20 for t.

$\dfrac{70}{20} = \dfrac{20r}{20}$ To undo the multiplication by 20, divide both sides by 20.

$3.5 = r$

The whales' average swimming rate is 3.5 mph.

	r	$\cdot$ t	= d
Gray whale	3.5	20	70

Self Check 3   An elevator travels at an average rate of 288 feet per minute. How long will it take the elevator to climb 30 stories, a distance of 360 feet?

A formula for converting temperatures: A message board flashes two temperature readings, one in degrees Fahrenheit and one in degrees Celsius. The Fahrenheit scale is used in the American system of measurement. The Celsius scale is used in the metric system. The formula that relates a Fahrenheit temperature F to a Celsius temperature C is:

$C = \dfrac{5}{9}(F - 32)$

EXAMPLE 4

Convert the temperature shown on the City Savings sign to degrees Fahrenheit.

Solution   Since the temperature C in degrees Celsius is 30°, we substitute 30 for C in the formula and solve for F.

$$C = \frac{5}{9}(F - 32)$$ This is the temperature conversion formula.

$$30 = \frac{5}{9}(F - 32)$$ Substitute 30 for C.

$$\frac{9}{5} \cdot 30 = \frac{9}{5} \cdot \frac{5}{9}(F - 32)$$ To undo the multiplication by $\frac{5}{9}$, multiply both sides by the reciprocal of $\frac{5}{9}$.

$$54 = F - 32$$ Do the multiplications.

$$54 + 32 = F - 32 + 32$$ To undo the subtraction of 32, add 32 to both sides.

$$86 = F$$

30°C is equivalent to 86°F.

Self Check 4   Change -175°C, the temperature on Saturn, to degrees Fahrenheit.

■ FORMULAS FROM GEOMETRY

To find the **perimeter** of a geometric figure, we find the distance around the figure by computing the sum of the lengths of its sides. Perimeter is measured in linear units, such as inches, feet, yards, and meters. The **area** of a figure is the amount of surface that it encloses. Area is measured in square units, such as square inches, square feet, square yards, and square meters (denoted as in.^{2}, ft^2, yd^2, and m^2, respectively). Many formulas for perimeter and area are shown inside the front cover of the book.

EXAMPLE 5

The flag of Eritrea, a country in east Africa, is shown below.   **a.** Find the perimeter of the flag.   **b.** Find the area of the red triangular region of the flag.

Solution   **a.** The perimeter of the flag is given by the formula $P = 2l + 2w$, where l is the length and w is the width of the rectangle.

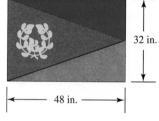

$$P = 2l + 2w$$
$$P = 2(48) + 2(32)$$ Substitute 48 for l and 32 for w.
$$= 96 + 64$$
$$= 160$$

The perimeter of the flag is 160 inches.

b. The area of a triangle is given by the formula $A = \frac{1}{2}bh$, where b is the length of the base and h is the height. With the triangle positioned as it is, the base is 32 inches and the height is 48 inches.

$$A = \frac{1}{2}bh$$

$$A = \frac{1}{2}(32)(48)$$ Substitute 32 for b and 48 for h.

$$= 16(48)$$ Multiply.

$$= 768$$

The area of the red triangular region of the flag is 768 in.^{2}.

Self Check 5   **a.** Find the perimeter of a square with sides 6 inches long.   **b.** Find the area of a triangle with base of 8 meters and height of 13 meters.

Formulas involving circles: A **circle** is the set of all points on a flat surface that are a fixed distance from a point called its **center.** A segment drawn from the center to a point on the circle is called a **radius.** Since a **diameter** of a circle is a segment passing through the center that joins two points on the circle, the diameter D of a circle is twice as long as its radius r. The perimeter of a circle is called its **circumference** C.

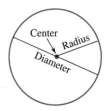

EXAMPLE 6

To the nearest tenth, find the area of a circle with a diameter of 14 feet.

Solution

The radius is one-half the diameter, or 7 feet. To find the area we substitute 7 for r in the formula for the area of a circle and proceed as follows.

Notation

We found the area of the circle to be *exactly* 49π ft^2. This form of the answer is convenient, but not very informative. To get a better feel for the area, we computed $49 \cdot \pi$ and rounded to the nearest tenth.

$A = \pi r^2$ πr^2 means $\pi \cdot r^2$.

$A = \pi(7)^2$ Substitute 7 for r.

$\quad = 49\pi$ Evaluate the exponential expression: $7^2 = 49$. The exact area is 49π ft^2.

$\quad \approx 153.93804$ Using a scientific calculator, enter these numbers and press these keys: $49 \times \pi =$. If you do not have a calculator, use 3.14 as an approximation of π.

To the nearest tenth, the area is 153.9 ft^2.

Self Check 6   To the nearest hundredth, find the circumference of the circle.

The **volume** of a three-dimensional geometric solid is the amount of space it encloses. Volume is measured in cubic units, such as cubic inches, cubic feet, and cubic meters (denoted as in.^{3}, ft^3, and m^3, respectively). Many formulas for volume are shown inside the front cover of the book.

EXAMPLE 7

Finding volumes.   To the nearest tenth, find the volume of the cylinder.

Solution

Since the radius of a circle is one-half its diameter, the radius of the cylinder is $\frac{1}{2}(6 \text{ cm}) = 3$ cm. The height of the cylinder is 12 cm. We substitute 3 for r and 12 for h in the formula for volume and proceed as follows.

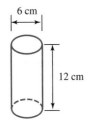

$V = \pi r^2 h$ $\pi r^2 h$ means $\pi \cdot r^2 \cdot h$.

$V = \pi(3)^2(\mathbf{12})$ Substitute 3 for r and 12 for h.

$\quad = \pi(9)(12)$ Evaluate the exponential expression.

$\quad = 108\pi$ Multiply. The exact volume is 108π cm^3.

$\quad \approx 339.2920066$ Use a calculator.

To the nearest tenth, the volume is 339.3 cubic centimeters. This can be written as 339.3 cm^3.

Self Check 7   Find the volume of each figure: **a.** a rectangular solid with length 7 inches, width 12 inches, and height 15 inches;   and   **b.** a cone whose base has radius 12 meters and whose height is 9 meters. Give the answer to the nearest tenth.

■ SOLVING FOR A SPECIFIED VARIABLE

Suppose we wish to find the bases of several triangles whose areas and heights are known. It could be tedious to substitute values for A and h into the formula and then repeatedly solve the formula for b. A better way is to solve the formula $A = \frac{1}{2}bh$ for b first, and then substitute values for A and h and compute b directly.

To **solve an equation for a variable** means to isolate that variable on one side of the equation, with all other terms on the opposite side.

EXAMPLE 8

Solve $A = \frac{1}{2}bh$ for b.

Solution

$$A = \frac{1}{2}bh$$ We must isolate b on one side of the equation.

$$2 \cdot A = 2 \cdot \frac{1}{2}bh$$ To clear the equation of the fraction, multiply both sides by 2.

$$2A = bh$$ Simplify.

$$\frac{2A}{h} = \frac{bh}{h}$$ To undo the multiplication by h, divide both sides by h.

$$\frac{2A}{h} = b$$ On the right-hand side, remove the common factor of h: $\dfrac{b\overset{1}{\cancel{h}}}{\underset{1}{\cancel{h}}} = b$.

$$b = \frac{2A}{h}$$ Reverse the sides to write b on the left.

Self Check 8   Solve $V = lwh$ for w.

EXAMPLE 9

Solve $P = 2l + 2w$ for l.

Solution

$$P = 2l + 2w$$ We must isolate l on one side of the equation.

$$P - 2w = 2l + 2w - 2w$$ To undo the addition of $2w$, subtract $2w$ from both sides.

$$P - 2w = 2l$$ Combine like terms: $2w - 2w = 0$.

$$\frac{P - 2w}{2} = \frac{2l}{2}$$ To undo the multiplication by 2, divide both sides by 2.

$$\frac{P - 2w}{2} = l$$ Simplify the right-hand side.

Caution

In Example 9, do not try to simplify the result this way:

$$l = \frac{P - \overset{1}{\cancel{2}}w}{\underset{1}{\cancel{2}}}$$

This step is incorrect because 2 is not a factor of the entire numerator.

We can write the result as $l = \dfrac{P - 2w}{2}$.

Self Check 9   Solve $P = 2l + 2w$ for w.

EXAMPLE 10

In Chapter 3, we will work with equations that involve the variables x and y, such as $2y - 4 = 3x$. Solve this equation for y.

Solution

We must isolate y on one side of the equation.

$$2y - 4 = 3x$$

$$2y - 4 + 4 = 3x + 4$$ To undo the subtraction of 4, add 4 to both sides.

$$2y = 3x + 4$$ Do the addition.

$$\frac{2y}{2} = \frac{3x + 4}{2}$$ To undo the multiplication by 2, divide both sides by 2.

$$y = \frac{3x}{2} + \frac{4}{2}$$ On the right-hand side, write $\frac{3x+4}{2}$ as the sum of two fractions with like denominators, $\frac{3x}{2}$ and $\frac{4}{2}$.

$$y = \frac{3}{2}x + 2$$ Write $\frac{3x}{2}$ as $\frac{3}{2}x$. Simplify: $\frac{4}{2} = 2$.

Self Check 10   Solve $3y + 12 = x$ for y.

EXAMPLE 11

Solve $V = \pi r^2 h$ for r^2.

Solution

We must isolate r^2 on one side of the equation.

$$V = \pi r^2 h$$

$$\frac{V}{\pi h} = \frac{\pi r^2 h}{\pi h}$$ To undo the multiplication by π and h on the right-hand side, divide both sides by πh.

$$\frac{V}{\pi h} = r^2$$ Remove the common factors of π and h: $\frac{\overset{1}{\cancel{\pi}} r^2 \overset{1}{\cancel{h}}}{\underset{1}{\cancel{\pi}} \underset{1}{\cancel{h}}} = r^2$.

$$r^2 = \frac{V}{\pi h}$$ Reverse the sides of the equation so that r^2 is on the left.

Caution

When solving for a variable, that variable must be isolated on one side of the equation.

Self Check 11   Solve $a^2 + b^2 = c^2$ for b^2.

Answers to Self Checks   **1.** $1,510.50   **2.** 2.5 years   **3.** 1.25 minutes   **4.** $-283°$F   **5. a.** 24 in.,   **b.** 52 m^2 **6.** 43.98 ft   **7. a.** 1,260 in.^{3},   **b.** 1,357.2 m^3 **8.** $w = \frac{V}{lh}$ **9.** $w = \frac{P - 2l}{2}$ **10.** $y = \frac{1}{3}x - 4$ **11.** $b^2 = c^2 - a^2$

2.5   **STUDY SET**

VOCABULARY   **Fill in the blanks.**

1. A _____ is an equation that is used to state a known relationship between two or more variables.

2. The _____ of a three-dimensional geometric solid is the amount of space it encloses.

3. The distance around a geometric figure is called its _____.

4. A _____ is the set of all points on a flat surface that are a fixed distance from a point called its center.

5. A line segment drawn from the center of a circle to a point on the circle is called a _____.

6. The amount of surface that is enclosed by a geometric figure is called its _____.

7. The perimeter of a circle is called its _____.

8. A line segment passing through the center of a circle and connecting two points on the circle is called a _____.

CONCEPTS

9. Use variables to write the formula relating the following:
   a. Time, distance, rate
   b. Markup, retail price, cost
   c. Costs, revenue, profit
   d. Interest rate, time, interest, principal
   e. Circumference, radius

10. Complete the table.

Principal ·	rate ·	time =	interest
$2,500	5%	2 yr	
$15,000	4.8%	1 yr	

11. Complete the table to find how far light and sound travel in 60 seconds.   (*Hint:* mi/sec means miles per second.)

	Rate ·	time =	distance
Light	186,282 mi/sec	60 sec	
Sound	1,088 ft/sec	60 sec	

12. Give the name of each figure.

a.

b.

c.

d.

e.

f.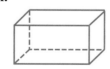

13. Tell which concept, perimeter, circumference, area, or volume, should be used to find the following:
   a. The amount of storage in a freezer
   b. How far a bicycle tire rolls in one revolution

c. The amount of land making up the Sahara Desert

d. The distance around a Monopoly game board

14. Tell which unit of measurement, ft, ft^2, or ft^3, would be appropriate when finding the following:
   a. The amount of storage inside a safe
   b. The ground covered by a sleeping bag lying on the floor
   c. The distance the tip of an airplane propeller travels in one revolution
   d. The size of the trunk of a car

15. a. Write an expression for the perimeter of the figure.

2 cm
$(x + 3)$ cm

   b. Write an expression for the area of the figure.

16. WHEELCHAIRS
   a. Find the diameter of the rear wheel.
   b. Find the radius of the front wheel.

12.5 in.
5 in.

NOTATION   Complete the solution.

17. Solve $Ax + By = C$ for y.

$$Ax + By = C$$
$$Ax + By - \boxed{} = C - \boxed{}$$
$$\boxed{} = C - Ax$$
$$\frac{By}{\boxed{}} = \frac{C - Ax}{\boxed{}}$$
$$y = \frac{C - Ax}{B}$$

18. Enter the missing formulas in each table.
   a. The table contains information about an investment earning simple interest.

	?	·	?	·	?	=	?
Certificate of deposit	$3,500		0.04		1 yr		$140

b. The table contains information about a trip made by a cross-country skier.

	?	·	?	=	?
Skier	3 mph		2 hr		6 mi

19. a. Approximate π to the nearest hundredth.

   b. What does 98π mean?

   c. In the formula for the volume of a cylinder, $V = \pi r^2 h$, what does r represent? What does h represent?

20. a. What does ft^2 mean?

   b. What does in.^3 mean?

PRACTICE Use a formula to solve each problem.

21. SWIMMING In 1930, a man swam down the Mississippi River from Minneapolis to New Orleans, a total of 1,826 miles. He was in the water for 742 hours. To the nearest tenth, what was his average swimming rate?

22. ROSE PARADE Rose Parade floats travel down the 5.5-mile-long parade route at a rate of 2.5 mph. How long will it take a float to complete the route if there are no delays?

23. HOLLYWOOD Figures for the summer of 1998 showed that the movie *Saving Private Ryan* had U.S. box-office receipts of $190 million. What were the production costs to make the movie if, at that time, the studio had made a $125 million profit?

24. SERVICE CLUBS After expenses of $55.15 were paid, a Rotary Club donated $875.85 in proceeds from a pancake breakfast to a local health clinic. How much did the pancake breakfast gross?

25. ENTREPRENEURS To start a mobile dog-grooming service, a woman borrowed $2,500. If the loan was for 2 years and the amount of interest was $175, what simple interest rate was she charged?

26. BANKING Three years after opening an account that paid 6.45% annually, a depositor withdrew the $3,483 in interest earned. How much money was left in the account?

27. METALLURGY Change 2,212°C, the temperature at which silver boils, to degrees Fahrenheit. Round to the nearest degree.

28. LOW TEMPERATURES Cryobiologists freeze living matter to preserve it for future use. They can work with temperatures as low as −270°C. Change this to degrees Fahrenheit.

29. VALENTINE'S DAY Find the markup on a dozen roses if a florist buys them wholesale for $12.95 and sells them for $37.50.

30. STICKER PRICES The factory invoice for a minivan shows that the dealer paid $16,264.55 for the vehicle. If the sticker price of the van is $18,202, how much over factory invoice is the sticker price?

31. YO-YOS How far does a yo-yo travel during one revolution of the "around the world" trick if the length of the string is 21 inches?

32. HORSES A horse trots in a perfect circle around its trainer at the end of a 28-foot-long rope. How far does the horse travel as it circles the trainer once?

Solve each formula for the given variable.

33. $E = IR$; for R

34. $d = rt$; for t

35. $V = lwh$; for w

36. $I = Prt$; for r

37. $C = 2\pi r$; for r

38. $V = \pi r^2 h$; for h

39. $A = \dfrac{Bh}{3}$; for h

40. $C = \dfrac{Rt}{7}$; for R

41. $w = \dfrac{s}{f}$; for f

42. $P = \dfrac{ab}{c}$; for c

43. $P = a + b + c$; for b

44. $a + b + c = 180$; for a

45. $T = 2r + 2t$; for r

46. $y = mx + b$; for x

47. $Ax + By = C$; for x

48. $A = P + Prt$; for t

49. $K = \dfrac{1}{2}mv^2$; for m

50. $V = \dfrac{1}{3}\pi r^2 h$; for h

51. $A = \dfrac{a + b + c}{3}$; for c **52.** $x = \dfrac{a + b}{2}$; for b

53. $2E = \dfrac{T - t}{9}$; for t **54.** $D = \dfrac{C - s}{n}$; for s

55. $s = 4\pi r^2$; for r^2 **56.** $E = mc^2$; for c^2

57. $Kg = \dfrac{wv^2}{2}$; for v^2 **58.** $c^2 = a^2 + b^2$; for a^2

59. $V = \dfrac{4}{3}\pi r^3$; for r^3 **60.** $A = \dfrac{\pi r^2 S}{360}$; for r^2

61. $\dfrac{M}{2} - 9.9 = 2.1B$; for M

62. $\dfrac{G}{0.5} + 16r = -8t$; for G

63. $S = 2\pi rh + 2\pi r^2$; for h

64. $c = bn + 16t^2$; for t^2

65. $3x + y = 9$; for y **66.** $-5x + y = 4$

67. $3y - 9 = x$; for y **68.** $5y - 25 = x$; for y

69. $4y + 16 = -3x$; for y **70.** $6y + 12 = -5x$; for y

71. $A = \dfrac{1}{2}h(b + d)$; for b

72. $C = \dfrac{1}{4}s(t - d)$; for t

73. $\dfrac{7}{8}c + w = 9$; for c **74.** $\dfrac{3}{4}m - t = 5b$; for m

APPLICATIONS

75. PROPERTIES OF WATER The boiling point and the freezing point of water are to be given in both degrees Celsius and degrees Fahrenheit on the thermometer. Find the missing degree measures.

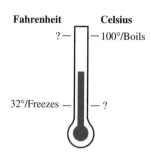

76. SPEED LIMITS Several state speed limits for trucks are shown. At each of these speeds, how far would a truck travel in $2\frac{1}{2}$ hours?

77. AVON PRODUCTS Complete the financial statement from the Hoover's Online business Web site.

Quarterly financials income statement (dollar amounts in millions except per share amounts)	Quarter ending Dec 02	Quarter ending Sep 02
Revenue	1,854.1	1,463.4
Cost of goods sold	679.5	506.5
Gross profit		

78. CREDIT CARDS The finance charge section of a person's credit card statement says, "annual percentage rate (APR) is 19.8%." Determine how much finance charges (interest) the card owner would have to pay if the account's average balance for the year was $2,500.

79. CARPENTRY Find the perimeter and area of the truss.

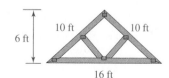

80. CAMPERS Find the area of the window of the camper shell on the next page.

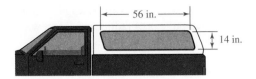

81. ARCHERY To the nearest tenth, find the circumference and area of the target.

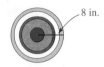

82. GEOGRAPHY The circumference of the Earth is about 25,000 miles. Find its diameter to the nearest mile.

83. LANDSCAPING Find the perimeter and the area of the redwood trellis.

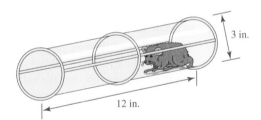

84. HAMSTER HABITATS Find the amount of space in the tube.

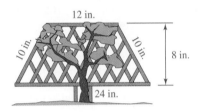

85. MEMORIALS The Vietnam Veterans Memorial is a black granite wall recognizing the more than 58,000 Americans who lost their lives or remain missing. Find the total area of the two triangular-shaped surfaces on which the names are inscribed.

86. SIGNAGE Find the perimeter and area of the service station sign.

87. RUBBER MEETS THE ROAD A sport truck tire has the road surface footprint shown here. Estimate the perimeter and area of the tire's footprint.

88. SOFTBALL The strike zone in fast-pitch softball is between the batter's armpit and the top of her knees, as shown. Find the area of the strike zone.

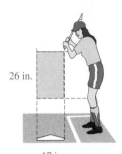

89. FIREWOOD Find the area on which the wood is stacked and the volume the cord of firewood occupies.

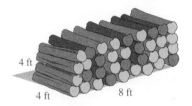

90. NATIVE AMERICAN DWELLINGS The teepees constructed by the Blackfoot Indians were cone-shaped tents made of long poles and animal hide, about 10 feet high and about 15 feet across at the ground. Estimate the volume of a teepee with these dimensions, to the nearest cubic foot.

91. IGLOOS During long journeys, some Canadian Inuit (Eskimos) built winter houses of snow blocks stacked in the dome shape shown on the next page. Estimate the volume of an igloo having an interior height of 5.5 feet to the nearest cubic foot.

92. PYRAMIDS   The Great Pyramid at Giza in northern Egypt is one of the most famous works of architecture in the world. Use the information in the illustration to find the volume to the nearest cubic foot.

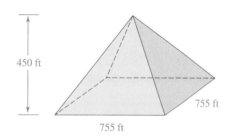

450 ft

755 ft

755 ft

93. BARBECUING   Use the fact that the fish is 18 inches long to find the area of the barbecue grill to the nearest square inch.

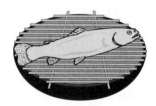

94. SKATEBOARDING   A half-pipe ramp used for skateboarding is in the shape of a semicircle with a radius of 8 feet. To the nearest tenth of a foot, what is the length of the arc that the skateboarder travels on the ramp?

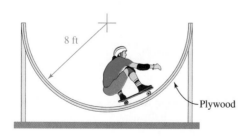

8 ft

Plywood

95. PULLEYS   The approximate length L of a belt joining two pulleys of radii r and R feet with centers D feet apart is given by the formula

$$L = 2D + 3.25(r + R)$$

Solve the formula for D.

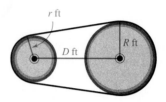

r ft

R ft

D ft

96. THERMODYNAMICS   The Gibbs free-energy function is given by $G = U - TS + pV$. Solve this formula for the pressure p.

WRITING

97. After solving $A = B + C + D$ for B, a student compared her answer with that at the back of the textbook.

Student's answer: $B = A - C - D$
Book's answer: $B = A - D - C$

Could this problem have two different-looking answers? Explain why or why not.

98. Suppose the volume of a cylinder is 28 cubic feet. Explain why it is incorrect to express the volume as 28^3 ft.

99. Explain the difference between what perimeter measures and what area measures.

100. Explain the error made below.

$$y = \frac{\overset{1}{3x + \overset{1}{2}}}{\underset{1}{\overset{1}{2}}}$$

REVIEW

101. Find 82% of 168.

102. 29.05 is what percent of 415?

103. What percent of 200 is 30?

104. A woman bought a coat for $98.95 and some gloves for $7.95. If the sales tax was 6%, how much did the purchase cost her?

CHALLENGE PROBLEMS

105. In mathematics, letters from the Greek alphabet are often used as variables. Solve the following equation for α (read as "alpha"), the first letter of the Greek alphabet.

$$-7(\alpha - \beta) - (4\alpha - \theta) = \frac{\alpha}{2}$$

106. When a car of mass m collides with a wall, the energy of the collision is given by the formula $E = \frac{1}{2}mv^2$. Compare the energy of two collisions: a car striking a wall at 30 mph, and at 60 mph.

2.6   More about Problem Solving

- Finding More than One Unknown
- Solving Number–Value Problems
- Solving Uniform Motion Problems
- Solving Geometric Problems
- Solving Investment Problems
- Solving Mixture Problems

In this section, we will solve several types of problems using the five-step problem-solving strategy.

■ FINDING MORE THAN ONE UNKNOWN

EXAMPLE 1

California coastline.   The first part of California's magnificent 17-Mile Drive begins at the Pacific Grove entrance and continues to Seal Rock. It is 1 mile longer than the second part of the drive, which extends from Seal Rock to the Lone Cypress. The final part of the tour winds through the Monterey Peninsula, eventually returning to the entrance. This part of the drive is 1 mile longer than four times the length of the second part. How long is each part of 17-Mile Drive?

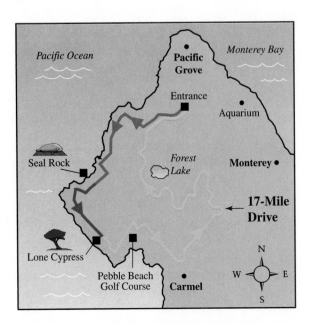

Analyze the Problem   The drive is composed of three parts. We need to find the length of each part. We can straighten out the winding 17-Mile Drive and model it with a line segment.

Form an Equation   Since the lengths of the first part and of the third part of the drive are related to the length of the second part, we will let x represent the length of that part. We then express the other lengths in terms of x. Let

$$x = \text{the length of the second part of the drive}$$
$$x + 1 = \text{the length of the first part of the drive}$$
$$4x + 1 = \text{the length of the third part of the drive}$$

Caution

For this problem, one common mistake is to let

x = the length of each part of the drive

The three parts of the drive have different lengths; x cannot represent three different distances.

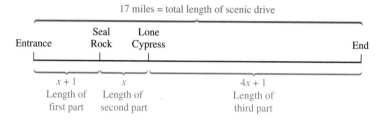

The sum of the lengths of the three parts must be 17 miles.

The length of part 1	plus	the length of part 2	plus	the length of part 3	equals	the total length.
$x + 1$	$+$	x	$+$	$4x + 1$	$=$	17

Solve the Equation

$$x + 1 + x + 4x + 1 = 17$$

$$6x + 2 = 17 \qquad \text{Combine like terms: } x + x + 4x = 6x \text{ and } 1 + 1 = 2.$$

$$6x = 15 \qquad \text{To undo the addition of 2, subtract 2 from both sides.}$$

$$\frac{6x}{6} = \frac{15}{6} \qquad \text{To undo the multiplication by 6, divide both sides by 6.}$$

$$x = 2.5$$

Recall that x represents the length of the second part of the drive. To find the lengths of the first and third parts, we evaluate $x + 1$ and $4x + 1$ for $x = 2.5$.

First part of drive   *Third part of drive*

$x + 1 = \mathbf{2.5} + 1$ $4x + 1 = 4(\mathbf{2.5}) + 1$ Substitute 2.5 for x.

$\quad\ \ = 3.5$ $\qquad\ \ = 11$

State the Conclusion   The first part of the drive is 3.5 miles long, the second part is 2.5 miles long, and the third part is 11 miles long.

Check the Result   Since 3.5 mi + 2.5 mi + 11 mi = 17 mi, the answers check.

■ SOLVING GEOMETRIC PROBLEMS

EXAMPLE 2   A gardener wants to use 62 feet of fencing bought at a garage sale to enclose a rectangular-shaped garden. Find the dimensions of the garden if its length is to be 4 feet longer than twice its width.

Analyze the Problem A sketch is often helpful when solving problems about geometric figures. We know that the length of the garden is to be 4 feet longer than twice the width. We also know that its perimeter is to be 62 feet. Recall that the perimeter of a rectangle is given by the formula $P = 2l + 2w$.

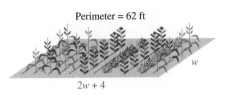

Perimeter = 62 ft

w

$2w + 4$

The Language of Algebra

Dimensions are measurements of length, width, and thickness. Perhaps you have viewed a 3-D (dimensional) movie wearing the special glasses.

Form an Equation Since the length of the garden is given in terms of the width, we will let $w =$ the width of the garden. Then the length $= 2w + 4$.

2	times	the length	plus	2	times	the width	is	the perimeter.
2	·	$(2w + 4)$	+	2	·	w	=	62

Solve the Equation

$2(2w + 4) + 2w = 62$ Be sure to write the parentheses so that the entire expression $2w + 4$ is multiplied by 2.

$4w + 8 + 2w = 62$ Use the distributive property to remove parentheses.

$6w + 8 = 62$ Combine like terms: $4w + 2w = 6w$.

$6w = 54$ To undo the addition of 8, subtract 8 from both sides.

$w = 9$ To undo the multiplication by 6, divide both sides by 6.

State the Conclusion The width of the garden is 9 feet. Since $2w + 4 = 2(9) + 4 = 22$, the length is 22 feet.

Check the Result If the garden has a width of 9 feet and a length of 22 feet, its length is 4 feet longer than twice the width ($2 \cdot 9 + 4 = 22$). Since its perimeter is $2 \cdot 22$ ft $+ 2 \cdot 9$ ft $= 62$ ft, the answers check.

EXAMPLE 3

Isosceles triangles. If the vertex angle of an isosceles triangle is 56°, find the measure of each base angle.

Analyze the Problem An **isosceles triangle** has two sides of equal length, which meet to form the **vertex angle.** In this case, the measurement of the vertex angle is 56°. We can sketch the triangle as shown. The **base angles** opposite the equal sides are also equal. We need to find their measure.

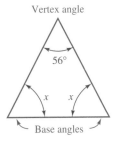

Vertex angle

56°

x x

Base angles

Form an Equation If we let $x =$ the measure of one base angle, the measure of the other base angle is also x. Since the sum of the angles of any triangle is 180°, the sum of the base angles and the vertex angle is 180°. We can use this fact to form the equation.

One base angle	plus	the other base angle	plus	the vertex angle	is	180°.
x	+	x	+	56	=	180

Solve the Equation

$$x + x + 56 = 180$$

$$2x + 56 = 180 \quad \text{Combine like terms: } x + x = 2x.$$

$$2x = 124 \quad \text{To undo the addition of 56, subtract 56 from both sides.}$$

$$x = 62 \quad \text{To undo the multiplication by 2, divide both sides by 2.}$$

State the Conclusion   The measure of each base angle is 62°.

Check the Result   Since $62° + 62° + 56° = 180°$, the answer checks.

■ SOLVING NUMBER–VALUE PROBLEMS

Some problems deal with items that have monetary value. In these problems, we must distinguish between the *number of* and the *value of* the items. For problems of this type, we will use the fact that

Number · value = total value

EXAMPLE 4

Dining area improvements.   A restaurant owner needs to purchase some tables, chairs, and dinner plates for the dining area of her establishment. She plans to buy four chairs and four plates for each new table. She also plans to buy 20 additional plates in case of breakage. If a table costs $100, a chair $50, and a plate $5, how many of each can she buy if she takes out a loan for $6,500 to pay for the new items?

Analyze the Problem   We know the *value* of each item: Tables cost $100, chairs cost $50, and plates cost $5 each. We need to find the *number* of tables, chairs, and plates she can purchase for $6,500.

Form an Equation   The number of chairs and plates she needs depends on the number of tables she buys. So we let t = the number of tables to be purchased. Since every table requires four chairs and four plates, she needs to order $4t$ chairs. Because 20 additional plates are needed, she should order $(4t + 20)$ plates. We can organize the facts of the problem in a table.

	Number	· Value	= Total value
Tables	t	100	$100t$
Chairs	$4t$	50	$50(4t)$
Plates	$4t + 20$	5	$5(4t + 20)$

Enter this information first.   Multiply to get each of these entries.

We can use the information in the last column of the table to form an equation.

The value of the tables	plus	the value of the chairs	plus	the value of the plates	equals	the total value of the purchase.
$100t$	+	$50(4t)$	+	$5(4t + 20)$	=	6,500

Solve the Equation

$$100t + 50(4t) + 5(4t + 20) = 6,500$$
$$100t + 200t + 20t + 100 = 6,500 \quad \text{Do the multiplications.}$$
$$320t + 100 = 6,500 \quad \text{Combine like terms.}$$
$$320t = 6,400 \quad \text{Subtract 100 from both sides.}$$
$$t = 20 \quad \text{Divide both sides by 320.}$$

To find the number of chairs and plates to buy, we evaluate $4t$ and $4t + 20$ for $t = 20$.

Chairs: $4t = 4(20)$ **Plates:** $4t + 20 = 4(20) + 20$ Substitute 20 for t.
$\qquad\qquad = 80$ $\qquad\qquad\qquad\qquad = 100$

State the Conclusion   The owner needs to buy 20 tables, 80 chairs, and 100 plates.

Check the Result   The total value of 20 tables is 20($100) = $2,000, the total value of 80 chairs is 80($50) = $4,000, and the total value of 100 plates is 100($5) = $500. Because the total purchase is $2,000 + $4,000 + $500 = $6,500, the answers check.

■ SOLVING INVESTMENT PROBLEMS

To find the amount of simple interest I an investment earns, we use the formula

$$I = Prt$$

where P is the principal, r is the annual rate, and t is the time in years.

EXAMPLE 5

Paying tuition. A college student invested the $12,000 inheritance he received and decided to use the annual interest earned to pay his tuition costs of $945. The highest rate offered by a bank at that time was 6% annual simple interest. At this rate, he could not earn the needed $945, so he invested some of the money in a riskier, but more profitable, investment offering a 9% return. How much did he invest at each rate?

Analyze the Problem   We know that $12,000 was invested for 1 year at two rates: 6% and 9%. We are asked to find the amount invested at each rate so that the total return would be $945.

Form an Equation   Let $x =$ the amount invested at 6%. Then $12,000 - x =$ the amount invested at 9%. To organize the facts of the problem, we enter the principal, rate, time, and interest earned in a table.

	P	$\cdot$ r	$\cdot$ $t =$	I
Bank	x	0.06	1	$0.06x$
Riskier investment	$12,000 - x$	0.09	1	$0.09(12,000 - x)$

Enter this information first.   Multiply to get each of these entries.

We can use the information in the last column of the table to form an equation.

The interest earned at 6%	plus	the interest earned at 9%	equals	the total interest.
$0.06x$	$+$	$0.09(12{,}000 - x)$	$=$	945

Solve the Equation

$0.06x + 0.09(12{,}000 - x) = 945$	
$100[0.06x + 0.09(12{,}000 - x)] = 100(945)$	Multiply both sides by 100 to clear the equation of decimals.
$100(0.06x) + 100(0.09)(12{,}000 - x) = 100(945)$	Distribute the multiplication by 100.
$6x + 9(12{,}000 - x) = 94{,}500$	Do the multiplications by 100.
$6x + 108{,}000 - 9x = 94{,}500$	Use the distributive property.
$-3x + 108{,}000 = 94{,}500$	Combine like terms.
$-3x = -13{,}500$	Subtract 108,000 from both sides.
$x = 4{,}500$	Divide both sides by -3.

Success Tip

We can *clear an equation of decimals* by multiplying both sides by a power of 10. In Example 5, we multiply the hundredths by 100 to move each decimal point two places to the right:

$100(0.06) = 6$ $100(0.09) = 9$

State the Conclusion   The student invested $4,500 at 6% and $12,000 − $4,500 = $7,500 at 9%.

Check the Result   The first investment earned 0.06($4,500), or $270. The second earned 0.09($7,500), or $675. The total return was $270 + $675 = $945. The answers check.

■ SOLVING UNIFORM MOTION PROBLEMS

If we know the rate r at which we will be traveling and the time t we will be traveling at that rate, we can find the distance d traveled by using the formula

$$d = rt$$

EXAMPLE 6

Coast Guard rescues.   A cargo ship, heading into port, radios the Coast Guard that it is experiencing engine trouble and that its speed has dropped to 3 knots (3 nautical miles per hour). Immediately, a Coast Guard cutter leaves port and speeds at a rate of 25 knots directly toward the disabled ship, which is 21 nautical miles away. How long will it take the Coast Guard to reach the cargo ship?

Analyze the Problem   We know the *rate* of each ship (25 knots and 3 knots), and we know that they must close a *distance* of 21 nautical miles between them. We don't know the *time* it will take to do this.

Form an Equation   Let t = the time it takes for the ships to meet. Using $d = rt$, we find that $25t$ represents the distance traveled by the Coast Guard cutter and $3t$ represents the distance traveled by the cargo ship. We can organize the facts of the problem in a table.

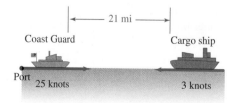

	r	$\cdot\ t$	$= d$
Coast Guard cutter	25	t	$25t$
Cargo ship	3	t	$3t$

Enter this information first.

We can use the information in the last column of the table to form an equation.

The distance the Coast Guard cutter travels	plus	the distance the cargo ship travels	equals	the initial distance between the two ships.
$25t$	$+$	$3t$	$=$	21

Solve the Equation

$$25t + 3t = 21$$

$$28t = 21 \qquad \text{Combine like terms.}$$

$$t = \frac{21}{28} \qquad \text{Divide both sides by 28.}$$

$$t = \frac{3}{4} \qquad \text{Simplify the fraction.}$$

State the Conclusion   The ships will meet in $\frac{3}{4}$ hr, or 45 minutes.

Check the Result   In $\frac{3}{4}$ hr, the Coast Guard cutter travels $25 \cdot \frac{3}{4} = \frac{75}{4}$ nautical miles, and the cargo ship travels $3 \cdot \frac{3}{4} = \frac{9}{4}$ nautical miles. Together, they travel $\frac{75}{4} + \frac{9}{4} = \frac{84}{4} = 21$ nautical miles. This is the initial distance between the ships; the answer checks.

■ SOLVING MIXTURE PROBLEMS

We now discuss how to solve mixture problems. In the first type, a *liquid mixture* of a desired strength is made from two solutions with different concentrations. In the second type, a *dry mixture* of a specified value is created from two differently priced components.

EXAMPLE 7

Mixing solutions.   A chemistry experiment calls for a 30% sulfuric acid solution. If the lab supply room has only 50% and 20% sulfuric acid solutions, how much of each should be mixed to obtain 12 liters of a 30% acid solution?

Analyze the Problem   The 50% solution is too strong and the 20% solution is too weak. We must find how much of each should be combined to obtain 12 liters of a 30% solution.

Form an Equation   If $x =$ the number of liters of the 50% solution used in the mixture, the remaining $(12 - x)$ liters must be the 20% solution.

The amount of pure acid in each solution is given by

Amount of solution · strength of solution = amount of pure acid

A table is helpful in organizing the facts of the problem.

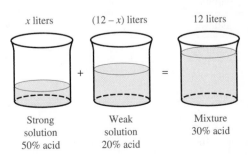

x liters $(12 - x)$ liters   12 liters

Strong solution 50% acid   +   Weak solution 20% acid   =   Mixture 30% acid

	Amount	· Strength	= Amount of acid
Strong	x	0.50	$0.50x$
Weak	$12 - x$	0.20	$0.20(12 - x)$
Mixture	12	0.30	$12(0.30)$

Enter this information first.   Multiply to get each of these entries.

We can use the information in the last column of the table to form an equation.

The acid in the 50% solution	plus	the acid in the 20% solution	equals	the acid in the final mixture.
$0.50x$	$+$	$0.20(12 - x)$	$=$	$12(0.30)$

Solve the Equation

$$0.50x + 0.20(12 - x) = 12(0.30)$$ 50% = 0.50, 20% = 0.20, and 30% = 0.30.

$$0.5x + 2.4 - 0.2x = 3.6$$ Distribute the multiplication by 0.20.

$$0.3x + 2.4 = 3.6$$ Combine like terms.

$$0.3x = 1.2$$ Subtract 2.4 from both sides.

$$\frac{0.3x}{0.3} = \frac{1.2}{0.3}$$ To undo the multiplication by 0.3, divide both sides by 0.3.

$$x = 4$$

Success Tip

We could begin by multiplying both sides of the equation by 10 to clear it of the decimals.

State the Conclusion   4 liters of 50% solution and $12 - 4 = 8$ liters of 20% solution should be used.

Check the Result   Acid in 4 liters of the 50% solution: $0.50(4) = 2.0$ liters.
Acid in 8 liters of the 20% solution: $0.20(8) = 1.6$ liters. ⟩ 3.6 liters
Acid in 12 liters of the 30% mixture: $0.30(12) = 3.6$ liters. The answers check.

EXAMPLE 8

Snack foods.   Because cashews priced at $9 per pound were not selling, a produce clerk decided to combine them with less expensive peanuts and sell the mixture for $7 per pound. How many pounds of peanuts, selling at $6 per pound, should be mixed with 50 pounds of cashews to obtain such a mixture?

Analyze the Problem   We need to determine how many pounds of peanuts to mix with 50 pounds of cashews to obtain a mixture worth $7 per pound.

Form an Equation   Let $x =$ the number of pounds of peanuts to use in the mixture. Since 50 pounds of cashews will be combined with the peanuts, the mixture will weigh $50 + x$ pounds. The value of the mixture and of each of the components of the mixture is given by

$$\text{Amount} \cdot \text{price} = \text{total value}$$

We can organize the facts of the problem in a table.

	Amount	· Price	= Total value
Peanuts	x	6	$6x$
Cashews	50	9	450
Mixture	$50 + x$	7	$7(50 + x)$

Enter this information first.   Multiply to get each of these entries.

We can use the information in the last column of the table to form an equation.

The value of the peanuts	plus	the value of the cashews	equals	the value of the mixture.
$6x$	$+$	450	$=$	$7(50 + x)$

Solve the Equation

$$6x + 450 = 7(50 + x)$$

$6x + 450 = 350 + 7x$ Distribute the multiplication by 7.

$450 = 350 + x$ Subtract $6x$ from both sides.

$100 = x$ Subtract 350 from both sides.

State the Conclusion   100 pounds of peanuts should be used in the mixture.

Check the Result

Value of 100 pounds of peanuts, at \$6 per pound: $100(6) = \$600$.

Value of 50 pounds of cashews, at \$9 per pound: $50(9) = \$450$. $\Big\} \$1,050$

Value of 150 pounds of the mixture, at \$7 per pound: \$1,050. The answer checks.

2.6   STUDY SET

VOCABULARY   **Fill in the blanks.**

1. The _____ of a triangle or a rectangle is the distance around it.

2. An _____ triangle is a triangle with two sides of the same length.

3. The equal sides of an isosceles triangle meet to form the _____ angle. The angles opposite the equal sides are called _____ angles, and they have equal measures.

4. When asked to find the dimensions of a rectangle, we are to find its _____ and _____.

CONCEPTS

5. A plumber wants to cut a 17-foot pipe into three sections. The longest section is to be three times as long as the shortest, and the middle-sized section is to be 2 feet longer than the shortest.
   a. Complete the diagram.

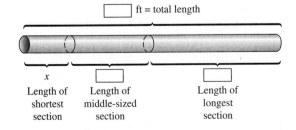

b. To solve this problem, an equation is formed, it is solved, and it is found that $x = 3$. How long is each section of pipe?

6. Complete the expression, which represents the perimeter of the rectangle shown.

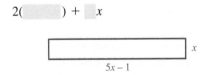

$$2(\qquad) + \boxed{}\, x$$

7. What is the sum of the measures of the angles of any triangle?

8. **a.** Complete the table, which shows the inventory of nylon brushes that a paint store carries.

	Number	·	Value	=	Total value
1 inch	$\frac{x}{2}$		4		
2 inch	x		5		
3 inch	$x + 10$		7		

b. Which type of brush does the store have the greatest number of?

c. What is the least expensive brush?

d. What is the total value of the inventory of nylon brushes?

9. In the advertisement, what are the principal, the rate, and the time for the investment opportunity shown?

> **Invest in Mini Malls!**
> Builder seeks daring people who want to earn big $$$$$$. In just 1 year, you will earn a gigantic 14% on an investment of only $30,000! Call now.

10. a. Complete the table, which gives the details about two investments made by a retired couple.

	P ·	r	· $t =$	I
Certificate of deposit	x	0.04	1	
Brother-in-law's business	$2x$	0.06	1	

b. How much more money was invested in the brother-in-law's business than in the certificate of deposit?

c. What is the total amount of interest the couple will make from these investments?

11. When a husband and wife leave for work, they drive in opposite directions. Their average speeds are different; however, their drives last the same amount of time. Complete the table, which gives the details of each person's commute.

	r	· $t =$	d
Husband	35	t	
Wife	45		

12. a. How many gallons of acid are there in the second barrel?

b. Suppose the contents of the two barrels are poured into an empty third barrel. How many gallons of liquid will the third barrel contain?

c. What would be a *reasonable* estimate of the concentration of the solution in the third barrel: 15%, 35%, or 60% acid?

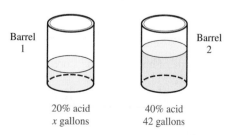

Barrel 1   20% acid x gallons

Barrel 2   40% acid   42 gallons

13. a. Two oil and vinegar salad dressings are combined to make a new mixture. Complete the table.

	Amount ·	Strength =	Pure vinegar
Strong	x	0.06	
Weak		0.03	
Mixture	10	0.05	

b. Two antifreeze solutions are combined to form a mixture. Complete the table.

	Amount ·	Strength =	Pure antifreeze
Strong	6	0.50	
Weak	x	0.25	
Mixture		0.30	

14. Use the information in the table to fill in the blanks. How many pounds of a _____ diet supplement worth $15.95 per pound should be mixed with _____ pounds of a vitamin diet supplement worth _____ per pound to obtain a _____ that is worth _____ per pound?

	Amount ·	Value =	Total value
Protein	x	15.95	15.95x
Vitamin	20	7.99	20(7.99)
Mixture	$x + 20$	12.50	12.50($x + 20$)

NOTATION

15. What concept about decimal multiplication is shown?

$$100(0.08) = 8$$

16. True or false: $x(0.09) = 0.09x$?

17. Suppose a rectangle has width w and length $2w - 3$. Explain why the expression $2 \cdot 2w - 3 + 2w$ does not represent the perimeter of the rectangle.

18. Write 5.5% as a decimal.

PRACTICE Solve each equation by first clearing it of decimals.

19. $0.08x + 0.07(15{,}000 - x) = 1{,}110$

20. $0.108x + 0.07(16{,}000 - x) = 1{,}500$

APPLICATIONS

21. CARPENTRY A 12-foot board has been cut into two sections, one twice as long as the other. How long is each section?

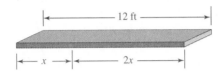

22. ROBOTICS The robotic arm will extend a total distance of 18 feet. Find the length of each section.

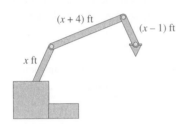

23. NATIONAL PARKS The Natchez Trace Parkway is a historical 444-mile route from Natchez, Mississippi, to Nashville, Tennessee. A couple drove the Trace in four days. Each day

they drove 6 miles more than the previous day. How many miles did they drive each day?

24. SOLAR HEATING One solar panel is 3.4 feet wider than the other. Find the width of each panel.

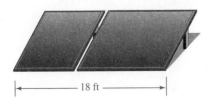

25. TOURING A rock group plans to travel for a total of 38 weeks, making three concert stops. They will be in Japan for 4 more weeks than they will be in Australia. Their stay in Sweden will be 2 weeks shorter than that in Australia. How many weeks will they be in each country?

26. LOCKS The three numbers of the combination for a lock are **consecutive integers,** and their sum is 81. (Consecutive integers follow each other, like 7, 8, 9.) Find the combination. (*Hint:* If x represents the smallest integer, $x + 1$ represents the next integer, and $x + 2$ represents the largest integer.)

27. COUNTING CALORIES A slice of pie with a scoop of ice cream has 850 calories. The calories in the pie alone are 100 more than twice the calories in the ice cream alone. How many calories are in each food?

28. WASTE DISPOSAL Two tanks hold a total of 45 gallons of a toxic solvent. One tank holds 6 gallons more than twice the amount in the other. How many gallons does each tank hold?

29. ACCOUNTING Determine the 2002 income of Sears, Roebuck and Co. for each quarter from the data in the graph. (Source: Hoover's Online Internet service.)

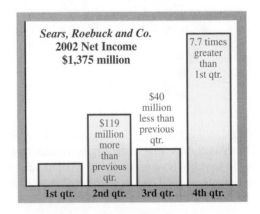

30. AMERICAN COLLEGE STUDENTS   A 1999–2000 survey found that the percent of college students that worked part time was 1% more than twice the percent that did not work. The percent that worked full time was 1% less than twice the percent that did not work. Find the missing percents in the graph.   (*Hint:* The sum of the percents is 100%.)

Most students work

Source: National Center for Education Statistics

31. ENGINEERING   A truss is in the form of an isosceles triangle. Each of the two equal sides is 4 feet shorter than the third side. If the perimeter is 25 feet, find the lengths of the sides.

32. FIRST AID   A sling is in the shape of an isosceles triangle with a perimeter of 144 inches. The longest side of the sling is 18 inches longer than either of the other two sides. Find the lengths of each side.

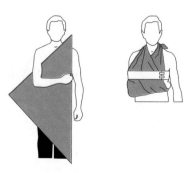

33. SWIMMING POOLS   The seawater Orthlieb Pool in Casablanca, Morocco, is the largest swimming pool in the world. With a perimeter of 1,110 meters, this rectangular-shaped pool is 30 meters longer than 6 times its width. Find its dimensions.

34. ART   The *Mona Lisa* was completed by Leonardo da Vinci in 1506. The length of the picture is 11.75 inches shorter than twice the width. If the perimeter of the picture is 102.5 inches, find its dimensions.

35. TV TOWERS   The two guy wires supporting a tower form an isosceles triangle with the ground. Each of the base angles of the triangle is 4 times the third angle (the vertex angle). Find the measure of the vertex angle.

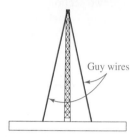

Guy wires

36. MOUNTAIN BICYCLES   For the bicycle frame shown, the angle that the horizontal crossbar makes with the seat support is 15° less than twice the angle at the steering column. The angle at the pedal gear is 25° more than the angle at the steering column. Find these three angle measures.

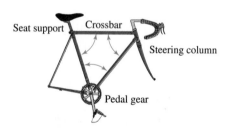

Seat support   Crossbar

Steering column

Pedal gear

37. COMPLEMENTARY ANGLES   Two angles are called **complementary angles** when the sum of their measures is 90°. Find the measures of the complementary angles shown here.

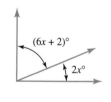

$(6x + 2)°$

$2x°$

38. SUPPLEMENTARY ANGLES   Two angles are called **supplementary angles** when the sum of their measures is 180°. Find the measures of the supplementary angles shown here.

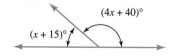

$(4x + 40)°$

$(x + 15)°$

39. RENTALS   The owners of an apartment building rent 1-, 2-, and 3-bedroom units. They rent equal numbers of each, with the monthly rents given in the table. If the total monthly income is $36,550, how many of each type of unit are there?

Unit	Rent
One-bedroom	$550
Two-bedroom	$700
Three-bedroom	$900

40. WAREHOUSING   A store warehouses 40 more portables than big-screen TV sets, and 15 more consoles than big-screen sets. Storage costs for the different TV sets are shown in the table. If storage costs $276 per month, how many big-screen sets are in stock?

Type of TV	Monthly cost
Portable	$1.50
Console	$4.00
Big-screen	$7.50

41. SOFTWARE   Three software applications are priced as shown. Spreadsheet and database programs sold in equal numbers, but 15 more word processing applications were sold than the other two combined. If the three applications generated sales of $72,000, how many spreadsheets were sold?

Software	Price
Spreadsheet	$150
Database	$195
Word processing	$210

42. INVENTORIES   With summer approaching, the number of air conditioners sold is expected to be double that of stoves and refrigerators combined. Stoves sell for $350, refrigerators for $450, and air conditioners for $500, and sales of $56,000 are expected. If stoves and refrigerators sell in equal numbers, how many of each appliance should be stocked?

43. INVESTMENTS   Equal amounts are invested in each of three accounts paying 7%, 8%, and 10.5% annually. If one year's combined interest income is $1,249.50, how much is invested in each account?

44. RETIREMENT   A professor wants to supplement her pension with investment interest. If she invests $28,000 at 6% interest, how much more would she have to invest at 7% to achieve a goal of $3,500 per year in supplemental income?

45. INVESTMENT PLANS   A financial planner recommends a plan for a client who has $65,000 to invest. (See the chart.) At the end of the presentation, the client asks, "How much will be invested at each rate?" Answer this question using the given information.

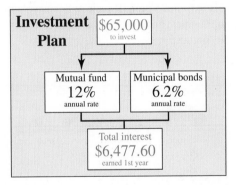

46. TAXES   On January 2, 2003, Terrell Washington opened two savings accounts. At the end of the year his bank mailed him the form shown below for income tax purposes. If a total of $15,000 was initially deposited and if no further deposits or withdrawals were made, how much money was originally deposited in account number 721?

USA HOME SAVINGS	Copy B For Recipient Interest Income
This is important tax information and is being furnished to the Internal Revenue Service.	OMB No. 1545-0112 **2003**
RECIPIENT'S name **TERRELL WASHINGTON**	Form 1099–iNT

Acct. Number	Annual Percent Yield	Early Withdrawal Penalty
822	5%	.00
721	4.5%	.00

Total Interest Income 720.00

47. FINANCIAL PLANNING   A plumber has a choice of two investment plans:

- An insured fund that pays 11% interest
- A risky investment that pays a 13% return

If the same amount invested at the higher rate would generate an extra $150 per year, how much does the plumber have to invest?

48. INVESTMENTS   The amount of annual interest earned by $8,000 invested at a certain rate is $200 less than $12,000 would earn at a rate 1% lower. At what rate is the $8,000 invested?

49. TORNADOES   During a storm, two teams of scientists leave a university at the same time in specially designed vans to search for tornadoes. The first team travels east at 20 mph and the second travels west at 25 mph. If their radios have a range of up to 90 miles, how long will it be before they lose radio contact?

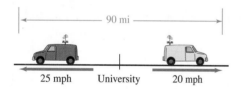

50. SEARCH AND RESCUE   Two search-and-rescue teams leave base at the same time looking for a lost boy. The first team, on foot, heads north at 2 mph and the other, on horseback, south at 4 mph. How long will it take them to search a combined distance of 21 miles between them?

51. AIR TRAFFIC CONTROL   An airliner leaves Berlin, Germany, headed for Montreal, Canada, flying at an average speed of 450 mph. At the same time, an airliner leaves Montreal headed for Berlin, averaging 500 mph. If the airports are 3,800 miles apart, when will the air traffic controllers have to make the pilots aware that the planes are passing each other?

52. SPEED OF TRAINS   Two trains are 330 miles apart, and their speeds differ by 20 mph. Find the speed of each train if they are traveling toward each other and will meet in 3 hours.

53. ROAD TRIPS   A car averaged 40 mph for part of a trip and 50 mph for the remainder. If the 5-hour trip covered 210 miles, for how long did the car average 40 mph?

54. CYCLING   A cyclist leaves his training base for a morning workout, riding at the rate of 18 mph. One hour later, his support staff leaves the base in a car going 45 mph in the same direction. How long will it take the support staff to catch up with the cyclist?

55. PHOTOGRAPHIC CHEMICALS   A photographer wishes to mix 2 liters of a 5% acetic acid solution with a 10% solution to get a 7% solution. How many liters of 10% solution must be added?

56. SALT SOLUTIONS   How many gallons of a 3% salt solution must be mixed with 50 gallons of a 7% solution to obtain a 5% solution?

57. ANTISEPTIC SOLUTIONS   A nurse wants to add water to 30 ounces of a 10% solution of benzalkonium chloride to dilute it to an 8% solution. How much water must she add?   (*Hint:* Water is 0% benzalkonium chloride.)

58. MAKING CHEESE   To make low-fat cottage cheese, milk containing 4% butterfat is mixed with milk containing 1% butterfat to obtain 15 gallons of a mixture containing 2% butterfat. How many gallons of the richer milk must be used?

59. MIXING FUELS   How many gallons of fuel costing $1.15 per gallon must be mixed with 20 gallons of a fuel costing $0.85 per gallon to obtain a mixture costing $1 per gallon?

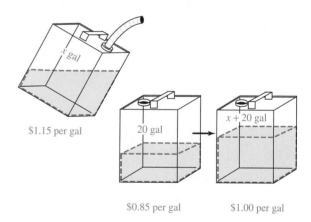

60. MIXING PAINT   Paint costing $19 per gallon is to be mixed with $3-per-gallon thinner to make 16 gallons of a paint that can be sold for $14 per gallon. How much paint thinner should be used?

61. BLENDING LAWN SEED   A store sells bluegrass seed for $6 per pound and ryegrass seed for $3 per pound. How much ryegrass must be mixed with 100 pounds of bluegrass to obtain a blend that will sell for $5 per pound?

62. BLENDING COFFEE   A store sells regular coffee for $4 a pound and gourmet coffee for $7 a pound. To get rid of 40 pounds of the gourmet coffee, a shopkeeper makes a blend to put on sale for $5 a pound. How many pounds of regular coffee should he use?

63. MIXING CANDY   Lemon drops worth $1.90 per pound are to be mixed with jelly beans that cost $1.20 per pound to make 100 pounds of a mixture worth $1.48 per pound. How many pounds of each candy should be used?

64. SNACK FOODS   A bag of peanuts is worth $.30 less than a bag of cashews. Equal amounts of peanuts and cashews are used to make 40 bags of a mixture that sells for $1.05 per bag. How much is a bag of cashews worth?

WRITING

65. Create a mixture problem of your own, and solve it.

66. Is it possible to mix a 10% sugar solution with a 20% sugar solution to get a 30% sugar solution?

67. A car travels at 60 mph for 15 minutes. Why can't we multiply the rate, 60, and the time, 15, to find the distance traveled by the car?

68. Create a geometry problem that could be answered by solving the equation $2w + 2(w + 5) = 26$.

REVIEW   Remove parentheses.

69. $-25(2x - 5)$

70. $-12(3a + 4b - 32)$

71. $-(-3x - 3)$

72. $\frac{1}{2}(4b - 8)$

73. $(4y - 4)4$

74. $3(5t + 1)2$

CHALLENGE PROBLEMS

75. EVAPORATION   How much water must be boiled away to increase the concentration of 300 milliliters of a 2% salt solution to a 3% salt solution?

76. TESTING   A teacher awarded 4 points for each correct answer and deducted 2 points for each incorrect answer when grading a 50-question true-false test. A student scored 56 points on the test, and did not leave any questions unanswered. How many questions did the student answer correctly?

ACCENT ON TEAMWORK

TRANSLATING KEY WORDS AND PHRASES

Overview: Students often say that the most challenging step of the five-step problem-solving strategy is forming an equation. This activity is designed to make that step easier by improving your translating skills.

Instructions: Form groups of 3 or 4 students. Select one person from your group to record the group's responses. Determine whether addition, subtraction, multiplication, or division is suggested by each of the following words or phrases. Then use the word or phrase in a sentence to illustrate its meaning.

deflate	recede	partition	evaporate	amplify
bisect	augment	hike	erode	boost
annexed	diminish	plummet	upsurge	wane
quadruple	corrode	taper off	trisect	broaden

GEOMETRIC SNACKS

Overview: This activity is designed to improve your ability to identify geometric figures and recall their perimeter, area, and volume formulas.

Instructions: Review the geometric figures and formulas inside the front cover. Then find some snack foods that have the shapes of the figures. For example, tortilla chips can be triangular in shape, and malted milk balls are spheres. If you are unable to find a particular shape already available, make a snack in that shape. Bring your collection of snacks to the next class. Form groups of 3 or 4 students. In your group, discuss the various shapes of the snacks, as well as their respective perimeter, area, and volume formulas.

COMPUTER SPREADSHEETS

Overview: In this activity, you will get some experience working with a spreadsheet.

Instructions: Form groups of 3 or 4 students. Examine the following spreadsheet, which consists of cells named by column and row. For example, 7 is entered in cell B3. In any cell you may enter data or a formula. For each formula in cells D1–D4 and E1–E4, the computer performs a calculation using values entered in other cells and prints the result in place of the formula. Find the value that will be printed in each formula cell. The symbol $*$ means multiply, $/$ means divide, and $\wedge$ means raise to a power.

	A	B	C	D	E
1	-8	20	-6	$= 2*B1 - 3*C1 + 4$	$= B1 - 3*A1\wedge2$
2	39	2	-1	$= A2/(B2 - C2)$	$= B3*B2*C2*2$
3	50	7	3	$= A3/5 + C3\wedge3$	$= 65 - 2*(B3 - 5)\wedge5$
4	6.8	-2.8	-0.5	$= 100*A4 + B4*C4$	$= A4/10 + A3/2*5$

KEY CONCEPT: SIMPLIFY AND SOLVE

Two of the most often used instructions in this book are **simplify** and **solve**. In algebra, we *simplify expressions* and we *solve equations and inequalities.*

To simplify an expression, we write it in a less complicated form. To do so, we apply the rules of arithmetic as well as algebraic concepts such as combining like terms, the distributive property, and the properties of 0 and 1.

To solve an equation or an inequality means to find the numbers that make the equation or inequality true when substituted for its variable. We use the addition, subtraction, multiplication, and division properties of equality or inequality to solve equations and inequalities. Quite often, we must simplify expressions on the left- or right-hand sides of an equation or inequality when solving it.

Use the procedures and the properties that we have studied to simplify the expression in part a and to solve the equation or inequality in part b.

Simplify

1. a. $-3x + 2 + 5x - 10$

2. a. $4(y + 2) - 3(y + 1)$

3. a. $\dfrac{1}{3}a + \dfrac{1}{3}a$

4. a. $-(2x + 10)$

5. a. $\dfrac{2}{3}(x - 2) - \dfrac{1}{6}(4x - 8)$

Solve

b. $-3x + 2 + 5x - 10 = 4$

b. $4(y + 2) = 3(y + 1)$

b. $\dfrac{1}{3}a + \dfrac{1}{3} = \dfrac{1}{2}$

b. $-2x \geq -10$

b. $\dfrac{2}{3}(x - 2) - \dfrac{1}{6}(4x - 8) = 0$

6. In the student's work on the right, where was the mistake made? Explain what the student did wrong.

Simplify: $2(x + 3) - x - 12$.

$$2(x + 3) - x - 12 = 2x + 6 - x - 12$$
$$= x - 6$$
$$0 = x - 6$$
$$0 + 6 = x - 6 + 6$$
$$\boxed{6 = x}$$

CHAPTER REVIEW

SECTION 2.1	Solving Equations

CONCEPTS

A number that makes an equation a true statement when substituted for the variable is called a *solution* of the equation.

REVIEW EXERCISES

Decide whether the given number is a solution of the equation.

1. $84, x - 34 = 50$

2. $3, 5y + 2 = 12$

3. $-30, \dfrac{x}{5} = 6$

4. $2, a^2 - a - 1 = 0$

5. $-3, 5b - 2 = 3b - 8$

6. $1, \dfrac{2}{y + 1} = \dfrac{12}{y + 1} - 5$

To *solve an equation,* isolate the variable on one side of the equation by undoing the operations performed on it.

Equations with the same solutions are called *equivalent equations.*

If the same number is added to, or subtracted from, both sides of an equation, an equivalent equation results.

If both sides of an equation are multiplied, or divided, by the same nonzero number, an equivalent equation results.

7. Fill in the blanks: To solve $x + 8 = 10$ means to find all the values of the _____ that make the equation a _____ statement.

Solve each equation. Check each result.

8. $x - 9 = 12$

9. $y + 15 = -32$

10. $a + 3.7 = 16.9$

11. $100 = -7 + r$

12. $120 = 15c$

13. $t - \dfrac{1}{2} = \dfrac{1}{2}$

14. $\dfrac{t}{8} = -12$

15. $3 = \dfrac{q}{2.6}$

16. $6b = 0$

17. $\dfrac{x}{14} = 0$

18. GEOMETRY   Find the unknown angle measure.

SECTION 2.2	**Problem Solving**

To solve a problem, follow these steps:

1. Analyze the problem.
2. Form an equation.
3. Solve the equation.
4. State the conclusion.
5. Check the result.

Drawing a diagram or creating a table is often helpful in problem solving.

19. WOMEN'S SOCCER   The U.S. National Women's team won the 1999 World Cup. On the 20-player roster were 3 goalkeepers, 6 defenders, 6 midfielders, and a group of forwards. How many forwards were on the team?

20. HISTORIC TOURS   A driving tour of three historic cities is an 858-mile round trip. Beginning in Boston, the drive to Philadelphia is 296 miles. From Philadelphia to Washington, D.C., is another 133 miles. How long will the return trip to Boston be?

21. CHROME WHEELS   Find the measure of the angle between each of the spokes on the wheel shown.

To solve applied percent problems, use the facts of the problem to write a percent sentence of the form:

    is   % of   .

Translate the sentence to mathematical symbols: *is* translates to an = symbol and *of* means multiply. Then, solve the resulting equation.

22. ADVERTISING   In 2001, $231 billion was spent on advertising in the United States. The circle graph gives the individual expenditures in percents. Find the amount of money spent on television advertising. Round to the nearest billion dollars.

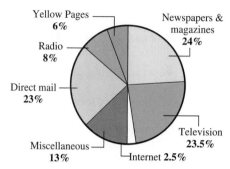

Based on data from *Advertising Age*

23. COST OF LIVING   A retired trucker receives a monthly Social Security check of $764. If she is to receive a 3.5% cost-of-living increase soon, how much larger will her check be?

24. 4.81 is 2.5% of what number?

25. FAMILY BUDGETS   It is recommended that a family pay no more than 30% of its monthly income (after taxes) on housing. If a family has an after-tax income of $1,890 per month and pays $625 in housing costs each month, are they within the recommended range?

To find *percent of increase or decrease,* find what percent the increase or decrease is of the original amount.

26. COLLECTIBLES   A collector of football trading cards paid $6 for a 1984 Dan Marino rookie card several years ago. If the card is now worth $100, what is the percent of increase in the card's value? (Round to the nearest one percent.)

| SECTION 2.3 | Simplifying Algebraic Expressions |

To *simplify* an algebraic expression means to write it in less complicated form.

The *distributive property:*
$a(b + c) = ab + ac$
$a(b - c) = ab - ac$
$a(b + c + d)$
$\quad = ab + ac + ad$

Simplify each expression.

27. $-4(7w)$

28. $-3r(-5)$

29. $3(-2x)(-4)$

30. $0.4(5.2f)$

31. $15\left(\dfrac{3}{5}a\right)$

32. $\dfrac{7}{2} \cdot \dfrac{2}{7}r$

Remove parentheses.

33. $5(x + 3)$

34. $-2(2x + 3 - y)$

35. $-(a - 4)$

36. $\dfrac{3}{4}(4c - 8)$

37. $40\left(\dfrac{x}{2} + \dfrac{4}{5}\right)$

38. $2(-3c - 7)(2.1)$

Like terms are terms with exactly the same variables raised to exactly the same powers.

To add or subtract like terms, combine their coefficients and keep the same variables with the same exponents.

Simplify each expression by combining like terms.

39. $8p + 5p - 4p$

40. $-5m + 2 - 2m - 2$

41. $n + n + n + n$

42. $5(p - 2) - 2(3p + 4)$

43. $55.7k - 55.6k$

44. $8a^3 + 4a^3 - 20a^3$

45. $\dfrac{3}{5}w - \left(-\dfrac{2}{5}w\right)$

46. $36\left(\dfrac{1}{9}h - \dfrac{3}{4}\right) + 36\left(\dfrac{1}{3}\right)$

47. Write an algebraic expression in simplified form for the perimeter of the triangle.

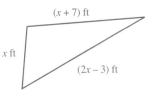

$(x + 7)$ ft

x ft

$(2x - 3)$ ft

SECTION 2.4

More about Solving Equations

To solve an equation means to find all the values of the variable that, when substituted for the variable, make a true statement.

An equation that is true for all values of its variable is called an *identity.*

An equation that is not true for any values of its variable is called a *contradiction.*

Solve each equation. Check the result.

48. $5x + 4 = 14$

49. $98.6 - t = 129.2$

50. $\dfrac{n}{5} - 2 = 4$

51. $\dfrac{b - 5}{4} = -6$

52. $5(2x - 4) - 5x = 0$

53. $-2(x - 5) = 5(-3x + 4) + 3$

54. $\dfrac{3}{4} = \dfrac{1}{2} + \dfrac{d}{5}$

55. $-\dfrac{2}{3}f = 4$

56. $\dfrac{3(2 - c)}{2} = \dfrac{-2(2c + 3)}{5}$

57. $\dfrac{b}{3} + \dfrac{11}{9} + 3b = -\dfrac{5}{6}b$

58. $3(a + 8) = 6(a + 4) - 3a$

59. $2(y + 10) + y = 3(y + 8)$

SECTION 2.5	**Formulas**

A *formula* is an equation that is used to state a known relationship between two or more variables.

Retail price: $r = c + m$

Profit: $p = r - c$

Distance: $d = rt$

Temperature:
$C = \frac{5}{9}(F - 32)$

Formulas from geometry:

Square: $P = 4s, A = s^2$

Rectangle: $P = 2l + 2w,$
$A = lw$

Triangle: $P = a + b + c$
$A = \frac{1}{2}bh$

Trapezoid:
$P = a + b + c + d$
$A = \frac{1}{2}h(b + d)$

Circle: $D = 2r$
$C = 2\pi r$
$A = \pi r^2$

Rectangular solid:
$V = lwh$

Cylinder: $V = \pi r^2 h$

Pyramid: $V = \frac{1}{3}Bh$
  (*B* is the area of the base)

Cone: $V = \frac{1}{3}\pi r^2 h$

Sphere: $V = \frac{4}{3}\pi r^3$

60. Find the markup on a CD player whose wholesale cost is $219 and whose retail price is $395.

61. One month, a restaurant had sales of $13,500 and made a profit of $1,700. Find the expenses for the month.

62. INDY 500   In 2002, the winner of the Indianapolis 500-mile automobile race averaged 166.499 mph. To the nearest hundredth of an hour, how long did it take him to complete the race?

63. JEWELRY MAKING   Gold melts at about 1,065°C. Change this to degrees Fahrenheit.

64. CAMPING   Find the perimeter of the air mattress.

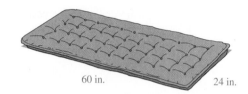

60 in.   24 in.

65. CAMPING   Find the amount of sleeping area on the top surface of the air mattress.

66. Find the area of a triangle with a base 17 meters long and a height of 9 meters.

67. Find the area of a trapezoid with bases 11 inches and 13 inches long and a height of 12 inches.

68. To the nearest hundredth, find the circumference of a circle with a radius of 8 centimeters.

69. To the nearest hundredth, find the area of the circle in Problem 68.

70. CAMPING   Find the approximate volume of the air mattress in Problem 64 if it is 3 inches thick.

71. Find the volume of a 12-foot cylinder whose circular base has a radius of 0.5 feet. Give the result to the nearest tenth.

72. Find the volume of a pyramid that has a square base, measuring 6 feet on a side, and a height of 10 feet.

73. HALLOWEEN   After being cleaned out, a spherical-shaped pumpkin has an inside diameter of 9 inches. To the nearest hundredth, what is its volume?

Solve each formula for the required variable.

74. $A = 2\pi rh$ for h

75. $A - BC = \dfrac{G - K}{3}$ for G

76. $a^2 + b^2 = c^2$ for b^2

77. $4y - 16 = 3x$ for y

| SECTION 2.6 | **More about Problem Solving** |

To solve problems, use the five-step problem-solving strategy.

1. Analyze the problem.
2. Form an equation.
3. Solve the equation.
4. State the conclusion.
5. Check the result.

78. SOUND SYSTEMS   A 45-foot-long speaker wire is to be cut into three pieces. One piece is to be 15 feet long. Of the remaining pieces, one must be 2 feet less than 3 times the length of the other. Find the length of the shorter piece.

79. AUTOGRAPHS   Kesha collected the autographs of 8 more television celebrities than she has of movie stars. Each TV celebrity autograph is worth $75 and each movie star autograph is worth $250. If her collection is valued at $1,900, how many of each type of autograph does she have?

80. ART HISTORY   *American Gothic* was painted in 1930 by Grant Wood. The length of the rectangular painting is 5 inches more than the width. Find the dimensions of the painting if it has a perimeter of $109\frac{1}{2}$ inches.

The sum of the measures of the angles of a triangle is 180°.

81. Find the missing angle measures of the triangle.

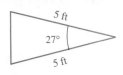

Total value
    = number · value
Interest = principal
     · rate · time
    $I = Prt$

82. Write an expression to represent the value of x video games each costing $45.

83. INVESTMENT INCOME   A woman has $27,000. Part is invested for 1 year in a certificate of deposit paying 7% interest, and the remaining amount in a cash management fund paying 9%. After 1 year, the total interest on the two investments is $2,110. How much is invested at each rate?

Distance = rate · time
    $d = rt$

84. WALKING AND BICYCLING   A bicycle path is 5 miles long. A man walks from one end at the rate of 3 mph. At the same time, a friend bicycles from the other end, traveling at 12 mph. In how many minutes will they meet?

The value v of a commodity is its price per pound p times the number of pounds n:

$$v = pn$$

85. MIXTURES   A store manager mixes candy worth 90¢ per pound with gumdrops worth $1.50 per pound to make 20 pounds of a mixture worth $1.20 per pound. How many pounds of each kind of candy does he use?

86. SOLUTIONS   How much acetic acid is in x gallons of a solution that is 12% acetic acid?

SECTION 2.7	Solving Inequalities

An *inequality* is a mathematical expression that contains a $>$, $<$, $\geq$, or $\leq$ symbol.

A *solution of an inequality* is any number that makes the inequality true.

A *parenthesis* indicates that a number is not on the graph. A *bracket* indicates that a number is included in the graph.

Interval notation can be used to describe a set of real numbers.

Solve each inequality. Write the solution set in interval notation and graph it.

87. $3x + 2 < 5$

88. $-\dfrac{3}{4}x \geq -9$

89. $\dfrac{3}{4} < \dfrac{d}{5} + \dfrac{1}{2}$

90. $5(3 - x) \leq 3(x - 3)$

91. $8 < x + 2 < 13$

92. $0 \leq 3 - 2x < 10$

93. SPORTS EQUIPMENT   The acceptable weight of Ping-Pong balls used in competition can range from 2.40 to 2.53 grams. Express this range using a compound inequality.

94. SIGNS   A large office complex has a strict policy about signs. Any sign to be posted in the building must meet three requirements:

- It must be rectangular in shape.
- Its width must be 18 inches.
- Its perimeter is not to exceed 132 inches.

What possible sign lengths meet these specifications?

CHAPTER 2 TEST ⊙

1. Is 3 a solution of $2x + 3 = 4x - 6$?

2. EXERCISING
   Find x.

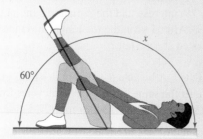

3. MULTIPLE BIRTHS IN THE UNITED STATES   In 2000, about 7,322 women gave birth to three or more babies at one time. This is about seven times the number of such births in 1971, 29 years earlier. How many multiple births occurred in 1971?

4. DOWN PAYMENTS   To buy a house, a woman was required to make a down payment of $11,400. What did the house sell for if this was 15% of the purchase price?

5. **SPORTS** In sports, percentages are most often expressed as three-place decimals instead of percents. For example, if a basketball player makes 75.8% of his free throws, the sports page will list this as .758. Use this format to complete the table.

All-time best regular-season winning percentages		
Team	Won–lost record	Winning percentage
1996 Chicago Bulls Basketball	72–10	
1972 Miami Dolphins Football	14–0	

6. **BODY TEMPERATURES** Suppose a person's body temperature rises from 98.6°F to 101.6°F. What is the percent increase? Round to the nearest one percent.

7. Find the expression that represents the perimeter of the rectangle.

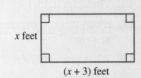

x feet

$(x + 3)$ feet

8. What property is illustrated below?

$$2(x + 7) = 2x + 2(7)$$

Simplify each expression.

9. $5(-4x)$

10. $-8(-7t)(4)$

11. $\dfrac{4}{5}(15a + 5) - 16a$

12. $-1.1d^2 - 3.8d^2 - d^2$

Solve each equation.

13. $5h + 8 - 3h + h = 8$

14. $\dfrac{4}{5}t = -4$

15. $\dfrac{11(b - 1)}{5} = 3b - 2$

16. $0.8x + 1.4 = 2.9 + 0.2x$

17. $\dfrac{m}{2} - \dfrac{1}{3} = \dfrac{1}{4}$

18. $23 - 5(x + 10) = -12$

19. Solve the equation for the variable indicated.
$A = P + Prt$; for r

20. On its first night of business, a pizza parlor brought in $445. The owner estimated his costs that night to be $295. What was the profit?

21. Find the Celsius temperature reading if the Fahrenheit reading is 14°.

22. **PETS** The spherical fishbowl is three-quarters full of water. To the nearest cubic inch, find the volume of water in the bowl.

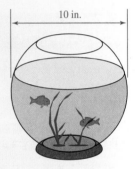

10 in.

23. **TRAVEL TIMES** A car leaves Rockford, Illinois, at the rate of 65 mph, bound for Madison, Wisconsin. At the same time, a truck leaves Madison at the rate of 55 mph, bound for Rockford. If the cities are 72 miles apart, how long will it take for the car and the truck to meet?

24. **SALT SOLUTIONS** How many liters of a 2% brine solution must be added to 30 liters of a 10% brine solution to dilute it to an 8% solution?

25. **GEOMETRY** If the vertex angle of an isosceles triangle is 44°, find the measure of each base angle.

26. **INVESTMENT PROBLEM** Part of $13,750 is invested at 9% annual interest, and the rest is invested at 8%. After one year, the accounts paid $1,185 in interest. How much was invested at the lower rate?

Solve each inequality. Write the solution set in interval notation and graph it.

27. $-8x - 20 \le 4$ **28.** $-4 \le 2(x + 1) < 10$

29. DRAFTING   In the illustration, the $\pm$ (read "plus or minus") symbol means that the width of a plug a manufacturer produces can range from $1.497 - 0.001$ inches to $1.497 + 0.001$ inches. Write the range of acceptable widths w for the plug using a compound inequality.

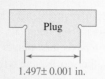

Plug

1.497 ± 0.001 in.

30. Solve: $2(y - 7) - 3y = -(y - 3) - 17$. Explain why the solution set is all real numbers.

CHAPTERS 1–2   CUMULATIVE REVIEW EXERCISES

1. Classify each of the following as an equation or an expression.
  a. $4m - 3 + 2m$ **b.** $4m = 3 + 2m$

2. Use the formula $t = \dfrac{w}{5}$ to complete the table.

Weight (lb)	Cooking time (hr)
15	
20	
25	

3. Give the prime factorization of 200.

4. Simplify: $\dfrac{24}{36}$.

5. Multiply: $\dfrac{11}{21}\left(-\dfrac{14}{33}\right)$.

6. COOKING   A recipe calls for $\frac{3}{4}$ cup of flour, and the only measuring container you have holds $\frac{1}{8}$ of a cup. How many $\frac{1}{8}$ cups of flour would you need to add to follow the recipe?

7. Add: $\dfrac{4}{5} + \dfrac{2}{3}$.

8. Subtract: $42\frac{1}{8} - 29\frac{2}{3}$.

9. Write $\dfrac{15}{16}$ as a decimal.

10. Multiply: $0.45(100)$.

11. Evaluate each expression.
  a. $|-65|$ **b.** $-|-12|$

12. What property of real numbers is illustrated below?

$x \cdot 5 = 5x$

Classify each number as a natural number, a whole number, an integer, a rational number, an irrational number, and a real number. Each number may have several classifications.

13. 3

14. -1.95

15. $\dfrac{17}{20}$

16. π

17. Write each product using exponents.
  a. $4 \cdot 4 \cdot 4$ **b.** $\pi \cdot r \cdot r \cdot h$

18. Perform each operation.
  a. $-6 + (-12) + 8$
  b. $-15 - (-1)$
  c. $2(-32)$
  d. $\dfrac{0}{35}$ **e.** $\dfrac{-11}{11}$

19. Write each phrase as an algebraic expression.
  a. The sum of the width w and 12.
  b. Four less than a number n.

20. SICK DAYS   Use the data in the table to find the average (mean) number of sick days used by this group of employees this year.

Name	Sick days	Name	Sick days
Chung	4	Ryba	0
Cruz	8	Nguyen	5
Damron	3	Tomaka	4
Hammond	2	Young	6

21. Complete the table.

x	$x^2 - 3$
-2	
0	
3	

22. Translate to mathematical symbols.

The loudness of a stereo speaker	is	2,000	divided by	the square of the distance of the listener from the speaker.

23. LAND OF THE RISING SUN   The flag of Japan is a red disc (representing sincerity and passion) on a white background (representing honesty and purity).
  a. What is the area of the rectangular-shaped flag?

  b. To the nearest tenth of a square foot, what is the area of the red disc?
  c. Use the results from parts a and b to find what percent of the area of the Japanese flag is occupied by the red disc.

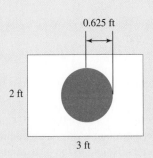

24. 45 is 15% of what number?

Let $x = -5$, $y = 3$, and $z = 0$. Evaluate each expression.

25. $(3x - 2y)z$

26. $\dfrac{x - 3y + |z|}{2 - x}$

27. $x^2 - y^2 + z^2$

28. $\dfrac{x}{y} + \dfrac{y + 2}{3 - z}$

Simplify each expression.

29. $-8(4d)$

30. $5(2x - 3y + 1)$

31. $2x + 3x - x$

32. $3a^2 + 6a^2 - 17a^2$

33. $\dfrac{2}{3}(15t - 30) + t - 30$ **34.** $5(t - 4) + 3t$

35. What is the length of the longest side of the triangle shown below?

36. Write an algebraic expression in simplest form for the perimeter of the triangle.

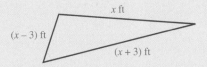

Solve each equation.

37. $3x - 4 = 23$

38. $\dfrac{x}{5} + 3 = 7$

39. $-5p + 0.7 = 3.7$

40. $\dfrac{y - 4}{5} = 3 - y$

41. $-\dfrac{4}{5}x = 16$

42. $\dfrac{1}{2} + \dfrac{x}{5} = \dfrac{3}{4}$

43. $-9(n + 2) - 2(n - 3) = 10$

44. $\frac{2}{3}(r - 2) = \frac{1}{6}(4r - 1) + 1$

45. Find the area of a rectangle with sides of 5 meters and 13 meters.

46. Find the volume of a cone that is 10 centimeters tall and has a circular base whose diameter is 12 centimeters. Round to the nearest hundredth.

47. Solve $V = \frac{1}{3}\pi r^2 h$ for r^2.

48. WORK   Physicists say that work is done when an object is moved a distance d by a force F. To find the work done, we can use the formula $W = Fd$. Find the work done in lifting the bundle of newspapers onto the workbench.   (*Hint:* The force that must be applied to lift the newspapers is equal to the weight of the newspapers.)

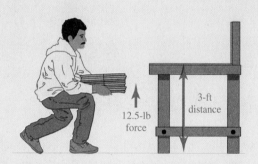

12.5-lb force

3-ft distance

49. WORK   See Exercise 48. Find the weight of a 1-gallon can of paint if the amount of work done to lift it onto the workbench is 28.35 foot-pounds.

50. Find the unknown angle measures.

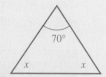

70°

x x

51. INVESTING   An investment club invested part of $10,000 at 9% annual interest and the rest at 8%. If the annual income from these investments was $860, how much was invested at 8%?

52. GOLDSMITH   How many ounces of a 40% gold alloy must be mixed with 10 ounces of a 10% gold alloy to obtain an alloy that is 25% gold?

Solve each inequality. Write the solution set in interval notation and graph it.

53. $x - 4 > -6$

54. $-6x \geq -12$

55. $8x + 4 \geq 5x + 1$

56. $-1 \leq 2x + 1 < 5$

Chapter

3

Linear Equations and Inequalities in Two Variables

Getty/Stone/Glen Allison

Snow skiing is one of our country's most popular recreational activities. Whether on the gentle incline of a cross-country trip or racing down a near-vertical mountainside, a skier constantly adapts to the steepness of the course. In this chapter, we discuss lines and a means of measuring their steepness, called *slope*. The concept of slope has a wide variety of applications, including roofing, road design, and handicap accessible ramps.

To learn more about the slope of a line, visit *The Learning Equation* on the Internet at http://tle.brookscole.com. (The log-in instructions are in the Preface.) For Chapter 3, the following online lessons are:

- *TLE* Lesson 6: Equations Containing Two Variables
- *TLE* Lesson 7: Rate of Change and the Slope of a Line

Relationships between two quantities can be described by a table, a graph, or an equation.

3.1   Graphing Using the Rectangular Coordinate System

- The Rectangular Coordinate System   • Graphing Mathematical Relationships
- Reading Graphs

It is often said, "A picture is worth a thousand words." That is certainly true when it comes to graphs. Graphs present data in an attractive and informative way. **Bar graphs** enable us to make quick comparisons, **line graphs** let us notice trends, and **circle graphs** show the relationship of the parts to the whole.

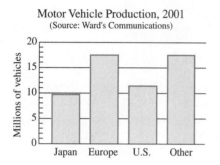

Motor Vehicle Production, 2001
(Source: Ward's Communications)

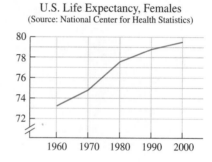

U.S. Life Expectancy, Females
(Source: National Center for Health Statistics)

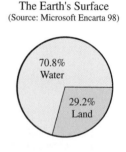

The Earth's Surface
(Source: Microsoft Encarta 98)

We will now introduce another type of graph that is widely used in mathematics called a *rectangular coordinate graph.*

■ THE RECTANGULAR COORDINATE SYSTEM

When designing the Gateway Arch in St. Louis, architects created a mathematical model called a **rectangular coordinate graph.** This graph, shown below on the right, is drawn on a grid called a **rectangular coordinate system.** This coordinate system is also called a **Cartesian coordinate system,** after the 17th-century French mathematician René Descartes.

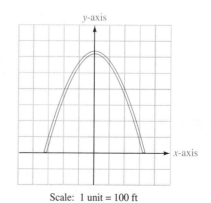

Scale: 1 unit = 100 ft

A rectangular coordinate system is formed by two perpendicular number lines. The horizontal number line is usually called the **x-axis,** and the vertical number line is usually called the **y-axis.** On the x-axis, the positive direction is to the right. On the y-axis, the positive direction is upward. Each axis should be scaled to fit the data. For example, the axes of the graph of the arch are scaled in units of 100 feet.

The point where the axes intersect is called the **origin.** This is the zero point on each axis. The axes form a **coordinate plane,** and they divide it into four regions called **quadrants,** which are numbered using Roman numerals.

The Language of Algebra

The word *axis* is used in mathematics and science. For example, Earth rotates on its *axis* once every 24 hours.

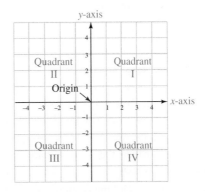

Each point in a coordinate plane can be identified by an **ordered pair** of real numbers x and y written in the form (x, y). The first number x in the pair is called the **x-coordinate,** and the second number y is called the **y-coordinate.** Some examples of such pairs are (3, −4), $\left(-1, -\frac{3}{2}\right)$, and (0, 2.5).

Notation

Don't be confused by this new use of parentheses. The notation (3, −4) represents a point on the coordinate plane, whereas 3(−4) indicates multiplication. Also, don't confuse the ordered pair with interval notation.

$$(3, -4)$$
$$\uparrow \qquad \uparrow$$
The x-coordinate   The y-coordinate

The process of locating a point in the coordinate plane is called **graphing** or **plotting** the point. Below, we use blue arrows to show how to graph the point with coordinates (3, −4). Since the x-coordinate, 3, is positive, we start at the origin and move 3 units to the *right* along the x-axis. Since the y-coordinate, −4, is negative, we then move *down* 4 units, and draw a dot. This locates the point (3, −4).

In the figure, red arrows are used to show how to plot the point (−4, 3). We start at the origin, move 4 units to the *left* along the x-axis, then move *up* 3 units and draw a dot. This locates the point (−4, 3).

The Language of Algebra

Note that the point (3, −4) has a different location than the point (−4, 3). Since the order of the coordinates of a point is important, we call them *ordered pairs.*

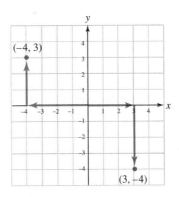

EXAMPLE 1

Plot each point and state the quadrant in which it lies.

a. $(4, 4)$ **b.** $\left(-1, -\frac{7}{2}\right)$ **c.** $(0, 2.5)$ **d.** $(-3, 0)$ **e.** $(0, 0)$

Solution

a. To plot the point $(4, 4)$, we begin at the origin, move 4 units to the *right* on the x-axis, and then move 4 units *up*. The point lies in quadrant I.

b. To plot the point $\left(-1, -\frac{7}{2}\right)$, we begin at the origin, move 1 unit to the *left*, and then move $\frac{7}{2}$ units, or $3\frac{1}{2}$ units, *down*. The point lies in quadrant III.

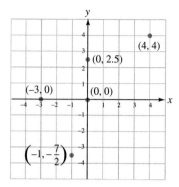

c. To plot the point $(0, 2.5)$, we begin at the origin and do not move right or left, because the x-coordinate is 0. Since the y-coordinate is positive, we move 2.5 units *up*. The point lies on the y-axis.

d. To plot the point $(-3, 0)$, we begin at the origin and move 3 units to the *left*. Since the y-coordinate is 0, we do not move up or down. The point lies on the x-axis.

e. To plot the point $(0, 0)$, we begin at the origin, and we remain there because both coordinates are 0. The point with coordinates $(0, 0)$ is the origin.

Success Tip

Points with an x-coordinate that is 0 lie on the y-axis. Points with a y-coordinate that is 0 lie on the x-axis. Points that lie on an axis are not considered to be in any quadrant.

Self Check 1

Plot the points:

a. $(2, -2)$ **b.** $(-4, 0)$ **c.** $\left(1.5, \frac{5}{2}\right)$ **d.** $(0, 5)$

EXAMPLE 2

Find the coordinates of points A, B, C, D, E, and F plotted below.

Notation

Points are labeled with capital letters. The notation $A(2, 3)$ indicates that point A has coordinates $(2, 3)$.

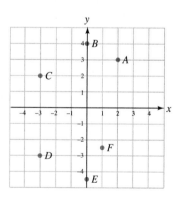

Solution

To locate point A, we start at the origin, move 2 units to the right, and then 3 units up. Its coordinates are $(2, 3)$. The coordinates of the other points are found in the same manner.

$B(0, 4)$ $C(-3, 2)$ $D(-3, -3)$ $E(0, -4.5)$ $F(1, -2.5)$

Self Check 2

Find the coordinates of each point.

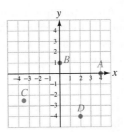

■ GRAPHING MATHEMATICAL RELATIONSHIPS

Every day, we deal with quantities that are related:

- The time it takes to cook a roast depends on the weight of the roast.
- The money we earn depends on the number of hours we work.
- The sales tax that we pay depends on the price of the item purchased.

We can use graphs to visualize such relationships. For example, suppose a tub is filling with water, as shown below. Obviously, the amount of water in the tub depends on how long the water has been running. To graph this relationship, we can use the measurements that were taken as the tub began to fill.

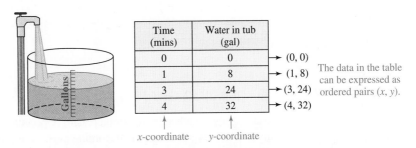

Time (mins)	Water in tub (gal)	
0	0	→ (0, 0)
1	8	→ (1, 8)
3	24	→ (3, 24)
4	32	→ (4, 32)

The data in the table can be expressed as ordered pairs (x, y).

x-coordinate   *y*-coordinate

The data in each row of the table can be written as an ordered pair and plotted on a rectangular coordinate system. Since the first coordinate of each ordered pair is a time, we label the *x*-axis *Time (min)*. The second coordinate is an amount of water, so we label the *y*-axis *Amount of water (gal)*. The *y*-axis is scaled in larger units (multiples of 4 gallons) because the size of the data ranges from 0 to 32 gallons.

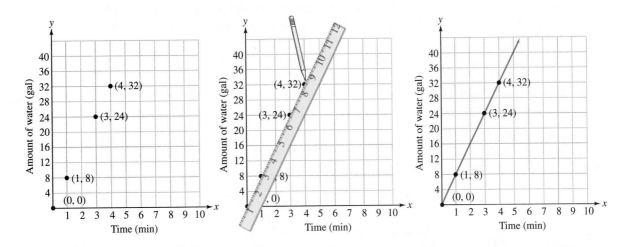

After plotting the ordered pairs, we use a straightedge to draw a line through the points. As we would expect, the completed graph shows that the amount of water in the tub increases steadily as the water is allowed to run.

We can use the graph to determine the amount of water in the tub at various times. For example, the green dashed line on the graph below shows that in 2 minutes, the tub will contain 16 gallons of water. This process, called **interpolation,** uses known information to predict values that are not known but are *within* the range of the data. The blue dashed line on the graph shows that in 5 minutes, the tub will contain 40 gallons of water. This process, called **extrapolation,** uses known information to predict values that are not known and are *outside* the range of the data.

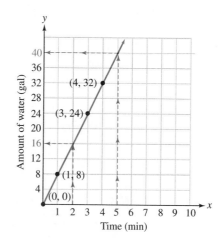

■ READING GRAPHS

Since graphs are becoming an increasingly popular way to present information, the ability to read and interpret them is becoming ever more important.

EXAMPLE 3

TV taping. The graph below shows the number of people in an audience before, during, and after the taping of a television show. Use the graph to answer the following questions.

a. How many people were in the audience when the taping began?
b. At what times were there exactly 100 people in the audience?
c. How long did it take the audience to leave after the taping ended?

The Language of Algebra

A rectangular coordinate system is a *grid*—a network of uniformly spaced perpendicular lines. At times, some large U.S. cities have such horrible traffic congestion that vehicles can barely move, if at all. The condition is called *gridlock.*

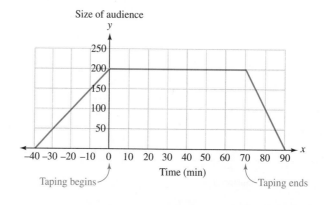

Solution   For each part of the solution, refer to the graph below. We can use the coordinates of specific points on the graph to answer these questions.

a. The time when the taping began is represented by 0 on the x-axis. The point on the graph directly above 0 is (0, 200). The y-coordinate indicates that 200 people were in the audience when the taping began.

b. We can draw a horizontal line passing through 100 on the y-axis. Since the line intersects the graph twice, at $(-20, 100)$ and at $(80, 100)$, there are two times when 100 people were in the audience. The x-coordinates of the points tell us those times: 20 minutes before the taping began, and 80 minutes after.

c. The x-coordinate of the point $(70, 200)$ tells us when the audience began to leave. The x-coordinate of $(90, 0)$ tells when the exiting was completed. Subtracting the x-coordinates, we see that it took $90 - 70 = 20$ minutes for the audience to leave.

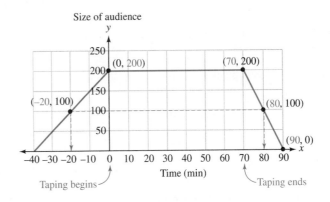

Self Check 3   Use the graph to answer the following questions.

a. At what times were there exactly 50 people in the audience?
b. How many people were in the audience when the taping took place?
c. When were the first audience members allowed into the taping session?

Answers to Self Checks   **1.**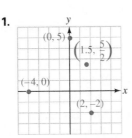

2. $A(4, 0)$; $B(0, 1)$; $C(-3.5, -2.5)$; $D(2, -4)$
3. a. 30 min before and 85 min after taping began,   **b.** 200,
c. 40 min before taping began

    3.1   **STUDY SET**

VOCABULARY   **Fill in the blanks.**

1. $(-1, -5)$ is called an _____ pair.

2. In the ordered pair $\left(-\frac{3}{2}, -5\right)$, the _____ is -5.

3. A rectangular coordinate system is formed by two perpendicular number lines called the _____ and the _____. The point where the axes cross is called the _____.

4. The *x*- and *y*-axes divide the coordinate plane into four regions called _____.

5. The point with coordinates (4, 2) can be graphed on a _____ coordinate system.

6. The process of locating the position of a point on a coordinate plane is called _____ the point.

CONCEPTS

7. Fill in the blanks.

    a. To plot the point with coordinates $(-5, 4)$, we start at the _____ and move 5 units to the _____ and then move 4 units _____.

    b. To plot the point with coordinates $\left(6, -\frac{3}{2}\right)$, we start at the _____ and move 6 units to the _____ and then move $\frac{3}{2}$ units _____.

8. In which quadrant is each point located?

    a. $(-2, 7)$ **b.** $(3, 16)$

    c. $(-1, -2.75)$ **d.** $(50, -16)$

    e. $\left(\frac{1}{2}, \frac{15}{16}\right)$ **f.** $(-6, \pi)$

9. a. In which quadrants are the second coordinates of points positive?

    b. In which quadrants are the first coordinates of points negative?

    c. In which quadrant do points with a negative *x*-coordinate and a positive *y*-coordinate lie?

    d. In which quadrant do points with a positive *x*-coordinate and a negative *y*-coordinate lie?

10. FARMING

    a. Write each row of data in the table as an ordered pair.

Rain (inches)	Bushels produced	
2	10	→
4	15	→
8	25	→

    b. Plot the ordered pairs on the following graph. Then draw a straight line through the points.

    c. Use the graph to determine how many bushels will be produced if 6 inches of rain fall.

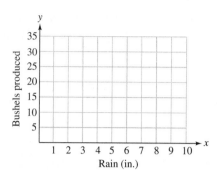

The graph that follows gives the heart rate of a woman before, during, and after an aerobic workout. In Problems 11–18, use the graph to answer the questions.

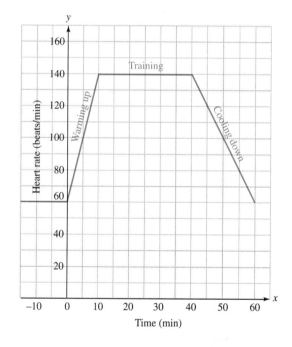

11. What was her heart rate before beginning the workout?

12. After beginning her workout, how long did it take the woman to reach her training-zone heart rate?

13. What was the woman's heart rate half an hour after beginning the workout?

14. For how long did the woman work out at her training zone?

15. At what time was her heart rate 100 beats per minute?

16. How long was her cool-down period?

17. What was the difference in the woman's heart rate before the workout and after the cool-down period?

18. What was her approximate heart rate 8 minutes after beginning?

19. BAR GRAPHS   Use the graph on page 184 to estimate the difference in the number of motor vehicles produced by Europe and the United States in 2001.

20. CIRCLE GRAPHS   The surface area of Earth is about 197,000,000 square miles. Use the graph on page 184 to find how many square miles are covered with water.

NOTATION

21. Explain the difference between (3, 5), 3(5), and 5(3 + 5).

22. In the table, which column contains values associated with the vertical axis of a graph?

x	y
2	0
5	3
−1	−3

23. Do these ordered pairs name the same point? $\left(2.5, -\frac{7}{2}\right), \left(2\frac{1}{2}, -3.5\right), \left(2.5, -3\frac{1}{2}\right)$

24. Do (3, 2) and (2, 3) represent the same point?

25. In the ordered pair (4, 5), is the number 4 associated with the horizontal or the vertical axis?

26. Fill in the blank: In the notation $A(4, 5)$, the capital letter A is used to name a _____.

PRACTICE

27. Complete the coordinates for each point.

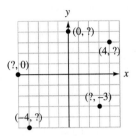

28. Find the coordinates of points A, B, C, D, E, and F.

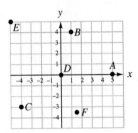

29. Graph each point: $(-3, 4), (4, 3.5), \left(-2, -\frac{5}{2}\right),$ $(0, -4), \left(\frac{3}{2}, 0\right), (3, -4).$

30. Graph each point: $(4, 4), (0.5, -3), (-4, -4),$ $(0, -1), (0, 0), (0, 3), (-2, 0).$

APPLICATIONS

31. CONSTRUCTION   The following graph shows a side view of a bridge design. Find the coordinates of each rivet, weld, and anchor.

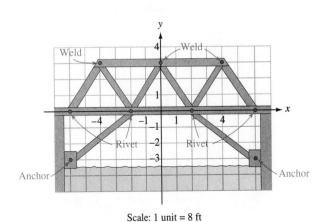

Scale: 1 unit = 8 ft

32. GOLF To correct her swing, the golfer is videotaped and then has her image displayed on a computer monitor so that it can be analyzed by a golf pro. Give the coordinates of the points that are highlighted on the arc of her swing.

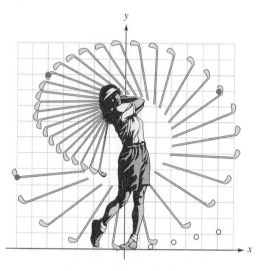

33. BATTLESHIP In the game Battleship, the player uses coordinates to drop depth charges from a battleship to hit a hidden submarine. What coordinates should be used to make three hits on the exposed submarine shown? Express each answer in the form (letter, number).

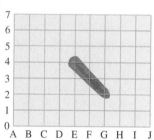

34. DENTISTRY Orthodontists describe teeth as being located in one of four *quadrants* as shown below.
  a. How many teeth are in the *upper left quadrant*?

  b. Why would the upper left quadrant appear on the right in the illustration?

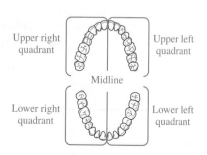

35. MAPS Use coordinates that have the form (number, letter) to locate each of the following on the map: Rockford, Mount Carroll, Harvard, and the intersection of state Highway 251 and U.S. Highway 30.

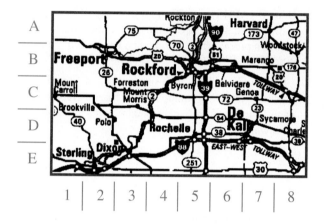

36. WATER PRESSURE The graphs show how the path of a stream of water changes when the hose is held at two different angles.
  a. At which angle does the stream of water shoot up higher? How much higher?

  b. At which angle does the stream of water shoot out farther? How much farther?

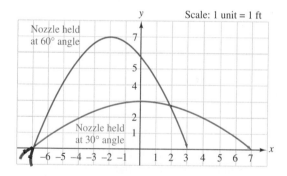

37. GEOMETRY Three vertices (corners) of a rectangle are the points $(2, 1)$, $(6, 1)$, and $(6, 4)$. Find the coordinates of the fourth vertex. Then find the area of the rectangle.

38. GEOMETRY Three vertices (corners) of a right triangle are the points $(-1, -7)$, $(-5, -7)$, and $(-5, -2)$. Find the area of the triangle.

39. THE MILITARY The table below shows the number of miles that a tank can be driven on a given number of gallons of diesel fuel. Write the data in the table as ordered pairs and plot them. Then draw a straight line through the points.

   a. How far can the tank go on 7 gallons of fuel?

   b. How many gallons of fuel are needed to travel a distance of 20 miles?

   c. How far can the tank go on 6.5 gallons of fuel?

Fuel (gal)	Distance (mi)
2	10
3	15
5	25

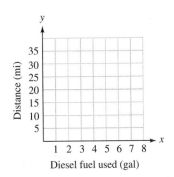

41. DEPRECIATION The table below shows the value (in thousands of dollars) of a car at various lengths of time after its purchase. Write the data in the table as ordered pairs and plot them. Then draw a straight line passing through the points.

   a. What does the point (3, 7) on the graph tell you?

   b. Find the value of the car when it is 7 years old.

   c. After how many years will the car be worth $2,500?

Age (yr)	Value ($1,000)
3	7
4	5.5
5	4

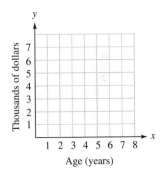

40. BOATING The table below shows the cost to rent a sailboat for a given number of hours. Write the data in the table as ordered pairs and plot them. Then draw a straight line through the points.

   a. What does it cost to rent the boat for 3 hours?

   b. For how long can the boat be rented for $60?

Rental time (hr)	Cost ($)
2	20
4	30
9	55

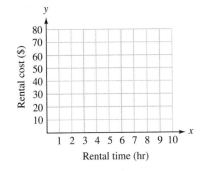

42. SWIMMING The table below shows the number of people at a public swimming pool at various times during the day. Write the data in the table as ordered pairs and plot them. (On the *x*-axis, 0 represents noon, 1 represents 1 PM, and so on.) Then draw a straight line passing through the points.

   a. How many people will be at the pool at 6 PM?

   b. At what time will there be 250 people at the pool?

   c. When will the number of people at the pool be half of what it was at noon?

Time	Number of people
0	350
3	200
5	100

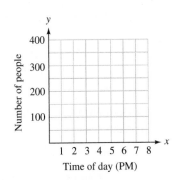

In Problems 43–44, refer to the following information. The approximate population of the United States for the years 1950–2000 is given by the straight line graph shown below.

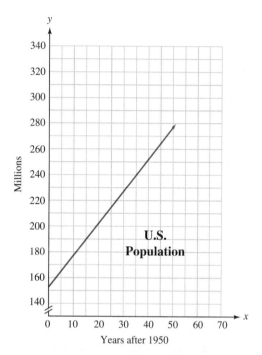

Years after 1950

43. CENSUS An official count of the population, known as the Census, is conducted every 10 years in the United States, as required by the Constitution. Use the graph to estimate the Census numbers.

Census year	U.S. Population (millions)
1950	
1960	
1970	
1980	
1990	
2000	

44. EXTRAPOLATION On the graph, use a straightedge to predict the Census numbers for 2010 and 2020.

Census year	U.S. Population (millions)
2010	
2020	

WRITING

45. Explain why the point $(-3, 3)$ is not the same as the point $(3, -3)$.

46. Explain how to plot the point $(-2, 5)$.

47. Explain why the coordinates of the origin are $(0, 0)$.

48. Explain this diagram.

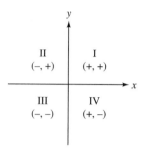

REVIEW

49. Solve $AC = \frac{2}{3}h - T$ for h.

50. Solve: $5(x + 1) \le 2(x - 3)$. Write the solution set in interval notation and graph it.

51. Evaluate: $\dfrac{-4(4 + 2) - 2^3}{|-12 - 4(5)|}$.

52. Simplify: $\dfrac{24}{54}$.

CHALLENGE PROBLEMS

53. In what quadrant does a point lie if the *sum* of its coordinates is negative and the *product* of its coordinates is positive?

54. Draw a line segment $\overline{AB}$ with endpoints $A(6, 5)$ and $B(-4, 5)$. Suppose that the x-coordinate of a point C is the average of the x-coordinates of points A and B, and the y-coordinate of point C is the average of the y-coordinates of points A and B. Find the coordinates of point C. Why is C called the midpoint of $\overline{AB}$?

3.2 Graphing Linear Equations

- Solutions of Equations in Two Variables
- Constructing Tables of Solutions
- Graphing Linear Equations
- Applications

In this section, we discuss equations that contain two variables. Such equations are often used to describe algebraic relationships between two quantities. To see a mathematical picture of these relationships, we will construct graphs of their equations.

■ SOLUTIONS OF EQUATIONS IN TWO VARIABLES

We have previously solved **equations in one variable.** For example, $x + 3 = 9$ is an equation in x. If we subtract 3 from both sides, we see that 6 is the solution. To verify this, we replace x with 6 and note that the result is a true statement: $9 = 9$.

In this chapter, we extend our equation-solving skills to find solutions of **equations in two variables.** To begin, let's consider $y = x - 1$, an equation in x and y.

A solution of $y = x - 1$ is a *pair* of values, one for x and one for y, that make the equation true. To illustrate, suppose x is 5 and y is 4. Then we have:

$$y = x - 1$$
$$4 \overset{?}{=} 5 - 1 \quad \text{Substitute 5 for } x \text{ and 4 for } y.$$
$$4 = 4 \qquad \text{True.}$$

Since the result is a true statement, $x = 5$ and $y = 4$ is a solution of $y = x - 1$. We write the solution as the ordered pair (5, 4), with the value of x listed first. We say that (5, 4) *satisfies* the equation.

In general, a **solution of an equation in two variables** is an ordered pair of numbers that makes the equation a true statement.

> **Notation**
>
> Equations in two variables often involve the variables x and y. However, other letters can be used. For example, $a - 3b = 5$ and $n = 4m + 6$ are equations in two variables.

EXAMPLE 1   Is $(-1, -3)$ a solution of $y = x - 1$?

Solution   We substitute -1 for x and -3 for y and see whether the resulting equation is true.

$$y = x - 1$$
$$-3 \overset{?}{=} -1 - 1 \quad \text{Substitute } -1 \text{ for } x \text{ and } -3 \text{ for } y.$$
$$-3 = -2$$

Since $-3 = -2$ is false, $(-1, -3)$ is *not* a solution.

Self Check 1   Is (9, 8) a solution of $y = x - 1$?

We have seen that solutions of equations in two variables are written as ordered pairs. If only one of the values of an ordered-pair solution is known, we can substitute it into the equation to determine the other value.

EXAMPLE 2   Complete the solution $(-5,)$ of the equation $y = -2x + 3$.

Solution   In the ordered pair, the x-value is -5; the y-value is not known. To find y, we substitute -5 for x in the equation and evaluate the right-hand side.

$$y = -2x + 3$$
$$y = -2(-5) + 3 \quad \text{Substitute } -5 \text{ for } x.$$
$$y = 10 + 3 \quad \text{Do the multiplication.}$$
$$y = 13$$

The completed ordered pair is $(-5, 13)$.

Self Check 2   Complete the solution $(-2, \quad)$ of the equation $y = 4x - 2$.

Solutions of equations in two variables are often listed in a **table of solutions** (or **table of values**).

EXAMPLE 3

Complete the table of solutions for $3x + 2y = 5$.

x	y	(x, y)
7		(7,)
	4	(, 4)

Solution   In the first row, we are given an x-value of 7. To find the corresponding y-value, we substitute 7 for x and solve for y.

$$3x + 2y = 5$$
$$3(7) + 2y = 5 \quad \text{Substitute 7 for } x.$$
$$21 + 2y = 5 \quad \text{Do the multiplication.}$$
$$2y = -16 \quad \text{Subtract 21 from both sides.}$$
$$y = -8 \quad \text{Divide both sides by 2.}$$

A solution of $3x + 2y = 5$ is $(7, -8)$.
    In the second row, we are given a y-value of 4. To find the corresponding x-value, we substitute 4 for y and solve for x.

$$3x + 2y = 5$$
$$3x + 2(4) = 5 \quad \text{Substitute 4 for } y.$$
$$3x + 8 = 5 \quad \text{Do the multiplication.}$$
$$3x = -3 \quad \text{Subtract 8 from both sides.}$$
$$x = -1 \quad \text{Divide both sides by 3.}$$

Another solution is $(-1, 4)$. The completed table is as follows:

x	y	(x, y)
7	-8	$(7, -8)$
-1	4	$(-1, 4)$

Self Check 3 Complete the table of solutions for $3x + 2y = 5$.

x	y	(x, y)
	-2	$(\ \ , -2)$
5		$(5, \ \ )$

CONSTRUCTING TABLES OF SOLUTIONS

To find a solution of an equation in two variables, we can select a number, substitute it for one of the variables, and find the corresponding value of the other variable. For example, to find a solution of $y = x - 1$, we can select a value for x, say, -4, substitute -4 for x in the equation, and find y.

x	y	(x, y)
-4	-5	$(-4, -5)$

$y = x - 1$
$y = -4 - 1$ Substitute -4 for x.
$y = -5$

The ordered pair $(-4, -5)$ is a solution. We list it in the table on the left.

To find another solution of $y = x - 1$, we select another value for x, say, -2, and find the corresponding y-value.

x	y	(x, y)
-4	-5	$(-4, -5)$
-2	-3	$(-2, -3)$

$y = x - 1$
$y = -2 - 1$ Substitute -2 for x.
$y = -3$

A second solution is $(-2, -3)$, and we list it in the table of solutions.

If we let $x = 0$, we can find a third ordered pair that satisfies $y = x - 1$.

x	y	(x, y)
-4	-5	$(-4, -5)$
-2	-3	$(-2, -3)$
0	-1	$(0, -1)$

$y = x - 1$
$y = 0 - 1$ Substitute 0 for x.
$y = -1$

A third solution is $(0, -1)$, which we also add to the table of solutions.

We can find a fourth solution by letting $x = 2$, and a fifth solution by letting $x = 4$.

x	y	(x, y)
-4	-5	$(-4, -5)$
-2	-3	$(-2, -3)$
0	-1	$(0, -1)$
2	1	$(2, 1)$
4	3	$(4, 3)$

$y = x - 1$ $y = x - 1$
$y = 2 - 1$ Substitute 2 for x. $y = 4 - 1$ Substitute 4 for x.
$y = 1$ $y = 3$

A fourth solution is $(2, 1)$ and a fifth solution is $(4, 3)$. We add them to the table.

Since we can choose any real number for x, and since any choice of x will give a corresponding value of y, it is apparent that the equation $y = x - 1$ has *infinitely many solutions*. We have found five of them: $(-4, -5)$, $(-2, -3)$, $(0, -1)$, $(2, 1)$, and $(4, 3)$.

GRAPHING LINEAR EQUATIONS

It would be impossible to list the infinitely many solutions of the equation $y = x - 1$. To show all of its solutions, we draw a mathematical "picture" of them. We call this picture the *graph of the equation.*

To graph $y = x - 1$, we plot the ordered pairs shown in the table on a rectangular coordinate system. Then we draw a straight line through the points, because *the graph of any solution of $y = x - 1$ will lie on this line.* Furthermore, every point on this line represents a solution. We call the line the **graph of the equation;** it represents all of the solutions of $y = x - 1$.

$$y = x - 1$$

x	y	(x, y)
-4	-5	$(-4, -5)$
-2	-3	$(-2, -3)$
0	-1	$(0, -1)$
2	1	$(2, 1)$
4	3	$(4, 3)$

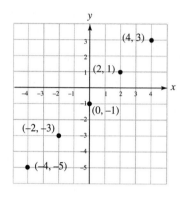

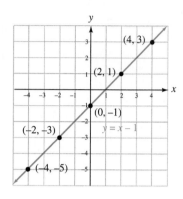

Construct a table of solutions.   Plot the ordered pairs.   Draw a straight line through the points. This is the *graph of the equation*.

The equation $y = x - 1$ is said to be *linear* because its graph is a line. By definition, a linear equation in two variables is any equation that can be written in the following **general** (or **standard**) **form.**

Linear Equations   A **linear equation in two variables** is an equation that can be written in the form

$$Ax + By = C$$

where A, B, and C are real numbers and A and B are not both 0.

Success Tip

The exponent on each variable of a linear equation is an understood 1. For example, $y = 2x + 4$ can be thought of as $y^1 = 2x^1 + 4$.

Some more examples of linear equations are

$$5x - 6y = 10, \qquad 3y = -2x - 12, \qquad \text{and} \qquad y = 2x + 4$$

Linear equations can be graphed in several ways. Generally, the form in which an equation is written determines the method that we use to graph it. To graph linear equations solved for y, such as $y = 2x + 4$, we can use the following method.

Graphing Linear Equations Solved for y

1. Find three solutions of the equation by selecting three values for x and calculating the corresponding values of y.
2. Plot the solutions on a rectangular coordinate system.
3. Draw a straight line passing through the points. If the points do not lie on a line, check your computations.

EXAMPLE 4

Graph: $y = 2x + 4$.

Solution   To find three solutions of this linear equation, we select three values of x that will make the computations easy. Then we find each corresponding value of y.

Success Tip

When selecting x-values for a table of solutions, a rule-of-thumb is to choose a negative number, a positive number, and 0. When $x = 0$, the computations to find y are usually quite simple.

If $x = -2$	**If** $x = 0$	**If** $x = 2$
$y = 2x + 4$	$y = 2x + 4$	$y = 2x + 4$
$y = 2(-2) + 4$	$y = 2(0) + 4$	$y = 2(2) + 4$
$y = -4 + 4$	$y = 0 + 4$	$y = 4 + 4$
$y = 0$	$y = 4$	$y = 8$
$(-2, 0)$ is a solution.	$(0, 4)$ is a solution.	$(2, 8)$ is a solution.

We enter the results in a table of solutions and plot the points. Then we draw a straight line through the points and label it $y = 2x + 4$.

Success Tip

Since two points determine a line, only two points are needed to graph a linear equation. However, we should plot a third point as a check. If the three points do not lie on a straight line, then at least one of them is in error.

$y = 2x + 4$

x	y	(x, y)
-2	0	$(-2, 0)$
0	4	$(0, 4)$
2	8	$(2, 8)$

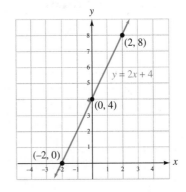

Self Check 4   Graph: $y = 2x - 3$.

EXAMPLE 5

Graph: $y = -3x$.

Solution   To find three solutions, we begin by choosing three x-values: $-1, 0$, and 1. Then we find the corresponding values of y. If $x = -1$, we have

$$y = -3x$$
$$y = -3(-1) \qquad \text{Substitute } -1 \text{ for } x.$$
$$y = 3$$

$(-1, 3)$ is a solution.

In a similar manner, we find the y-values for x-values of 0 and 1, and record the results in a table of solutions. After plotting the ordered pairs, we draw a straight line through the points and label it $y = -3x$.

$$y = -3x$$

x	y	(x, y)
-1	3	$(-1, 3)$
0	0	$(0, 0)$
1	-3	$(1, -3)$

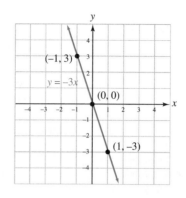

Self Check 5   Graph: $y = -4x$.

EXAMPLE 6

Graph: $3y = -2x - 12$.

Solution   The graph of $3y = -2x - 12$ can be found by solving for y and graphing the *equivalent equation* that results. To isolate y, we proceed as follows.

$$3y = -2x - 12$$

$$\frac{3y}{3} = \frac{-2x}{3} - \frac{12}{3} \qquad \text{To undo the multiplication by 3, divide both sides by 3.}$$

$$y = -\frac{2}{3}x - 4 \qquad \text{Write } \frac{-2x}{3} \text{ as } -\frac{2}{3}x. \text{ Simplify: } \frac{12}{3} = 4.$$

To find solutions of $y = -\frac{2}{3}x - 4$, each value of x must be multiplied by $-\frac{2}{3}$. This computation is made easier if we select x-values that are *multiples of 3,* such as -3, 0, and 6. For example, if $x = -3$, we have

$$y = -\frac{2}{3}x - 4$$

$$y = -\frac{2}{3}(-3) - 4 \qquad \text{Substitute } -3 \text{ for } x.$$

$$y = 2 - 4 \qquad\qquad \text{Do the multiplication: } -\frac{2}{3}(-3) = 2. \text{ This step is simpler if we choose}$$
$$\qquad\qquad\qquad\qquad x\text{-values that are multiples of 3.}$$

$$y = -2$$

$(-3, -2)$ is a solution.

Two more solutions, one for $x = 0$ and one for $x = 6$, are found in a similar way, and entered in a table. We plot the ordered pairs, draw a straight line through the points, and label the line as $y = -\frac{2}{3}x - 4$ or as $3y = -2x - 12$.

$$y = -\frac{2}{3}x - 4$$

x	y	(x, y)
-3	-2	$(-3, -2)$
0	-4	$(0, -4)$
6	-8	$(6, -8)$

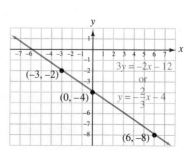

Self Check 6   Solve $2y = 5x + 2$ for y. Then graph the equation.

■ APPLICATIONS

When linear equations are used to model real-life situations, they are often written in variables other than x and y. In such cases, we must make the appropriate changes when labeling the table of solutions and the graph of the equation.

EXAMPLE 7

Cleaning windows.   The linear equation $A = -0.03n + 32$ estimates the amount A of glass cleaner (in ounces) that is left in the bottle after the sprayer trigger has been pulled a total of n times. Graph the equation and use the graph to estimate the amount of cleaner that is left after 500 sprays.

Solution   Since A depends on n in the equation $A = -0.03n + 32$, solutions will have the form (n, A). To find three solutions, we begin by selecting three values of n. Because the number of trials cannot be negative, and the computations to find A involve decimal multiplication, we select 0, 100, and 1,000. For example, if $n = 100$, we have

$$A = -0.03n + 32$$
$$A = -0.03(100) + 32$$
$$A = -3 + 32 \qquad \text{Do the multiplication: } -0.03(100) = -3.$$
$$A = 29$$

$(100, 29)$ is a solution.   After 100 sprays, 29 ounces of cleaner are left in the bottle.

In a similar manner, solutions are found for $n = 0$ and $n = 1,000$, and listed in the following table. Then the ordered pairs are plotted and a straight line is drawn through the points.

To graphically estimate the amount of solution that is left after 500 sprays, we draw the dashed blue lines, as shown. Reading on the vertical A-axis, we see that after 500 sprays, about 17 ounces of glass cleaner would be left.

$$A = -0.03n + 32$$

n	A	(n, A)
0	32	$(0, 32)$
100	29	$(100, 29)$
1,000	2	$(1,000, 2)$

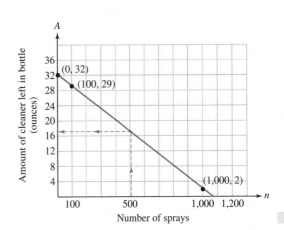

Answers to Self Checks   **1.** yes   **2.** $(-2, -10)$ **3.**

x	y	(x, y)
3	-2	$(3, -2)$
5	-5	$(5, -5)$

4.

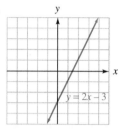

5.

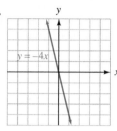

6.

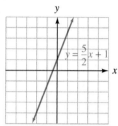

3.2   STUDY SET

VOCABULARY   Fill in the blanks.

1. We say $y = 2x + 5$ is an equation in _____ variables, x and y.

2. A _____ of an equation in two variables is an ordered pair of numbers that makes the equation a true statement.

3. Solutions of equations in two variables are often listed in a _____ of solutions.

4. The line that represents all of the solutions of a linear equation is called the _____ of the equation.

5. The equation $y = 3x + 8$ is said to be _____ because its graph is a line.

6. The _____ form of a linear equation in two variables is $Ax + By = C$.

7. A linear equation in two variables has _____ many solutions.

8. Two points _____ a line.

CONCEPTS

9. Consider the equation $y = -2x + 6$.
  a. How many variables does the equation contain?
  b. Does $(4, -2)$ satisfy the equation?
  c. Is $(-3, 0)$ a solution?
  d. How many solutions does this equation have?

10. To graph a linear equation, three solutions were found, they were plotted (in black), and a straight line was drawn through them, as shown below.
  a. Construct the table of solutions for this graph.
  b. From the graph, determine three other solutions of the equation.

x	y	(x, y)

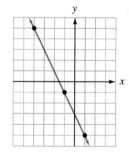

11. The graph of $y = -2x - 3$ is shown in Problem 10. Fill in the blanks: Every point on the graph represents an ordered-pair _____ of $y = -2x - 3$ and every ordered-pair solution is a _____ on the graph.

12. The graph of a linear equation is shown on the next page.
  a. If the coordinates of point M are substituted into the equation, will the result be true or false?
  b. If the coordinates of point N are substituted into the equation, will the result be true or false?

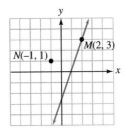

13. A student found three solutions of a linear equation and plotted them as shown in part (a) of the illustration.

   a. What conclusion can be made?

   b. What is wrong with the graph of $y = x - 3$, shown in illustration (b)?

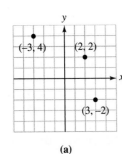   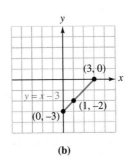

        (a)   (b)

14. a. Rewrite the linear equation $y = \frac{1}{2}x + 7$ showing the understood exponents on the variables.

$$y^{\square} = \frac{1}{2}x^{\square} + 7$$

   b. Explain why $y = x^2 + 2$ and $y = x^3 - 4$ are not linear equations.

15. Solve each equation for y.

   a. $5y = 10x + 5$

   b. $3y = -5x - 6$

   c. $-7y = -x + 21$

16. a. Complete three lines of the table of solutions for $y = \frac{4}{5}x + 2$. Use the three values of x that make the computations the easiest.

x	y	(x, y)
-5		
-3		
0		
4		
10		

b. Complete three lines of the table of solutions for $T = 0.6r + 560$. Use the three values of r that make the computations the easiest.

r	T	(r, T)
-12		
-10		
0		
8		
100		

NOTATION   **Complete the solution.**

17. Verify that $(-2, 6)$ is a solution of $y = -x + 4$.

$$y = -x + 4$$
$$\overset{?}{=} -(\quad) + 4$$
$$6 \overset{?}{=} \quad + 4$$
$$6 =$$

18. Determine whether each statement is true or false.

   a. $\dfrac{9x}{8} = \dfrac{9}{8}x$ **b.** $-\dfrac{1}{6}x = -\dfrac{x}{6}$

   c. When we divide both sides of $2y = 3x + 10$ by 2, we obtain $y = 3x + 5$.

19. Complete the labeling of the table of solutions and graph of $c = -a + 4$.

		$(\quad , \quad)$
-1	5	$(-1, 5)$
0	4	$(0, 4)$
2	2	$(2, 2)$

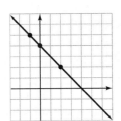

20. A table of solutions for a linear equation is shown below. When constructing the graph of the equation, how would you scale the x-axis and the y-axis?

x	y	(x, y)
-20	600	$(-20, 600)$
5	100	$(5, 100)$
35	-500	$(35, -500)$

PRACTICE Determine whether each equation has the given ordered pair as a solution.

21. $y = 5x - 4$; $(1, 1)$

22. $y = -2x + 3$; $(2, -1)$

23. $y = -\frac{3}{4}x + 8$; $(-8, 12)$

24. $y = \frac{1}{6}x - 2$; $(-12, 4)$

25. $7x - 2y = 3$; $(2, 6)$

26. $10x - y = 10$; $(0, 0)$

27. $x + 12y = -12$; $(0, -1)$

28. $-2x + 3y = 0$; $(-3, -2)$

For each equation, complete the solution.

29. $y = -5x - 4$; $(-3,\ \ )$

30. $y = 8x + 30$; $(-6,\ \ )$

31. $4x - 5y = -4$; $(\ , 4)$

32. $7x + y = -12$; $(\ \ , 2)$

Complete each table of solutions.

33. $y = 2x - 4$

x	y	(x, y)
8		
	8	

34. $y = 3x + 1$

x	y	(x, y)
-3		
	-2	

35. $3x - y = -2$

x	y	(x, y)
-5		
	-1	

36. $5x - 2y = -15$

x	y	(x, y)
5		
	0	

Construct a table of solutions and then graph each equation.

37. $y = 2x - 3$

38. $y = 3x + 1$

39. $y = 5x - 4$

40. $y = 6x - 3$

41. $y = x$

42. $y = 4x$

43. $y = -3x + 2$

44. $y = -2x + 1$

45. $y = -x - 1$

46. $y = -x + 2$

47. $y = \frac{x}{3}$

48. $y = -\frac{x}{3} - 1$

49. $y = -\frac{1}{2}x$

50. $y = \frac{3}{4}x$

51. $y = \frac{3}{8}x - 6$

52. $y = \frac{5}{6}x - 5$

53. $y = \frac{2}{3}x - 2$

54. $y = -\frac{3}{2}x + 2$

Solve each equation for y and then graph it.

55. $7y = -2x$

56. $6y = -4x$

57. $3y = 12x + 15$

58. $5y = 20x - 30$

59. $5y = x + 20$

60. $4y = x - 16$

61. $y + 1 = 7x$

62. $y - 3 = 2x$

APPLICATIONS

63. BILLIARDS The path traveled by the black eight ball on a game-winning shot is described by two linear equations. Complete the table of solutions for each equation and then graph the path of the ball.

$y = 2x - 4$

x	y	(x, y)
1		
2		
4		

$y = -2x + 12$

x	y	(x, y)
4		
6		
8		

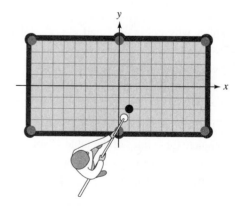

64. PING-PONG The path traveled by a Ping-Pong ball is described by two linear equations. Complete the table of solutions for each equation and then graph the path of the ball.

$y = \frac{1}{2}x + \frac{3}{2}$

x	y	(x, y)
7		
3		
-3		

$y = -\frac{1}{2}x - \frac{3}{2}$

x	y	(x, y)
-3		
-5		
-7		

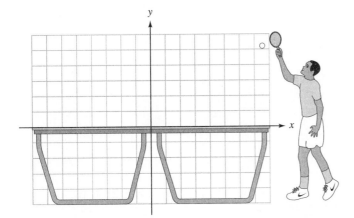

65. HOUSEKEEPING The linear equation $A = -0.02n + 16$ estimates the amount A of furniture polish (in ounces) that is left in the bottle after the sprayer trigger has been pulled a total of n times. Graph the equation and use the graph to estimate the amount of polish that is left after 650 sprays.

66. SHARPENING PENCILS The linear equation $L = -0.04t + 8$ estimates the length L (in inches) of a pencil after it has been inserted into a sharpener and the handle turned a total of t times. Graph the equation and use the graph to estimate the length of the pencil after 75 turns of the handle.

67. NFL TICKETS The average ticket price p to a National Football League game during the years 1990–2002 is approximated by $p = \frac{9}{4}t + 23$, where t is the number of years after 1990. Graph this equation and use the graph to predict the average ticket price in 2010. (Source: Team Marketing Report, NFL.)

68. U.S. AUTOMOBILE ACCIDENTS The number n of lives saved by seat belts during the years 1995–2001 is estimated by $n = 392t + 9,970$, where t is the number of years after 1995. Graph this equation and use the graph to predict the number of lives that will be saved by seat belts in 2020. (Source: Bureau of Transportation Statistics.)

69. RAFFLES A private school is going to sell raffle tickets as a fund raiser. Suppose the number n of raffle tickets that will be sold is predicted by the equation $n = -20p + 300$, where p is the price of a raffle ticket in dollars. Graph the equation and use the graph to predict the number of raffle tickets that will be sold at a price of $6.

70. CATS The number n of cat owners (in millions) in the U.S. during the years 1994–2002 is estimated by $n = \frac{3}{5}t + 31.5$, where t is the number of years after 1994. Graph this equation and use the graph to predict the number of cat owners in the U.S. in 2014. (Source: Pet Food Institute.)

WRITING

71. When we say that $(-2, -6)$ is a solution of $y = x - 4$, what do we mean?

72. What is a table of solutions?

73. What does it mean when we say that a linear equation in two variables has infinitely many solutions?

74. A linear equation and a graph are two ways of mathematically describing a relationship between two quantities. Which do you think is more informative and why?

75. From geometry, we know that two points determine a line. Explain why it is a good practice when graphing linear equations to find and plot three solutions instead of just two.

76. On a quiz, students were asked to graph $y = 3x - 1$. One student made the table of solutions on the left. Another student made the table on the right. The tables are completely different. Which table is incorrect? Or could they both be correct? Explain.

x	y	(x, y)
0	-1	$(0, -1)$
2	5	$(2, 5)$
3	8	$(3, 8)$

x	y	(x, y)
-2	-7	$(-2, -7)$
-1	-4	$(-1, -4)$
1	2	$(1, 2)$

REVIEW

77. Simplify: $-(-5 - 4c)$.

78. Denote the set of integers.

79. Evaluate: $-2^2 + 2^2$.

80. Find the volume, to the nearest tenth, of a sphere with radius 6 feet.

81. Evaluate: $1 + 2[-3 - 4(2 - 8^2)]$.

82. Solve: $-2(a + 3) = 3(a - 5)$.

CHALLENGE PROBLEMS   **Graph each of the following *nonlinear* equations in two variables by constructing a table of solutions consisting of seven ordered pairs. These equations are called nonlinear, because their graphs are not straight lines.**

83. $y = x^2 + 1$

84. $y = x^3 - 2$

85. $y = |x| - 2$

86. $y = (x + 2)^2$

3.3   More about Graphing Linear Equations

- Intercepts   • The Intercept Method   • Graphing Horizontal and Vertical Lines
- Information from Intercepts   • Graphing Calculators

In this section, we graph a linear equation by determining the points where the graph intersects the x-axis and the y-axis. These points are called the *intercepts* of the graph.

■ INTERCEPTS

The graph of $y = 2x - 4$ is shown below. We see that the graph crosses the y-axis at the point $(0, -4)$; this point is called the **y-intercept** of the graph. The graph crosses the x-axis at the point $(2, 0)$; this point is called the **x-intercept** of the graph.

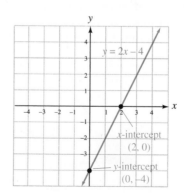

EXAMPLE 1   For each graph, identify the x-intercept and the y-intercept.

a. 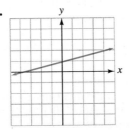   **b.** 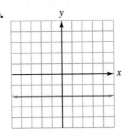   **c.**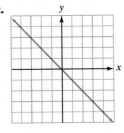

Solution   **a.** The graph crosses the x-axis at $(-4, 0)$. This is the x-intercept. The graph crosses the y-axis at $(0, 1)$. This is the y-intercept.

     b. Since the horizontal line does not cross the x-axis, there is no x-intercept. The graph crosses the y-axis at $(0, -2)$. This is the y-intercept.

     c. The graph crosses the x-axis and the y-axis at the same point, the origin. Therefore the x-intercept is $(0, 0)$ and the y-intercept is $(0, 0)$.

Self Check 1   Identify the x-intercept and the y-intercept of the graph.

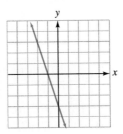

From the previous examples, we see that a y-intercept has an x-coordinate of 0, and an x-intercept has a y-coordinate of 0. These observations suggest the following procedures for finding the intercepts of a graph from its equation.

Finding Intercepts	To find the y-intercept, substitute 0 for x in the given equation and solve for y. To find the x-intercept, substitute 0 for y in the given equation and solve for x.

■ THE INTERCEPT METHOD

Plotting the x- and y-intercepts of a graph and drawing a straight line through them is called the **intercept method of graphing a line.** This method is useful when graphing linear equations written in the general form $Ax + By = C$.

EXAMPLE 2   Graph $x - 3y = 6$ by finding the intercepts.

Solution   To find the y-intercept, let $x = 0$ and solve for y. To find the x-intercept, let $y = 0$ and solve for x.

The Language of Algebra

The point where a line *intersects* the *x*- or *y*-axis is called an intercept. The word *intersect* means to cut through or cross. A famous tourist attraction in Southern California is the *intersection* of Hollywood Blvd. & Vine St.

y-intercept		*x-intercept*	
$x - 3y = 6$		$x - 3y = 6$	
$0 - 3y = 6$	Substitute 0 for *x*.	$x - 3(0) = 6$	Substitute 0 for *y*.
$-3y = 6$		$x - 0 = 6$	
$y = -2$	Divide both sides by -3.	$x = 6$	

The *y*-intercept is $(0, -2)$ and the *x*-intercept is $(6, 0)$. Since each intercept of the graph is a solution of the equation, we enter the intercepts in a table of solutions.

As a check, we find one more point on the line. We select a convenient value for *x*, say, 3, and find the corresponding value of *y*.

$$x - 3y = 6$$
$$3 - 3y = 6 \quad \text{Substitute 3 for } x.$$
$$-3y = 3 \quad \text{Subtract 3 from both sides.}$$
$$y = -1 \quad \text{Divide both sides by } -3.$$

Therefore, $(3, -1)$ is a solution. It is also entered in the table.

The intercepts and the check point are plotted, a straight line is drawn through them, and the line is labeled $x - 3y = 6$.

$$x - 3y = 6$$

x	*y*	*(x, y)*	
0	-2	$(0, -2)$	← *y*-intercept
6	0	$(6, 0)$	← *x*-intercept
3	-1	$(3, -1)$	← check point

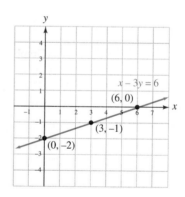

Self Check 2   Graph $x - 2y = 2$ by finding the intercepts.

The computations for finding intercepts can be simplified if we realize what logically follows when we substitute 0 for *y* or 0 for *x* in an equation written in the form $Ax + By = C$.

EXAMPLE 3   Graph $4x + 3y = -12$ by finding the intercepts.

Solution   When we substitute 0 for *x*, it follows that the term $4x$ will be equal to 0. Therefore, to find the *y*-intercept, we can cover $4x$ and solve the equation that remains for *y*.

$$\boxed{} + 3y = -12 \quad \text{If } x = 0, \text{ then } 4x = 4(0) = 0. \text{ Cover this term.}$$
$$y = -4 \quad \text{To solve } 3y = -12, \text{ divide both sides by 3.}$$

The *y*-intercept is $(0, -4)$.

When we substitute 0 for *y*, it follows that the term $3y$ will be equal to 0. Therefore, to find the *x*-intercept, we can cover $3y$ and solve the equation that remains for *x*.

$4x$ $= -12$ If $y = 0$, then $3y = 3(0) = 0$. Cover this term.

$x = -3$ To solve $4x = -12$, divide both sides by 4.

The x-intercept is $(-3, 0)$.

A third solution can be found by selecting a convenient value for x and finding the corresponding value for y. If we choose $x = -6$, we find that $y = 4$. The solution $(-6, 4)$ is entered in the table, and the equation is graphed as shown.

$$4x + 3y = -12$$

x	y	(x, y)
0	-4	$(0, -4)$
-3	0	$(-3, 0)$
-6	4	$(-6, 4)$

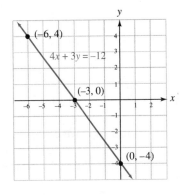

Self Check 3   Graph $2x + 5y = -10$ by finding the intercepts.

EXAMPLE 4

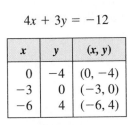

Graph $3x = -5y + 8$ by finding the intercepts.

Solution   We find the intercepts and select $x = 1$ to find a check point.

y-intercept: $x = 0$	*x-intercept: $y = 0$*	*Check point: $x = 1$*
$3x = -5y + 8$	$3x = -5y + 8$	$3x = -5y + 8$
$3(0) = -5y + 8$	$3x = -5(0) + 8$	$3(1) = -5y + 8$
$0 = -5y + 8$	$3x = 8$	$3 = -5y + 8$
$-8 = -5y$	$x = \dfrac{8}{3}$	$-5 = -5y$
$\dfrac{8}{5} = y$	$x = 2\frac{2}{3}$	$1 = y$
$1\frac{3}{5} = y$		

The y-intercept is $\left(0, 1\frac{3}{5}\right)$, the x-intercept is $\left(2\frac{2}{3}, 0\right)$, and the check point is $(1, 1)$. The ordered pairs are plotted as shown.

Success Tip

When graphing, it is often helpful to write any coordinates that are improper fractions as mixed numbers. For example: $\left(\frac{8}{3}, 0\right) = \left(2\frac{2}{3}, 0\right)$.

$$3x = -5y + 8$$

x	y	(x, y)
0	$1\frac{3}{5}$	$\left(0, 1\frac{3}{5}\right)$
$\frac{8}{3} = 2\frac{2}{3}$	0	$\left(2\frac{2}{3}, 0\right)$
1	1	$(1, 1)$

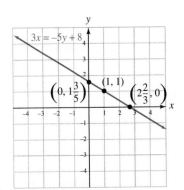

Self Check 4   Graph $8x = -4y + 15$ by finding the intercepts.

■ GRAPHING HORIZONTAL AND VERTICAL LINES

Equations such as $y = 4$ and $x = -3$ are linear equations, because they can be written in the general form $Ax + By = C$.

| $y = 4$ | is equivalent to | $0x + 1y = 4$ |
| $x = -3$ | is equivalent to | $1x + 0y = -3$ |

We now discuss how to graph these types of linear equations.

EXAMPLE 5

Graph: $y = 4$.

Solution   We can write the equation in general form as $0x + y = 4$. Since the coefficient of x is 0, the numbers chosen for x have no effect on y. The value of y is always 4. For example, if $x = 2$, we have

$$0x + y = 4 \quad \text{This is the original equation written in general form.}$$
$$0(2) + y = 4 \quad \text{Substitute 2 for } x.$$
$$y = 4 \quad \text{Simplify the left-hand side.}$$

One solution is $(2, 4)$. To find two more solutions, we choose $x = 0$ and $x = -3$. For any x-value, the y-value is always 4, so we enter $(0, 4)$ and $(-3, 4)$ in the table. If we plot the ordered pairs and draw a straight line through the points, the result is a horizontal line. The y-intercept is $(0, 4)$ and there is no x-intercept.

$y = 4$

x	y	(x, y)
2	4	$(2, 4)$
0	4	$(0, 4)$
-3	4	$(-3, 4)$

↑ Choose any number for x.   ↑ Each value of y must be 4.

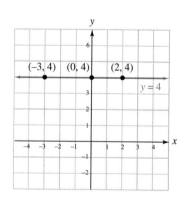

Self Check 5   Graph: $y = -2$.

EXAMPLE 6

Graph: $x = -3$.

Solution   We can write the equation in general form as $x + 0y = -3$. Since the coefficient of y is 0, the numbers chosen for y have no effect on x. The value of x is always -3. For example, if $y = -2$, we have

$$x + 0y = -3 \quad \text{This is the original equation written in general form.}$$
$$x + 0(-2) = -3 \quad \text{Substitute } -2 \text{ for } y.$$
$$x = -3 \quad \text{Simplify the left-hand side.}$$

One solution is $(-3, -2)$. To find two more solutions, we choose $y = 0$ and $y = 3$. For any y-value, the x-value is always -3, so we enter $(-3, 0)$ and $(-3, 3)$ in the table. If we plot the ordered pairs and draw a straight line through the points, the result is a vertical line. The x-intercept is $(-3, 0)$ and there is no y-intercept.

$$x = -3$$

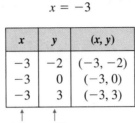

x	y	(x, y)
-3	-2	$(-3, -2)$
-3	0	$(-3, 0)$
-3	3	$(-3, 3)$

Each value of x must be -3.   Choose any number for y.

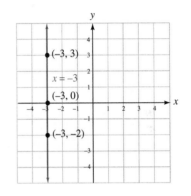

Self Check 6   Graph: $x = 4$.

From the results of Examples 5 and 6, we have the following facts.

Equations of Horizontal and Vertical Lines	The equation $y = b$ represents the horizontal line that intersects the y-axis at $(0, b)$. The equation $x = a$ represents the vertical line that intersects the x-axis at $(a, 0)$.

The graph of the equation $y = 0$ has special significance; it is the x-axis. Similarly, the graph of the equation $x = 0$ is the y-axis.

The Language of Algebra

Two *parallel* lines are always the same distance apart. For example, think of the rails of train tracks. When graphing lines, remember that $y = b$ is *parallel* to the x-axis and $x = a$ is *parallel* to the y-axis.

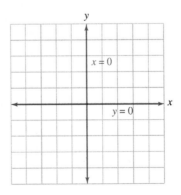

■ INFORMATION FROM INTERCEPTS

The ability to read and interpret graphs is a valuable skill. When analyzing a graph, we should locate and examine the intercepts. As the following example illustrates, the coordinates of the intercepts can yield useful information.

EXAMPLE 7

Camcorders. The number of feet of videotape that remain on a cassette depends on the number of minutes of videotaping that has already occurred. The following graph shows the relationship between these two quantities for a cassette in standard play mode. What information do the intercepts give about the cassette?

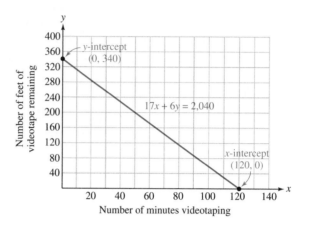

Solution
The *y*-intercept of (0, 340) indicates that when 0 minutes of taping have occurred, 340 feet of videotape are available. That is, the cassette contains 340 feet of videotape.

The *x*-coordinate of (120, 0) indicates that when 120 minutes of videotaping have occurred, 0 feet of tape are available. In other words, the cassette can hold 120 minutes, or 2 hours, of videotaping.

Courtesy of Texas Instruments

■ GRAPHING CALCULATORS

So far, we have graphed linear equations by making tables of solutions and plotting points. A graphing calculator can make the task of graphing much easier.

However, a graphing calculator does not take the place of a working knowledge of the topics discussed in this chapter. It should serve as an aid to enhance your study of algebra.

The Viewing Window
The screen on which a graph is displayed is called the **viewing window.** The **standard window** has settings of

$$\text{Xmin} = -10, \qquad \text{Xmax} = 10, \qquad \text{Ymin} = -10, \qquad \text{and} \qquad \text{Ymax} = 10$$

which indicate that the minimum *x*- and *y*-coordinates used in the graph will be -10, and that the maximum *x*- and *y*-coordinates will be 10.

Graphing an Equation
To graph $y = x - 1$ using a graphing calculator, we press the $\boxed{Y =}$ key and enter $x - 1$ after the symbol Y_1. Then we press the $\boxed{\text{GRAPH}}$ key to see the graph.

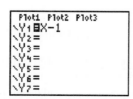
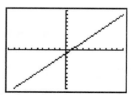

Changing the Viewing Window   We can change the viewing window by pressing the WINDOW key and entering -4 for the minimum x- and y-coordinates and 4 for the maximum x- and y-coordinates. Then we press the GRAPH key to see the graph of $y = x - 1$ in more detail.

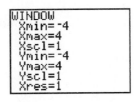   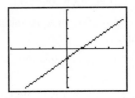

Solving an Equation for y   To graph $3x + 2y = 12$, we must first solve the equation for y.

$$3x + 2y = 12$$
$$2y = -3x + 12 \qquad \text{Subtract } 3x \text{ from both sides.}$$
$$y = -\frac{3}{2}x + 6 \qquad\qquad \text{Divide both sides by 2.}$$

Next, we press the WINDOW key to reenter the standard window settings and press the Y = key to enter $y = -\frac{3}{2}x + 6$. Then we press the GRAPH key to see the graph.

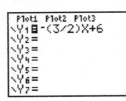   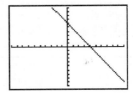

Answers to Self Checks   **1.** $(-1, 0); (0, -3)$ **2.**

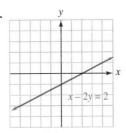

3.

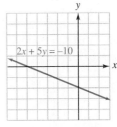

4.

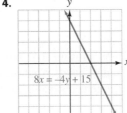

5.

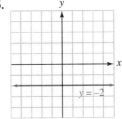

6.

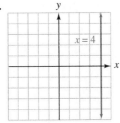

3.3   STUDY SET

VOCABULARY   Fill in the blanks.

1. We say $5x + 3y = 10$ is an equation in _____ variables, x and y.

2. $2x - 3y = 6$ is a _____ equation; its graph is a line.

3. The equation $2x - 3y = 7$ is written in _____ form.

4. The _____ of a line is the point where the line intersects the x-axis.

5. The y-intercept of a line is the point where the line _____ the y-axis.

6. The graph of $y = 4$ is a _____ line, with y-intercept $(0, 4)$.

CONCEPTS   Identify the intercepts of each graph.

7.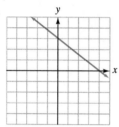

8.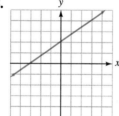

9.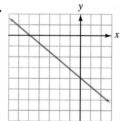

10.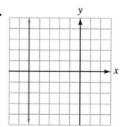

11.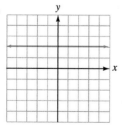

12.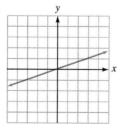

13. Estimate the intercepts of the line in the graph.

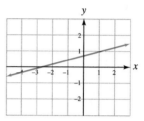

14. Fill in the blanks.
    a. To find the y-intercept of the graph of a line, substitute _____ for x in the equation and solve for ___.
    b. To find the x-intercept of the graph of a line, substitute _____ for y in the equation and solve for ___.

15. Consider the linear equation $3x + 2y = 6$.
    a. If we let $x = 0$, which term of the equation is equal to 0?
    b. Solve the equation that remains. What is the y-intercept of the graph of $3x + 2y = 6$?

16. In the table of solutions, which entry is the y-intercept of the graph and which entry is the x-intercept of the graph?

x	y	(x, y)
6	0	$(6, 0)$
0	-2	$(0, -2)$
-3	-3	$(-3, -3)$

17. What is the maximum number of intercepts that a line may have? What is the minimum number of intercepts that a line may have?

18. It is known that the value of a certain piece of farm machinery will steadily decrease after it is purchased.
   a. From the graph, which intercept tells the purchase price of the machinery? What was that price?

   b. Which intercept tells when the machinery will have lost all of its value? When is that?

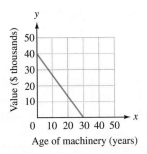

19. Match each graph with its equation
   a. $x = 2$ **b.** $y = 2$ **c.** $y = 2x$
   d. $2x - y = 2$ **e.** $y = 2x + 2$ **f.** $y = -2x$

i. 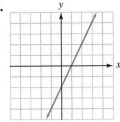   **ii.**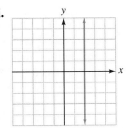

iii. 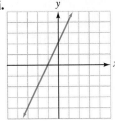   **iv.**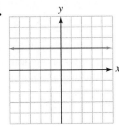

v. 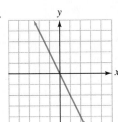   **vi.**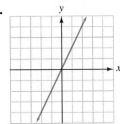

20. What linear equation could have the table of solutions shown below?

x	y	(x, y)
1	8	$(1, 8)$
0	8	$(0, 8)$
-1	8	$(-1, 8)$

NOTATION

21. a. Does the point $(0, 6)$ lie on the x-axis or the y-axis?

   b. Is it correct to say that the point $(0, 0)$ lies on the x-axis *and* on the y-axis?

22. True or false: $x = 5$ is equivalent to $1x + 0y = 5$.

23. What is the equation of the x-axis? What is the equation of the y-axis?

24. Write any coordinates that are improper fractions as mixed numbers.
   a. $\left(\frac{7}{2}, 0\right)$ **b.** $\left(0, -\frac{17}{3}\right)$

PRACTICE   **Use the intercept method to graph each equation.**

25. $4x + 5y = 20$ **26.** $3x + 4y = 12$

27. $x - y = -3$ **28.** $x - y = 3$

29. $5x + 15y = -15$ **30.** $8x + 4y = -24$

31. $x + 2y = -2$ **32.** $x + 2y = -4$

33. $4x - 3y = 12$ **34.** $5x - 10y = 20$

35. $3x + y = -3$ **36.** $2x - y = -2$

37. $9x - 4y = -9$ **38.** $5x - 4y = -15$

39. $8 = 3x + 4y$ **40.** $9 = 2x + 3y$

41. $4x - 2y = 6$ **42.** $6x - 3y = 3$

43. $3x - 4y = 11$ **44.** $5x - 4y = 13$

45. $9x + 3y = 10$ **46.** $4x + 4y = 5$

47. $3x = -15 - 5y$ **48.** $x = 5 - 5y$

49. $-4x = 8 - 2y$ **50.** $-5x = 10 + 5y$

51. $7x = 4y - 12$ **52.** $7x = 5y - 15$

53. $y - 3x = -\dfrac{4}{3}$ **54.** $y - 2x = -\dfrac{9}{8}$

Graph each equation.

55. $y = 4$

56. $y = -3$

57. $x = -2$

58. $x = 5$

59. $y = -\dfrac{1}{2}$

60. $y = \dfrac{5}{2}$

61. $x = \dfrac{4}{3}$

62. $x = -\dfrac{5}{3}$

63. $y - 2 = 0$

64. $x + 1 = 0$

65. $-2x + 3 = 11$

66. $-3y + 2 = 5$

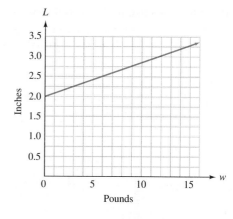

APPLICATIONS

67. CHEMISTRY   The relationship between the temperature and volume of a gas at a constant pressure is graphed below. The T-intercept of this graph is a very important scientific fact. It represents the lowest possible temperature, called **absolute zero.**

  a. Estimate absolute zero.

  b. What is the volume of the gas when the temperature is absolute zero?

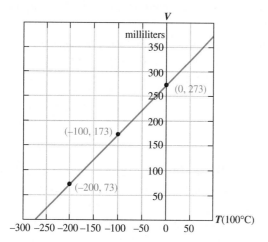

68. PHYSICS   The graph shows the length L of a stretched spring (in inches) as different weights w (in pounds) are attached to it. What information about the spring does the L-intercept give us?

69. LANDSCAPING   A developer is going to purchase x trees and y shrubs to landscape a new office complex. The trees cost \$50 each and the shrubs cost \$25 each. His budget is \$5,000. This situation is modeled by the equation $50x + 25y = 5,000$. Use the intercept method to graph it.

  a. What information is given by the y-intercept?

  b. What information is given by the x-intercept?

70. THE MOTOR CITY   The linear equation $y = -192,000x + 1,850,000$ models the population y of Detroit, Michigan, where x is the number of decades since 1950. Without graphing, find the y-intercept of the graph. Then explain what it means.

WRITING

71. To graph $3x + 2y = 12$, a student found the intercepts and a check point, and graphed them, as shown on the left. Instead of drawing a crooked line through the points, what should he have done?

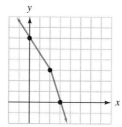

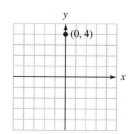

72. A student graphed the linear equation $y = 4$, as shown above on the right. Explain his error.

73. How do we find the intercepts of the graph of an equation without having to graph the equation?

74. In Section 3.2, we discussed a method to graph $y = 2x - 3$. In Section 3.3, we discussed a method to graph $2x + 3y = 6$. Briefly explain the steps involved in each method.

REVIEW

75. Simplify $\dfrac{3 \cdot 5 \cdot 5}{3 \cdot 5 \cdot 5 \cdot 5}$ by removing the common factors.

76. Simplify: $4\left(\dfrac{d}{2} - 3\right) - 5\left(\dfrac{2}{5}d - 1\right)$.

77. Translate: Six less than twice x.

78. Is -5 a solution of $2(3x + 10) = 5x + 6$?

CHALLENGE PROBLEMS

79. Where will the line $y = b$ intersect the line $x = a$?

80. Write an equation of the line that has an x-intercept of $(4, 0)$ and a y-intercept of $(0, 3)$.

3.4 The Slope of a Line

- Finding the Slope of a Line from Its Graph   • The Slope Formula
- Slopes of Horizontal and Vertical Lines   • Applications of Slope
- Rates of Change

In Sections 3.2 and 3.3, we graphed linear equations. All of the graphs were similar in one sense—they were lines. However, the lines slanted in different ways and had varying degrees of steepness. In this section, we introduce a means of measuring the steepness of a line. We call this measure the *slope of the line,* and it can be found in several ways.

■ FINDING THE SLOPE OF A LINE FROM ITS GRAPH

The **slope of a line** is a comparison of the vertical change to the corresponding horizontal change as we move along the line. The comparison is expressed as a **ratio** (a quotient of two numbers).

As an example, let's find the slope of the line graphed on the next page. To begin, we select two points on the line, $P(4, 2)$ and $Q(10, 7)$. As we move from point P to point Q, the y-coordinates change from 2 to 7. Therefore, the vertical change, called the **rise,** is $7 - 2$ or 5 units.

As we move from point P to point Q, the x-coordinates change from 4 to 10. Therefore, the horizontal change, called the **run,** is $10 - 4$ or 6 units.

The slope of a line is defined to be *the ratio of the vertical change to the horizontal change.* So we have

$$\text{slope} = \frac{\text{vertical change}}{\text{horizontal change}} = \frac{\text{change in } y}{\text{change in } x} = \frac{\text{rise}}{\text{run}} = \frac{5}{6}$$

The slope of the line is $\frac{5}{6}$. This indicates that there is a vertical change (rise) of 5 units for each horizontal change (run) of 6 units.

The Language of Algebra

Ratios are used in many settings. Mechanics speak of gear *ratios.* Colleges advertise their student-to-teacher *ratios.* Banks calculate debt-to-income *ratios* for loan applicants.

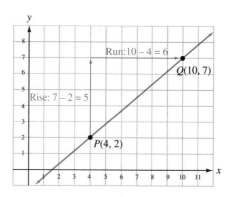

EXAMPLE 1

Find the slope of the line graphed below.

Pick a point on the line that also lies on the intersection of two grid lines.

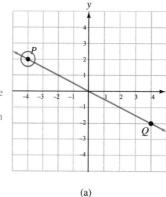

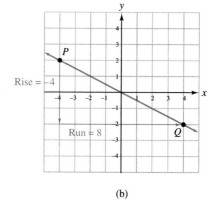

(a)   (b)

Solution   We begin by choosing two points on the line, P and Q, as shown in illustration (a). One way to move from P to Q is shown in illustration (b). Starting at P, we move downward, a rise of -4, and then to the right, a run of 8, to reach Q. These steps create a right triangle called a **slope triangle.**

The Language of Algebra

The symbol m is used to denote the slope of a line. Many historians credit this to the fact that it is the first letter of the French word *monter,* meaning to ascend or to climb.

To find the slope of the line, we write a ratio of the rise to the run. By tradition, the letter m is used to denote slope, so we have

$$m = \frac{\text{rise}}{\text{run}}$$ Slope is the ratio (quotient) of rise to run.

$$m = \frac{-4}{8}$$ Substitute -4 for the rise and 8 for the run.

$$m = -\frac{1}{2}$$ Simplify the fraction.

Success Tip

When drawing a slope triangle, remember that upward movements are positive, downward movements are negative, movements to the right are positive, and movements to the left are negative.

The slope of the line is $-\frac{1}{2}$.

The two-step process to move from P to Q can be reversed. Starting at P, we can move to the right, a run of 8; and then downward, a rise of -4, to reach Q. With this approach, the slope triangle is above the line. When we form the ratio to find the slope, we get the same result as before:

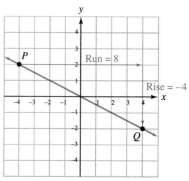

$$m = \frac{\text{rise}}{\text{run}} = \frac{-4}{8} = -\frac{1}{2}$$

Self Check 1   Find the slope of the line shown above using two points different from those used in the solution of Example 1.

The identical answers from Example 1 and its Self Check illustrate an important fact about slope: The same value will be obtained no matter which two points on a line are used to find the slope.

■ THE SLOPE FORMULA

We can generalize the graphic method for finding slope to develop a slope formula. To begin, we select two points on a line, as shown in the figure below. Call them P and Q. To distinguish between the coordinates of these points, we use **subscript notation.**

The Language of Algebra

The prefix *sub* means below or beneath, as in submarine or subway. In x_2, the *subscript* 2 is written lower than the variable.

- Point P is denoted as $P(x_1, y_1)$.   Read as "point P with coordinates of x sub 1 and y sub 1."

- Point Q is denoted as $Q(x_2, y_2)$.   Read as "point Q with coordinates of x sub 2 and y sub 2."

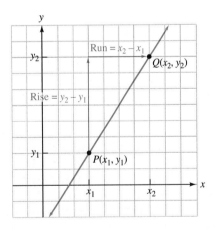

As we move from point P to point Q, the rise is the difference of the y-coordinates: $y_2 - y_1$. The run is the difference of the x-coordinates: $x_2 - x_1$. Since the slope is the ratio $\frac{\text{rise}}{\text{run}}$, we have the following formula for calculating slope.

Slope of a Line	The **slope** of a line passing through points (x_1, y_1) and (x_2, y_2) is

$$m = \frac{\text{vertical change}}{\text{horizontal change}} = \frac{\text{change in } y}{\text{change in } x} = \frac{\text{rise}}{\text{run}} = \frac{y_2 - y_1}{x_2 - x_1} \quad \text{if } x_2 \neq x_1.$$

EXAMPLE 2   Find the slope of the line passing through $(1, 2)$ and $(3, 8)$. Then graph the line.

Solution   When using the slope formula, it makes no difference which point you call (x_1, y_1) and which point you call (x_2, y_2). If we let (x_1, y_1) be $(1, 2)$ and (x_2, y_2) be $(3, 8)$, then

$$m = \frac{y_2 - y_1}{x_2 - x_1}$$ This is the slope formula.

$$m = \frac{8 - 2}{3 - 1}$$ Substitute 8 for y_2, 2 for y_1, 3 for x_2, and 1 for x_1.

$$m = \frac{6}{2}$$ Do the subtractions.

$$m = 3$$ Simplify. Think of this as a $\frac{3}{1}$ rise-to-run ratio.

Notation

We can write slopes that are integers in $\frac{\text{rise}}{\text{run}}$ form by writing them as fractions with a denominator of 1. For example, $m = 3 = \frac{3}{1}$ or $m = -5 = \frac{-5}{1}$.

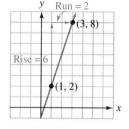

The slope of the line is 3. The graph of the line, including the slope triangle, is shown here. Note that we obtain the same value for the slope if we let $(x_1, y_1) = (3, 8)$ and $(x_2, y_2) = (1, 2)$.

$$m = \frac{y_2 - y_1}{x_2 - x_1} = \frac{2 - 8}{1 - 3} = \frac{-6}{-2} = 3$$

Self Check 2   Find the slope of the line passing through (2, 1) and (4, 11).

Caution   When using the slope formula, be sure to subtract the y-coordinates and the x-coordinates in the same order. Otherwise, your answer will have the wrong sign.

$$m \neq \frac{y_2 - y_1}{x_1 - x_2} \quad \text{and} \quad m \neq \frac{y_1 - y_2}{x_2 - x_1}$$

EXAMPLE 3   Find the slope of the line that passes through $(-2, 4)$ and $(5, -6)$ and graph the line.

Solution   Since we know the coordinates of two points on the line, we can find its slope. If (x_1, y_1) is $(-2, 4)$ and (x_2, y_2) is $(5, -6)$, then

Notation

Slopes are normally written as fractions, sometimes as decimals, but never as mixed numbers.

As with any fractional answer, always express slope in lowest terms.

$$m = \frac{y_2 - y_1}{x_2 - x_1}$$ This is the slope formula.

$$m = \frac{-6 - 4}{5 - (-2)}$$ Substitute -6 for y_2, 4 for y_1, 5 for x_2, and -2 for x_1.

$$m = -\frac{10}{7}$$ Do the subtractions. We may write the result as $\frac{-10}{7}$ or $-\frac{10}{7}$.

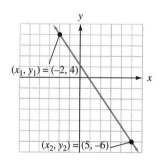

The slope of the line is $-\frac{10}{7}$. In the graph, we see that the line falls from left to right—a fact indicated by its negative slope.

Self Check 3   Find the slope of the line that passes through $(-1, -2)$ and $(1, -7)$.

From the previous examples, we see that the slope of the line in Example 2 was positive and the slopes of the lines in Examples 1 and 3 were negative. In general, lines that rise from left to right have a positive slope. Lines that fall from left to right have a negative slope.

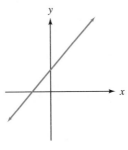

Positive slope   **Negative slope**

When we compare lines with positive slopes, we see that the larger the slope, the steeper the line. For example, a line with slope 3 is steeper than a line with slope $\frac{5}{6}$, and a line with slope $\frac{5}{6}$ is steeper than a line with slope $\frac{1}{4}$.

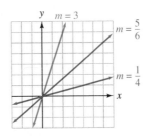

■ SLOPES OF HORIZONTAL AND VERTICAL LINES

In the next two examples, we calculate the slope of a horizontal line and we show that a vertical line has no defined slope.

EXAMPLE 4   Find the slope of the line $y = 3$.

Solution   The graph of $y = 3$ is a horizontal line. To find its slope, we need to know two points on the line. From the graph, we select $(-2, 3)$ and $(3, 3)$. If (x_1, y_1) is $(-2, 3)$ and (x_2, y_2) is $(3, 3)$, we have

$$m = \frac{y_2 - y_1}{x_2 - x_1}$$ This is the slope formula.

$$m = \frac{3 - 3}{3 - (-2)}$$ Substitute 3 for y_2, 3 for y_1, 3 for x_2, and -2 for x_1.

$$m = \frac{0}{5}$$ Simplify the numerator and the denominator.

$$m = 0$$

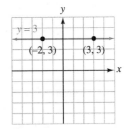

The slope of the line $y = 3$ is 0.

The y-coordinates of any two points on a horizontal line will be the same, and the x-coordinates will be different. Thus, the numerator of

$$\frac{y_2 - y_1}{x_2 - x_1}$$

will always be zero, and the denominator will always be nonzero. Therefore, the slope of a horizontal line is zero.

EXAMPLE 5

If possible, find the slope of the line $x = -2$.

Solution   The graph of $x = -2$ is a vertical line. To find its slope, we need to know two points on the line. From the graph, we select $(-2, 3)$ and $(-2, -1)$. If (x_2, y_2) is $(-2, 3)$ and (x_1, y_1) is $(-2, -1)$, we have

$$m = \frac{y_2 - y_1}{x_2 - x_1}$$ This is the slope formula.

$$m = \frac{3 - (-1)}{-2 - (-2)}$$ Substitute 3 for y_2, -1 for y_1, -2 for x_2, and -2 for x_1.

$$m = \frac{4}{0}$$ Simplify the numerator and the denominator.

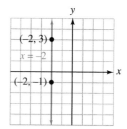

Since division by zero is undefined, $\frac{4}{0}$ has no meaning. The slope of the line $x = -2$ is undefined.

The y-coordinates of any two points on a vertical line will be different, and the x-coordinates will be the same. Thus, the numerator of

$$\frac{y_2 - y_1}{x_2 - x_1}$$

will always be nonzero, and the denominator will always be zero. Therefore, the slope of a vertical line is undefined.

We now summarize the results from Examples 4 and 5.

Slopes of Horizontal and Vertical Lines   Horizontal lines (lines with equations of the form $y = b$) have a slope of 0.
Vertical lines (lines with equations of the form $x = a$) have undefined slope.

The Language of Algebra

Undefined and *0* do not mean the same thing. A horizontal line has a defined slope; it is 0. A vertical line does not have a defined slope; we say its slope is *undefined.*

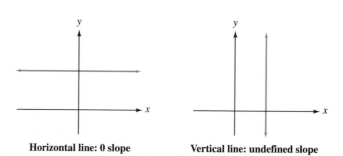

Horizontal line: 0 slope   Vertical line: undefined slope

■ APPLICATIONS OF SLOPE

The concept of slope has many applications. For example, architects use slope when designing ramps and roofs. Truckers must be aware of the slope, or *grade,* of the roads they travel. Mountain bikers ride up rocky trails and snow skiers speed down steep slopes.

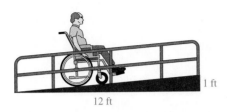

The Americans with Disabilities Act provides a guideline for the steepness of a ramp. The maximum slope for a wheelchair ramp is 1 foot of rise for every 12 feet of run: $m = \frac{1}{12}$.

The **grade** of an incline is its slope expressed as a percent: A 15% grade means a rise of 15 feet for every run of 100 feet: $m = \frac{15}{100}$.

EXAMPLE 6   *Architecture.*   **Pitch** is the incline of a roof expressed as a ratio of the vertical rise to the horizontal run. Find the pitch of the roof shown in the illustration.

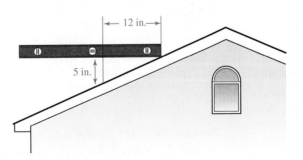

Solution   From the definition, we recognize that the pitch of a roof is simply its slope. In the illustration, a level is used to create a slope triangle. The rise is 5 and the run is 12.

$$m = \frac{\text{rise}}{\text{run}}$$

$$= \frac{5}{12}$$

The roof has a $\frac{5}{12}$ pitch.

■ RATES OF CHANGE

We have seen that the slope of a line is a *ratio* of two numbers. For many applications, however, we often attach units to a slope calculation. When we do so, we say that we have found a **rate of change.**

EXAMPLE 7

Checking accounts.   A checking plan at a bank charges customers a fixed monthly fee plus a small service charge for each check written. The relationship between the monthly cost y and the number x of checks written is graphed below. At what rate does the monthly cost change?

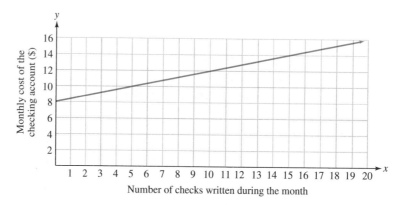

Number of checks written during the month

Solution   To find the rate of change, we find the slope of the line and attach the proper units. Two points on the line are $(5, 10)$ and $(15, 14)$. If we let $(x_1, y_1) = (5, 10)$ and $(x_2, y_2) = (15, 14)$, we have

$$\text{Rate of change} = \frac{(y_2 - y_1) \text{ dollars}}{(x_2 - x_1) \text{ checks}}$$ This is the slope formula with the appropriate units attached.

$$= \frac{(14 - 10) \text{ dollars}}{(15 - 5) \text{ checks}}$$ Substitute 14 for y_2, 10 for y_1, 15 for x_2, and 5 for x_1.

$$= \frac{4 \text{ dollars}}{10 \text{ checks}}$$ Do the subtractions.

$$= \frac{2 \text{ dollars}}{5 \text{ checks}}$$ Simplify the fraction.

The Language of Algebra

The preposition *per* means for each, or for every. When we say the rate of change is 40¢ *per* check, we mean 40¢ for each check.

The monthly cost of the checking account increases \$2 for every 5 checks written.

We can express $\frac{2}{5}$ in decimal form by dividing the numerator by the denominator. Then we can write the rate of change in two other ways, using the word *per*, which indicates division.

$$\text{Rate of change} = \$0.40 \text{ per check}$$ or $$\text{Rate of change} = 40¢ \text{ per check}$$

Answers to Self Checks   **1.** $-\dfrac{1}{2}$ **2.** 5   **3.** $-\dfrac{5}{2}$

3.4   STUDY SET

VOCABULARY   **Fill in the blanks.**

1. A _____ is the quotient of two numbers.

2. The _____ of a line is a measure of the line's steepness.

3. The _____ of a line is defined to be the ratio of the change in y to the change in x.

4. $m = \dfrac{\phantom{\text{horizontal change}}}{\text{horizontal change}} = \dfrac{\text{change in } y}{} = \dfrac{\text{rise}}{}$

5. The rate of _____ of a linear relationship can be found by finding the slope of the graph of the line and attaching the proper units.

6. _____ lines have a slope of 0. Vertical lines have _____ slope.

CONCEPTS

7. Fill in the blanks.

    a. A line with positive slope _____ from left to right.

    b. A line with negative slope _____ from left to right.

8. Which line graphed has

    a. a positive slope?

    b. a negative slope?

    c. zero slope?

    d. undefined slope?

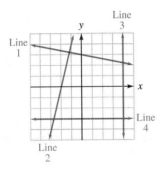

9. Suppose the rise of a line is 2 and the run is 15. Write the ratio of rise to run.

10. Consider the following graph of the line and the slope triangle.

    a. What is the rise?

    b. What is the run?

    c. What is the slope of the line?

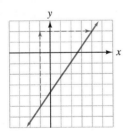

11. Consider the graph of the line and the slope triangle shown in the next column.

    a. What is the rise?

    b. What is the run?

    c. What is the slope of the line?

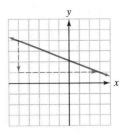

12. Which two labeled points should be used to find the slope of the line?

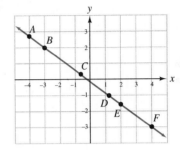

13. In this problem, you are to find the slope of the line graphed below by drawing a slope triangle.

    a. Find the slope using points A and B.

    b. Find the slope using points B and C.

    c. Find the slope using points A and C.

    d. What observation is suggested by your answers to parts a, b, and c?

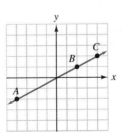

14. Evaluate each expression.

    a. $\dfrac{10 - 4}{6 - 5}$ **b.** $\dfrac{-1 - 1}{-2 - (-7)}$

15. Express each of the following slope calculations in a better way.

    a. $m = \dfrac{0}{6}$ **b.** $m = \dfrac{8}{0}$

16. Simplify each slope.

a. $m = \dfrac{3}{12}$ **b.** $m = -\dfrac{9}{6}$

c. $m = \dfrac{-4}{4}$ **d.** $m = \dfrac{-10}{-5}$

17. The *grade* of an incline is its slope expressed as a percent. What grade is represented by each of the following slopes?

a. $m = \dfrac{2}{5}$ **b.** $m = \dfrac{3}{20}$

18. GROWTH RATES   Refer to the graph. The slope of the line is 3. Fill in the correct units: The rate of change of the boy's height is   3 ▭ per ▭ .

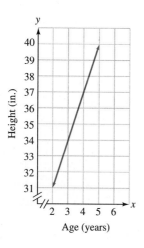

NOTATION

19. What is the formula used to find the slope of the line passing through (x_1, y_1) and (x_2, y_2)?

20. Fill in the blanks to state the slope formula in words: m equals y _____ two minus y _____ one
_____ x sub _____ minus x sub _____.

21. Explain the difference between y^2 and y_2.

22. Consider the points $(7, 2)$ and $(-4, 1)$. If we let $y_2 = 1$, then what is x_2?

PRACTICE   **Find the slope of each line, if possible.**

23.

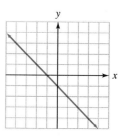

24.

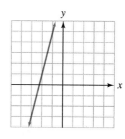

25.

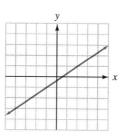

26.

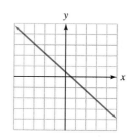

27.

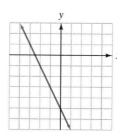

28.

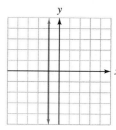

29.

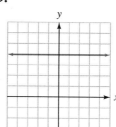

30.

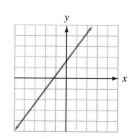

31.

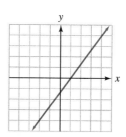

32.

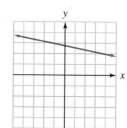

Find the slope of the line passing through the given points, when possible.

33. (2, 4) and (1, 3)

34. (1, 3) and (2, 5)

35. (3, 4) and (2, 7)

36. (3, 6) and (5, 2)

37. (0, 0) and (4, 5)

38. (4, 3) and (7, 8)

39. (−3, 5) and (−5, 6)

40. (6, −2) and (−3, 2)

41. (−2, −2) and (−12, −8)

42. (−1, −2) and (−10, −5)

43. (5, 7) and (−4, 7)

44. (−1, −12) and (6, −12)

45. (8, −4) and (8, −3)

46. (−2, 8) and (−2, 15)

47. (−6, 0) and (0, −4)

48. (0, −9) and (−6, 0)

49. (−2.5, 1.75) and (−0.5, −7.75)

50. (6.4, −7.2) and (−8.8, 4.2)

Determine the slope of the graph of the line that has the given table of solutions.

51.

x	y	(x, y)
−3	−1	(−3, −1)
1	2	(1, 2)
5	5	(5, 5)

52.

x	y	(x, y)
−3	6	(−3, 6)
0	2	(0, 2)
3	−2	(3, −2)

53.

x	y	(x, y)
−3	6	(−3, 6)
0	6	(0, 6)
3	6	(3, 6)

54.

x	y	(x, y)
4	−5	(4, −5)
4	0	(4, 0)
4	3	(4, 3)

Find the slope of each line, if possible.

55. $x = 6$

56. $y = -2$

57. $y = 0$

58. $x = 0$

59. $x = -2$

60. $y = 8$

61. $y = -3$

62. $x = 6$

APPLICATIONS

63. POOL DESIGN   Find the slope of the bottom of the swimming pool as it drops off from the shallow end to the deep end.

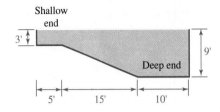

64. DRAINAGE   To measure the amount of fall (slope) of a concrete patio slab, a 10-foot-long 2-by-4, a 1-foot ruler, and a level were used. Find the amount of fall in the slab.

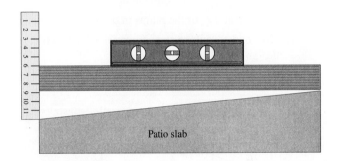

65. GRADE OF A ROAD   The vertical fall of the road shown in the illustration is 264 feet for a horizontal run of 1 mile. Find the slope of the decline and use that information to complete the roadside warning sign for truckers.

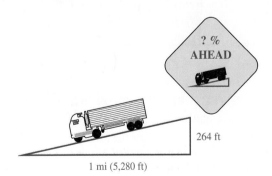

66. TREADMILLS For each height setting listed in the table, find the resulting slope of the jogging surface of the treadmill. Express each incline as a percent.

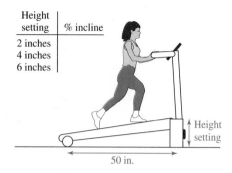

Height setting	% incline
2 inches	
4 inches	
6 inches	

Height setting

50 in.

67. ENGINEERING The illustrations show two ramp designs.

   a. Find the slope of the ramp in design 1.

   b. Find the slopes of the ramps in design 2.

   c. Give one advantage and one drawback of each design.

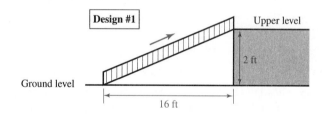

Design #1   Upper level   2 ft   Ground level   16 ft

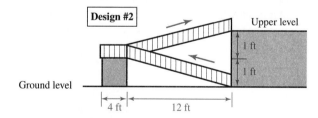

Design #2   Upper level   1 ft   1 ft   Ground level   4 ft   12 ft

68. ARCHITECTURE Since the pitch of the roof of the house shown is to be $\frac{2}{5}$, there will be a 2-foot rise for every 5-foot run. Draw the roof line if it is to pass through the given black points. Find the coordinates of the peak of the roof.

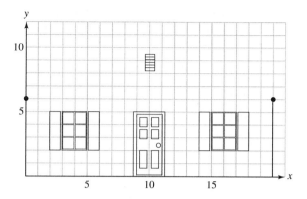

69. IRRIGATION The graph shows the number of gallons of water remaining in a reservoir as water is discharged from it to irrigate a field. Find the rate of change in the number of gallons of water in the reservoir.

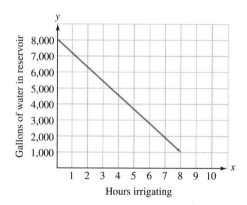

Gallons of water in reservoir

Hours irrigating

70. COMMERCIAL JETS Examine the graph and consider trips of more than 7,000 miles by a Boeing 777. Use a rate of change to estimate how the maximum payload decreases as the distance traveled increases.

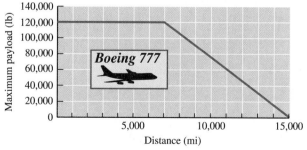

Maximum payload (lb)

Boeing 777

Distance (mi)

Based on data from Lawrence Livermore National Laboratory and *Los Angeles Times* (October 22, 1998).

71. MILK PRODUCTION The following graph approximates the amount of milk produced per cow in the U.S. for the years 1993–2002. Find the rate of change.

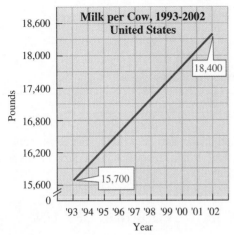

Source: United States Department of Agriculture

72. WAL-MART The graph below approximates the net sales of Wal-Mart for the years 1991–2002.
  a. Find the rate of change in sales for the years 1991–1998.
  b. Find the rate of change in sales for the years 1998–2002.

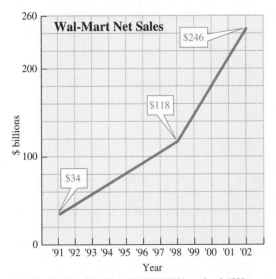

Based on data from Wal-Mart, *USA TODAY* (November 6, 1998), and Hoover's online.

WRITING

73. Explain why the slope of a vertical line is undefined.

74. How do we distinguish between a line with positive slope and a line with negative slope?

75. Give an example of a rate of change that government officials might be interested in knowing so they can plan for the future needs of our country.

76. Explain the difference between a rate of change that is positive and one that is negative. Give an example of each.

REVIEW

77. HALLOWEEN CANDY A candy maker wants to make a 60-pound mixture of two candies to sell for $2 per pound. If black licorice bits sell for $1.90 per pound and orange gumdrops sell for $2.20 per pound, how many pounds of each should be used?

78. MEDICATIONS A doctor prescribes an ointment that is 2% hydrocortisone. A pharmacist has 1% and 5% concentrations in stock. How many ounces of each should the pharmacist use to make a 1-ounce tube?

CHALLENGE PROBLEMS

79. Use the concept of slope to determine whether $A(-50, -10)$, $B(20, 0)$, and $C(34, 2)$ all lie on the same straight line.

80. A line having slope $\frac{2}{3}$ passes through the point $(10, -12)$. What is the y-coordinate of another point on the line whose x-coordinate is 16?

3.5 Slope–Intercept Form

- Slope–Intercept Form of the Equation of a Line
- Using the Slope and y-Intercept to Graph a Line
- Writing the Equation of a Line   • Parallel and Perpendicular Lines
- Applications

Linear equations appear in many forms. Some examples are:

$$y = 2x + 1, \qquad 3x - 5y = 15, \qquad 8y = 6x + 7, \qquad \text{and} \qquad x = -4$$

Of all of the ways in which a linear equation can be written, one form, called *slope–intercept form,* is probably the most useful. When an equation is written in this form, two important features of its graph are evident.

■ SLOPE–INTERCEPT FORM OF THE EQUATION OF A LINE

To explore the relationship between a linear equation and its graph, let's consider $y = 2x + 1$ and its graph.

$$y = 2x + 1$$

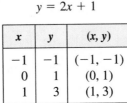

x	y	(x, y)
-1	-1	$(-1, -1)$
0	1	$(0, 1)$
1	3	$(1, 3)$

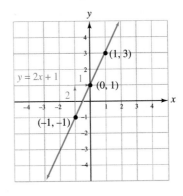

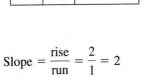

$$\text{Slope} = \frac{\text{rise}}{\text{run}} = \frac{2}{1} = 2$$

A close examination of the equation and the graph leads to two observations:

- The graph crosses the y-axis at 1. This is the same as the constant term in $y = 2x + \mathbf{1}$.
- The slope of the line is 2. This is the same as the coefficient of x in $y = \mathbf{2}x + 1$.

It appears that the slope and y-intercept of the graph of $y = 2x + 1$ can be determined from the equation.

$$y = 2x + 1$$

The slope of the line is 2.   The y-intercept is $(0, 1)$.

These observations suggest the following form of an equation of a line.

| Slope–Intercept Form of the Equation of a Line | If a linear equation is written in the form |

$$y = mx + b$$

the graph of the equation is a line with slope m and y-intercept $(0, b)$.

EXAMPLE 1

Find the slope and the y-intercept of the graph of each equation.

a. $y = 6x - 2$　　**b.** $y = -\dfrac{5}{4}x$　　**c.** $y = \dfrac{x}{2} + 3$　　**d.** $y = 5 + 12x$

Solution　**a.** If we write the subtraction as the addition of the opposite, the equation will be in $y = mx + b$ form:

$$y = 6x + (-2)$$
$$\uparrow \qquad \uparrow$$
$$y = mx + \quad b$$

Since $m = 6$ and $b = -2$, the slope of the line is 6 and the y-intercept is $(0, -2)$.

Caution

For equations in $y = mx + b$ form, the slope of the line is the *coefficient* of x, not the x-term. For example, the graph of $y = 6x - 5$ has slope 6, *not* $6x$.

b. Writing $y = -\dfrac{5}{4}x$ in slope–intercept form, we have

$$y = -\frac{5}{4}x + 0 \qquad \text{Add 0 to make the value of } b \text{ obvious.}$$

Since $m = -\dfrac{5}{4}$ and $b = 0$, the slope of the line is $-\dfrac{5}{4}$ and the y-intercept is $(0, 0)$.

c. Since $\dfrac{x}{2}$ means $\dfrac{1}{2}x$, we can rewrite $y = \dfrac{x}{2} + 3$ as

$$y = \frac{1}{2}x + 3$$

We see that $m = \dfrac{1}{2}$ and $b = 3$, so the slope of the line is $\dfrac{1}{2}$ and the y-intercept is $(0, 3)$.

d. We can use the commutative property of addition to reorder the terms on the right-hand side of the equation so that it is in $y = mx + b$ form.

$$y = 12x + 5$$

The slope is 12 and the y-intercept is $(0, 5)$.

Self Check 1　Find the slope and the y-intercept:

a. $y = -5x - 1$　　**b.** $y = \dfrac{7}{8}x$　　**c.** $y = 5 - \dfrac{x}{3}$

The equation of any nonvertical line can be written in slope–intercept form. To do so, we apply the properties of equality to solve for y.

EXAMPLE 2   Find the slope and y-intercept of the line whose equation is $8x + y = 9$.

Solution   The slope and y-intercept are not immediately apparent because the equation is not in slope–intercept form. To write it in $y = mx + b$ form, we isolate y on the left-hand side.

$$8x + y = 9$$
$$8x + y - 8x = -8x + 9 \qquad \text{To undo the addition of } 8x, \text{ subtract } 8x \text{ from both sides.}$$

$$y = -8x + 9 \qquad \text{On the left-hand side, combine like terms: } 8x - 8x = 0.$$

The slope is -8.   The y-intercept is $(0, 9)$.

Self Check 2   Find the slope and y-intercept of the line whose equation is $9x + y = -4$.

EXAMPLE 3   Find the slope and y-intercept of the line with the given equation.

a. $x + 4y = 16$ **b.** $-9x - 3y = 11$

Solution   **a.** To write the equation in slope–intercept form, we solve for y.

$$x + 4y = 16$$
$$x + 4y - x = -x + 16 \qquad \text{To undo the addition of } x, \text{ subtract } x \text{ from both sides.}$$
$$4y = -x + 16 \qquad \text{Simplify the left-hand side.}$$
$$\frac{4y}{4} = \frac{-x + 16}{4} \qquad \text{To undo the multiplication by 4, divide both sides by 4.}$$
$$y = \frac{-x}{4} + \frac{16}{4} \qquad \text{On the right-hand side, rewrite } \tfrac{-x + 16}{4} \text{ as the sum of two fractions with like denominators, } \tfrac{-x}{4} \text{ and } \tfrac{16}{4}.$$
$$y = -\frac{1}{4}x + 4 \qquad \text{Write } \tfrac{-x}{4} \text{ as } -\tfrac{1}{4}x. \text{ Simplify: } \tfrac{16}{4} = 4.$$

Since $m = -\frac{1}{4}$ and $b = 4$, the slope is $-\frac{1}{4}$ and the y-intercept is $(0, 4)$.

b. To write the equation in $y = mx + b$ form, we isolate y on the left-hand side.

$$-9x - 3y = 11$$
$$-3y = 9x + 11 \qquad \text{To eliminate the term } -9x \text{ on the left-hand side, add } 9x \text{ to both sides: } -9x + 9x = 0.$$
$$\frac{-3y}{-3} = \frac{9x}{-3} + \frac{11}{-3} \qquad \text{To undo the multiplication by } -3, \text{ divide both sides by } -3.$$
$$y = -3x - \frac{11}{3} \qquad \text{Simplify.}$$

Since $m = -3$ and $b = -\frac{11}{3}$, the slope is -3 and the y-intercept is $\left(0, -\frac{11}{3}\right)$.

Self Check 3   Find the slope and y-intercept of the line whose equation is $10x + 2y = 7$.

■ USING THE SLOPE AND *y*-INTERCEPT TO GRAPH A LINE

If we know the slope and *y*-intercept of a line, we can graph the line. To illustrate this, we graph $y = 5x - 4$, a line with slope 5 and *y*-intercept $(0, -4)$.

We begin by plotting the *y*-intercept. If we write the slope as $\frac{5}{1}$, we see that the rise is 5 and the run is 1. From $(0, -4)$, we move 5 units upward and then 1 unit to the right. This locates a second point on the line, $(1, 1)$. Then we draw a line through the two points. The result is a line with *y*-intercept $(0, -4)$ and slope 5.

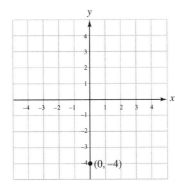

Plot the *y*-intercept, $(0, -4)$.

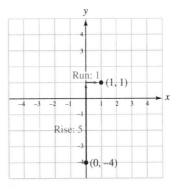

From the *y*-intercept, draw the rise and run components of the slope triangle.

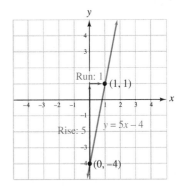

Use a straightedge to draw a line through the two points.

EXAMPLE 4

Graph the line whose equation is $y = -\frac{4}{3}x + 2$.

Solution

The slope of the line is $-\frac{4}{3}$, which can be expressed as $\frac{-4}{3}$. After plotting the *y*-intercept, $(0, 2)$, we move 4 units downward and then 3 units to the right. This locates a second point on the line, $(3, -2)$. From this point, we can move another 4 units downward and 3 units to the right, to locate a *third point* on the line, $(6, -6)$. Then we draw a line through the three points to obtain a line with *y*-intercept $(0, 2)$ and slope $-\frac{4}{3}$.

Caution

When using the *y*-intercept and the slope to graph a line, remember to draw the slope triangle from the *y*-intercept, *not* from the origin.

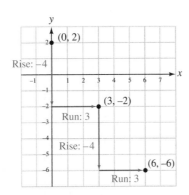

Plot the *y*-intercept. From $(0, 2)$, draw the rise and run components of a slope triangle. From $(3, -2)$, draw another slope triangle.

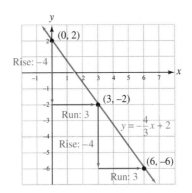

Use a straightedge to draw a line through the three points.

Self Check 4   Graph the line whose equation is $y = -\frac{5}{6}x + 2$.

■ WRITING THE EQUATION OF A LINE

If we are given the slope and y-intercept of a line, we can write an equation of the line by substituting for m and b in the slope–intercept form.

EXAMPLE 5   Write an equation of the line with slope -1 and y-intercept $(0, 9)$.

Solution   If the slope is -1 and the y-intercept is $(0, 9)$, then $m = -1$ and $b = 9$.

$y = mx + b$ This is the slope–intercept form.
$y = -1x + 9$ Substitute -1 for m and 9 for b.
$y = -x + 9$ Simplify: $-1x = -x$.

The equation of the line with slope -1 and y-intercept $(0, 9)$ is $y = -x + 9$.

Self Check 5   Write the equation of the line with slope 1 and y-intercept $(0, -12)$.

■ PARALLEL AND PERPENDICULAR LINES

Two lines that lie in the same plane are **parallel** if they do not intersect. When graphed, parallel lines have the same slope, but different y-intercepts.

Parallel Lines	Two different lines with the same slope are parallel.

EXAMPLE 6   Graph $y = -\dfrac{2}{3}x$ and $y = -\dfrac{2}{3}x + 3$ on the same coordinate system.

Solution   The graph of the first equation is a line with slope $-\frac{2}{3}$ and y-intercept $(0, 0)$. The graph of the second equation is a line with slope $-\frac{2}{3}$ and y-intercept $(0, 3)$. Since the lines have the same slope, they are parallel.

The Language of Algebra

The word *parallel* is used in many settings: drivers *parallel* park, and gymnasts perform on the *parallel* bars.

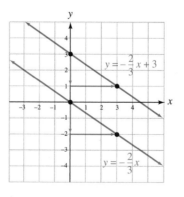

Self Check 6   Graph $y = \dfrac{5}{2}x - 2$ and $y = \dfrac{5}{2}x$ on the same coordinate system.

Unlike parallel lines, **perpendicular lines** intersect. And more important, they intersect to form four right angles (angles with measure 90°). The two lines graphed below are perpendicular. In the figure, the symbol ⌐ is used to denote a right angle.

The Language of Algebra

The word *perpendicular* is used in construction. For example, the monument shown is *perpendicular* to the ground.

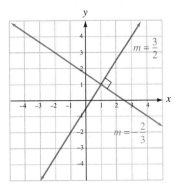

The product of the slopes of two (nonvertical) perpendicular lines is -1. To illustrate this, consider the lines in the illustration, with slopes $\frac{3}{2}$ and $-\frac{2}{3}$. If we find the product of their slopes, we have

$$\frac{3}{2}\left(-\frac{2}{3}\right) = -\frac{6}{6} = -1$$

Note that the slopes of the lines in this example, $\frac{3}{2}$ and $-\frac{2}{3}$, are **negative** (or **opposite**) **reciprocals.** We can use the term *negative reciprocal* to express the relationship between the slopes of perpendicular lines in an alternate way.

Slopes of Perpendicular Lines

1. Two nonvertical lines are perpendicular if the product of the slopes is -1, that is, if their slopes are negative reciprocals.

   In symbols, two lines with slopes m_1 and m_2 are perpendicular if

$$m_1 \cdot m_2 = -1 \qquad \text{or} \qquad m_1 = -\frac{1}{m_2}$$

2. A horizontal line with 0 slope is perpendicular to a vertical line with undefined slope.

EXAMPLE 7

Determine whether the graphs of $y = -5x + 6$ and $y = \frac{x}{5} - 2$ are parallel, perpendicular, or neither.

Solution   The slope of the line $y = -5x + 6$ is -5. The slope of the line $y = \frac{x}{5} - 2$ is $\frac{1}{5}$. $\left(\text{Recall that } \frac{x}{5} = \frac{1}{5}x.\right)$ Since the slopes are not equal, the lines are not parallel. If we find the product of their slopes, we have

$$-5\left(\frac{1}{5}\right) = -\frac{5}{5} = -1 \qquad -5 \text{ and } \frac{1}{5} \text{ are negative reciprocals.}$$

Since the product of their slopes is -1, the lines are perpendicular.

Self Check 7   Determine whether the graphs of $y = 4x + 6$ and $y = \frac{1}{4}x$ are parallel, perpendicular, or neither.

■ APPLICATIONS

In the next example, as a means of making the equation more descriptive, we replace x and y in $y = mx + b$ with two other variables.

EXAMPLE 8

Group discounts.   To promote group sales for an Alaskan cruise, a travel agency reduces the regular cost of $4,500 by $5 for each person traveling in the group.

a. Write a linear equation in slope–intercept form that finds the cost c of the cruise, if a group of p people travel together.

b. Use the equation to determine the cost if a group of 55 retired teachers travel together.

Solution   a. Since the cost c of the cruise depends on the number p of people traveling in the group, the equation will have the form $c = mp + b$. We need to determine m and b.

Cruise to Alaska

$4,500 per person

Group discounts available*

*For groups of up to 100

   The cost of the cruise steadily *decreases* as the number of people in the group increases. This rate of change, -5 dollars per person, is the slope of the graph of the equation. Thus m is -5.

   If a group of 0 people take the cruise, there will be no discount; the cruise will cost $4,500. Written as an ordered pair of the form (p, c), we have $(0, 4,500)$. When graphed, this would be the c-intercept. Thus, b is 4,500.

   Substituting for m and b, we obtain the linear equation that models this situation.

$$c = -5p + 4,500$$

b. To find the cost of the cruise for a group of 55, we proceed as follows:

$$c = -5p + 4,500$$
$$c = -5(55) + 4,500 \quad \text{Substitute 55 for } p, \text{ the number of people in the group.}$$
$$c = -275 + 4,500$$
$$= 4,225$$

If a group of 55 people travel together, the Alaskan cruise will cost each person $4,225.

Self Check 8   Write a linear equation in slope–intercept form that finds the cost c of the cruise if a $10-per-person discount is offered for groups.

Answers to Self Checks   1. a. $m = -5, (0, -1)$
  b. $m = \frac{7}{8}, (0, 0)$
  c. $m = -\frac{1}{3}, (0, 5)$
2. $m = -9; (0, -4)$
3. $m = -5; \left(0, \frac{7}{2}\right)$

4.
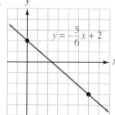

5. $y = x - 12$

6.
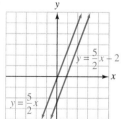

7. neither
8. $c = -10p + 4,500$

3.5   STUDY SET

VOCABULARY   Fill in the blanks.

1. The equation $y = mx + b$ is called the
   _____ form of the equation of a line.

2. The graph of the linear equation $y = mx + b$ has a
   _____ of $(0, b)$ and a _____ of m.

3. _____ lines do not intersect.

4. The slope of a line is a _____ of change.

5. The numbers $\frac{5}{6}$ and $-\frac{6}{5}$ are called negative
   _____. Their product is -1.

6. The product of the slopes of _____ lines
   is -1.

CONCEPTS

7. Tell whether each equation is in slope–intercept form.
   a. $7x + 4y = 2$ b. $5y = 2x - 3$
   c. $y = 6x + 1$ d. $x = 4y - 8$
   e. $y = \frac{x}{5} - 3$ f. $y = 2x$

8. a. How do we solve $4x + y = 9$ for y?

   b. How do we solve $-2x + y = 9$ for y?

9. a. To solve $5y = 10x + 20$ for y, both sides of the
   equation were divided by 5. Complete the solution.

   $$\frac{5y}{5} = \frac{10x}{5} + \frac{20}{5}$$

   $$\boxed{} = \boxed{} + \boxed{}$$

   b. To solve $-2y = 6x - 12$ for y, both sides of the
   equation were divided by -2. Complete the
   solution.

   $$\frac{-2y}{-2} = \frac{6x}{-2} - \frac{12}{-2}$$

   $$\boxed{} = \boxed{} \quad 6$$

10. Examine the work shown in the following graph. An
    equation in slope–intercept form is in the process of
    being graphed.
    a. What is the y-intercept of the line?
    b. What is the slope of the line?
    c. What equation is being graphed?

d. One more step needs to be completed. What is it?

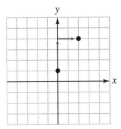

11. Use the graph of the line to determine m and b. Then
    write the equation of the line in slope–intercept form.

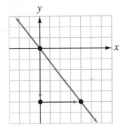

12. Find the negative reciprocal of each number.

Number	Negative reciprocal
6	
$\frac{7}{8}$	
$-\frac{1}{4}$	
1	

13. Fill in the blanks.
    a. Two different lines with the same slope are
       _____.
    b. If the slopes of two lines are negative reciprocals,
       the lines are _____.
    c. The product of the slopes of perpendicular lines is
       _____.

14. a. What is the *y*-intercept of Line 1?

   b. What do Line 1 and Line 2 have in common? How are they different?

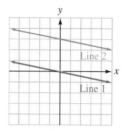

15. The slope of Line 1 shown in the following illustration is 2.

   a. What is the slope of Line 2?

   b. What is the slope of Line 3?

   c. What is the slope of Line 4?

   d. Which lines have the same *y*-intercept?

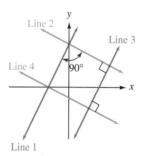

16. NAVIGATION   The graph shows the recommended speed at which a ship should proceed into head waves of various heights.

   a. What information does the *y*-intercept of the graph give?

   b. What is the rate of change in the recommended speed of the ship as the wave height increases?

   c. Write the equation of the graph.

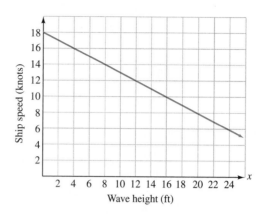

NOTATION   Complete the solution by solving the equation for *y*. Then find the slope and the *y*-intercept of its graph.

17.
$$2x + 5y = 15$$
$$2x + 5y - = + 15$$
$$= -2x + 15$$
$$\frac{5y}{} = \frac{-2x}{} + \frac{15}{}$$
$$y = -\frac{2}{5}x + $$

The slope is _____ and the *y*-intercept is _____ .

18. What is the slope–intercept form of the equation of a line?

19. Simplify each expression.

   a. $\dfrac{8x}{2}$ **b.** $\dfrac{8x}{6}$

   c. $\dfrac{-8x}{-8}$ **d.** $\dfrac{-16}{8}$

20. Tell whether each statement is true or false.

   a. $\dfrac{x}{6} = \dfrac{1}{6}x$ **b.** $\dfrac{5}{3}x = \dfrac{5x}{3}$

21. What does the symbol ⌐ denote?

22. Write the phrase *ninety degrees* in symbols.

PRACTICE   Find the slope and the *y*-intercept of the graph of each equation.

23. $y = 4x + 2$ **24.** $y = -4x - 2$

25. $y = -5x - 8$ **26.** $y = 7x + 3$

27. $4x - 2 = y$ **28.** $6x - 1 = y$

29. $y = \dfrac{x}{4} - \dfrac{1}{2}$

30. $y = \dfrac{x}{15} - \dfrac{3}{4}$

31. $y = \dfrac{1}{2}x + 6$

32. $y = \dfrac{4}{5}x - 9$

33. $y = 6 - x$

34. $y = 12 + 4x$

35. $x + y = 8$

36. $x - y = -30$

37. $6y = x - 6$

38. $2y = x + 20$

39. $7y = -14x + 49$

40. $9y = -27x + 36$

41. $-4y = 6x - 4$

42. $-6y = 8x + 6$

43. $2x + 3y = 6$

44. $4x + 5y = 25$

45. $3x - 5y = 15$

46. $x - 6y = 6$

47. $-6x + 6y = -11$

48. $-4x + 4y = -9$

49. $y = x$

50. $y = -x$

51. $y = -5x$

52. $y = 14x$

53. $y = -2$

54. $y = 30$

55. $-5y - 2 = 0$

56. $3y - 13 = 0$

Write an equation of the line with the given slope and y-intercept. Then graph it.

57. Slope 5, y-intercept $(0, -3)$

58. Slope -2, y-intercept $(0, 1)$

59. Slope $\dfrac{1}{4}$, y-intercept $(0, -2)$

60. Slope $\dfrac{1}{3}$, y-intercept $(0, -5)$

61. Slope -3, y-intercept $(0, 6)$

62. Slope 4, y-intercept $(0, -1)$

63. Slope $-\dfrac{8}{3}$, y-intercept $(0, 5)$

64. Slope $-\dfrac{7}{6}$, y-intercept $(0, 2)$

Find the slope and the y-intercept of the graph of each equation. Then graph the equation.

65. $y = 3x + 3$

66. $y = -3x + 5$

67. $y = -\dfrac{x}{2} + 2$

68. $y = \dfrac{x}{3}$

69. $y = -3x$

70. $y = -4x$

71. $4x + y = -4$

72. $2x + y = -6$

73. $3x + 4y = 16$

74. $2x + 3y = 9$

75. $10x - 5y = 5$

76. $4x - 2y = 6$

For each pair of equations, determine whether their graphs are parallel, perpendicular, or neither.

77. $y = 6x + 8$
$y = 6x$

78. $y = 3x - 15$
$y = -\dfrac{1}{3}x + 4$

79. $y = x$
$y = -x$

80. $y = \dfrac{1}{2}x - \dfrac{4}{5}$
$y = 0.5x + 3$

81. $y = -2x - 9$
$y = 2x - 9$

82. $y = \dfrac{3}{4}x + 1$
$y = \dfrac{4}{3}x - 5$

83. $x - y = 12$
$-2x + 2y = -23$

84. $y = -3x + 1$
$3y = x - 5$

85. $x = 9$
$y = 8$

86. $-x + 4y = 10$
$2y + 16 = -8x$

APPLICATIONS

87. PRODUCTION COSTS   A television production company charges a basic fee of \$5,000 and then \$2,000 an hour when filming a commercial.
  a. Write a linear equation that describes the relationship between the total production costs c and the hours h of filming.
  b. Use your answer to part a to find the production costs if a commercial required 8 hours of filming.

88. COLLEGE FEES Each semester, students enrolling at a community college must pay tuition costs of $20 per unit as well as a $40 student services fee.

   a. Write a linear equation that gives the total fees t to be paid by a student enrolling at the college and taking x units.

   b. Use your answer to part a to find the enrollment cost for a student taking 12 units.

89. CHEMISTRY A portion of a student's chemistry lab manual is shown below. Use the information to write a linear equation relating the temperature F (in degrees Fahrenheit) of the compound to the time t (in minutes) elapsed during the lab procedure.

Chem. Lab #1 Aug. 13
Step 1: Removed compound from freezer @ –10°F.

Step 2: Used heating unit to raise temperature of compound 5° F every minute.

90. INCOME PROPERTY Use the information in the newspaper advertisement to write a linear equation that gives the amount of income A (in dollars) the apartment owner will receive when the unit is rented for m months.

APARTMENT FOR RENT
1 bedroom/1 bath, with garage
$500 per month +
$250 nonrefundable security fee.

91. EMPLOYMENT SERVICE A policy statement of LIZCO, Inc., is shown below. Suppose a secretary had to pay an employment service $500 to get placed in a new job at LIZCO. Write a linear equation that tells the secretary the actual cost c of the employment service to her m months after being hired.

Policy no. 23452–A new hire will be reimbursed by LIZCO for any employment service fees paid by the employee at the rate of $20 per month.

92. VIDEOTAPES A VHS videocassette contains 800 feet of tape. In the long play mode (LP), it plays 10 feet of tape every 3 minutes. Write a linear equation that relates the number of feet f of tape yet to be played and the number of minutes m the tape has been playing.

93. SEWING COSTS A tailor charges a basic fee of $20 plus $5 per letter to sew an athlete's name on the back of a jacket.

   a. Write a linear equation that will find the cost c to have a name containing x letters sewn on the back of a jacket.

   b. Graph the equation.

   c. Suppose the tailor raises the basic fee to $30. On your graph from part b, draw the new graph showing the increased cost.

94. SALAD BARS For lunch, a delicatessen offers a "Salad and Soda" special where customers serve themselves at a well-stocked salad bar. The cost is $1.00 for the drink and 20¢ an ounce for the salad.

   a. Write a linear equation that will find the cost c of a "Salad and Soda" lunch when a salad weighing x ounces is purchased.

   b. Graph the equation.

   c. How would the graph from part b change if the delicatessen began charging $2.00 for the drink?

   d. How would the graph from part b change if the cost of the salad changed to 30¢ an ounce?

95. PROFESSIONAL HOCKEY Use the following facts to write a linear equation in slope–intercept form that approximates the average price of a National Hockey League ticket for the years 1995–2002.

   • Let t represent the number of years since 1995 and c the average cost of a ticket.

   • In 1995, the average ticket price was $33.50.

   • From 1995 to 2002, the average ticket price increased $2 per year.

(Source: Team Marketing Report, NHL)

96. COMPUTER DRAFTING The illustration shows a computer-generated drawing of an automobile engine mount. When the designer clicks the mouse on a line of the drawing, the computer finds the equation of the line. Determine whether the two lines selected in the drawing are perpendicular.

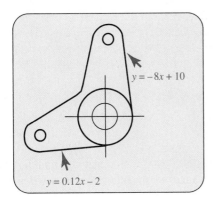

$y = -8x + 10$

$y = 0.12x - 2$

WRITING

97. Why is $y = mx + b$ called the slope–intercept form of the equation of a line?

98. On a quiz, a student was asked to find the slope of the graph of $y = 2x + 3$. She answered: $m = 2x$. Her instructor marked it wrong. Explain why the answer is incorrect.

REVIEW

99. CABLE TV   A 186-foot television cable is to be cut into four pieces. Find the length of each piece if each successive piece is 3 feet longer than the previous one.

100. INVESTMENTS   Joni received $25,000 as part of a settlement in a class action lawsuit. She invested some money at 10% and the rest at 9% simple interest rates. If her total annual income from these two investments was $2,430, how much did she invest at each rate?

CHALLENGE PROBLEMS

101. If the graph of $y = mx + b$ passes through quadrants I, II, and IV, what can be known about the constants m and b?

102. The equation $y = \frac{3}{4}x - 5$ is in slope–intercept form. Write it in general form, $Ax + By = C$, where $A > 0$.

KEY CONCEPT: DESCRIBING LINEAR RELATIONSHIPS

In Chapter 3, we discussed ways to mathematically describe linear relationships between two quantities using equations and graphs.

EQUATIONS IN TWO VARIABLES

The general form of the equation of a line is $Ax + By = C$. Two very useful forms of the equation of a line are the slope–intercept form and the point–slope form.

1. Write the equation of a line with a slope of -3 and a y-intercept of $(0, -4)$.

2. Write the equation of the line that passes through $(5, 2)$ and $(-5, 0)$. Give the answer in slope–intercept form.

3. CRICKETS   The equation $T = \frac{1}{4}c + 40$ predicts the outdoor temperature T in degrees Fahrenheit using the number c of cricket chirps per minute. Find the temperature if a cricket chirps 160 times in one minute.

4. U.S. HEALTH CARE   For the year 1990, the per capita health care expenditure was about \$2,660. Since then, the rate of increase has been about \$209 per year. Write a linear equation to model this. Let x represent the number of years since 1990 and let y represent the yearly per capita expenditure. Use your answer to predict the per capita expenditure in 2020. (Source: Centers for Medicare and Medicaid Services)

RECTANGULAR COORDINATE GRAPHS

The graph of an equation is a "picture" of all of its solutions. A thorough examination of a graph can yield a lot of useful information.

5. Complete the table of solutions for $2x - 4y = 8$. Then graph the equation.

$$2x - 4y = 8$$

x	y
0	
	0
-2	

6. a. What information does the y-intercept give?

   b. What is the slope of the line and what does it tell?

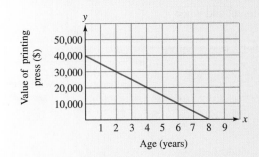

7. a. Find a point on the line.

   b. Determine the slope of the line.

   c. Write the equation of the line in slope–intercept form.

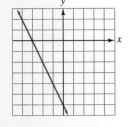

8. Write the equation of the line that passes through $(1, -1)$ and is parallel to the line graphed to the right.

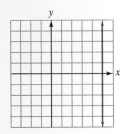

CHAPTER REVIEW

Graphing Using the Rectangular Coordinate System

CONCEPTS

A *rectangular coordinate system* is composed of a horizontal number line called the *x*-axis and a vertical number line called the *y*-axis.

To *graph* ordered pairs means to locate their position on a coordinate system.

The two axes divide the coordinate plane into four regions called *quadrants*.

REVIEW EXERCISES

1. Graph the points with coordinates $(-1, 3)$, $(0, 1.5)$, $(-4, -4)$, $\left(2, \frac{7}{2}\right)$, and $(4, 0)$.

2. HAWAIIAN ISLANDS   Estimate the coordinates of Oahu using an ordered pair of the form (longitude, latitude).

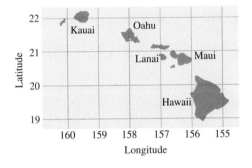

3. In what quadrant does the point $(-3, -4)$ lie?

4. What are the coordinates of the origin?

5. GEOMETRY   Three vertices (corners) of a square are the points $(-5, 4)$, $(-5, -2)$, and $(1, -2)$. Find the coordinates of the fourth vertex and find the area of the square.

6. COLLEGE ENROLLMENTS   The graph gives the number of students enrolled at a college for the period from 4 weeks before to 5 weeks after the semester began.

   a. What was the maximum enrollment and when did it occur?

   b. How many students had enrolled 2 weeks before the semester began?

   c. When was enrollment 2,250?

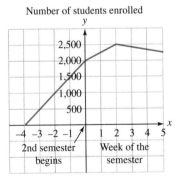

SECTION 3.2

Graphing Linear Equations

A *solution* of an equation in two variables is an ordered pair of numbers that makes the equation a true statement.

An equation whose graph is a straight line and whose variables are raised to the first power is called a *linear equation.*

The *general* or *standard form* of a linear equation is $Ax + By = C$, where A, B, and C are real numbers and A and B are not both zero.

To graph a linear equation solved for y:

1. Find three solutions by selecting three x-values and finding the corresponding y-values.

2. Plot each ordered-pair solution.

3. Draw a straight line through the points.

7. Is $(-3, -2)$ a solution of $y = 2x + 4$?

8. Complete the table of solutions for $3x + 2y = -18$.

x	y	(x, y)
-2		
	3	

9. Which of the following equations are not linear equations?

$8x - 2y = 6 \qquad y = x^2 + 1 \qquad y = x \qquad 3y = -x + 4 \qquad y - x^3 = 0$

Graph each equation by constructing a table of solutions.

10. $y = 4x - 2$

11. $5y = -5x + 15$ (Solve for y first.)

12. The graph of a linear equation is shown here.

    a. When the coordinates of point A are substituted into the equation, will a true or false statement result?

    b. When the coordinates of point B are substituted into the equation, will a true or false statement result?

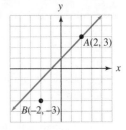

13. BIRTHDAY PARTIES   A restaurant offers a party package for children that includes everything: food, drinks, cake, and party favors. The cost c, in dollars, is given by the linear equation $c = 8n + 50$, where n is the number of children attending the party. Graph the equation and use the graph to estimate the cost of a party if 18 children attend.

SECTION 3.3

More about Graphing Linear Equations

The point where a line intersects the x-axis is called the *x-intercept.* The point where a line intersects the y-axis is called the *y-intercept.*

14. Identify the x- and y-intercepts of the graph.

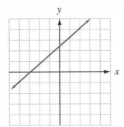

To find the y-intercept, substitute 0 for x in the given equation and solve for y. To find the x-intercept, substitute 0 for y in the given equation and solve for x.

The equation $y = b$ represents the horizontal line that intersects the y-axis at $(0, b)$. The equation $x = a$ represents the vertical line that intersects the x-axis at $(a, 0)$.

15. Graph $-4x + 2y = 8$ by finding its x- and y-intercepts.

16. Graph: $y = 4$.

17. Graph: $x = -1$.

18. DEPRECIATION   The graph shows how the value of some sound equipment decreased over the years. Find the intercepts of the graph. What information do the intercepts give about the equipment?

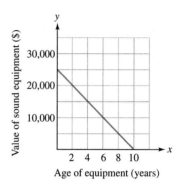

| SECTION 3.4 | The Slope of a Line |

The *slope m* of a line is a number that measures "steepness" by finding the ratio $\frac{\text{rise}}{\text{run}}$.

$$m = \frac{\text{change in the } y\text{-values}}{\text{change in the } x\text{-values}}$$

Lines that rise from left to right have a *positive slope,* and lines that fall from left to right have a *negative slope.* Horizontal lines have a slope of zero. Vertical lines have *undefined* slope.

If (x_1, y_1) and (x_2, y_2) are two points on a nonvertical line, the slope m of the line is

$$m = \frac{y_2 - y_1}{x_2 - x_1}$$

In each case, find the slope of the line.

19.

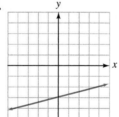

20.

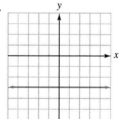

21. The line with the table of solutions shown below

x	y	(x, y)
2	-3	$(2, -3)$
4	-17	$(4, -17)$

22. The line passing through points $(1, -4)$ and $(3, -7)$

The *pitch* of a roof is its slope.

The *grade* of an incline or decline is its slope expressed as a percent.

When units are attached to a slope it becomes a *rate of change.*

23. CARPENTRY   Trusses like the one shown here will be used to construct the roof of a shed. Find the pitch of the roof.

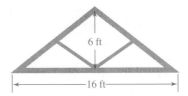

24. HANDICAP ACCESSIBILITY   Find the grade of the ramp. Round to the nearest tenth of a percent.

25. TOURISM   The graph shows the number of international travelers to the United States from 1986 to 2000, in two-year increments.

   a. Between 1992 and 1994 the largest decline in the number of visitors occurred. What was the rate of change?

   b. Between 1986 and 1988 the largest increase in the number of visitors occurred. What was the rate of change?

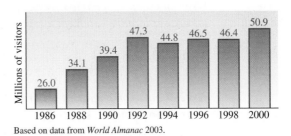

Based on data from *World Almanac* 2003.

| SECTION 3.5 | **Slope–Intercept Form** |

If a linear equation is written in *slope–intercept* form,

$$y = mx + b$$

the graph of the equation is a line with slope m and y-intercept $(0, b)$.

Find the slope and the y-intercept of each line.

26. $y = \dfrac{3}{4}x - 2$

27. $y = -4x$

28. $y = \dfrac{x}{8} + 10$

29. $7x + 5y = -21$

30. Write an equation of the line with slope -6 and y-intercept $(0, 4)$.

31. Find the slope and the y-intercept of the line whose equation is $9x - 3y = 15$. Then graph it.

The *rate of change* is the slope of the graph of a linear equation.

32. COPIERS   A business buys a used copy machine that, when purchased, has already produced 75,000 copies.

    a. If the business plans to run 300 copies a week, write a linear equation that would find the number of copies c the machine has made in its lifetime after the business has used it for w weeks.

    b. Use your result in part a to predict the total number of copies that will have been made on the machine 1 year, or 52 weeks, after being purchased by the business.

Two lines with the same slope are *parallel*.

The product of the slopes of *perpendicular* lines is -1.

33. Without graphing, determine whether graphs of the given pairs of lines would be parallel, perpendicular, or neither.

    a. $y = -\dfrac{2}{3}x + 6$

         $y = -\dfrac{2}{3}x - 6$

    b. $x + 5y = -10$

         $y = 5x$

| SECTION 3.6 | **Point–Slope Form** |

If a line with slope m passes through the point (x_1, y_1), the equation of the line in *point–slope* form is

$$y - y_1 = m(x - x_1)$$

Write an equation of a line with the given slope that passes through the given point. Give the answer in slope–intercept form and graph the equation.

34. $m = 3, (1, 5)$

35. $m = -\dfrac{1}{2}, (-4, -1)$

Write an equation of the line with the following characteristics. Give the answer in slope–intercept form.

36. passing through $(3, 7)$ and $(-6, 1)$

37. horizontal, passing through $(6, -8)$

38. CAR REGISTRATION   When it was 2 years old, the annual registration fee for a Dodge Caravan was $380. When it was 4 years old, the registration fee dropped to $310. If the relationship is linear, write an equation that gives the registration fee f in dollars for the van when it is x years old.

| SECTION 3.7 | **Graphing Linear Inequalities** |

An ordered pair (x, y) is a *solution* of an inequality in x and y if a true statement results when the variables are replaced by the coordinates of the ordered pair.

39. Determine whether each ordered pair is a solution of $2x - y \leq -4$.

    a. $(0, 5)$

    b. $(2, 8)$

    c. $(-3, -2)$

    d. $\left(\dfrac{1}{2}, -5\right)$

To graph a linear inequality:

1. Graph the *boundary line.* Draw a solid line if the inequality contains ≤ or ≥ and a broken line if it contains < or >.

2. Pick a *test point* on one side of the boundary. Use the origin if possible. Replace x and y with the coordinates of that point. If the inequality is satisfied, shade the side that contains the point. If the inequality is not satisfied, shade the other side.

Graph each inequality.

40. $x - y < 5$

41. $2x - 3y \geq 6$

42. $y \leq -2x$

43. $y < -4$

44. The graph of a linear inequality is shown. Would a true or a false statement result if the coordinates of

   a. point A were substituted into the inequality?

   b. point B were substituted into the inequality?

   c. point C were substituted into the inequality?

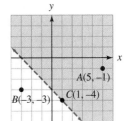

45. WORK SCHEDULES   A student told her employer that during the school year, she would be available for up to 30 hours a week, working either 3- or 5-hour shifts. If x represents the number of 3-hour shifts she works and y represents the number of 5-hour shifts she works, the inequality $3x + 5y \leq 30$ shows the possible combinations of shifts she can work. Graph the inequality, then find three possible combinations.

46. Explain the difference between an equation and an inequality.

CHAPTER 3 TEST

The graph shows the number of dogs being boarded in a kennel over a 3-day holiday weekend.

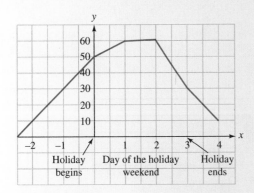

1. How many dogs were in the kennel 2 days before the holiday?

2. What is the maximum number of dogs that were boarded on the holiday weekend?

3. When were there 30 dogs in the kennel?

4. What information does the y-intercept of the graph give?

5. Draw a rectangular coordinate system and label each quadrant.

6. Complete the table of solutions for the linear equation.

$$x + 4y = 6$$

x	y	(x, y)
2		
	3	

7. Is $(-3, -4)$ a solution of $3x - 4y = 7$?

8. The graph of a linear equation is shown below.

    a. If the coordinates of point C are substituted into the equation, will the result be true or false?

    b. If the coordinates of point D are substituted into the equation, will the result be true or false?

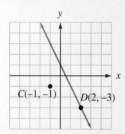

9. Graph: $y = \dfrac{x}{3}$.

10. Graph: $8x + 4y = -24$.

11. What are the x- and y-intercepts of the graph of $2x - 3y = 6$?

12. Find the slope of the line.

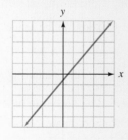

13. Find the slope of the line passing through $(-1, 3)$ and $(3, -1)$.

14. What is the slope of a vertical line?

15. What is the slope of a line that is perpendicular to a line with slope $-\dfrac{7}{8}$?

16. When graphed, are the lines $y = 2x + 6$ and $y = 2x$ parallel, perpendicular, or neither?

In Problems 17 and 18, refer to the illustration at the bottom of the page that shows the elevation changes in a 26-mile marathon course.

17. Find the rate of change of the decline on which the woman is running.

18. Find the rate of change of the incline on which the man is running.

19. Graph: $x = -4$.

20. Graph the line passing through $(-2, -4)$ having a slope of $\dfrac{2}{3}$.

21. Find the slope and the y-intercept of $x + 2y = 8$.

22. Write an equation of the line passing through $(-2, 5)$ with slope 7. Give the answer in slope–intercept form.

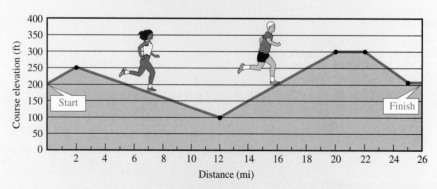

23. DEPRECIATION   After it is purchased, a $15,000 computer loses $1,500 in resale value every year. Write a linear equation that gives the resale value v of the computer x years after being purchased.

24. Determine whether (6, 1) is a solution of $2x - 4y \geq 8$.

25. WATER HEATERS   The scatter diagram shows how excessively high temperatures affect the life of a water heater. Write an equation of the line that models the data for water temperatures between 140° and 180°. Let T represent the temperature of the water in degrees Fahrenheit and y represent the expected life of the heater in years. Give the answer in slope–intercept form.

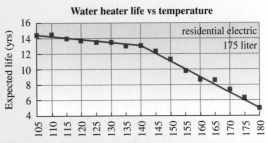

Water heater life vs temperature

residential electric
175 liter

Expected life (yrs)

Water: stored temperature (Fahrenheit)

Source: www.uniongas.com/WaterHeating

26. Graph the inequality $x - y > -2$.

CHAPTERS 1–3   CUMULATIVE REVIEW EXERCISES

1. UNITED AIRLINES   On May 2, 2003, UAL Corporation, the parent company of United Airlines, announced its 11th straight quarterly loss. (See the graph below.)
   a. During this time span, in which quarter was the loss the greatest?
   b. Estimate the corporation's losses for the year 2002.

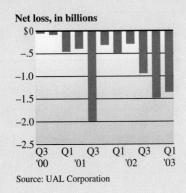

Net loss, in billions

$0
−.5
−1.0
−1.5
−2.0
−2.5

Q3   Q1   Q3   Q1   Q3   Q1
'00   '01   '02   '03

Source: UAL Corporation

2. Give the prime factorization of 108.

3. Write $\frac{1}{250}$ as a decimal.

4. Determine whether each statement is true or false.
   a. Every whole number is an integer.
   b. Every integer is a real number.
   c. 0 is a whole number, an integer, and a rational number.

5. PENNIES   A 2002 telephone survey of adults asked whether the penny should be discontinued from the national currency. The results are shown in the circle graph. If 781 people favored keeping the penny, how many took part in the survey?

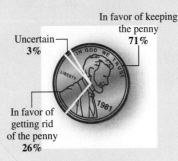

In favor of keeping the penny
71%

Uncertain
3%

In favor of getting rid of the penny
26%

Based on data from Coinstar

6. Evaluate: $\left| \dfrac{(6-5)^4 - (-21)}{-27 + 4^2} \right|$.

7. Evaluate $b^2 - 4ac$ for $a = 2$, $b = -8$, and $c = 4$.

8. Suppose x sheets from a 500-sheet ream of paper have been used. How many sheets are left?

9. How many terms does the algebraic expression $3x^2 - 2x + 1$ have? What is the coefficient of the second term?

10. Use the distributive property to remove parentheses.
  a. $2(x + 4)$ **b.** $2(x - 4)$
  c. $-2(x + 4)$ **d.** $-2(x - 4)$

Simplify each expression.

11. $5a + 10 - a$ **12.** $-7(9t)$

13. $-2b^2 + 6b^2$ **14.** $5(-17)(0)(2)$

15. $(a + 2) - (a - 2)$ **16.** $-4(-5)(-8a)$

17. $-y - y - y$ **18.** $\dfrac{3}{2}(4x - 8) + x$

Solve each equation.

19. $3x - 5 = 13$ **20.** $1.2 - x = -1.7$

21. $\dfrac{2x}{3} - 2 = 4$ **22.** $\dfrac{y - 2}{7} = -3$

23. $-3(2y - 2) - y = 5$ **24.** $9y - 3 = 6y$

25. $\dfrac{1}{3} + \dfrac{c}{5} = -\dfrac{3}{2}$ **26.** $5(x + 2) = 5x - 2$

27. $-x = -99$ **28.** $3c - 2 = \dfrac{11(c - 1)}{5}$

29. HIGH HEELS   Find x.

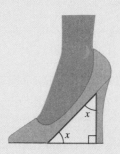

30. Solve for h:

$$S = 2\pi rh + 2\pi r^2$$

31. Find the perimeter and the area of the gauze pad of the bandage.

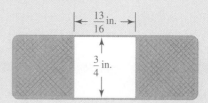

32. Two sides of an isosceles triangle are 3 feet and 4 feet long. What are the possible perimeters of the triangle?

33. Complete the table.

	% acid	Liters	Amount of acid
50% solution	0.50	x	
25% solution	0.25	$13 - x$	
30% mixture	0.30	13	

34. ROAD TRIPS   A bus, carrying the members of a marching band, and a truck, carrying their instruments, leave a high school at the same time. The bus travels at 60 mph and the truck at 50 mph. In how many hours will they be 75 miles apart?

35. MIXING CANDY   Candy corn worth $1.90 per pound is to be mixed with black gumdrops that cost $1.20 per pound to make 200 pounds of a mixture worth $1.48 per pound. How many pounds of each candy should be used?

Solve each inequality. Write the solution set in interval notation and graph it.

36. $-\dfrac{3}{16}x \geq -9$

37. $8x + 4 > 3x + 4$

38. Is $(-2, 4)$ a solution of $y = 2x - 8$?

Graph each equation.

39. $y = x$ **40.** $4y + 2x = -8$

41. What is the slope of the graph of the line $y = 5$?

42. What is the slope of the line passing through $(-2, 4)$ and $(5, -6)$?

43. ROOFING   What is the pitch of the roof?

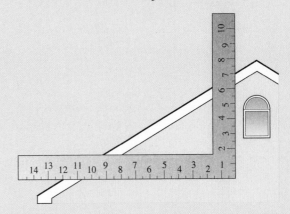

44. Find the slope and the y-intercept of the graph of the line described by $4x - 6y = -12$.

45. Write an equation of the line that has slope -2 and y-intercept $(0, 1)$.

46. Write an equation of the line that has slope $-\dfrac{7}{8}$ and passes through $(2, -9)$. Express the answer in point–slope form.

47. Is $(-6, 0)$ a solution of $y \geq -x - 6$?

48. Graph the inequality $x < 4$ on a rectangular coordinate system.

47. COMPARING INVESTMENTS Two certificates of deposit (CDs) pay interest at rates that differ by 1%. Money invested for 1 year in the first CD earns $175 interest. The same principal invested in the second CD earns $200. Find the two rates of interest.

48. COMPARING INTEREST RATES Two bond funds pay interest at rates that differ by 2%. Money invested for 1 year in the first fund earns $315 interest. The same amount invested in the second fund earns $385. Find the lower rate of interest.

WRITING

49. In Example 4, one inlet pipe could fill an oil tank in 7 days, and another could fill the same tank in 9 days. We were asked to find how long it would take if both pipes were used. Explain why each of the following approaches is incorrect.

The time it would take to fill the tank

- is the *sum* of the lengths of time it takes each pipe to fill the tank: 7 days + 9 days = 16 days.
- is the *difference* in the lengths of time it takes each pipe to fill the tank: 9 days − 7 days = 2 days.
- is the *average* of the lengths of time it takes each pipe to fill the tank:

$$\frac{7 \text{ days} + 9 \text{ days}}{2} = \frac{16 \text{ days}}{2} = 8 \text{ days}$$

50. Write a shared-work problem that can be modeled by the equation

$$\frac{x}{3} + \frac{x}{4} = 1$$

REVIEW

51. When expressed as a decimal, is $\frac{7}{9}$ a terminating or a repeating decimal?

52. Solve: $x + 20 = 4x - 1 + 2x$.

53. List the set of integers.

54. Solve: $4x^2 + 8x = 0$.

55. Evaluate $2x^2 + 5x - 3$ for $x = -3$.

56. Solve $T - R = ma$ for R.

CHALLENGE PROBLEMS

57. RIVER TOURS A river boat tour begins by going 60 miles upstream against a 5-mph current. There, the boat turns around and returns with the current. What still-water speed should the captain use to complete the tour in 5 hours?

58. TRAVEL TIME A company president flew 680 miles one way in the corporate jet but returned in a smaller plane that could fly only half as fast. If the total travel time was 6 hours, find the speeds of the planes.

59. SALES A dealer bought some radios for a total of $1,200. She gave away 6 radios as gifts, sold the rest for $10 more than she paid for each radio, and broke even. How many radios did she buy?

60. FURNACE REPAIRS A repairman purchased several furnace-blower motors for a total cost of $210. If his cost per motor had been $5 less, he could have purchased one additional motor. How many motors did he buy at the regular rate?

6.8 Proportions and Similar Triangles

- Ratios, Rates, and Proportions   • Solving Proportions   • Problem Solving
- Similar Triangles

In this section, we will discuss a problem-solving tool called a *proportion*. A proportion is a type of rational equation that involves two *ratios* or two *rates*.

■ RATIOS, RATES, AND PROPORTIONS

Ratios enable us to compare numerical quantities. Here are some examples.

- To prepare fuel for a lawnmower, gasoline is mixed with oil in a 50 to 1 ratio.
- In the stock market, winning stocks might outnumber losers by a ratio of 7 to 4.
- Gold is combined with other metals in the ratio of 14 to 10 to make 14-karat jewelry.

Ratios   A **ratio** is the quotient of two numbers or the quotient of two quantities that have the same units.

There are three common ways to write a ratio: as a fraction, using the word *to,* or with a colon. For example, the comparison of the number of winning stocks to the number of losing stocks mentioned earlier can be written as

$$\frac{7}{4}, \qquad 7 \text{ to } 4, \qquad \text{or} \qquad 7:4$$

Each of these forms can be read as "the ratio of 7 to 4."

EXAMPLE 1

Translate each phrase into a ratio written in fractional form: **a.** The ratio of 5 to 9   and **b.** 12 ounces to 2 pounds.

Solution   **a.** The ratio of 5 to 9 is written $\frac{5}{9}$.

b. To write a ratio of two quantities with the same units, we must express 2 pounds in terms of ounces. Since 1 pound = 16 ounces, 2 pounds = 32 ounces. The ratio of 12 ounces to 32 ounces can be simplified so that no units appear in the final form.

Notation

A ratio that is the quotient of two quantities having the same units should be simplified so that no units appear in the final answer.

$$\frac{12 \text{ ounces}}{32 \text{ ounces}} = \frac{3 \cdot \overset{1}{\cancel{4}} \text{ ounces}}{\underset{1}{\cancel{4}} \cdot 8 \text{ ounces}} = \frac{3}{8}$$

Self Check 1   Translate each phrase into a ratio written in fractional form: **a.** The ratio of 15 to 2 and   **b.** 12 hours to 2 days.

A quotient that compares quantities with different units is called a **rate.** For example, if the 495-mile drive from New Orleans to Dallas takes 9 hours, the average rate of speed is the quotient of the miles driven and the length of time the trip takes.

$$\text{Average rate of speed} = \frac{495 \text{ miles}}{9 \text{ hours}} = \frac{\overset{1}{\cancel{9}} \cdot 55 \text{ miles}}{\underset{1}{\cancel{9}} \cdot 1 \text{ hours}} = \frac{55 \text{ miles}}{1 \text{ hour}}$$

Rates   A **rate** is a quotient of two quantities that have different units.

If two ratios or two rates are equal, we say that they are *in proportion.*

Proportion   A **proportion** is a mathematical statement that two ratios or two rates are equal.

Some examples of proportions are

The Language of Algebra

The word *proportion* implies a comparative relationship in size. For a picture to appear realistic, the artist must draw the shapes in the proper *proportion*. Remember the Y2K scare? The massive computer failures predicted by some experts were blown way *out of proportion*.

$$\frac{1}{2} = \frac{3}{6}, \qquad \frac{3 \text{ waiters}}{7 \text{ tables}} = \frac{9 \text{ waiters}}{21 \text{ tables}}, \qquad \text{and} \qquad \frac{a}{b} = \frac{c}{d}$$

- The proportion $\frac{1}{2} = \frac{3}{6}$ can be read as "1 is to 2 as 3 is to 6."
- The proportion $\frac{3 \text{ waiters}}{7 \text{ tables}} = \frac{9 \text{ waiters}}{21 \text{ tables}}$ can be read as "3 waiters is to 7 tables as 9 waiters is to 21 tables."
- The proportion $\frac{a}{b} = \frac{c}{d}$ can be read as "a is to b as c is to d."

Each of the four numbers in a proportion is called a **term.** The first and fourth terms are called the **extremes,** and the second and third terms are called the **means.**

$$\begin{array}{l} \text{First term} \longrightarrow a \\ \text{Second term} \longrightarrow b \end{array} = \begin{array}{l} c \longleftarrow \text{Third term} \\ d \longleftarrow \text{Fourth term} \end{array} \qquad a \text{ and } d \text{ are the extremes. } b \text{ and } c \text{ are the means.}$$

For the proportion $\frac{a}{b} = \frac{c}{d}$, we can show that the product of the extremes, ad, is equal to the product of the means, bc, by multiplying both sides of the proportion by bd, and observing that $ad = bc$.

$$\frac{a}{b} = \frac{c}{d}$$

$$bd \cdot \frac{a}{b} = bd \cdot \frac{c}{d} \qquad \text{To clear the fractions, multiply both sides by the LCD, } bd.$$

$$ad = bc \qquad \text{Simplify: } \frac{b}{b} = 1 \text{ and } \frac{d}{d} = 1.$$

Since $ad = bc$, the product of the extremes equals the product of the means.

The same products ad and bc can be found by multiplying diagonally in the proportion $\frac{a}{b} = \frac{c}{d}$. We call ad and bc **cross products.**

The Fundamental Property of Proportions   In a proportion, the product of the extremes is equal to the product of the means.

$$\text{If } \frac{a}{b} = \frac{c}{d}, \text{ then } ad = bc \qquad \text{and} \qquad \text{if } ad = bc, \text{ then } \frac{a}{b} = \frac{c}{d}.$$

EXAMPLE 2

Determine whether each equation is a proportion: **a.** $\dfrac{3}{7} = \dfrac{9}{21}$ and   **b.** $\dfrac{8}{3} = \dfrac{13}{5}$.

Solution   In each case, we check to see whether the product of the extremes is equal to the product of the means.

a. The product of the extremes is $3 \cdot 21 = 63$. The product of the means is $7 \cdot 9 = 63$. Since the cross products are equal, $\frac{3}{7} = \frac{9}{21}$ is a proportion.

$$3 \cdot 21 = 63 \qquad 7 \cdot 9 = 63$$

$$\frac{3}{7} \times \frac{9}{21}$$

b. The product of the extremes is $8 \cdot 5 = 40$. The product of the means is $3 \cdot 13 = 39$. Since the cross products are not equal, the equation is not a proportion: $\frac{8}{3} \neq \frac{13}{5}$.

$$8 \cdot 5 = 40 \qquad 3 \cdot 13 = 39$$

$$\frac{8}{3} \times \frac{13}{5}$$

Self Check 2   Determine whether the equation is a proportion: $\dfrac{6}{13} = \dfrac{24}{53}$.

■ SOLVING PROPORTIONS

The fundamental property of proportions provides us with a way to solve proportions.

EXAMPLE 3   Solve: $\dfrac{12}{18} = \dfrac{4}{x}$.

Solution   To solve for x, we set the cross products equal.

$$\frac{12}{18} = \frac{4}{x}$$

$12 \cdot x = 18 \cdot 4$ In a proportion, the product of the extremes equals the product of the means.

$12x = 72$ Do the multiplications.

$\dfrac{12x}{12} = \dfrac{72}{12}$ To isolate x, divide both sides by 12.

$x = 6$

Caution

Remember that a cross product is the product of the means or the extremes of a *proportion.* For example, it would be incorrect to try to compute cross products to solve $\frac{12}{18} = \frac{4}{x} + \frac{1}{2}$. It is not a proportion. The right-hand side is not a ratio.

Check: To check the result, we substitute 6 for x in $\dfrac{12}{18} = \dfrac{4}{x}$ and find the cross products.

$$12 \cdot 6 = 72 \qquad 18 \cdot 4 = 72$$

$$\frac{12}{18} \overset{?}{\times} \frac{4}{6}$$

Since the cross products are equal, the solution of $\dfrac{12}{18} = \dfrac{4}{x}$ is 6.

Self Check 3   Solve: $\dfrac{15}{x} = \dfrac{25}{40}$.

EXAMPLE 4

Solve: $\dfrac{2a + 1}{4} = \dfrac{10}{8}$.

Solution

$$\dfrac{2a + 1}{4} = \dfrac{10}{8}$$

$$8(2a + 1) = 40 \qquad \text{In a proportion, the product of the extremes equals the product of the means.}$$

$$16a + 8 = 40 \qquad \text{Distribute the multiplication by 8.}$$

$$16a + 8 - 8 = 40 - 8 \qquad \text{Subtract 8 from both sides.}$$

$$16a = 32 \qquad \text{Combine like terms.}$$

$$\dfrac{16a}{16} = \dfrac{32}{16} \qquad \text{Divide both sides by 16.}$$

$$a = 2$$

The solution is 2.

Success Tip

Since proportions are rational equations, they can also be solved by multiplying both sides by the LCD. For Example 4, an alternate approach is to multiply both sides by 8:

$$8\left(\dfrac{2a + 1}{4}\right) = 8\left(\dfrac{10}{8}\right)$$

Self Check 4

Solve: $\dfrac{3x - 1}{2} = \dfrac{12.5}{5}$.

■ **PROBLEM SOLVING**

We can use proportions to solve many problems. If we are given a ratio (or rate) comparing two quantities, the words of the problem can be translated to a proportion, and we can solve it to find the unknown.

EXAMPLE 5

Grocery shopping. If 6 apples cost $1.38, how much will 16 apples cost?

Solution

Analyze the Problem We know the cost of 6 apples; we are to find the cost of 16 apples.

Form a Proportion Let c = the cost of 16 apples. If we compare the number of apples to their cost, we know that the two rates are equal.

6 apples is to $1.38 as 16 apples is to $c.

$$\text{6 apples} \longrightarrow \dfrac{6}{1.38} = \dfrac{16}{c} \longleftarrow \text{16 apples}$$
$$\text{Cost of 6 apples} \longrightarrow \qquad \qquad \longleftarrow \text{Cost of 16 apples}$$

Solve the Proportion

$$6 \cdot c = 1.38(16) \qquad \text{In a proportion, the product of the extremes equals the product of the means.}$$

$$6c = 22.08 \qquad \text{Multiply: } 1.38(16) = 22.08.$$

$$\dfrac{6c}{6} = \dfrac{22.08}{6} \qquad \text{Divide both sides by 6.}$$

$$c = 3.68$$

State the Conclusion Sixteen apples will cost $3.68.

Check the Result 16 apples are about 3 times as many as 6 apples, which cost $1.38. If we multiply $1.38 by 3, we get an estimate of the cost of 16 apples: $1.38 \cdot 3 = $4.14. The result, $3.68, seems reasonable.

Self Check 5   If 9 tickets to a concert cost $112.50, how much will 15 tickets cost?

Caution   When solving problems using proportions, we must make sure that the units of both numerators are the same and the units of both denominators are the same. In Example 5, it would be incorrect to write

Cost of 6 apples ⟶ $\dfrac{1.38}{6} = \dfrac{16}{c}$ ⟵ 16 apples
6 apples ⟶ ⟵ Cost of 16 apples

EXAMPLE 6

The Language of Algebra

Architects, interior decorators, landscapers, and automotive engineers are a few of the professionals who construct *scale* drawings or *scale* models of the projects they are designing.

Miniatures.   A **scale** is a ratio (or rate) that compares the size of a model, drawing, or map to the size of an actual object. The scale indicates that 1 inch on the model carousel is equivalent to 160 inches on the actual carousel. How wide should the model be if the actual carousel is 35 feet wide?

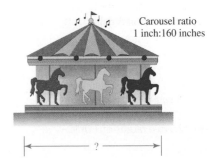

Carousel ratio
1 inch:160 inches

Analyze the Problem   We are asked to determine the width of the miniature carousel, if a ratio of 1 inch to 160 inches is used. We would like the width of the model to be given in inches, not feet, so we will express the 35-foot width of the actual carousel as $35 \cdot 12 = 420$ inches.

Form a Proportion   Let $w =$ the width of the model. The ratios of the dimensions of the model to the corresponding dimensions of the actual carousel are equal.

1 inch is to 160 inches as w inches is to 420 inches.

model ⟶ $\dfrac{1}{160} = \dfrac{w}{420}$ ⟵ model
actual ⟶ ⟵ actual

Solve the Proportion

$420 = 160w$ In a proportion, the product of the extremes is equal to the product of the means.

$\dfrac{420}{160} = \dfrac{160w}{160}$ Divide both sides by 160.

$2.625 = w$ Simplify.

State the Conclusion   The width of the miniature carousel should be 2.625 in., or $2\dfrac{5}{8}$ in.

Check the Result   A width of $2\dfrac{5}{8}$ in. is approximately 3 in. When we write the ratio of the model's approximate width to the width of the actual carousel, we get $\dfrac{3}{420} = \dfrac{1}{140}$, which is about $\dfrac{1}{160}$. The answer seems reasonable.

When shopping, *unit prices* can be used to compare costs of different sizes of the same brand to determine the best buy. The **unit price** gives the cost per unit, such as cost per ounce, cost per pound, or cost per sheet. We can find the unit price of an item using a proportion.

EXAMPLE 7   *Comparison shopping.*   Which size of toothpaste is the better buy?

$2.19

$2.79

Solution   To find the unit price for each tube, we let x = the price of 1 ounce of toothpaste. Then we set up and solve the following proportions.

The Language of Algebra

A unit price indicates the cost of 1 unit of an item, such as 1 ounce of bottled water or 1 pound of hamburger. In advanced mathematics, we study unit circles—circles that have a radius of 1 unit.

For the 4-ounce tube:

Ounces → $\dfrac{4}{2.19} = \dfrac{1}{x}$ ← Ounce
Price →   ← Price

$$4x = 2.19$$

$$x = \frac{2.19}{4}$$

$$x \approx 0.55$$ The unit price is approximately $0.55.

For the 6-ounce tube:

Ounces → $\dfrac{6}{2.79} = \dfrac{1}{x}$ ← Ounce
Price →   ← Price

$$6x = 2.79$$

$$x = \frac{2.79}{6}$$

$$x \approx 0.47$$ The unit price is approximately $0.47.

The price of 1 ounce of toothpaste from the 4-ounce tube is about 55¢. The price for 1 ounce of toothpaste from the 6-ounce tube is about 47¢. Since the 6-ounce tube has the lower unit price, it is the better buy.

Self Check 7   Which is the better buy: 3 pounds of hamburger for $6.89 or 5 pounds for $12.49?

■ SIMILAR TRIANGLES

If two angles of one triangle have the same measures as two angles of a second triangle, the triangles have the same shape. Triangles with the same shape, but not necessarily the same size, are called **similar triangles.** In the following figure, $\triangle ABC \sim \triangle DEF$. (Read the symbol $\sim$ as "is similar to.")

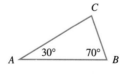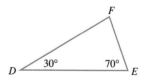

Property of Similar Triangles   If two triangles are **similar,** all pairs of corresponding sides are in proportion.

For the similar triangles shown above, the following proportions are true.

$$\frac{AB}{DE} = \frac{BC}{EF}, \qquad \frac{BC}{EF} = \frac{CA}{FD}, \qquad \text{and} \qquad \frac{CA}{FD} = \frac{AB}{DE}$$ Read AB as "the length of segment AB."

EXAMPLE 8   *Finding the height of a tree.*   A tree casts a shadow 18 feet long at the same time as a woman 5 feet tall casts a shadow 1.5 feet long. Find the height of the tree.

Solution   **Analyze the Problem**   The figure shows the similar triangles determined by the tree and its shadow and the woman and her shadow. Since the triangles are similar, the lengths of their corresponding sides are in proportion. We can use this fact to find the height of the tree.

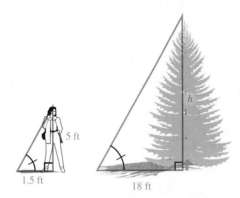

Each triangle has a right angle. Since the sun's rays strike the ground at the same angle, the angles highlighted with a tick mark have the same measure. Therefore, two angles of the smaller triangle have the same measures as two angles of the larger triangle; the triangles are similar.

5 ft

1.5 ft

18 ft

Form a Proportion   If we let h = the height of the tree, we can find h by solving the following proportion.

$$\frac{h}{5} = \frac{18}{1.5} \qquad \frac{\text{Height of the tree}}{\text{Height of the woman}} = \frac{\text{Length of shadow of the tree}}{\text{Length of shadow of the woman}}$$

Solve the Proportion

$$1.5h = 5(18) \qquad \text{In a proportion, the product of the extremes equals the product of the means.}$$

$$1.5h = 90 \qquad \text{Multiply.}$$

$$\frac{1.5h}{1.5} = \frac{90}{1.5} \qquad \text{Divide both sides by 1.5.}$$

$$h = 60 \qquad \tfrac{90}{1.5} = 60.$$

State the Conclusion   The tree is 60 feet tall.

Check the Result $\dfrac{18}{1.5} = 12$ and $\dfrac{60}{5} = 12$. The ratios are the same. The result checks.

Self Check 8   Find the height of the tree in Example 8 if the woman is 5 feet 6 inches tall.

Answers to Self Checks   **1. a.** $\frac{15}{2}$, **b.** $\frac{1}{4}$ **2.** no   **3.** 24   **4.** 2   **5.** $187.50   **7.** 3 pounds for $6.89
8. 66 ft

6.8   STUDY SET

VOCABULARY   Fill in the blanks.

1. A _____ is the quotient of two numbers or the quotient of two quantities with the same units. A _____ is a quotient of two quantities that have different units.

2. A _____ is a mathematical statement that two ratios or two rates are equal.

3. The _____ of the proportion $\frac{2}{x} = \frac{16}{40}$ are 2, x, 16, and 40.

4. In $\frac{50}{3} = \frac{x}{9}$, the terms 50 and 9 are called the
_____ and the terms 3 and x are called the
_____ of the proportion.

5. The product of the extremes and the product of the means of a proportion are also known as _____ products.

6. A _____ is a ratio (or rate) that compares the size of a model, drawing, or map to the size of an actual object.

7. Examples of _____ prices are $1.65 per gallon, 17¢ per day, and $50 per foot.

8. Two triangles with the same shape, but not necessarily the same size, are called _____ triangles.

CONCEPTS

9. WEST AFRICA   Write the ratio (in fractional form) of the number of red stripes to the number of white stripes on the flag of Liberia.

10. Fill in the blanks: In a proportion, the product of the extremes is _____ to the product of the means.

If $\frac{a}{b} = \frac{c}{d}$, then ____ = ____.

11. What are the cross products for each proportion?

    a. $\frac{6}{5} = \frac{12}{10}$ b. $\frac{15}{2} = \frac{45}{x}$

12. a. Is 45 a solution of $\frac{5}{3} = \frac{75}{x}$?

    b. Is -2 a solution of $\frac{a+4}{8} = \frac{3}{16}$?

13. SNACK FOODS   In a sample of 25 bags of potato chips, 2 were found to be underweight. Complete the following proportion that could be used to find the number of underweight bags that would be expected in a shipment of 1,000 bags of potato chips.

number of bags → $\frac{}{}$ = $\frac{}{}$ ← number of bags
number underweight → $\qquad$ $\qquad$ ← number underweight

14. MINIATURES   A model of a "high wheeler" bicycle is to be made using a scale of 2 inches to 15 inches. The following proportion was set up to determine the height of the front wheel of the model. Explain the error.

$$\frac{2}{15} = \frac{48}{h}$$

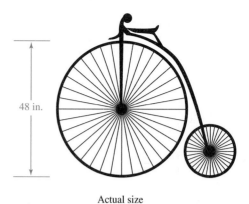

Actual size

15. GROCERY SHOPPING   Examine the following pricing stickers. Which item is the better buy?

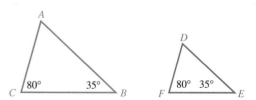

AQUACLEAR WATER	AQUACLEAR WATER
1.79	4.49
12- 8 OZ BOTTLES	24- 12 OZ BOTTLES

16. Complete the following proportion that can be used to find the unit price of facial tissue if a box of 85 tissues sells for $1.19.

price → $\frac{1.19}{85}$ = $\frac{x}{}$ ← price
number of sheets →   ← number of sheets

17. Two similar triangles are shown. Fill in the blanks to make the proportions true.

$\frac{AB}{DE} = \frac{}{EF}$ $\frac{BC}{} = \frac{CA}{FD}$ $\frac{CA}{FD} = \frac{AB}{}$

18. The two triangles shown in the following illustration are similar. Complete the proportion.

$\frac{x}{} = \frac{}{}$

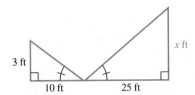

3 ft

10 ft   25 ft

x ft

NOTATION **Complete the solution.**

19. Solve for *x*: $\dfrac{12}{18} = \dfrac{x}{24}$.

$$12 \cdot 24 = 18 \cdot \boxed{}$$
$$\boxed{} = 18x$$
$$\frac{288}{\boxed{}} = \frac{18x}{\boxed{}}$$
$$\boxed{} = x$$

20. Write the ratio of 25 to 4 in two forms.

21. Write each ratio in simplified form.

  a. $\dfrac{12}{15}$ **b.** $\dfrac{9 \text{ crates}}{7 \text{ crates}}$

22. Fill in the blanks: The proportion $\dfrac{20}{1.6} = \dfrac{100}{8}$ can be read: 20 is to 1.6 _____ 100 is _____ 8.

23. Fill in the blank: We read $\triangle XYZ \sim \triangle MNO$ as: triangle *XYZ* is _____ to triangle *MNO*.

24. Write the statement *x is approximately 0.75* using symbols.

PRACTICE **Write each ratio as a fraction in simplest form.**

25. 4 boxes to 15 boxes   **26.** 2 miles to 9 miles

27. 30 days to 24 days   **28.** 45 people to 30 people

29. 90 minutes to 3 hours   **30.** 20 inches to 2 feet

31. 13 quarts to 2 gallons   **32.** 11 dimes to 1 dollar

Tell whether each statement is a proportion.

33. $\dfrac{9}{7} = \dfrac{81}{70}$ **34.** $\dfrac{5}{2} = \dfrac{20}{8}$

35. $\dfrac{7}{3} = \dfrac{14}{6}$ **36.** $\dfrac{13}{19} = \dfrac{65}{95}$

37. $\dfrac{9}{19} = \dfrac{38}{80}$ **38.** $\dfrac{40}{29} = \dfrac{29}{22}$

Solve each proportion.

39. $\dfrac{2}{3} = \dfrac{x}{6}$ **40.** $\dfrac{3}{6} = \dfrac{x}{8}$

41. $\dfrac{5}{10} = \dfrac{3}{c}$ **42.** $\dfrac{7}{14} = \dfrac{2}{x}$

43. $\dfrac{6}{x} = \dfrac{8}{4}$ **44.** $\dfrac{4}{x} = \dfrac{2}{8}$

45. $\dfrac{x+1}{5} = \dfrac{3}{15}$ **46.** $\dfrac{x-1}{7} = \dfrac{2}{21}$

47. $\dfrac{x+7}{-4} = \dfrac{1}{4}$ **48.** $\dfrac{x+3}{12} = \dfrac{-7}{6}$

49. $\dfrac{5-x}{17} = \dfrac{13}{34}$ **50.** $\dfrac{4-x}{13} = \dfrac{11}{26}$

51. $\dfrac{2x-1}{18} = \dfrac{9}{54}$ **52.** $\dfrac{2x+1}{18} = \dfrac{14}{3}$

53. $\dfrac{x-1}{9} = \dfrac{2x}{3}$ **54.** $\dfrac{x+1}{4} = \dfrac{3x}{8}$

55. $\dfrac{8x}{3} = \dfrac{11x+9}{4}$ **56.** $\dfrac{3x}{16} = \dfrac{x+2}{5}$

57. $\dfrac{2}{3x} = \dfrac{x}{6}$ **58.** $\dfrac{y}{4} = \dfrac{4}{y}$

59. $\dfrac{b-5}{3} = \dfrac{2}{b}$ **60.** $\dfrac{2}{c} = \dfrac{c-3}{2}$

61. $\dfrac{x-1}{x+1} = \dfrac{2}{3x}$ **62.** $\dfrac{2}{x+6} = \dfrac{-2x}{5}$

Each pair of triangles is similar. Find the missing side length.

63.

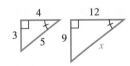

64.

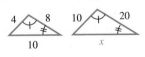

65.

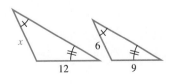

66.

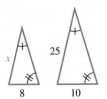

APPLICATIONS

67. GEAR RATIOS Write each ratio in two ways: as a fraction in simplest form and using a colon.

    a. The number of teeth of the larger gear to the number of teeth of the smaller gear

    b. The number of teeth of the smaller gear to the number of teeth of the larger gear

68. FACULTY–STUDENT RATIOS At a college, there are 300 faculty members and 2,850 students. Find the rate of faculty to students. (This is often referred to as the faculty to student ratio, even though the units are different.)

69. SHOPPING FOR CLOTHES If shirts are on sale at two for $25, how much do five shirts cost?

70. COMPUTING A PAYCHECK Billie earns $412 for a 40-hour week. If she missed 10 hours of work last week, how much did she get paid?

71. COOKING A recipe for spaghetti sauce requires four 16-ounce bottles of ketchup to make 2 gallons of sauce. How many bottles of ketchup are needed to make 10 gallons of sauce?

72. MIXING PERFUME A perfume is to be mixed in the ratio of 3 drops of pure essence to 7 drops of alcohol. How many drops of pure essence should be mixed with 56 drops of alcohol?

73. CPR A first aid handbook states that when performing cardiopulmonary resuscitation on an adult, the ratio of chest compressions to breaths should be 5:2. If 210 compressions were administered to an adult patient, how many breaths should have been given?

74. COOKING A recipe for wild rice soup follows. Find the amounts of chicken broth, rice, and flour needed to make 15 servings.

> **Wild Rice Soup**
>
> *A sumptuous side dish with a nutty flavor*
>
> | 3 cups chicken broth | 1 cup light cream |
> |---|---|
> | $\frac{2}{3}$ cup uncooked rice | 2 tablespoons flour |
> | $\frac{1}{4}$ cup sliced onions | $\frac{1}{8}$ teaspoon pepper |
> | $\frac{1}{2}$ cup shredded carrots | |
> | | Serves: 6 |

75. NUTRITION The table shows the nutritional facts about a 10-oz chocolate milkshake sold by a fast-food restaurant. Use the information to complete the table for the 16-oz shake. Round to the nearest unit when an answer is not exact.

	Calories	Fat (gm)	Protein (gm)
10-oz chocolate milkshake	355	8	9
16-oz chocolate milkshake			

76. STRUCTURAL ENGINEERING A portion of a bridge is shown. Use the fact that $\frac{AB}{BC}$ is in proportion to $\frac{FE}{ED}$ to find FE.

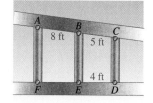

77. QUALITY CONTROL Out of a sample of 500 men's shirts, 17 were rejected because of crooked collars. How many crooked collars would you expect to find in a run of 15,000 shirts?

78. PHOTO ENLARGEMENTS The 3-by-5 photo is to be blown up to the larger size. Find x.

3 in.
5 in.

x in.
$6\frac{1}{4}$ in.

79. MIXING FUEL The instructions on a can of oil intended to be added to lawnmower gasoline are shown on the next page. Are these instructions correct? (*Hint:* There are 128 ounces in 1 gallon.)

Recommended	Gasoline	Oil
50 to 1	6 gal	16 oz

80. DRIVER'S LICENSES   Of the 50 states, Alabama has one of the highest ratios of licensed drivers to residents. If the ratio is $800:1,000$ and the population of Alabama is 4,500,000, how many residents of that state have a driver's license?

81. CROP DAMAGE   To estimate the ground squirrel population on his acreage, a farmer trapped, tagged, and then released a dozen squirrels. Two weeks later, the farmer trapped 35 squirrels and noted that 3 were tagged. Use this information to estimate the number of ground squirrels on his acreage.

82. CONCRETE   A $2:3$ concrete mix means that for every two parts of sand, three parts of gravel are used. How much sand should be used in a mix composed of 25 cubic feet of gravel?

83. MODEL RAILROADS   A model railroad engine is 9 inches long. If the scale is 87 feet to 1 foot, how long is a real engine?

84. MODEL RAILROADS   A model railroad caboose is 3.5 inches long. If the scale is 169 feet to 1 foot, how long is a real caboose?

85. BLUEPRINTS   The scale for the drawing shown means that a $\frac{1}{4}$-inch length $\left(\frac{1''}{4}\right)$ on the drawing corresponds to an actual size of 1 foot ($1'0''$). Suppose the length of the kitchen is $2\frac{1}{2}$ inches on the drawing. How long is the actual kitchen?

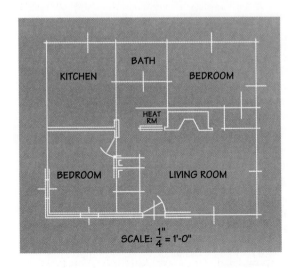

86. THE *TITANIC*   A $1:144$ scale model of the *Titanic* is to be built. If the ship was 882 feet long, find the length of the model?

For each of the following purchases, determine the better buy.

87. Trumpet lessons: 45 minutes for $25 or 60 minutes for $35

88. Memory for a computer: 128 megabytes for $26 or 512 megabytes for $110

89. Business cards: 100 for $9.99 or 150 for $12.99

90. Dog food: 20 pounds for $7.49 or 44 pounds for $14.99

91. Soft drinks: 6-pack for $1.50 or a case (24 cans) for $6.25

92. Donuts: A dozen for $6.24 or a baker's dozen (13) for $6.65

93. HEIGHT OF A TREE   A tree casts a shadow of 26 feet at the same time as a 6-foot man casts a shadow of 4 feet. Find the height of the tree.

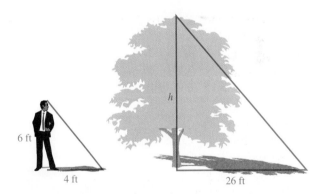

94. HEIGHT OF A BUILDING   A man places a mirror on the ground and sees the reflection of the top of a building, as shown. The two triangles in the illustration are similar. Find the height, h, of the building.

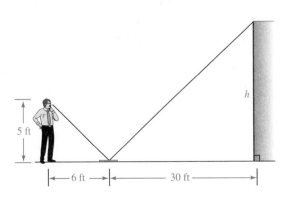

95. SURVEYING   To determine the width of a river, a surveyor laid out the similar triangles as shown. Find w.

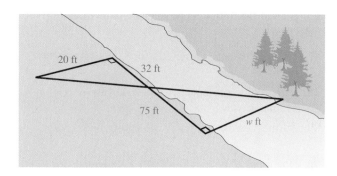

96. FLIGHT PATHS   An airplane ascends 100 feet as it flies a horizontal distance of 1,000 feet. How much altitude will it gain as it flies a horizontal distance of 1 mile?   (*Hint:* 5,280 feet = 1 mile.)

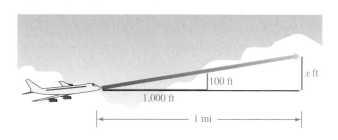

WRITING

97. Explain the difference between a ratio and a proportion.

98. Explain why the concept of cross products cannot be used to solve the equation

$$\frac{x}{3} - \frac{3x}{4} = \frac{1}{12}$$

99. What are similar triangles?

100. What is a unit price? Give an example.

REVIEW

101. Change $\frac{9}{10}$ to a percent.

102. Change $33\frac{1}{3}\%$ to a fraction.

103. Find 30% of 1,600.

104. SHOPPING   Maria bought a dress for 25% off the original price of $98. How much did the dress cost?

CHALLENGE PROBLEMS

105. Suppose $\frac{a}{b} = \frac{c}{d}$. Write three other proportions using a, b, c, and d.

106. Verify that $\frac{3}{5} = \frac{12}{20} = \frac{3 + 12}{5 + 20}$. Is the following rule always true? Explain.

$$\frac{a}{b} = \frac{c}{d} = \frac{a + c}{b + d}$$

ACCENT ON TEAMWORK

WHAT IS π?

Overview: In this activity, you will discover an important fact about the ratio of the circumference to the diameter of a circle.
Instructions: Form groups of 2 or 3 students. With a piece of string or a cloth tape measure, find the circumference and the diameter of objects that are circular in shape. You can measure anything that is round: for example, a coin, the top of a can, a tire, or a waste paper basket. Enter your results in a table, as shown below. Convert each measurement to a decimal, and then use a calculator to determine a decimal approximation of the ratio of the circumference C to diameter d.

Object	Circumference C	Diameter d	$\frac{C}{d}$ (approx.)
A quarter	$2\frac{15}{16}$ in. = 2.9375 in.	$\frac{15}{16}$ in. = 0.9375 in.	3.13333

Since early history, mathematicians have known that the ratio of the circumference to the diameter of a circle is the same for any size circle, approximately 3. Today, following centuries of study, we know that this ratio is exactly 3.141592653589 . . . .

$$\frac{C}{d} = 3.141592653589 \ldots$$

The Greek letter π (pi) is used to represent the ratio of circumference to diameter:

$$\pi = \frac{C}{d}, \qquad \text{where } \pi = 3.141592653589 \ldots$$

Are the ratios in your table numerically close to π? Give some reasons why they aren't exactly 3.141592653589 . . . . in each case.

USING PROPORTIONS WHEN COOKING

Overview: In this activity, you will use proportions to adjust the ingredients in your favorite recipe so that it would serve everyone in your class.

Instructions: Each student should bring his/her favorite recipe to class. Working in pairs, begin with the first recipe and determine the amount of each ingredient that is needed to make enough of it to serve the exact number of people in the class. For example, if the recipe serves 8 and there are 25 students and an instructor in the class, write and solve proportions to determine the amount of flour, sugar, milk, and so on, to make enough of the recipe to serve 26 people. Then do the same for the second recipe.

When finished, share with the class how you made the calculations, as well as any difficulties that you encountered adjusting the ingredients of the recipes.

KEY CONCEPT: EXPRESSIONS AND EQUATIONS

In this chapter, we have discussed procedures for simplifying rational expressions and procedures for solving rational equations.

SIMPLIFYING RATIONAL EXPRESSIONS

To simplify a rational expression:

1. Factor the numerator and denominator completely to determine all the factors common to both.

2. Remove factors equal to 1 by replacing each pair of factors common to the numerator and denominator with the equivalent fraction $\frac{1}{1}$.

This procedure is also used when multiplying and dividing rational expressions.

1. a. Simplify: $\dfrac{2x^2 - 8x}{x^2 - 6x + 8}$.

b. What common factor was removed?

2. a. Multiply: $\dfrac{x^2 + 2x + 1}{x} \cdot \dfrac{x^2 - x}{x^2 - 1}$.

b. What common factors were removed?

■ UNIT CONVERSIONS

Success Tip

Remember that unit conversion factors are equal to 1. Here are some examples:

$$\frac{12 \text{ in.}}{1 \text{ ft}} \quad \frac{60 \text{ min}}{1 \text{ hr}} \quad \frac{1 \text{ decade}}{10 \text{ yr}}$$

We can use the concepts discussed in this section to make conversions from one unit of measure to another. *Unit conversion factors* play an important role in this process. A **unit conversion factor** is a fraction that has value 1. For example, we can use the fact that 1 square yard = 9 square feet to form two unit conversion factors:

$$\frac{1 \text{ yd}^2}{9 \text{ ft}^2} = 1 \qquad \text{Read as "1 square yard per 9 square feet."} \qquad \frac{9 \text{ ft}^2}{1 \text{ yd}^2} = 1 \qquad \text{Read as "9 square feet per 1 square yard."}$$

Since a unit conversion factor is equal to 1, multiplying a measurement by a unit conversion factor does not change the measurement, it only changes the units of measure.

EXAMPLE 7

Carpeting. A roll of carpeting is 12 feet wide and 150 feet long. Find the number of square yards of carpeting on the roll.

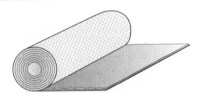

Solution   When unrolled, the carpeting forms a rectangular shape with an area of $12 \cdot 150 = 1,800$ square feet. We multiply 1,800 ft² by a unit conversion factor such that the units of ft² are removed and the units of yd² are introduced. Then we can remove units common to the numerator and denominator.

$$1,800 \text{ ft}^2 = \frac{1,800 \text{ ft}^2}{1} \cdot \frac{1 \text{ yd}^2}{9 \text{ ft}^2} \qquad \text{Multiply by a unit conversion factor that relates yd}^2 \text{ to ft}^2.$$

$$= \frac{1,800 \text{ ft}^2}{1} \cdot \frac{1 \text{ yd}^2}{9 \text{ ft}^2} \qquad \text{Remove the units of ft}^2 \text{ that are common to the numerator and denominator.}$$

$$= 200 \text{ yd}^2 \qquad \text{Divide 1,800 by 9.}$$

There are 200 yd² of carpeting on the roll.

EXAMPLE 8

The speed of light. The speed with which light moves through space is about 186,000 miles per second. Express this speed in miles per minute.

Solution   The speed of light can be expressed as $\frac{186,000 \text{ miles}}{1 \text{ sec}}$. We multiply this fraction by a unit conversion factor such that the units of seconds are removed and the units of minutes are introduced. Since 60 seconds = 1 minute, we will use $\frac{60 \text{ sec}}{1 \text{ min}}$.

$$\frac{186,000 \text{ miles}}{1 \text{ sec}} = \frac{186,000 \text{ miles}}{1 \text{ sec}} \cdot \frac{60 \text{ sec}}{1 \text{ min}} \qquad \text{Multiply by a unit conversion factor that relates seconds to minutes.}$$

$$= \frac{186,000 \text{ miles}}{1 \text{ sec}} \cdot \frac{60 \text{ sec}}{1 \text{ min}} \qquad \text{Remove the units of seconds that are common to the numerator and denominator.}$$

$$= \frac{11,160,000 \text{ miles}}{1 \text{ min}} \qquad \text{Multiply 186,000 and 60.}$$

The speed of light is about 11,160,000 miles per minute.

Appendix

Answers to Selected Exercises

Study Set Section 1.1 (page 6)

1. sum, difference   **3.** Variables   **5.** equation
7. horizontal, vertical   **9.** equation   **11.** algebraic
expression   **13.** algebraic expression   **15.** equation
17. a. multiplication, subtraction   **b.** x **19. a.** addition,
subtraction   **b.** m **21.**

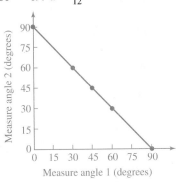

23. They determine that 15-year-old machinery is worth
$35,000.   **25.** $5 \cdot 6, 5(6)$ **27.** $34 \cdot 75, 34(75)$ **29.** $4x$
31. $3rt$ **33.** lw **35.** Prt **37.** $2w$ **39.** xy **41.** $\frac{32}{x}$
43. $\frac{90}{30}$ **45.** The product of 8 and 2 is 16.   **47.** The
difference of 11 and 9 is 2.   **49.** The product of 2 and x is 10.
51. The quotient of 66 and 11 is 6.   **53.** $p = 100 - d$
55. $7d = h$ **57.** $s = 3c$ **59.** $w = e + 1{,}200$
61. $p = r - 600$ **63.** $\frac{l}{4} = m$ **65.** 390, 400, 405
67. 1,300, 1,200, 1,100   **69.** $d = \frac{e}{12}$
71. 90, 60, 45, 30, 0

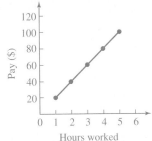

Study Set Section 1.2 (page 18)

1. prime   **3.** numerator, denominator   **5.** equivalent
7. least or lowest   **9.** 60   **11.** $\frac{4}{12} = \frac{1}{3}$ **13.** $\frac{2}{5}$ **15. a.** 1

b. 1   **17. a.** 3 times   **b.** 2 times   **19. a.** $\frac{5}{16}$ **b.** 1
c. $\frac{15}{48}$ **21.** 1, 2, 4, 5, 10, 20   **23.** 1, 2, 4, 7, 14, 28
25. $3 \cdot 5 \cdot 5$ **27.** $2 \cdot 2 \cdot 7$ **29.** $3 \cdot 3 \cdot 13$
31. $2 \cdot 2 \cdot 5 \cdot 11$ **33.** $\frac{3}{9}$ **35.** $\frac{24}{54}$ **37.** $\frac{35}{5}$ **39.** $\frac{1}{2}$ **41.** $\frac{4}{3}$
43. $\frac{3}{4}$ **45.** $\frac{9}{8}$ **47.** lowest terms   **49.** $\frac{4}{25}$ **51.** $\frac{3}{10}$
53. $\frac{8}{5}$ **55.** $\frac{3}{2}$ **57.** 70   **59.** $10\frac{1}{2}$ **61.** $13\frac{3}{4}$ **63.** $\frac{9}{10}$
65. $\frac{5}{8}$ **67.** $\frac{14}{5}$ **69.** 28   **71.** $1\frac{9}{11}$ **73.** $2\frac{1}{2}$ **75.** $\frac{6}{5}$
77. $\frac{5}{24}$ **79.** $\frac{19}{15}$ **81.** $\frac{3}{4}$ **83.** $\frac{17}{12}$ **85.** $\frac{22}{35}$ **87.** $\frac{1}{6}$ **89.** $\frac{9}{4}$
91. $1\frac{1}{4}$ **93.** $\frac{5}{9}$ **95. a.** $\frac{7}{32}$ in.   **b.** $\frac{3}{32}$ in.   **97.** $40\frac{1}{2}$ in.
103. The difference of 7 and 5 is 2.   **105.** The quotient of 30
and 15 is 2.   **107.** 150, 180

Study Set Section 1.3 (page 28)

1. whole   **3.** integers   **5.** negative, positive   **7.** rational
9. irrational   **11.** real   **13.** opposites
15. $\frac{6}{1}, \frac{-9}{1}, \frac{-7}{8}, \frac{7}{2}, \frac{-3}{10}, \frac{283}{100}$ **17.** 13 and -3 **19. a.** $<$
b. $>$ **c.** $>, <$ **d.** $>$ **21.** π in.   **23.** square root
25. is not equal to   **27.** Greek   **29.** $\frac{-4}{5}, \frac{4}{-5}$ **31.** 0.625
33. $0.0\overline{3}$ **35.** 0.42   **37.** $0.\overline{45}$ **39.** $>$ **41.** $>$ **43.** $>$
45. $<$ **47.** $<$ **49.** $=$ **51.** $=$ **53.** $>$ **55.** $>$
57. a. true   **b.** false   **c.** false   **d.** true
59. a. $-5 > -6$ **b.** $-25 < 16$
61.

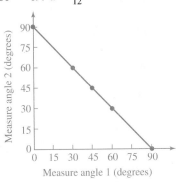

63. natural, whole, integers: 9; rational: 9, $\frac{15}{16}$, $3\frac{1}{8}$, 1.765;
irrational: 2π, 3π, $\sqrt{89}$; real: all   **65.** shell 1; $|-6| > |5|$
67. a. '00: $-\$81$ billion; '99: $-\$74$ billion; '02: $-\$70$ billion
b. '90; $-\$40$ billion   **73.** $\frac{4}{9}$ **75.** $\frac{6}{5}$ **77.** $\frac{13}{30}$

Study Set Section 1.4 (page 37)

1. signed   **3.** opposites   **5.** identity
7. $-1 + (-1) = -4$ **9.** -5 **11.** -3 **13. a.** 0   **b.** a
c. a **d.** $(b + c)$ **15.** positive   **17. a.** $1 + (-5)$
b. $-80.5 + 15$ **c.** $(20 + 4)$ **19. a.** 0   **b.** 0   **c.** -6
d. $-\frac{15}{16}$ **e.** 0   **f.** 0   **21.** $x + y = y + x$ **23.** $8 + 9$

25. -2 **27.** 2   **29.** -8 **31.** 8   **33.** 0   **35.** -77
37. 4   **39.** -35 **41.** -8.2 **43.** -20.1 **45.** 0.2
47. $-\frac{1}{8}$ **49.** $\frac{5}{12}$ **51.** $-\frac{9}{10}$ **53.** 16   **55.** -15
57. -21 **59.** -26 **61.** 0   **63.** 4   **65.** -5 **67.** 1
69. -3.2 **71.** 10   **73.** 215   **75.** -112 **77.** 2,150 m
79. $-18, -6, -5, -4$ **81. a.** 3,660.66, 1,408.78
b. $-1,242.86$ **83.** $89 million   **85.** southward, 132 km
87. $2.1 million

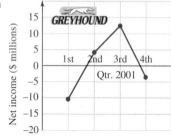

89. true   **91.** -9 and 3

Study Set Section 1.5 (page 44)

1. opposites, inverses   **3.** range   **5. a.** -12 **b.** $\frac{1}{5}$
c. -2.71 **d.** 0   **7. a.** number   **b.** opposite
9. $+(-9)$ **11.** no   **13.** $-10 + (-8) + (-23) + 5 + 34$
15. a. -500 **b.** y **17.** -3 **19.** -13 **21.** 11
23. -21 **25.** -6 **27.** 1   **29.** 12   **31.** 2   **33.** 40
35. 0   **37.** 5   **39.** -9 **41.** -88 **43.** 12   **45.** 0
47. -4 **49.** -2 **51.** $-\frac{1}{2}$ **53.** $-\frac{5}{16}$ **55.** $-\frac{5}{12}$
57. -1.1 **59.** -3.5 **61.** -2.3 **63.** 4.6   **65.** 22
67. -25 **69.** -11 **71.** -50 **73.** -7 **75.** -1
77. -1 **79.** 0   **81.** 160°F   **83.** 1,030 ft   **85.** $-5.75°$
87. 428 B.C. (-428) **89.** left; -8 **95.** $2 \cdot 3 \cdot 5$ **97.** $\frac{21}{56}$
99. true

Study Set Section 1.6 (page 54)

1. product, quotient   **3.** commutative   **5.** undefined
7. -5 **9.** positive   **11.** 1   **13. a.** One of the numbers is 0.
b. They are reciprocals (multiplicative inverses).   **15. a.** NEG
b. not possible to tell   **c.** POS   **d.** NEG   **17. a.** a
b. $a(bc)$ **c.** 0   **d.** a **e.** 1   **19. a.** associative property
of multiplication   **b.** multiplicative inverse   **c.** commutative
property of multiplication   **d.** multiplication property of 1
21. a. $-4(-5) = 20$ **b.** $\frac{16}{-8} = -2$ **23.** -16 **25.** 54
27. -60 **29.** -24 **31.** -800 **33.** 36   **35.** 2.4
37. -0.48 **39.** 0.99   **41.** -15.12 **43.** $-\frac{3}{8}$ **45.** $\frac{1}{12}$
47. $-\frac{3}{20}$ **49.** $\frac{15}{16}$ **51.** -520 **53.** 0   **55.** 0   **57.** 60
59. 84   **61.** 120   **63.** $\frac{1}{24}$ **65.** -720 **67.** 10   **69.** 3
71. -2 **73.** -4 **75.** -1 **77.** 1   **79.** -4 **81.** -20
83. -0.005 **85.** 0   **87.** undefined   **89.** $-\frac{5}{12}$ **91.** $\frac{15}{4}$
93. $1\frac{1}{2}$ **95.** -4.7 **97.** 30.3   **99.** -67 **101.** -6
103. $-72°$ **105.** -280 **107.** $-193°$ F   **109.** $-$43.32
million   **111.** $-$614,516   **113. a.** 5, -10 **b.** 2.5, -5
c. 7.5, -15 **d.** 10, -20 **119.** -5 **121.** $1.08\overline{3}$
123. $\frac{3}{7}$

Study Set Section 1.7 (page 65)

1. base, exponent   **3.** power   **5.** order   **7. a.** 54, 34
b. 34; multiplication is to be done before addition.
9. innermost: parentheses; outermost: brackets
11. a. subtraction, power, addition, multiplication   **b.** power,
multiplication, subtraction, addition   **13. a.** subtraction
b. division   **15. a.** subtraction   **b.** power   **c.** power
d. power   **17. a.** 3   **b.** x **c.** 1   **d.** 1   **19. a.** -5
b. 5   **21.** 3, 9, 18   **23.** 3^4 **25.** $10^2 k^3$ **27.** $8\pi r^3$
29. $6x^2 y^3$ **31.** 36   **33.** -256 **35.** -125 **37.** $-1,296$
39. 0.16   **41.** $-\frac{8}{125}$ **43.** -17 **45.** 192   **47.** 38
49. 80   **51.** -34 **53.** -28 **55.** 194   **57.** -44
59. 0   **61.** -38 **63.** -8 **65.** 12   **67.** 8
69. undefined   **71.** 201   **73.** 50   **75.** 20   **77.** -396
79. 343   **81.** 360   **83.** 12   **85.** -10 **87.** undefined
89. 59   **91.** 28   **93.** 1,000   **95.** -54 **97.** $\frac{1}{8}$ **99.** -8
101. 31   **103.** -39 **105.** -27 **107.** -8 **109.** 11
111. $-\frac{8}{9}$ **113.** 1   **115.** 10   **117.** 12   **119.** -1
121. 2^2 square units, 3^2 square units, 4^2 square units
123. $2,106   **125. a.** $11,875   **b.** $95   **127.** 81 in.
133. a. ii   **b.** iii   **c.** iv   **d.** i

Study Set Section 1.8 (page 75)

1. expressions   **3.** constant   **5.** evaluate   **7.** expression,
equation   **9. a.** 3   **b.** 11   **c.** -6 **d.** -9
11. a. term   **b.** factor   **c.** factor   **d.** term   **e.** factor
f. term   **13. a.** 7, 14, 21, $7w$ **b.** 1, 2, 3, $\frac{s}{60}$
15. a. $x =$ weight of the car; $2x - 500 =$ weight of the van
b. 3,500 lb   **17.** 5, 30; 10, $10d$; 50, $50(x + 5)$
19. 5, 25, 45   **21. a.** $8y$ **b.** $2cd$ **c.** $15sx$ **d.** $-9a^3 b^2$
23. $l + 15$ **25.** $50x$ **27.** $\frac{w}{l}$ **29.** $P + p$
31. $k^2 - 2,005$ **33.** $J - 500$ **35.** $\frac{1,000}{n}$ **37.** $p + 90$
39. $35 + h + 300$ **41.** $p - 680$ **43.** $4d - 15$
45. $2(200 + t)$ **47.** $|a - 2|$ **49.** 300; $60h$ **51. a.** $3y$
b. $\frac{f}{3}$ **53.** $29x¢$ **55.** $\frac{c}{6}$ **57.** $5b$ **59.** $5(x + 2)$
61. $-1, -2, -28$ **63.** 41, 11, 2   **65.** 150, -450
67. 0, 0, 5   **69.** 20   **71.** -12 **73.** -5 **75.** 156
77. $-\frac{1}{5}$ **79.** 17   **81.** 36   **83.** 230   **85.** 50
87. 48, 64, 48, 0   **89.** $-37°$ C, $-64°$ C   **91.** $1\frac{23}{64}$ in.^{2}
97. 60   **99.** -225

Key Concept (page 81)

1. f   **2.** j   **3.** h   **4.** a   **5.** b   **6.** e   **7.** c   **8.** i
9. d   **10.** g   **11.** $C = p + t$ (Answers may vary depending
on the variables chosen.)   **12.** $b = 2t$ (Answers may vary
depending on the variables chosen.)   **13.** $x + 4 =$ amount of
business ($ millions) in the year with the celebrity
14. 1, 41, 97

Chapter Review (page 82)

1. 1 hr; 100 cars   **2.** 100   **3.** 7 P.M.   **4.** The difference of
15 and 3 is 12.   **5.** The sum of 15 and 3 is 18.   **6.** The

quotient of 15 and 3 is 5. **7.** The product of 15 and 3 is 45.
8. $4 \cdot 9$; $4(9)$ **9.** $\frac{9}{3}$ **10.** $8b$ **11.** Prt **12.** equation
13. expression **14.** 10, 15, 25 **15. a.** $2 \cdot 12, 3 \cdot 8$
(answers may vary) **b.** $2 \cdot 2 \cdot 6$ (answers may vary)
c. 1, 2, 3, 4, 6, 8, 12, 24 **16.** $3^3 \cdot 2$ **17.** $7^2 \cdot 3$
18. $11 \cdot 7 \cdot 5$ **19.** prime **20.** 1 **21.** 0 **22.** $\frac{4}{7}$ **23.** $\frac{4}{3}$
24. $\frac{40}{64}$ **25.** $\frac{36}{3}$ **26.** $\frac{7}{64}$ **27.** $\frac{5}{21}$ **28.** $\frac{16}{45}$ **29.** $3\frac{1}{4}$
30. $\frac{2}{5}$ **31.** $\frac{5}{22}$ **32.** $\frac{11}{12}$ **33.** $\frac{5}{18}$ **34.** $\frac{17}{96}$ in. **35.** 0
36. $-\$65$ billion **37.** -206 ft **38.** $<$ **39.** $>$ **40.** $\frac{7}{10}$
41. $\frac{14}{3}$ **42.** 0.004 **43.** $0.7\overline{72}$
44.

45. false **46.** false **47.** true **48.** true **49.** natural: 8;
whole: 0, 8; integers: 0, -12, 8; rational: $-\frac{4}{5}$, 99.99, 0, -12, $4\frac{1}{2}$,
$0.666\ldots$, 8; irrational: $\sqrt{2}$; real: all **50.** $>$ **51.** $<$
52. -82 **53.** 12 **54.** -7 **55.** 0 **56.** -11
57. -12.3 **58.** $-\frac{3}{16}$ **59.** 11 **60.** commutative property
of addition **61.** associative property of addition
62. addition property of opposites **63.** addition property of 0
64. -1 **65.** -10 **66.** 3 **67.** $\frac{9}{16}$ **68.** -4 **69.** -19
70. -49 **71.** -15 **72.** 5.7 **73.** -10 **74.** -29
75. 65,233 ft **76.** -56 **77.** 54 **78.** 12 **79.** 36
80. 6.36 **81.** -2 **82.** $-\frac{2}{15}$ **83.** 0 **84.** associative
property of multiplication **85.** commutative property of
multiplication **86.** multiplication property of 1
87. inverse property of multiplication **88.** 3 **89.** $-\frac{1}{3}$
90. -1 **91.** -4 **92.** 3 **93.** $-\frac{6}{5}$ **94.** undefined
95. -4.5 **96.** high: 2, low: -3 **97.** high: 4, low: -6
98. 8^5 **99.** a^4 **100.** $9\pi r^2$ **101.** x^3y^4 **102.** 81
103. $-\frac{8}{27}$ **104.** 32 **105.** 50 **106.** 4; power,
multiplication, subtraction, addition **107.** 17 **108.** -48
109. -9 **110.** 44 **111.** -420 **112.** $-\frac{14}{19}$ **113.** 113
114. 0 **115.** $\$20$ **116.** 3 **117.** 1 **118.** 2, -5
119. 16, -5, 25 **120.** $\frac{1}{2}$, 1 **121.** 9.6, -1 **122.** $h + 25$
123. $s - 15$ **124.** $\frac{1}{2}t$ **125.** $(n + 4)$ in. **126.** $(b - 4)$ in.
127. $10d$ **128.** $(x - 5)$ years **129.** 30, $10d$
130. 0, 19, -16 **131.** 40 **132.** -36

Chapter 1 Test (page 90)

1. $\$24$ **2.** 5 hr **3.** 3, 20, 70
4. $2 \cdot 2 \cdot 3 \cdot 3 \cdot 5 = 2^2 \cdot 3^2 \cdot 5$ **5.** $\frac{2}{5}$ **6.** $\frac{3}{2} = 1\frac{1}{2}$ **7.** $\frac{25}{36}$
8. $10\frac{1}{15}$ **9.** $\$3.57$ **10.** $0.8\overline{3}$
11.

12. a. true **b.** false **c.** true **d.** true **14. a.** $>$
b. $<$ **c.** $<$ **d.** $>$ **15.** a gain of 0.6 of a rating point
16. -2 **17.** $\frac{3}{8}$ **18.** -6 **19.** -30 **20.** 2

21. -2.44 **22.** 0 **23.** -3 **24.** 0 **25.** 50 **26.** $-\frac{27}{125}$
27. 14 **28.** associative property of addition **29. a.** 9^5
b. $3x^2z^3$ **30.** 170 **31.** 36 **32.** -12 **33.** -100
34. 36 **35.** 4, 17, -59 **36.** $2w + 7$ **37.** $x - 2$
38. $25q\,\cent$ **40.** 3; 5

Study Set Section 2.1 (page 100)

1. equation **3.** check **5.** equivalent **7.** isolate
9. a. $x + 5 = 7$ **b.** subtract 5 from both sides
11. a. $x + 6$ **b.** neither **c.** no **d.** yes **13.** 24
15. n **17. a.** c, c **b.** c, c **19. a.** x **b.** y **c.** t
d. h **21.** 15, 15, 30, 30 **23. a.** is possibly equal to
b. $27°$ **25.** yes **27.** no **29.** no **31.** no **33.** no
35. no **37.** no **39.** yes **41.** yes **43.** 3 **45.** 71
47. 9 **49.** 0 **51.** -9 **53.** -3 **55.** -2.3 **57.** -36
59. 13 **61.** $\frac{8}{9}$ **63.** $\frac{7}{25}$ **65.** 4 **67.** 41 **69.** 0
71. 1 **73.** -6 **75.** 20 **77.** 0.5 **79.** 45 **81.** 0
83. -105 **85.** 21 **87.** -2.64 **89.** 1,251,989
91. -28 **93.** $65°$ **95.** $38°$ **101.** 0 **103.** $45 - x$

Study Set Section 2.2 (page 110)

1. variable **3.** variable, equation, solve **5.** amount,
percent, base **7.** $x + 371 + 479 = 1{,}240$
9. $x + 11{,}000 = 13{,}500$ **11.** $x + 5 + 8 + 16 = 31$
13. ▬ is ▬ % of ▬? **15.** $12 = 0.40 \cdot x$
17. a. 0.35 **b.** 0.035 **c.** 3.5 **d.** 0.005 **19.** 312
21. 26% **23.** 300 **25.** 46.2 **27.** 2.5% **29.** 1,464
31. $6x = 330$ **33.** 63 **35.** $\$322.00$ **37.** 27 min
39. 16 **41.** 5 **43.** 54 **45.** 975 mi. **47.** 54 ft
49. $135°$ **51.** 0.48 oz **53.** $\$684$ billion **55.** 78.125%
57. 19% **59.** 120 **61. a.** 5 g; 25% **b.** 20 g
63. 1994–1995; about 9.8% **65.** 12% **71.** $\frac{12}{5} = 2\frac{2}{5}$
73. no

Study Set Section 2.3 (page 121)

1. simplify **3.** expressions, equations **5.** opposite
7. coefficient **9. a.** 5, 6, 30 **b.** $-8, 2, 4$ **11.** They are
not like terms. **13.** -1, sign **15. a.** $3a, 2a$ **b.** 10, 12
c. none **d.** $9y^2, -8y^2$ **17. a.** $4 + 6, 10$
b. $30 - 50, -20$ **c.** 27 **19. a.** $6(h - 4)$ **b.** $-(z + 16)$
21. no, yes, no, no, yes, yes **23.** $63m$ **25.** $-35q$
27. $300t$ **29.** $11.2x$ **31.** g **33.** $5x$ **35.** $6y$ **37.** s
39. $-20r$ **41.** $60c$ **43.** $-96m$ **45.** $5x + 15$
47. $36c - 42$ **49.** $24t + 16$ **51.** $0.4x - 1.6$
53. $5t + 5$ **55.** $-12x - 20$ **57.** $-78c + 18$
59. $-2w + 4$ **61.** $9x + 10$ **63.** $9r - 16$ **65.** $-x + 7$
67. $5.6y - 7$ **69.** $40d + 50$ **71.** $-12r - 60$
73. $x + y - 5$ **75.** $6x - 21y - 16z$ **77.** $20x$ **79.** 0
81. 0 **83.** r **85.** $37y$ **87.** $-s^3$ **89.** 5 **91.** $-10r$
93. $3a$ **95.** $-3x$ **97.** x **99.** $\frac{4}{5}t$ **101.** $0.4r$
103. $7z - 15$ **105.** $-2x + 5$ **107.** $20d - 66$
109. $-3c - 1$ **111.** $s - 12$ **113.** $12c + 34$
115. $8x - 9$ **117.** $12x$ **119.** $(4x + 8)$ ft **123.** 0
125. 2

Study Set Section 2.4 (page 131)

1. equal   **3.** original   **5.** identity   **7.** subtraction, multiplication   **9.** multiplying   **11.** $-\frac{5}{4}$ **13.** 30   **15.** 6
17. 7, 7, 28, 2, 2   **19. a.** -1 **b.** $\frac{3}{5}$ **21.** 6   **23.** 5
25. -7 **27.** -20 **29.** 4   **31.** 2.9   **33.** $\frac{10}{3}$ **35.** -4
37. $-\frac{8}{3}$ **39.** 12   **41.** -48 **43.** -12 **45.** 5
47. $-\frac{17}{4}$ **49.** 0.04   **51.** -6 **53.** 0   **55.** $\frac{1}{7}$ **57.** $\frac{1}{4}$
59. -1 **61.** -41 **63.** 1   **65.** $\frac{9}{2}$ **67.** -7.2
69. -82 **71.** 0   **73.** -20 **75.** 3   **77.** 28   **79.** $-\frac{12}{5}$
81. $\frac{2}{15}$ **83.** $\frac{27}{5}$ **85.** $\frac{52}{9}$ **87.** $\frac{5}{4}$ **89.** -5 **91.** 80
93. 4   **95.** all real numbers   **97.** no solution   **99.** no solution   **101.** all real numbers   **103.** 2,991,980   **109.** 0
111. $\frac{1}{64}$ **113.** $16x$

Study Set Section 2.5 (page 139)

1. formula   **3.** perimeter   **5.** radius   **7.** circumference
9. a. $d = rt$ **b.** $r = c + m$ **c.** $p = r - c$ **d.** $I = Prt$
e. $C = 2\pi r$ **11.** 11,176,920 mi, 65,280 ft   **13. a.** volume
b. circumference   **c.** area   **d.** perimeter
15. a. $(2x + 10)$ cm   **b.** $(2x + 6)$ cm^2
17. Ax, Ax, By, B, B **19. a.** 3.14   **b.** $98 \cdot \pi$ **c.** the radius of the cylinder; the height of the cylinder   **21.** 2.5 mph
23. $65 million   **25.** 3.5%   **27.** 4,014°F   **29.** $24.55
31. about 132 in.   **33.** $R = \frac{E}{I}$ **35.** $w = \frac{V}{lh}$ **37.** $r = \frac{C}{2\pi}$
39. $h = \frac{3A}{B}$ **41.** $f = \frac{s}{w}$ **43.** $b = P - a - c$
45. $r = \frac{T - 2t}{2}$ **47.** $x = \frac{C - By}{A}$ **49.** $m = \frac{2K}{v^2}$
51. $c = 3A - a - b$ **53.** $t = T - 18E$ **55.** $r^2 = \frac{s}{4\pi}$
57. $v^2 = \frac{2Kg}{w}$ **59.** $r^3 = \frac{3V}{4\pi}$ **61.** $M = 4.2B + 19.8$
63. $h = \frac{S - 2\pi r^2}{2\pi r}$ **65.** $y = 9 - 3x$ **67.** $y = \frac{1}{3}x + 3$
69. $y = -\frac{3}{4}x - 4$ **71.** $b = \frac{2A}{h} - d$ or $b = \frac{2A - hd}{h}$
73. $c = \frac{72 - 8w}{7}$ **75.** 212°F, 0°C   **77.** 1,174.6, 956.9
79. 36 ft, 48 ft^2 **81.** 50.3 in., 201.1 in.^{2}
83. 56 in., 144 in.^{2} **85.** 2,450 ft^2 **87.** 27.75 in., 47.8125 in.^{2} **89.** 32 ft^2, 128 ft^3 **91.** 348 ft^3
93. 254 in.^{2} **95.** $D = \frac{L - 3.25r - 3.25R}{2}$ **101.** 137.76
103. 15%

Study Set Section 2.6 (page 153)

1. perimeter   **3.** vertex, base   **5. a.** $17, x + 2, 3x$
b. 3 ft, 5 ft, 9 ft   **7.** 180°   **9.** $30,000, 14%, 1 yr
11. $35t, t, 45t$ **13. a.** $0.06x, 10 - x, 0.03(10 - x), 0.05(10)$
b. $0.50(6), 0.25(x), 6 + x, 0.30(6 + x)$ **15.** To multiply a decimal by 100, move the decimal point two places to the right.
17. Parentheses are needed: $2(2w - 3) + 2w$ **19.** 6,000
21. 4 ft, 8 ft   **23.** 102 mi, 108 mi, 114 mi, 120 mi
25. Australia: 12 wk; Japan: 16 wk; Sweden: 10 wk   **27.** 250 calories in ice cream, 600 calories in pie   **29.** in millions of dollars: $110, $229, $189, $847   **31.** 7 ft, 7 ft, 11 ft
33. 75 m by 480 m   **35.** 20°   **37.** 22°, 68°   **39.** 17
41. 90   **43.** $4,900   **45.** $42,200 at 12%, $22,800 at 6.2%

47. $7,500   **49.** 2 hr   **51.** 4 hr into the flights   **53.** 4 hr
55. $1\frac{1}{3}$ liters   **57.** 7.5 oz   **59.** 20 gal   **61.** 50 lb
63. 40 lb lemon drops, 60 lb jelly beans   **69.** $-50x + 125$
71. $3x + 3$ **73.** $16y - 16$

Study Set Section 2.7 (page 167)

1. inequality   **3.** solve   **5.** interval   **7. a.** true
b. false   **c.** true   **d.** false   **9. a.** $-2 \le 17$ **b.** $x > 32$
11. a. same   **b.** positive   **13. a.**
b. $(8, \infty)$ **c.** all real numbers greater than 8   **15.** three
17. a. is less than, is greater than   **b.** is greater than, or equal to   **19.** [, (, ∞, $-\infty$ **21.** 5, 5, 12, 4, 4, 3
23. $(-\infty, 5)$
25. $(-3, 1]$
27. $x < -1, (-\infty, -1)$ **29.** $-7 < x \le 2, (-7, 2]$
31. $x > 3, (3, \infty)$
33. $x < -1, (-\infty, -1)$
35. $g \ge 10, [10, \infty)$
37. $x \ge 3, [3, \infty)$
39. $y \le -40, (-\infty, -40]$
41. $x > \frac{6}{7}, \left(\frac{6}{7}, \infty\right)$
43. $x \le 0.4, (-\infty, 0.4]$
45. $y \ge 20, [20, \infty)$
47. $x \ge -24, [-24, \infty)$
49. $n \le 2, (-\infty, 2]$
51. $m < 0, (-\infty, 0)$
53. $x \ge -10, [-10, \infty)$
55. $x < -2, (-\infty, -2)$
57. $x < -\frac{11}{4}, \left(-\infty, -\frac{11}{4}\right)$
59. $x \le -1, (-\infty, -1]$
61. $x \ge -13, [-13, \infty)$
63. $x > 0, (0, \infty)$

65. $x \leq 1.5$, $(-\infty, 1.5]$

67. $a > 6$, $(6, \infty)$

69. $x \geq \frac{9}{4}$, $\left[\frac{9}{4}, \infty\right)$

71. $x \leq 20$, $(-\infty, 20]$

73. $n > \frac{5}{4}$, $\left(\frac{5}{4}, \infty\right)$

75. $y \leq \frac{1}{8}$, $\left(-\infty, \frac{1}{8}\right]$

77. $x \leq \frac{3}{2}$, $\left(-\infty, \frac{3}{2}\right]$

79. $x \geq 3$, $[3, \infty)$

81. $7 < x < 10$, $(7, 10)$

83. $-10 \leq x \leq 0$, $[-10, 0]$

85. $-6 \leq c \leq 10$, $[-6, 10]$

87. $2 \leq x < 3$, $[2, 3)$

89. $-5 < x < -2$, $(-5, -2)$

91. $-1 \leq x < 2$, $[-1, 2)$

93. $x \geq 0.03$, $[0.03, \infty)$

95. 98% or better   **97.** 27 mpg or better
99. $0 \text{ ft} < s \leq 19 \text{ ft}$ **101.** $x \geq 35 \text{ ft}$
103. a. $0° < a \leq 18°$ **b.** $18° \leq a \leq 50°$
c. $30° \leq a \leq 37°$ **d.** $75° \leq a < 90°$
105. a. $26 \text{ lb} \leq w \leq 31 \text{ lb}$ **b.** $12 \text{ lb} \leq w \leq 14 \text{ lb}$
c. $18.5 \text{ lb} \leq w \leq 20.5 \text{ lb}$ **d.** $11 \text{ lb} \leq w \leq 13 \text{ lb}$
109. -125 **111.** $1, -3, 6$

Key Concept (page 171)

1. a. $2x - 8$ **b.** $x = 6$ **2. a.** $y + 5$ **b.** $y = -5$
3. a. $\frac{2}{3}a$ **b.** $a = \frac{1}{2}$ **4. a.** $-2x - 10$ **b.** $x \leq 5$
5. a. 0   **b.** all real numbers   **6.** The mistake is on the third line. The student made an equation out of the answer, which is $x - 6$, by writing $0 =$ on the left. Then the student solved that equation.

Chapter Review (page 172)

1. yes   **2.** no   **3.** no   **4.** no   **5.** yes   **6.** yes
7. variable, true   **8.** 21   **9.** -47 **10.** 13.2   **11.** 107
12. 8   **13.** 1   **14.** -96 **15.** 7.8   **16.** 0   **17.** 0
18. 160°   **19.** 5   **20.** 429 mi   **21.** 60°   **22.** \$54 billion
23. \$26.74   **24.** 192.4   **25.** no   **26.** 1,567%
27. $-28w$ **28.** $15r$ **29.** $24x$ **30.** $2.08f$ **31.** $9a$

32. r **33.** $5x + 15$ **34.** $-4x - 6 + 2y$ **35.** $-a + 4$
36. $3c - 6$ **37.** $20x + 32$ **38.** $-12.6c - 29.4$ **39.** $9p$
40. $-7m$ **41.** $4n$ **42.** $-p - 18$ **43.** $0.1k$ **44.** $-8a^3$
45. w **46.** $4h - 15$ **47.** $(4x + 4) \text{ ft}$ **48.** 2
49. -30.6 **50.** 30   **51.** -19 **52.** 4   **53.** 1   **54.** $\frac{5}{4}$
55. -6 **56.** 6   **57.** $-\frac{22}{75}$ **58.** identity; all real numbers
59. contradiction; no solution   **60.** \$176   **61.** \$11,800
62. 3.00 hr   **63.** 1,949°F   **64.** 168 in.   **65.** 1,440 in.^{2}
66. 76.5 m^2 **67.** 144 in.^{2} **68.** 50.27 cm
69. 201.06 cm^2 **70.** 4,320 in.^{3} **71.** 9.4 ft^3 **72.** 120 ft^3
73. 381.70 in.^{3} **74.** $h = \frac{A}{2\pi r}$ **75.** $G = 3A - 3BC + K$
76. $b^2 = c^2 - a^2$ **77.** $y = \frac{3}{4}x + 4$ **78.** 8 ft   **79.** 12, 4
80. 24.875 in. $\times$ 29.875 in. $\left(24\frac{7}{8} \text{ in.} \times 29\frac{7}{8} \text{ in.}\right)$
81. 76.5°, 76.5°   **82.** \$45x   **83.** \$16,000 at 7%, \$11,000 at 9%   **84.** 20   **85.** 10 lb of each   **86.** $0.12x$ gal
87. $x < 1$, $(-\infty, 1)$

88. $x \leq 12$, $(-\infty, 12]$

89. $d > \frac{5}{4}$, $\left(\frac{5}{4}, \infty\right)$

90. $x \geq 3$, $[3, \infty)$

91. $6 < x < 11$, $(6, 11)$

92. $-\frac{7}{2} < x \leq \frac{3}{2}$, $\left(-\frac{7}{2}, \frac{3}{2}\right]$

93. $2.40 \text{ g} \leq w \leq 2.53 \text{ g}$ **94.** The sign length must be 48 inches or less

Chapter 2 Test (page 178)

1. no   **2.** 120°   **3.** 1,046   **4.** \$76,000   **5.** .878, 1.000
6. 3%   **7.** $(4x + 6) \text{ ft}$ **8.** the distributive property
9. $-20x$ **10.** $224t$ **11.** $-4a + 4$ **12.** $-5.9d^2$ **13.** 0
14. -5 **15.** $-\frac{1}{4}$ **16.** 2.5   **17.** $\frac{7}{6}$ **18.** -3
19. $r = \frac{A - P}{Pt}$ **20.** \$150   **21.** $-10°$ C   **22.** 393 in.^{3}
23. $\frac{3}{5}$ hr   **24.** 10 liters   **25.** 68°   **26.** \$5,250
27. $x \geq -3$, $[-3, \infty)$

28. $-3 \leq x < 4$, $[-3, 4)$

29. $1.496 \text{ in.} \leq w \leq 1.498 \text{ in.}$

Cumulative Review Exercises Chapters 1–2 (page 180)

1. a. expression   **b.** equation   **2.** 3, 4, 5
3. $2 \cdot 2 \cdot 2 \cdot 5 \cdot 5 = 2^3 \cdot 5^2$ **4.** $\frac{2}{3}$ **5.** $-\frac{2}{9}$ **6.** 6
7. $\frac{22}{15} = 1\frac{7}{15}$ **8.** $12\frac{11}{24}$ **9.** 0.9375   **10.** 45   **11. a.** 65
b. -12 **12.** the commutative property of multiplication
13. natural number, whole number, integer, rational number, real number   **14.** rational number, real number   **15.** rational number, real number   **16.** irrational number, real number

17. a. 4^3 **b.** $\pi r^2 h$ **18. a.** -10 **b.** -14 **c.** -64
d. 0 **e.** -1 **19. a.** $w + 12$ **b.** $n - 4$ **20.** 4
21. $1, -3, 6$ **22.** $l = \frac{2,000}{d^2}$ (Answers may vary depending on
the variables chosen.) **23. a.** $6\,\text{ft}^2$ **b.** $1.2\,\text{ft}^2$ **c.** 20%
24. 300 **25.** 0 **26.** -2 **27.** 16 **28.** 0 **29.** $-32d$
30. $10x - 15y + 5$ **31.** $4x$ **32.** $-8a^2$ **33.** $11t - 50$
34. $8t - 20$ **35.** $(x + 3)$ ft **36.** $3x$ ft **37.** 9 **38.** 20
39. -0.6 **40.** $\frac{19}{6}$ **41.** -20 **42.** $\frac{5}{4}$ **43.** -2 **44.** no
solution, contradiction **45.** $65\,\text{m}^2$ **46.** $376.99\,\text{cm}^3$
47. $r^2 = \frac{3V}{\pi h}$ **48.** 37.5 ft-lb **49.** 9.45 lb **50.** $55°, 55°$
51. $\$4,000$ **52.** 10 oz
53. $x > -2, (-2, \infty)$

54. $x \le 2, (-\infty, 2]$

55. $x \ge -1, [-1, \infty)$

56. $-1 \le x < 2, [-1, 2)$

Study Set Section 3.1 (page 189)

1. ordered **3.** x-axis, y-axis, origin **5.** rectangular
7. a. origin, left, up **b.** origin, right, down **9. a.** I and II
b. II and III **c.** II **d.** IV **11.** 60 beats/min **13.** 140
beats/min **15.** 5 min and 50 min after starting **17.** no
difference **19.** about 6 million vehicles **21.** $(3, 5)$ is an
ordered pair, $3(5)$ indicates multiplication, and $5(3 + 5)$ is an
expression containing grouping symbols. **23.** yes
25. horizontal **27.** $(4, 3), (0, 4), (-5, 0), (-4, -5), (3, -3)$
29.

31. rivets: $(-6, 0), (-2, 0),$
$(2, 0), (6, 0)$; welds: $(-4, 3),$
$(0, 3), (4, 3)$; anchors: $(-6, -3),$
$(6, -3)$

33. $(E, 4), (F, 3), (G, 2)$ **35.** Rockford $(5, B)$, Mount Carroll
$(1, C)$, Harvard $(7, A)$, intersection $(5, E)$ **37.** $(2, 4)$; 12 sq.
units **39. a.** 35 mi **b.** 4 gal **c.** 32.5 mi
41. a. A 3-year-old car is worth $\$7,000$. **b.** $\$1,000$
c. 6 yr **43.** $152, 179, 202, 227, 252, 277$
49. $h = \frac{3(AC + T)}{2}$ **51.** -1

Study Set Section 3.2 (page 202)

1. two **3.** table **5.** linear **7.** infinitely **9. a.** 2
b. yes **c.** no **d.** infinitely many **11.** solution, point
13. a. At least one point is in error. The points should lie on a
straight line. Check the computations. **b.** The line is too
short. Arrowheads are not drawn. **15. a.** $y = 2x + 1$
b. $y = -\frac{5}{3}x - 2$ **c.** $y = \frac{1}{7}x - 3$ or $y = \frac{x}{7} - 3$
17. $6, -2, 2, 6$ **19.** a, c, a, c **21.** yes **23.** no **25.** no

27. yes **29.** 11 **31.** 4 **33.** $12, (8, 12), 6, (6, 8)$
35. $-13, (-5, -13), -1, (-1, -1)$
37.

39.

41.

43.

45.

47.

49.

51.

53.

55.

57.

59.

61.

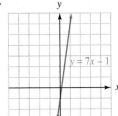

$y = 7x - 1$

63. $-2, (1, -2), 0, (2, 0), 4,$
$(4, 4); 4, (4, 4), 0, (6, 0), -4,$
$(8, -4)$

65. 3 oz

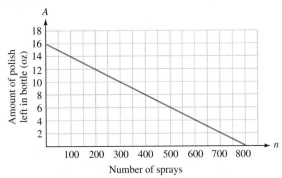

Amount of polish left in bottle (oz)

Number of sprays

67. about $70   **69.** about 180   **77.** $5 + 4c$ **79.** 0
81. 491

Study Set Section 3.3 (page 214)

1. two   **3.** general/standard   **5.** intersects/crosses
7. x-intercept: $(4, 0)$ y-intercept: $(0, 3)$ **9.** x-intercept:
$(-5, 0)$ y-intercept: $(0, -4)$ **11.** y-intercept: $(0, 2)$
13. y-intercept: $\left(0, \frac{2}{3}\right)$; x-intercept: $\left(-2\frac{1}{2}, 0\right)$ **15. a.** $3x$
b. $(0, 3)$ **17.** 2; 1   **19. a.** ii   **b.** iv   **c.** vi   **d.** i
e. iii   **f.** v   **21. a.** y-axis   **b.** yes   **23.** $y = 0; x = 0$
25.

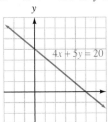

$4x + 5y = 20$

27.

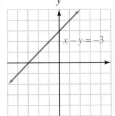

$x - y = -3$

29.

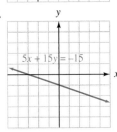

$5x + 15y = -15$

31.

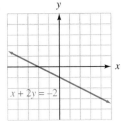

$x + 2y = -2$

33.

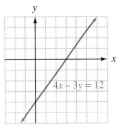

$4x - 3y = 12$

35.

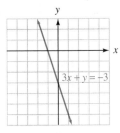

$3x + y = -3$

37.

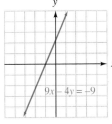

$9x - 4y = -9$

39.

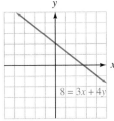

$8 = 3x + 4y$

41.

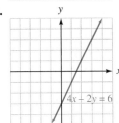

$4x - 2y = 6$

43.

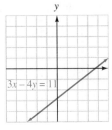

$3x - 4y = 11$

45.

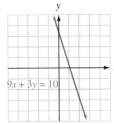

$9x + 3y = 10$

47.

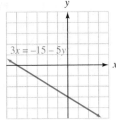

$3x = -15 - 5y$

49.

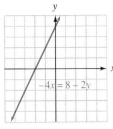

$-4x = 8 - 2y$

51.

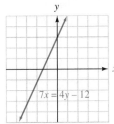

$7x = 4y - 12$

53.

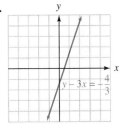

$y - 3x = -\frac{4}{3}$

55.

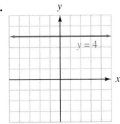

$y = 4$

57.

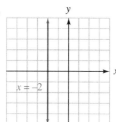

59.

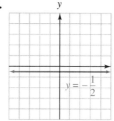

61.

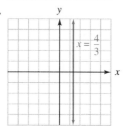

63.

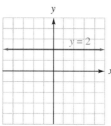

65.

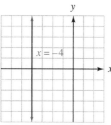

67. a. about $-270°C$
b. 0 milliliters

69. a. If only shrubs are purchased, he can buy 200.
b. If only trees are purchased, he can buy 100.   **75.** $\frac{1}{5}$
77. $2x - 6$

Study Set Section 3.4 (page 224)

1. ratio   **3.** slope   **5.** change   **7. a.** rises   **b.** falls
9. $\frac{2}{15}$ **11. a.** -3 **b.** 8   **c.** $-\frac{3}{8}$ **13. a.** $\frac{1}{2}$ **b.** $\frac{1}{2}$
c. $\frac{1}{2}$ **d.** When finding the slope of a line, any two points on
the line give the same result.   **15. a.** $m = 0$ **b.** undefined
17. a. 40%   **b.** 15%   **19.** $m = \frac{y_2 - y_1}{x_2 - x_1}$ **21.** y^2 means
$y \cdot y$ and y_2 means y sub 2.   **23.** $\frac{2}{3}$ **25.** $\frac{4}{3}$ **27.** -2
29. 0   **31.** $-\frac{1}{5}$ **33.** 1   **35.** -3 **37.** $\frac{5}{4}$ **39.** $-\frac{1}{2}$
41. $\frac{3}{5}$ **43.** 0   **45.** undefined   **47.** $-\frac{2}{3}$ **49.** -4.75
51. $m = \frac{3}{4}$ **53.** $m = 0$ **55.** undefined   **57.** 0
59. undefined   **61.** 0   **63.** $-\frac{2}{5}$ **65.** $\frac{1}{20}$; 5%   **67. a.** $\frac{1}{8}$
b. $\frac{1}{12}$ **c.** 1: less expensive, steeper; 2: not as steep, more
expensive   **69.** -875 gal per hr   **71.** 300 lb per yr
77. 40 lb licorice; 20 lb gumdrops

Study Set Section 3.5 (page 237)

1. slope–intercept   **3.** parallel   **5.** reciprocals   **7. a.** no
b. no   **c.** yes   **d.** no   **e.** yes   **f.** yes   **9. a.** y, $2x$, 4
b. y, $-3x$, $+$ **11.** $y = -\frac{5}{4}x$ **13. a.** parallel
b. perpendicular   **c.** -1 **15. a.** $-\frac{1}{2}$ **b.** 2   **c.** $-\frac{1}{2}$
d. Line 1 and Line 2   **17.** $2x$, $-2x$, $5y$, 5, 5, 5, 3, $-\frac{2}{5}$, $(0, 3)$

19. a. $4x$ **b.** $\frac{4x}{3}$ **c.** x **d.** -2 **21.** a right angle
23. $4, (0, 2)$ **25.** $-5, (0, -8)$ **27.** $4, (0, -2)$
29. $\frac{1}{4}, \left(0, -\frac{1}{2}\right)$ **31.** $\frac{1}{2}, (0, 6)$ **33.** $-1, (0, 6)$
35. $-1, (0, 8)$ **37.** $\frac{1}{6}, (0, -1)$ **39.** $-2, (0, 7)$
41. $-\frac{3}{2}, (0, 1)$ **43.** $-\frac{2}{3}, (0, 2)$ **45.** $\frac{3}{5}, (0, -3)$
47. $1, \left(0, -\frac{11}{6}\right)$ **49.** $1, (0, 0)$ **51.** $-5, (0, 0)$
53. $0, (0, -2)$ **55.** $0, \left(0, -\frac{2}{5}\right)$
57. $y = 5x - 3$

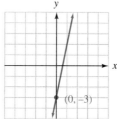

59. $y = \frac{1}{4}x - 2$

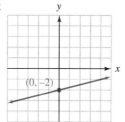

61. $y = -3x + 6$

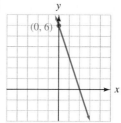

63. $y = -\frac{8}{3}x + 5$

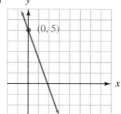

65.

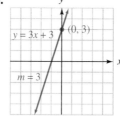

67.

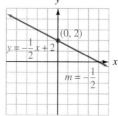

69.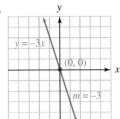

71.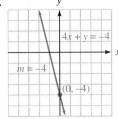

73.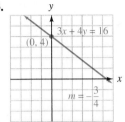

75.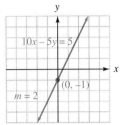

77. parallel **79.** perpendicular **81.** neither **83.** parallel
85. perpendicular **87. a.** $c = 2{,}000h + 5{,}000$
b. \$21,000 **89.** $F = 5t - 10$ **91.** $c = -20m + 500$
93. a. $c = 5x + 20$
c.

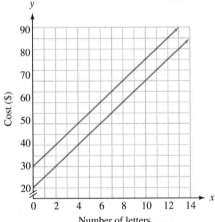

95. $c = 2t + 33.50$ **99.** 42 ft, 45 ft, 48 ft, 51 ft

Study Set Section 3.6 (page 247)

1. point–slope **3. a.** point–slope **b.** slope–intercept
5. a. $x + 6$ **b.** $y + 9$ **7.** $-\frac{5}{2}$ **9. a.** yes **b.** yes
11. a. $(-2, -3)$ **b.** $\frac{5}{6}$ **c.** $(4, 2)$ **13. a.** no **b.** no
c. yes **d.** yes **15.** (67, 170), (79, 220)
17. $y - y_1 = m(x - x_1)$ **19.** point–slope, y, slope–intercept
21. $y - 1 = 3(x - 2)$ **23.** $y + 1 = -\frac{4}{5}(x + 5)$
25. $y = \frac{1}{5}x - 1$ **27.** $y = -5x - 37$ **29.** $y = -\frac{4}{3}x + 4$
31. $y = -\frac{11}{6}x - \frac{7}{3}$ **33.** $y = -\frac{2}{3}x + 2$ **35.** $y = 8x + 4$
37. $y = -3x$ **39.** $y = 2x + 5$ **41.** $y = -\frac{1}{2}x + 1$
43. $y = 5$ **45.** $y = \frac{1}{10}x + \frac{1}{2}$ **47.** $x = -8$
49. $y = \frac{1}{4}x - \frac{5}{4}$ **51.** $x = 4$ **53.** $y = 5$

55.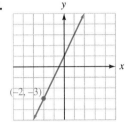

57.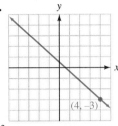

59.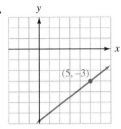

61.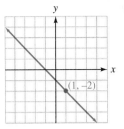

63. $h = 3.9r + 28.9$ **65.** $y = -\frac{2}{5}x + 4$, $y = -7x + 70$,
$x = 10$ **67. a.** $y = -40m + 920$ **b.** 440 yd^3
69. $l = \frac{25}{4}r + \frac{1}{4}$ **71. a.** $y = -\frac{1}{4}x + \frac{117}{4}$ or
$y = -0.25x + 29.25$ **b.** 19.25 gal **77.** 17 in. by 39 in.

Study Set Section 3.7 (page 258)

1. inequality **3.** solution **5.** boundary **7.** point
9. a. false **b.** false **c.** true **d.** false **11. a.** no
b. yes **c.** no **d.** no **13. a.** no **b.** yes **15.** the
half-plane opposite that in which the test point lies
17. a. yes **b.** no **c.** no **d.** yes **19. a.** horizontal
b. vertical **21. a.** is less than **b.** is greater than
c. is less than or equal to **d.** is greater than or equal to
23. $\leq, \geq$ **25.**

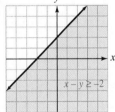

27.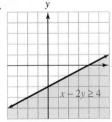

29.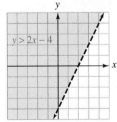

31.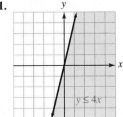

33.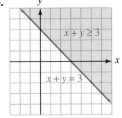

35.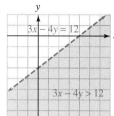

37.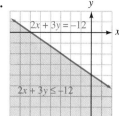

59.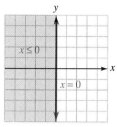

61.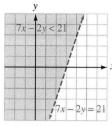

39.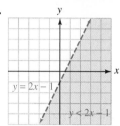

41.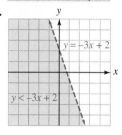

63.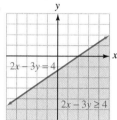

65.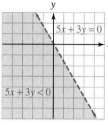

43.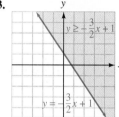

45.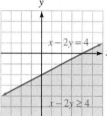

67. ii   **69.** (10, 10), (20, 10), (10, 20); answers may vary

71. (50, 50), (30, 40), (40, 40); answers may vary

77. $t = \dfrac{A - P}{Pr}$ **79.** $15x + 22$

Key Concept (page 263)

1. $y = -3x - 4$ **2.** $y = \frac{1}{5}x + 1$ **3.** 80°F

4. $y = 209x + 2{,}660$; \$8,930   **5.** $-2, 4, -3$

47.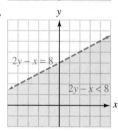

49.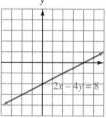

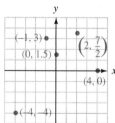

6. a. When new, the press cost \$40,000.   **b.** $-5{,}000$; the value of the press decreased \$5,000/yr

51.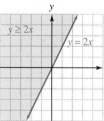

53.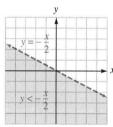

7. a. $(-2, -2)$ (answers may vary)   **b.** -2

c. $y = -2x - 6$ **8.** $x = 1$

Chapter Review (page 264)

1. 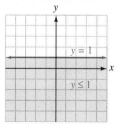   **2.** (158, 21.5)   **3.** quadrant III

55.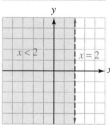

57.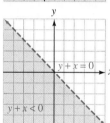

4. (0, 0)   **5.** (1, 4); 36 square units   **6. a.** 2,500; week 2

b. 1,000   **c.** 1st week and 5th week   **7.** yes

8. $-6, (-2, -6), -8, (-8, 3)$ **9.** $y = x^2 + 1$ and $y - x^3 = 0$

10.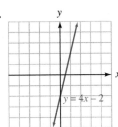

11.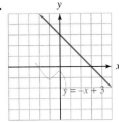

35. $y = -\frac{1}{2}x - 3$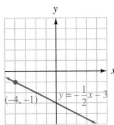

12. a. true   **b.** false   **13.** about $195
14. $(-3, 0), (0, 2.5)$ **15.** *x*-intercept: $(-2, 0)$; *y*-intercept: $(0, 4)$

16.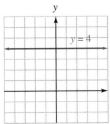

36. $y = \frac{2}{3}x + 5$ **37.** $y = -8$ **38.** $f = -35x + 450$
39. a. yes   **b.** yes   **c.** yes   **d.** no

40.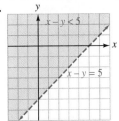

41.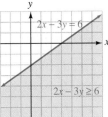

17.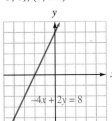

18. $(0, 25{,}000)$; the equipment was originally valued at $25,000. $(10, 0)$. In 10 years, the sound equipment had no value.

42.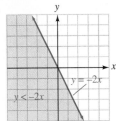

43.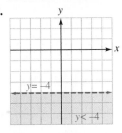

44. a. true   **b.** false   **c.** false

19. $\frac{1}{4}$ **20.** 0   **21.** -7 **22.** $-\frac{3}{2}$ **23.** $\frac{3}{4}$ **24.** 8.3%
25. a. -1.25 million people per yr   **b.** 4.05 million people per yr   **26.** $m = \frac{3}{4}$; *y*-intercept: $(0, -2)$ **27.** $m = -4$; *y*-intercept: $(0, 0)$ **28.** $m = \frac{1}{8}$; *y*-intercept $(0, 10)$
29. $m = -\frac{7}{5}$; *y*-intercept $\left(0, -\frac{21}{5}\right)$ **30.** $y = -6x + 4$
31. $m = 3$; *y*-intercept: $(0, -5)$.

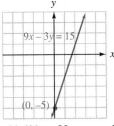

45. $(2, 4), (5, 3), (6, 2)$ answers may vary   **46.** An equation contains an $=$ symbol. An inequality contains one of the symbols $<, \leq, >,$ or $\geq$.

Chapter 3 Test (page 269)

1. 10   **2.** 60   **3.** 1 day before and the 3rd day of the holiday
4. 50 dogs were in the kennel when the holiday began.
5. 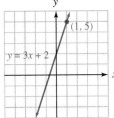   **6.** 1, $(2, 1)$, -6, $(-6, 3)$ **7.** yes

32. a. $c = 300w + 75{,}000$ **b.** 90,600   **33. a.** parallel
b. perpendicular   **34.** $y = 3x + 2$

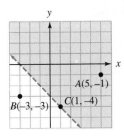

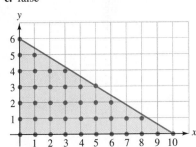

51. $\frac{2x^2-1}{x(x+1)}$ **53.** $\frac{35x^2+x+5}{5x(x+5)}$ **55.** $\frac{17t+42}{(t+3)(t+2)}$

57. $\frac{2x^2+11x}{(2x-1)(2x+3)}$ **59.** $\frac{4a+1}{(a+2)^2}$ **61.** $\frac{4m^2+10m+6}{(m-2)(m+5)}$

63. $\frac{14s+58}{(s+3)(s+7)}$ **65.** $\frac{12a+26}{(a+1)(a+3)^2}$ **67.** $-\frac{4c+6}{(2c+1)(c-3)}$

69. $\frac{b-1}{2(b+1)}$ **71.** $\frac{1}{a+1}$ **73.** $\frac{3}{s-3}$ **75.** $\frac{x+2}{x-2}$

77. $-\frac{2}{x-3}$ **79.** $\frac{17h-2}{12(h-2)(h+2)}$ **81.** $\frac{1}{(y+3)(y+4)}$

83. $\frac{s^2+8s+4}{(s+4)(s+1)(s+1)}$ **85.** $\frac{2x+13}{(x-8)(x-1)(x+2)}$

87. $-\frac{1}{2(x-2)}$ **89.** $\frac{6x+8}{x}$ **91.** $\frac{a^2b-3}{a^2}$ **93.** $\frac{x^2-4x+9}{x-4}$

95. $-\frac{4x+3}{x+1}$ **97.** $-\frac{2}{a-4}$ **99.** $\frac{1}{r+2}$ **101.** $\frac{2y+7}{y-1}$

103. $\frac{20x+9}{6x^2}$ cm **109.** 8; (0, 2) **111.** 0

Study Set Section 6.5 (page 464)

1. complex, complex **3.** reciprocal **5.** single, reciprocal

7. a. $\frac{x-3}{4}$ **b.** yes **c.** $\frac{1}{12}-\frac{x}{6}$ **d.** no

9. a. $y, 3, 6$, and y **b.** $6y$ **c.** $\frac{6y}{6y}$ **11.** $2x$ **13.** $4y^2$

15. $\frac{4x^2}{15}\big/\frac{16x}{25}$ **17.** $\frac{5x}{12}$ **19.** $\frac{8}{9}$ **21.** $\frac{x^2}{y}$ **23.** $\frac{n^3}{8}$ **25.** $\frac{1-3x}{5+2x}$

27. $\frac{5}{4}$ **29.** $\frac{10}{3}$ **31.** $18x$ **33.** $\frac{2-5y}{6}$ **35.** $\frac{6d+12}{d}$

37. $\frac{1}{2}$ **39.** $\frac{5}{7}$ **41.** $\frac{x^3}{14}$ **43.** $\frac{s^2-s}{2+2s}$ **45.** $-\frac{x^2}{2}$ **47.** $\frac{1+x}{2+x}$

49. $\frac{14x}{9}$ **51.** $-\frac{t}{32}$ **53.** $\frac{8}{4c+5c^2}$ **55.** $\frac{b-5ab}{3ab-7a}$

57. $\frac{3-x}{x-1}$ **59.** $\frac{b+9}{8a}$ **61.** $\frac{32h-1}{96h+6}$ **63.** $\frac{xy}{y+x}$

65. $\frac{1}{x+2}$ **67.** $\frac{1}{x+3}$ **69.** $\frac{5t^2}{27}$ **71.** $\frac{m-2}{6}$ **73.** $\frac{y}{x-2y}$

75. $\frac{m^2+n^2}{m^2-n^2}$ **77.** $\frac{x}{x-2}$ **79.** $\frac{3}{14}$ **81.** $\frac{R_1R_2}{R_2+R_1}$

87. 1 **89.** $\frac{81}{256r^8}$ **91.** $\frac{r^{10}}{9}$

Study Set Section 6.6 (page 473)

1. rational **3.** clear **5.** quadratic **7. a.** yes **b.** no
9. a. 3, 0 **b.** 3, 0 **c.** 3, 0 **11.** y **13.** $(x+8)(x-8)$
15. $(x+2)(x-2)$ **17.** 12, 1, 10x
19. $2a, 2a, 2a, 2a, 2a, 4, 7, 3$ **21.** multiplication;
$fpq = f \cdot p \cdot q$ **23.** 1 **25.** $\frac{3}{5}$ **27.** 7 **29.** 3 **31.** no
solution; 5 is extraneous **33.** $-4, 4$ **35.** 1 **37.** no
solution; 0 is extraneous **39.** $-3, 3$ **41.** -12 **43.** -40
45. -48 **47.** $-\frac{5}{9}$ **49.** $-\frac{12}{7}$ **51.** $\frac{11}{4}$ **53.** -1 **55.** 6
57. 1 **59.** 4 **61.** no solution; -2 is extraneous
63. $2, -5$ **65.** $-4, 3$ **67.** $-2, 1$ **69.** 2 **71.** 0
73. $3, -4$ **75.** $1, -9$ **77.** -5 **79.** $P = nrt$
81. $d = \frac{bc}{a}$ **83.** $A = \frac{h(b+d)}{2}$ **85.** $a = \frac{b}{b-1}$
87. $r = \frac{E-IR}{I}$ **89.** $r = \frac{st}{s-t}$ **91.** $L^2 = 6dF - 3d^2$
93. $R = \frac{HB}{B-H}$ **95.** $r = \frac{r_1r_2}{r_2+r_1}$ **101.** $x(x+4)$
103. $(2x+3)(x-1)$ **105.** $(x^2+9)(x+3)(x-3)$

Study Set Section 6.7 (page 483)

1. distance, rate, time **3.** interest, principal, rate, time
5. iii **7.** $t = \frac{d}{r}$ **9. a.** 0.09 **b.** 3.5% **11.** $\frac{1}{3}$ **13.** $\frac{x}{4}$
15. $\frac{50}{r}, \frac{75}{r-0.02}$ **17.** $6\frac{1}{9}$ days **19.** 4 **21.** 2 **23.** 5

25. $\frac{2}{3}, \frac{3}{2}$ **27.** 8 **29.** $2\frac{2}{9}$ hr **31.** $4\frac{4}{9}$ hr **33.** 8 hr

35. 20 min **37.** $1\frac{4}{5}$ hr = 1.8 hr **39.** 4 mph **41.** 1st: $1\frac{1}{2}$

ft per sec; 2nd: $\frac{1}{2}$ ft per sec **43.** $\frac{300}{255+x}, \frac{210}{255-x}$, 45 mph

45. Credit union: 4%; bonds: 6% **47.** 7% and 8%
51. repeating **53.** $\{\ldots, -4, -3, -2, -1, 0, 1, 2, 3, 4, \ldots\}$
55. 0

Study Set Section 6.8 (page 493)

1. ratio, rate **3.** terms **5.** cross **7.** unit **9.** $\frac{6}{5}$

11. a. 60, 60 **b.** 15x, 90 **13.** 25, 2, 1,000, x **15.** 24
twelve-oz bottles **17.** BC, EF, DE **19.** x, 288, 18, 18, 16

21. a. $\frac{4}{5}$ **b.** $\frac{9}{7}$ **23.** similar **25.** $\frac{4}{15}$ **27.** $\frac{5}{4}$ **29.** $\frac{1}{2}$

31. $\frac{13}{8}$ **33.** no **35.** yes **37.** no **39.** 4 **41.** 6

43. 3 **45.** 0 **47.** -8 **49.** $-\frac{3}{2}$ **51.** 2 **53.** $-\frac{1}{5}$

55. -27 **57.** $2, -2$ **59.** $6, -1$ **61.** $-\frac{1}{3}, 2$ **63.** 15

65. 8 **67. a.** $\frac{3}{2}, 3:2$ **b.** $\frac{2}{3}, 2:3$ **69.** $62.50 **71.** 20

73. 84 **75.** 568, 13, 14 **77.** 510 **79.** not exactly, but
close **81.** 140 **83.** 65 ft, 3 in. **85.** 10 ft **87.** 45
minutes for $25 **89.** 150 for $12.99 **91.** 6-pack for $1.50

93. 39 ft **95.** $46\frac{7}{8}$ ft **101.** 90% **103.** 480

Key Concept (page 499)

1. a. $\frac{2x}{x-2}$ **b.** $x-4$ **2. a.** $x+1$ **b.** $x, x-1, x+1$
3. a. $\frac{2x^2-1}{x(x+1)}$ **b.** $\frac{x}{x}, \frac{x+1}{x+1}$ **4. a.** $\frac{3(n^2-n-2)}{n^2}$ **b.** $3n$
5. a. 2 **b.** b **6. a.** 5 **b.** $(s+2)(s-1)$ **7. a.** 2, 4
b. $4(y-6)$ **8. a.** $b = \frac{a}{1-a}$ **b.** ab

Chapter Review (page 500)

1. $4, -4$ **2.** $-\frac{3}{7}$ **3.** $\frac{1}{2x}$ **4.** $\frac{5}{2x}$ **5.** $\frac{x}{x+1}$ **6.** $a-2$
7. -1 **8.** $-\frac{1}{x+3}$ **9.** $\frac{x}{x-1}$ **10.** does not simplify
11. $\frac{4}{3}$ **12.** x is not a common factor of the numerator and the
denominator; x is a term of the numerator. **13.** 150 mg
14. $\frac{3x}{y}$ **15.** 96 **16.** $\frac{x-1}{x+2}$ **17.** $\frac{2x}{x+1}$ **18.** $\frac{3y}{2}$
19. $\frac{1}{x(x-1)}$ **20.** $-x-2$ **21. a.** yes **b.** no **c.** yes
d. yes **22.** $\frac{1}{3}$ mile per minute **23.** $\frac{1}{3d}$ **24.** 1
25. $\frac{2x+2}{x-7}$ **26.** $\frac{1}{a-4}$ **27.** $9x$ **28.** $8x^3$ **29.** $m(m-8)$
30. $(5x+1)(5x-1)$ **31.** $(a+5)(a-5)$
32. $(2t+7)(t+5)^2$ **33.** $\frac{63}{7a}$ **34.** $\frac{2xy+x}{x(x-9)}$ **35.** $\frac{2b+14}{6(b-5)}$
36. $\frac{9r^2-36r}{(r+1)(r-4)(r+5)}$ **37.** $\frac{a-7}{7a}$ **38.** $\frac{x^2+x-1}{x(x-1)}$
39. $\frac{1}{t+1}$ **40.** $\frac{x^2+4x-4}{2x^2}$ **41.** $\frac{b+6}{b-1}$ **42.** $\frac{6c+8}{c}$
43. $\frac{14n+58}{(n+3)(n+7)}$ **44.** $\frac{4t+1}{(t+2)^2}$ **45.** $\frac{1}{(a+3)(a+2)}$
46. $\frac{17y-2}{12(y-2)(y+2)}$ **47.** yes **48.** $\frac{14x+28}{(x+6)(x-1)}$ units,
$\frac{12}{(x+6)(x-1)}$ square units **49.** $\frac{n^3}{14}$ **50.** $\frac{r+9}{8s}$ **51.** $\frac{1+y}{1-y}$
52. $\frac{21}{3a+10a^2}$ **53.** x^2+3 **54.** $\frac{y-5xy}{3xy-7x}$ **55.** 3 **56.** no
solution; 5 is extraneous **57.** 3 **58.** 2, 4 **59.** 0

Index